D0171139

Broken

Broken

Can the Senate Save Itself and the Country?

Ira Shapiro

ROWMAN & LITTLEFIELD
Lanham • Boulder • New York • London

Published by Rowman & Littlefield
A wholly owned subsidiary of The Rowman & Littlefield Publishing Group, Inc.
4501 Forbes Boulevard, Suite 200, Lanham, Maryland 20706
www.rowman.com

Unit A, Whitacre Mews, 26-34 Stannary Street, London SE11 4AB

British Library Cataloguing in Publication Information Available

Library of Congress Cataloging-in-Publication Data Available

978-1-5381-0582-5 (cloth)
978-1-5381-0583-2 (electronic)

♾️™ The paper used in this publication meets the minimum requirements of American National Standard for Information Sciences—Permanence of Paper for Printed Library Materials, ANSI/NISO Z39.48-1992.

Printed in the United States of America

To my children, Susanna and Brian, and my grandchildren, Zev and Jacob:
our hope for the future.

The Senate, the great anchor of the government . . . Such an institution may be some times necessary as a defense to the people against their own temporary errors and delusions.

—James Madison letter to Thomas Jefferson;
Federal Papers #63 (1787)

The American Senate, in my opinion, was the premier spark of brilliance that emerged from the collective intellect of the Constitution's framers.

—Senator Robert C. Byrd (1988)

One thing I never heard in my time overseas is "I wish we had a Senate like yours."

—James Fallows (2010)

Contents

Acknowledgments

$\mathcal{I}$t is cliché to observe that writing a book is a lonely endeavor. Fortunately, I benefited greatly, as I'm sure most authors do, from the encouragement and support of friends and family. I am particularly grateful for the astute comments and suggestions from friends who are terrific students of politics and policy, representing various stages of my life: Brandeis University: Walt and Edie Mossberg, Larry Joseph, and Alan Ehrenhalt; the Senate: Margaret and Al Crenshaw, Brian Conboy, and Ken Ackerman; the Office of the United States Trade Representative (USTR): Jennifer Haverkamp and Vanessa Sciarra; and, more recent friends, who epitomize the talent of the next generation: Joseph Marks, Marta McClellan Ross, and Joe Frederici.

Special thanks go to my administrative assistant, Carmela Lupica ("Lena") for her help in all aspects of the book, including research, editing, and production. It greatly helped that Lena was on the Hill almost as long ago as I was, so she found working on the book to be quite absorbing, even when I was somewhat less organized than would have been optimal.

I owe a great debt of gratitude to Jonathan Sisk, vice president and senior acquisitions editor for American government, public policy, and American history, at Rowman & Littlefield. Jon encouraged me to write the book, persuaded Rowman & Littlefield to publish it, and to bring out an updated edition of *The Last Great Senate*—all of which make Jon quite indispensable to this project. Kate Powers, assistant acquisitions editor, has been a constant source of support and help in bringing the book to completion.

In this venture, as in everything in my life for the past half century, my wife, Nancy, was my greatest supporter and my best adviser. Love you!

Introduction

May you have a strong foundation when the winds of changes shift.

—Bob Dylan, "Forever Young"

*O*n June 25, 2017, as the turbulent Trump presidency passed the five-month mark, the Sunday morning talk shows featured no fewer than ten U.S. senators discussing the president's firing of FBI director James Comey, its impact on the investigations of Russian interference in the 2016 election and possible collusion by the Trump campaign, and the increasingly heated debate over the future of the Affordable Care Act. It was one of those days that remind us of the central role that senators play in our national political conversation and in the working—or failing—of our political system. It was a day when many other Americans shared my interest in, if not my obsession with, the Senate.

I confess to a love of the Senate that goes back more than fifty years. I recall the thrilling summer of 1964 when Hubert Humphrey and Everett Dirksen led the Senate in breaking the southern filibuster to pass the Civil Rights Act; in 1966, J. William Fulbright, wearing sunglasses to shield his eyes for the television lights, convening the hearings that exposed the folly of the escalation of the Vietnam War; in 1968, when Eugene McCarthy and Robert Kennedy stepped forward to prevent President Lyndon Johnson from seeking another term; and in 1973, being part of nation riveted as Sam Ervin and Howard Baker led their select committee in exposing the abuses of power that would become known as "Watergate." Long before Lin-Manuel Miranda's *Hamilton*, the Senate was "the room where it happened."

Like Hamilton and Burr in their era, and so many other young people in the crisis times of the 1960s and 1970s, I wanted to be in the room where it happened. I got a job as a summer intern for Jacob Javits, the great senator from New York, and started working in the Senate one day after my graduation from

1

college in 1969. Enthralled by the experience that summer—Richard Nixon's first year as president—I focused on coming back to the Senate full time after law school. Gaylord Nelson, the visionary environmentalist from Wisconsin who founded Earth Day, gave me that opportunity, hiring me as his legislative legal counsel.

The Senate I joined in October 1975 had just completed what was probably the most extraordinary decade in its history. In the fall of 1963, the Senate had been virtually paralyzed, hopelessly divided over President Kennedy's civil rights legislation, and seemingly unable to make progress on virtually any domestic issues. But with the assassination of Kennedy and the determination of President Lyndon Johnson, the Senate broke the southern filibuster, making possible the passage of the Civil Rights Act of 1964, the greatest legislative accomplishment in our history. The Senate went on from there to play a key role in the range of Great Society legislation, which still forms the foundation of much of American life. After its unwise acquiescence in the Tonkin Gulf Resolution, which Johnson misused as a license to widen America's involvement in Vietnam, the Senate became the forum for debating and ultimately stopping the war.

In 1973, the Watergate Committee worked, in tandem with the press, the courts, and the special prosecutor, to hold Richard Nixon and his administration accountable for their crimes and their cover-up. In 1975, the Senate empowered a select committee, chaired by Frank Church, to investigate the abuses of the intelligence community. Reacting to the "imperial presidency" of Johnson and Nixon, the Senate (and the House) reasserted congressional prerogatives, giving themselves powerful new instruments—the Budget Act and the War Powers Act—for checking the Executive.

In short, the Senate was in the forefront of every major issue during a decade of crisis in our country. Dealing with civil rights, war and peace, presidential power, and Supreme Court nominations, the Senate seemed to have a special relationship to the Constitution. It occupied a unique role in our country, just as the Founders had intended.

The magnetic pull that the Senate exerted on me was not unique. During this period, the Senate was the place to be, where a young man or woman could come to Washington, hitch their star to a major national figure, make a mark at an early age, and derive priceless experience in politics and government. It was no accident that the staff of the Senate and senators of this era included young men and women who would be future senators and congressional leaders: George Mitchell, Tom Daschle, Lamar Alexander, Mitch McConnell, Susan Collins, Tom Foley, Fred Thompson, Jane Harman, Norm Dicks, Nancy Pelosi, Steny Hoyer, Chris Van Hollen, Ted Kaufman, Angus King; future press and media luminaries: Tim Russert, Chris Matthews, Mark Shields, Lawrence O'Donnell, George Will, Jeff Greenfield, Colby King, Steven

Pearlstein; future White House chiefs of staff: Leon Panetta, John Podesta, Ken Duberstein, Josh Bolten; a future Secretary of State, Madeleine Albright; two future Supreme Court justices, Stephen Breyer and Elena Kagan; and a future president, Bill Clinton. They trained in the right place. As Justice Oliver Wendell Holmes once wrote about those who had been young during the Civil War: "In our youth, to our great good fortune, our hearts were touched with fire."

By late 1975, Nixon had resigned, and the Vietnam War was over. The crisis that had gripped the country for a decade had finally abated, but a very strong Senate remained active and assertive. I found my work as absorbing and fulfilling as I had hoped, and I stayed twelve years. Many people stayed longer and accomplished more, but I had an unusual range of experiences: working on the personal staff of senators, as well as committee and leadership staffs; running a special Senate committee; serving in the majority and in the minority; working on domestic and foreign policy issues, ranging from national security wiretapping to the Senate ethics code to completing the Metrorail system. Quite possibly, no one ever had the privilege of working for as many distinguished senators: in addition to Javits and Nelson, Abraham Ribicoff (D-CT), Robert Byrd (D-WV), Thomas Eagleton (D-MO), and finishing with Jay Rockefeller (D-WV) as his first chief of staff. Javits entered the Senate in 1957; Rockefeller retired from the Senate at the end of 2014. The men that I worked for spanned nearly sixty years of Senate history.

I left the Senate at the end of 1987, returning to private law practice. A few years later, I got a different vantage point on the Senate starting in 1993, when I joined the Clinton administration as General Counsel to the U.S. Trade Representative. The Finance Committee members, led by the inimitable Daniel Patrick Moynihan and Bob Packwood and their staffs, were superb to deal with: consummate professionals, focused on substance, cooperating in a bipartisan way, determined to help chart a new U.S. trade policy to deal with the opportunities and challenges presented by a globalized world after the Berlin Wall came down. In 1995, I had the privilege to be confirmed rapidly and unanimously by the Senate for ambassadorial status, even though Senator Jesse Helms, whose views were almost completely antithetical to mine, chaired the committee considering my nomination.

Then, starting some time in the 1990s, along with many other people who shared my reverence for the institution, I sadly watched the Senate decline.

The trust, mutual respect, and bipartisanship that had characterized the Senate of the 1960s and 1970s, which carried over through the 1980s, vanished abruptly as the partisan divide became a chasm. The Senate, which had been almost a demilitarized zone where partisan politics was concerned, became just another part of "the permanent campaign." Compromise, the sine qua non of politics, became a dirty word. Moderates became fewer, and an endangered class; many chose to retire six or twelve years earlier than anticipated. The Senate, whose wisdom the nation relied on in times of crisis, approved the exorbitant Bush tax cuts, rushed to judgment on the war in Iraq, and spent its time second-guessing a Florida court about the mental state of Terri Schiavo. Robert Byrd, the keeper of the Senate flame, ripped the "supine Senate" that allowed George W. Bush to intrude on Congress's authority to declare war and appropriate funds. In 2005, political historian Lewis L. Gould wrote that "a profound sense of crisis now surrounds the Senate and its members."

As Barack Obama came to the presidency, I began writing the book that would become *The Last Great Senate: Courage and Statesmanship in Times of Crisis.* I discovered something that was in plain sight but had not been recognized—the great Senate of the 1960s and 1970s—and I wrote about its closing years, during the Carter presidency. I wanted to recall those superb senators, what they accomplished individually, but more important, how they worked together enabling the Senate to act in the national interest. Jonathan Martin, political correspondent for the *New York Times*, who was then at *Politico*, wrote: "Instead of lamenting the present gridlock in the capital, Shapiro, a veteran Congressional aide turned Washington lawyer, decided to glorify the past. . . . Shapiro depicts the end of the 1970s as the conclusion to a golden era of modern American political history—a period where giants in both parties worked together to produce sweeping legislative achievements."

Even as I wrote about "the last great Senate" I hoped that the challenges facing Barack Obama and the country would inspire a Senate comeback—if not to greatness, at least to respectability. Astonishingly, exactly the opposite took place. The Senate's decline turned into a downward spiral, constantly accelerating. Even a national economic emergency—750,000 jobs disappearing in January 2009—was not enough to produce even a trace of bipartisan cooperation. The Senate Republicans decided to oppose Obama's proposals even before he made any. Hyperpartisanship and gridlock became the order of the day—every day. The disgust of the public was matched only by the despair of many senators about what the Senate had become. Michael Bennet (D-CO), one of the brightest young senators, told me in 2012: "We don't do any legislating. We just wait for [Senate leaders] McConnell and Reid to come out and give us our orders." Olympia Snowe, a respected moderate, retired, after observing bitterly: "We have been miniaturized." The Senate had become ground zero for the dysfunction of our government—the political institution that had declined the longest and failed the worst.

In 2012, reviewing the dismal record, I wrote that the Senate needed "new rules, new attitudes and new leaders." In both 2013 and 2015, with many senators calling for "regular order"—the opportunity to produce legislation in committee and offer amendments on the floor—the Senate scored early bipartisan accomplishments. But the positive accomplishments could not continue as the parties battled over executive and judicial nominations. In 2013, Democratic Leader Harry Reid took the unprecedented action of changing the Senate rules by majority vote—the so-called nuclear option—to overcome the obstruction to Obama executive and judicial (federal judges below the Supreme Court) nominations by Republican leader Mitch McConnell. In 2016, McConnell retaliated and raised the ante by simply refusing to consider any nomination that President Obama would make to fill the Supreme Court vacancy caused by Justice Antonin Scalia's death. The Senate's downward spiral continued to accelerate; there was apparently no bottom. Not coincidentally, the public anger about gridlock and disgust with Congress and both parties continued to rise.

I conceived of this book in 2016 as the presidential election entered its final months. Like virtually everyone else, I thought Hillary Clinton would be elected; I was shocked and depressed by the nearly universal view that she was destined to be a failed president, unable to overcome the gridlock and hyper-partisanship. The evidence was unmistakable that our vaunted political system, the pride of our country, was in deep crisis. My book was going to explain why the key to her success—and the only possible path forward for the recovery of our political system—was a rejuvenated Senate.

We all know the forces that have caused our politics to decline: the polarization of the parties and the "permanent campaign" that leaves little common ground and no time for governing; the impact of 24/7 cable news, the social media, and a political conversation conducted on Twitter; the staggering cost of campaigns and the demands of fundraising; the influence of outside groups and "dark money." The crisis of American democracy requires many changes, particularly with respect to how we finance campaigns, conduct elections, and establish congressional districts. But those reforms will take years to enact, if they can be enacted at all. In contrast, the Senate combines constitutional authority and responsibility with the potential to change rapidly.

Whatever else is going on, those hundred men and women can change the way they operate; they do not have to be talented and committed individuals trapped in a dysfunctional institution. They can stop being blind partisans and go back to being real senators, focused on collective action for the national interest. They have an obligation to rise above the partisanship, not simply mirror or exacerbate it. Many of them are already doing so, and it would not take many more to provide sixty to seventy senators who could ensure that the Senate once again became what Walter F. Mondale called "the nation's mediator," the place where the parties come together to hammer our principled compromises in the national interest. The book I envisioned would describe how the Senate worked at its best; when and why it had declined; and the vital importance of its recovery. In particular, I wanted to show the increased power of the leaders, at the expenses of the committees and individual senators, had gone much too far and contributed mightily to the Senate's decline.

The stunning election of Donald J. Trump made the Senate's role even more crucial, and the need for its recovery much more urgent. Trump did not create the crisis facing American democracy, although his ability to win the presidency certainly resulted in significant part from widespread public anger and disgust with the hyperpartisanship, gridlock, and our deeply degraded political discourse. Trump's campaign revealed fault lines in our country much deeper than we had recognized, and then exacerbated them. He came to the presidency with a complete absence of qualifications—the first person ever to hold the office without having previous government or military experience. The divisive and vitriolic nature of his campaign raised profound questions about his views and temperament, his vision of America and its democratic system, and his tolerance for disagreement with his views. Only the Senate has the power to help Trump succeed as president, if he chose to govern seriously, or to act as a check on him if he chose a radical or authoritarian path.

The book has two parts. Part I traces the history of the Senate from the election of 1980 to the election of 2016. Any book covering that span of time reflects the author's choices about what is important. Because I see the Senate's decline as accelerating over time, I have tried to tell the story by giving more attention to more recent events as the trajectory of the decline steepened. I have selected the events that strike me as most illuminating. While it's not generally a pretty picture, I have also tried to include events and anecdotes that illustrate the Senate's great potential to serve the country.

Part II of the book comes closer to journalism, written in real time, during the first six months of 2017 when the divided and diminished Senate meets the insurgent president. It is an astonishing and unprecedented moment in our history—the most dangerous since 1861 when Abraham Lincoln became president with the nation on the brink of civil war. The framers of the Constitution conceived of the Senate as a check on the passions of the time that could rip through the House of Representatives, and on a president who could be overreaching in asserting his power. Given the fears that prompted the framers' work, this is indeed the Senate's defining moment. If the Senate continues to be broken, it will fail the test of history and richly deserve the frustration, anger, and despair with which it is commonly viewed. If, however, the Senate steps up to the unprecedented challenges posed by this president, it can save itself and the country, rebuilding public confidence and restoring public trust.

Any author writing about a topic of current resonance lives in fear of the months between when the manuscript goes to press and when the book comes out. That is certainly true in this case, as the Trump presidency features shocking and unprecedented developments weekly, and sometimes daily. But it seems safe to say that the Senate will be simultaneously engaged in trying to save the American health care system and in an investigation of Russian interference in the 2016 presidential election, including possible collusion between the Trump campaign and Russia, which could lead to President Trump's impeachment, removal, or resignation. I fervently hope that in a few years some other author will be able to write *Another Great Senate: Just When We Needed It Most.*

Part I

FROM HALLOWED GROUND
TO SCORCHED EARTH

• *1* •

McConnell's Power Play

$\mathcal{I}$n the second week of February 2016, the New Hampshire primary confirmed the unexpected rise of Donald J. Trump to be the Republican frontrunner. Political analysts of all stripes explained endlessly, and unconvincingly, why Trump would surely flame out. Because of Trump, the presidential campaign had already riveted the attention of Americans and observers around the world. Other forms of entertainment—from movies to books to sports—all found reduced audiences as Americans turned on the cable news and strapped in for a presidential year already unlike any other in history.

In contrast to the uncertainty and tumult of the presidential campaign, on Capitol Hill, the Senate, for the first time in years, was taking care of business, racking up legislative accomplishments.[1] Mitch McConnell (R–KY), the thirty-year Senate veteran, had achieved his life goal by becoming Senate majority leader in January 2015 after eight years as minority leader. McConnell had pledged to restore the Senate to being the great deliberative body that the framers of the Constitution had, in their wisdom, intended it to be.[2] He promised to rejuvenate the committee process so that legislation could be developed thoughtfully and taken to the Senate floor where it would be subject to an open amendment process and free-wheeling debate. McConnell had also pledged that senators would go back to working five-day weeks. He proclaimed that under his leadership the Senate would not be "the hollow shell of an institution" that his predecessor Harry Reid (D–NV) had created.[3]

The promised turnabout seemed to be underway. McConnell, notoriously guarded and controlled in his comments, was unusually expansive, even happy, as he reviewed the accomplishments of the Senate in his first year as leader.[4] A more open amendment process allowed more vigorous debate and a series of bipartisan legislative accomplishments: a new formula to pay doctors treating Medicare patients based on the quality of care they provided rather than the amount of care; a transportation bill that shored up the highway trust fund and allowed the continued repair of America's roads; a massive spending bill that funded the government through October 2016; an education reform bill that gave states a larger say on how to improve schools and evaluate teachers; and a security visa waiver that allowed citizens from thirty-eight "friendly" countries easy access to the United States while requiring stricter visa reviews for individuals from Iran, Iraq, Sudan, and Syria who were residents of those countries, or had visited them in the past five years. Bob Corker (R–TN) and Ben Cardin (D–MD), leaders of the Foreign Relations Committee, engineered an ingenious bipartisan compromise to carve out a limited role for Congress in reviewing the nuclear pact with Iran.

"They've really nailed down some festering issues that have been on the agenda for quite a while," noted Sarah Binder, a leading expert on Congress at the Brookings Institution. "And they've done it in this sort of remarkably bipartisan way."[5]

McConnell generously praised the Democrats for their contributions to the legislation, noting that they had been good collaborators.[6] He even showed a previously undetected wry sense of humor, describing working constructively with the White House to win Trade Promotion Authority for President Obama as "almost an out-of-body experience."[7] McConnell was in his element, successfully pursuing his political objectives while doing a more than respectable job of leading a Senate comeback.

A comeback was certainly long overdue. No one disputed that the Senate, which had been a crown jewel of our political system, had sunk to an all-time low.[8] In July 2015, former Senate leaders Tom Daschle (D–SD) and Trent Lott (R–MS) released a new book, *Crisis Point*. Daschle and Lott represent the epitome of Washington's political establishment. After a combined fifty-nine years in Congress, they continue to work in Washington as strategic advisers, lobbyists, board members, and leading participants in the Bipartisan Policy Center. They have many incentives not to be critical of Capitol Hill, and have a natural reluctance to criticize their successors as Senate leaders. Consequently, their unflinching words carry an extra force:

> America's strength has always come from its unique diversity—its willingness to not just permit but encourage competing viewpoints in order to strengthen the whole. The adversarial system, embedded by the Founding Fathers into our system of government, was meant to spur debate, challenge complacency, and drive progress. It has sustained our Republic for over 225 years, but we have to face a sad truth: *it has stopped working.* In fact, it has begun to work against us . . .

Our system of checks and balances was not designed to encourage the kind of inertia plaguing our current leaders in Washington. The quality of our United States Congress—and, by extension, the American government— continues to grow increasingly dysfunctional. . . . The center can no longer hold under such mindless and unprecedented partisanship; it is no exaggeration to say that the state of our democracy is as bad as we've ever seen it.[9]

Then, in a further unmistakable shot at the current Senate leaders, Daschle and Lott observed: "Bipartisan negotiation is the pumping blood of democracy, and it has run dry in the current Washington landscape. . . . Today's leaders don't practice bipartisanship and the environment of the nation's capital doesn't allow for it. The common ground has been stripped and scorched, allowing no community to grow."[10] McConnell did not actually need any further incentive as he tried to lead the Senate back from its nadir, but proving his predecessors wrong would have powerful appeal.

By 2016, Mitch McConnell had been a Senate fixture for so long that it was sometimes hard to grasp the magnitude of his accomplishments. Even when he served as minority leader, all legislation, as well as executive and judicial nominations, had to come through McConnell, who had unified the Senate Republicans to an unprecedented degree. The Senate's arcane rules and procedures gave a unified minority an extraordinary ability to permit action or obstruct it. If political power can be defined as the ability to achieve your political objectives and preventing your opponents from achieving theirs, no one in America was more powerful than Mitch McConnell—including the president of the United States.

As far back as early 2011, an *Atlantic* profile of McConnell by Joshua Green, titled "Strict Obstructionist," described McConnell as "the master manipulator and strategist—the unheralded architect of the Republican resurgence."[11] For the first six years of the Obama presidency, McConnell had "come to embody a kind of oppositional politics that critics say has left voters cynical about Washington, the Senate all but dysfunctional, and the Republican Party without a positive agenda or message."[12] Consequently, when he became majority leader, McConnell was in an excellent position to deliver on his promise to rejuvenate the Senate. Because McConnell was the principal cause of the gridlock, once he decided to become a constructive player the Senate could change rapidly. The Senate Democrats could gnash their teeth at the situation in which they found themselves, but McConnell knew he could count on them. By their nature, they wanted government to work and loved to legislate. As Chuck Schumer (D-NY), soon to be the Democratic leader, would say plaintively: "We're Democrats. We cannot just block everything. We believe in government."[13]

McConnell could savor his position even more because of how he had dramatically reversed his fortunes over the course of two years. As the 2012 elections approached, McConnell was virtually measuring the drapes in the majority leader's office because the Senate seemed ready to go Republican. The *Huffington Post* had called it "McConnell's moment," and he described himself as "prepared, and more than a little eager."[14] Thus, Obama's reelection in 2012 and a sweeping victory for the Senate Democrats, who retained every contested seat that they had held, and added two more, stunned him. Bitterly disappointed, McConnell recognized the real possibility that he would never reach his goal of being majority leader. Moreover, the polls indicated that he was so unpopular in Kentucky that he might be defeated in his race for a sixth term. He faced a tough primary challenge from a Tea Party Republican Matt Bevin, and the prospect of a fierce fight with a Democrat if he got through the primary. Chagrined that he was apparently the most endangered Republican incumbent, McConnell gave serious thought to not running again.[15]

Characteristically, he persevered. McConnell ran a relentless campaign against Bevin and defeated him comfortably. There was not that much room to the right of Mitch McConnell, even in a Republican Party increasingly influenced by its Tea Party wing. At the same time, McConnell took the lead in ensuring that Republicans chosen for Senate seats would be strong general election candidates. He helped identify appealing candidates who won Senate seats, like Thom Tillis, who had been majority leader of the North Carolina state senate; David Perdue, the CEO of Reebok, who ran in Georgia; and Joni Ernst and Tom Cotton, Iraq war veterans, who ran in Iowa and Arkansas. He orchestrated a concerted effort to defeat every Tea Party challenger so that there would be no repeat of 2012 when extreme Republican nominees lost Senate seats that could have easily been won in Missouri and Indiana.[16] With that accomplished, McConnell turned his focus to his own race, and decisively defeated Alison Lundergan Grimes, a promising but inexperienced challenger. Kentucky's voters were reminded of what it meant to have a senator who was a Senate leader, and the argument for staying with McConnell proved compelling. Throughout 2013 to 2014, McConnell still found time for his day job: being President Obama's principal nemesis, thwarting virtually every Obama initiative. On election night, Mitch McConnell not only won his own race but also gained a Senate majority. It was a political tour de force.

McConnell, understandably proud of what he had accomplished, came out with a memoir in early 2016, aptly titled *The Long Game*. He began 2016 knowing that the game still had to go through him, now more than ever—and then the game changed dramatically.

On February 13, 2016, Justice Antonin Scalia, the leading voice for the conservative wing of the Supreme Court, died, giving President Obama the opportunity to nominate a justice at a time when the Court was evenly divided between its liberal and conservative wings on virtually every key issue. No issue mattered more to the right wing of the Republican Party than the Supreme Court. The Senate, which had handled many controversial Supreme Court nominations, expected to face one more.

McConnell responded with extraordinary, even unseemly, speed.[17] About an hour after the announcement of Justice Scalia's death, when other political leaders were expressing condolences, McConnell announced that the Senate should not confirm a replacement for Justice Scalia until after the 2016 election. "The American people should have a voice in the selection of their next Supreme Court justice," McConnell intoned. "Therefore, this vacancy should not be filled until we have a new president."

"The swiftness of McConnell's statement . . . stunned White House officials who had expected the Kentucky Republican to block their nominee with every tool at his disposal, but didn't imagine the combative GOP leader would issue an instant, categorical rejection of anyone Obama chose to nominate," *Politico* reported. Despite McConnell's statement, there was no precedent for the Senate to refuse to consider a Supreme Court nominee in an election year; it had done so for justices nominated by Lyndon Johnson in 1968 and by Ronald Reagan in 1988.

Senator Patrick Leahy (D-VT), the longest serving senator, blasted McConnell for a blatantly political move when the Senate's calendar appeared to be open most of the summer: "Cancel one of the vacations, one of the recesses," Leahy said. "If this was November, then I could see . . . at least making the argument. But it's February." Charles Grassley (R-IA), who chaired the Judiciary Committee, brushed Leahy's argument aside. "This president, above all others, has made no bones about his goal to use the courts to circumvent Congress and push through his own agenda," Grassley said. "It only makes sense that we defer to the American people who will elect a new president to select the next Supreme Court Justice."[18]

Legal scholars expressed outrage, pointing out that McConnell's action was unprecedented in American history.[19] The White House floated the possibility of nominating Brian Sandoval, the Republican governor of Nevada.[20] Democrats were hopeful when Republicans senators Susan Collins (R-ME) and Jerry Moran (R-KS) said that a nominee put forth by Obama should receive a hearing. (Moran reversed course quickly under intense fire from the Republican right wing.[21]) The debate further escalated when President Obama nominated Merrick Garland, the universally admired chief judge of the D.C. Circuit Court of Appeals. Surely, many thought, McConnell would not be able to hold his troops together to stonewall an extraordinarily qualified nominee who was known to be only slightly left of center. "The Senate Republicans will sacrifice their majority and their best shot at the White House on the altar of Ted Cruz if they block this nomination," said one Democratic strategist. Many Democrats predicted that McConnell's power play would backfire by energizing the Democratic base, particularly in key Senate races.[22] Grassley, eighty-two years old, seeking his seventh term in Iowa, seemed uniquely vulnerable.[23] The Democrats found a seemingly formidable candidate, former lieutenant governor Patty Judge, and turned up the heat through paid media.

In the end, McConnell triumphed across the board. Donald Trump's astonishing campaign and the vitriolic contest against Hillary Clinton dominated the political landscape and drowned out even an issue as important as the selection of a Supreme Court justice. It would be hard to identify many votes that were cast or voters that were mobilized for Hillary Clinton or Senate Democratic candidates because Mitch McConnell had prevented President Obama from nominating a Supreme Court justice. By contrast, McConnell's move galvanized many conservative voters to put aside their misgivings about Donald Trump because of the overriding importance of who would nominate the next Supreme Court justice.[24] Virtually all the close Senate races swung to the Republicans in the end. Grassley won reelection in a landslide.

In 2016, Donald Trump, a billionaire celebrity reality TV star, won the presidential election after the intervention of Russia and FBI director James Comey. Against that surreal background, anything else may look like politics as usual. But in fact, Senator McConnell's unprecedented action was an exercise of raw political power unmatched in American history. It was a moment that crystallized just how polarized our politics had become and how badly the institutions and guardrails in our system had eroded. Outrageous acts of partisan obstruction had gradually become normal, and the principal architect of obstruction usually won.

McConnell did not need time to consult because he knew that his Senate Republican colleagues would either strongly agree with him or that they reluctantly swallow their concerns and go along. He could make the decision alone because only he could balance what he was gaining—the Supreme Court seat if a Republican president was elected—against what he was losing—the promising Senate comeback that he had hoped to lead.

McConnell often expressed his reverence for the Senate, and at some level, he certainly loved it. But he never put the interests of the Senate first; he had repeatedly made decisions and taken actions that had sacrificed and diminished the Senate. Perhaps he calculated that "the long game" would always give him other opportunities to atone. Or perhaps he had simply embraced the famous motto of Vince Lombardi: "Winning isn't everything. It's the only thing." In either case, by the end of 2016, Mitch McConnell, undeniably one of the strongest Senate leaders in history, stood tall amid the wreckage of a Senate that the senators and the American people regarded as broken.

In the Shadow of Mansfield's Great Senate

$\mathcal{T}$he words of Tom Daschle and Trent Lott carried special force because they were veteran senators and Senate leaders. But the views they expressed were common knowledge long before their book came out. As Jonathan Martin, national political correspondent for the *New York Times*, then at *Politico*, observed in 2012: "Vast forests have lost their trees to books, articles and dissertations commenting on American political dysfunction."[1] Unmistakably, hyperpartisanship produced gridlock, resulting in public anger and a profound loss of confidence in Washington.

The Senate is ground zero for America's political dysfunction. It is the political institution that has failed Americans the longest and the worst. America is a strong enough country to survive a few bad years, but the Senate has been in decline for several decades, and the decline continued to accelerate, turning into a downward spiral that reached a new low with Senator McConnell's decision not to consider an Obama nominee to replace Justice Scalia. The Senate's failure is particularly crippling because it is supposed to be the balance wheel and the moderating force in our system—the place where the two parties come together to find common ground through vigorous debate and principled compromises to advance the national interest. But to perform its role as "the nation's mediator," the Senate requires a degree of bipartisan comity that has long been lost. Without that bipartisan comity, the Senate not only reflects the polarization in the country; it exacerbates it by demonstrating it constantly at the highest and most visible level of government.

The Senate's long decline is acutely painful to a generation of Americans who grew up with a special attachment to it. The year 2017 marked the centennial of President John F. Kennedy, whose life and presidency were tragically shortened when he was assassinated in Dallas on November 22, 1963. We remember John Kennedy as a politician of extraordinary intellect and charisma. A war hero and an author, the scion of a glamorous family, the first Roman Catholic to reach the White House, Kennedy would have been a formidable presidential candidate if he had been a governor or a university president. But in 1960, there is no doubt that Kennedy benefited from how deeply embedded the Senate had become in the nation's consciousness in the previous decade.

AMERICANS DISCOVER THE SENATE

The Senate had first gained the attention of many Americans in 1939 with Frank Capra's film *Mr. Smith Goes to Washington*, starring Jimmy Stewart as the idealistic young lawyer appointed to the Senate who battles political corruption in Washington. The film, widely regarded as a classic, captured eleven Academy Award nominations and catapulted Stewart to stardom. Recent real-life filibusters by senators Rand Paul (R-KY) and Ted Cruz (R-TX) still draw unfavorable comparison to Stewart's valiant effort.

But the Senate truly seized the attention of the American public in 1950 when Estes Kefauver (D-TN), a little-known senator from Tennessee, began an extraordinary series of investigative hearings into organized crime in America. The "Kefauver hearings," as they became universally known, took place in fourteen cities around the country.[2] They illuminated the workings of the Mafia, and forced J. Edgar Hoover, the FBI director, to admit that organized crime was a national problem. Television was still very new in America, and the Kefauver hearings became the first nationally shared television experience, viewed by more than thirty million Americans in their homes, bars, restaurants, and movie theaters. At one time, an astonishing 72 percent of Americans expressed familiarity with the committee's work.

During eight days of hearings in New York in March 1951, more than fifty witnesses described the highest-ranking crime syndicate in America, an organization allegedly led by Frank Costello, who had taken over from Lucky Luciano. "The week of March 12, 1951, will occupy a special place in history," *Life* magazine reported. "People had suddenly gone indoors into living rooms, taverns, and clubrooms, auditoriums and back-offices. There, in eerie half-light, looking at millions of small frosty screens, people sat as if charmed. Never had the attention of the nation been riveted so completely on a single matter." *Time* magazine wrote: "From Manhattan as far west as the coaxial cable ran, the U.S. adjusted itself to Kefauver's schedule. Dishes stood in sinks, babies went unfed, business sagged, and department stores emptied while the hearings went on."

At virtually the same time, President Harry Truman fired General Douglas MacArthur for insubordination and violating civilian control of the military by widening the war in Korea beyond what Truman had authorized him to do.[3] The public anger toward Truman, an unpopular president, for firing MacArthur, one of the greatest national heroes, was astonishingly intense. There was an outcry for Truman to be impeached and for MacArthur to run for president. The general returned to the United States like a conquering hero, receiving ticker-tape parades in several cities. The Senate Armed Services Committee, chaired by Richard Russell (D-GA), held a searching set of hearings that put Truman's decision and MacArthur's behavior in a much different light; the public outcry ended, and the old general faded away.

In 1954, the country became again enthralled by the Permanent Subcommittee on Investigations hearings into Senator Joseph McCarthy's (R-WI) charges of communism in the army. The hearings produced one of the most famous moments in American political history when Joseph Welch, the army's chief counsel, challenged McCarthy: "At long last, have you left no sense of decency?" That dramatic exchange highlighted a hearing that sent McCarthy's popularity into a tailspin and opened the door to his censure by the Senate, ending the "Red Scare" that he had done so much to precipitate.

In 1955, Kennedy, a little-known Massachusetts senator, wrote *Profiles in Courage*, eloquently describing inordinate acts of political courage and sacrifice by eight of his congressional predecessors.[4] *Profiles in Courage* would become one of the most indelible phrases in American life. It also became one of the best-known political books ever written, earning the Pulitzer Prize and springboarding Kennedy to national prominence.

In 1957, William White, the Pulitzer Prize–winning biographer of Senator Robert Taft, wrote *Citadel: The Story of the U.S. Senate*, perhaps the most serious exploration of the Senate to date.[5] At the same time, White's reporting for the *New York Times* showed Majority Leader Lyndon Johnson working to pass the Civil Rights Act of 1957, a modest but important first legislative step to address the discrimination against black Americans.

Also in 1957, Senator John McClellan (D-AR) seized attention with a major set of investigative hearings into corruption and criminal activities among labor unions.[6] The tough, crime-fighting McClellan had a young, fiercely determined chief counsel, Robert F. Kennedy, who, as attorney general in his brother's administration, would continue his investigation of, and vendetta with, Teamster president Jimmy Hoffa.

In 1959, Allen Drury, another *New York Times* Senate correspondent, wrote *Advise and Consent*, a novel about a brutal Senate confirmation fight over Robert Leffingwell, the liberal nominated to be secretary of state. Nothing could quite match the Kefauver hearings in seizing the nation's consciousness, but *Advise and Consent* became the most famous political novel ever written. It spent 102 weeks on the best-seller list, and the movie version, with memorable scenes of Senate floor debate and off-the-floor intrigue, captivated many Americans. In 2009 Thomas Mallon, writing for the *New York Times Book Review,* observed: "Fifty years later, most of the subject matter remains recognizable. Drury's 99 men and lone woman wrestle with the issue of pre-emptive war, the degree of severity with which lying under oath must be viewed, and the way the cover up is invariably worse than the crime."[7] Scott Simon of *National Public Radio,* writing in the *Wall Street Journal,* put it succinctly: "Fifty years after publication and astounding success, Allen Drury's novel remains the definitive Washington tale."[8]

The remarkable visibility of the Senate throughout the 1950s certainly helped Kennedy reach the White House. Kennedy's extraordinary worldwide popularity and glamour further added to the luster of the Senate.

One of the great ironies is that through most of the 1950s, while the Senate became recognizable and fascinating to many Americans, it remained dominated by the southern senators who used their seniority, committee chairmanships, and the filibuster to bottle up civil rights and other progressive legislation. The Senate was, in the words of William White, "The South's undying revenge for Gettysburg . . . the only place in the country where the South did not lose the Civil War."[9] In the late 1950s, Majority Leader Lyndon Johnson used his extraordinary energy, cunning, and power to drag the conservative, often reactionary, Senate into the twentieth century. The Senate's progressive period would come later.

Of course, the self-important Senate always prompted some biting humor. It became common to say that "every senator looks in the mirror and sees a president." From 1960 when Kennedy captured the presidency, until today, nearly forty senators or former senators reached for the White House—several of them multiple times—with only Barack Obama replicating Kennedy's success of moving directly from the Senate to the White House.

But while it was easy to joke about it, the fact was only the presidency was a better job than being a senator. And what could be better preparation for the presidency than being involved in the full range of domestic and foreign policy issues that a senator confronted? Ed Muskie, Scoop Jackson, Hubert Humphrey, Howard Baker, Bob Dole, John McCain—none of them became presidents, but few doubted their ability to do the job if they reached the White House. Moreover, even the presidency was term limited. Senators could remain important players on the national scene for three or four or five six-year terms, ranging wide on issues and going deeply into the areas they cared most about. It was no accident that a basketball star (Bill Bradley) and two astronauts (John Glenn and Harrison Schmitt) reached for Senate seats. For many years, there were persistent rumors that Paul Newman or Warren Beatty would run. No one was really surprised when Robert Kennedy or Hillary Clinton sought a Senate seat. Being part of "the most exclusive club" provided a great opportunity to serve the country.

Of course, that was another time, before senators like Warren Rudman (R-NH), Olympia Snowe (R-ME), Evan Bayh (D-IN), Mel Martinez (R-FL), Jim Webb (D-VA), and many others left the Senate in disgust. It was long before the life of a senator came to consist of sitting around waiting for some senator to drop his "hold" that paralyzed the Senate; hoping for a chance to be on a Sunday talk show; going home every weekend to campaign; leaving the Senate office building for several hours each day to raise money; and being told by the party leader how to vote. In a memorable 2010 *New Yorker* article, George Packer described an endless, vapid debate, punctuated by a series of long quorum calls, and dubbed the Senate "the empty chamber."[10]

RECALLING MIKE MANSFIELD: THE GREATEST SENATE LEADER

Organizations—whether corporations, law firms, or NGOs—often try to learn by looking at "best practices." Where the Senate is concerned, there is a strong consensus about best practices, and what made the Senate work when it was at its peak. That discussion always starts the name with the taciturn professor of Asian history, an improbable politician, who became a senator from Montana, reluctantly accepted the post of majority leader, and then went on to be the longest serving and greatest majority leader: Mike Mansfield.

Born in New York, Mansfield moved to Montana to live with relatives after his mother died when he was seven. As a young man, he served in the army, navy, and marines, and developed a fascination for Asia where he served after World War I. He returned home to become a university professor of political science and history, but his deep interest in world affairs led him into politics. His intellect, honesty, and humility appealed to Montanans, who elected him first to the House and then to the Senate in 1952.

In 1960, when John Kennedy was elected president, Lyndon Johnson left the Senate to become Kennedy's vice president. A vigorous contest for the position of majority leader appeared likely between Hubert Humphrey of Minnesota, who had become the Senate's most visible and effective liberal, and George Smathers of Florida, a much more conservative, business-oriented senator, with a flamboyant personal life. Kennedy, less liberal than Humphrey, enjoyed Smathers's company but knew his limitations. Shortly after his election,

Kennedy called Mansfield, who was a close and trusted friend, and said that he wanted him to become majority leader. Startled by the president-elect's intervention into a Senate leadership race, Mansfield said that he had no interest in the position. He also expressed doubt that Kennedy, the first Catholic president, should also have Catholic leaders in both houses of Congress. Kennedy brushed that objection aside, telling Mansfield that he needed him to lead the Senate and move his legislative program. Mansfield reluctantly agreed. He went on to make history long after both Kennedy and Johnson were gone.

Perpetually sucking on a pipe, Mansfield was a man of few words, laconic in his personal style. He did not believe in the theatrics that had characterized Lyndon Johnson's Senate leadership. Nor did he believe in a Senate where the majority leader immodestly took credit for breaking seemingly impossible deadlocks. Mansfield was repelled by Johnson's exercise of raw power, which included intimidation; learning, and capitalizing on, senators' weaknesses; and punishing those who crossed him by denying them positions on major committees or depriving them of staff and office space. Tom Daschle and Trent Lott would write: "It's unlikely that [Mansfield] twisted one arm in his sixteen years in charge."

Even more fundamentally, Mansfield did not believe in a Senate dominated by the leaders and a handful of senior senators. He believed in a democratic, small-d, Senate, where all senators were adults, elected by their constituents, and all senators were equal. In fact, he even treated the senators in the minority as his equals. To a degree that stunned the senators, Mansfield believed in the "golden rule" and acted accordingly. He treated each senator the way he wanted to be treated himself, and he expected reciprocity.[11]

Most senators, starting with Minority Leader Everett Dirksen, doubted that Mansfield could possibly run the Senate along those lines. Under his leadership, the hundred senators, not the majority leader, were responsible for making the Senate work. By 1963, Mansfield's democratized Senate had become newly paralyzed. Very little legislation was moving; senators saw no reason to come to the Senate floor. Mansfield seemed unable to rouse the Senate from its torpor and made few efforts to do so. He received intense criticism in the press, led by reporters that Johnson had cultivated. Meanwhile, he contended with a virtual rebellion within the Senate, led by Russell Long of Louisiana and Thomas Dodd of Connecticut, who publicly pined for the return of a strong leader.

On Friday, November 22, 1963, Mansfield announced that on the following Monday, he would deliver a speech on the Senate floor addressing the questions that had been raised about his leadership. The speech that Mansfield prepared for delivery was remarkable for its clarity and honesty:

Descriptions of the Majority Leader, the senator from Montana, have ranged from a benign Mr. Chips to glamourless, to tragic mistake. As for being a tragic mistake, if that means I am neither a circus ringmaster, the master of ceremonies of a Senate night club, a tamer of Senate lions, or a wheeler and dealer, then I must accept too that title. . . . But as long as I have this responsibility, it will be discharged to the best of my ability by me as I am . . . I shall not don any Mandarin's robes or any skin other than that to which I am accustomed in order that I might look like a majority leader or sound like a majority leader.[12]

He closed with an eloquent explanation of how he viewed the Senate: "The Constitutional authority does not lie with the leadership. It lies with all of us individually, collectively and equally. . . . In the end, it is not the senators as individuals who are of fundamental importance. In the end, it is the institution of the Senate itself, as one of the foundations of the Constitution. It is the Senate as one of the rocks of the Republic."

Mansfield never delivered his speech. It had to be inserted in the *Congressional Record* because several hours after he informed the Senate of his intent to speak, the Senate and the country received word that President Kennedy had been assassinated in Dallas.

Mansfield never faced a question about his leadership again. Galvanized by the tragedy of Kennedy's assassination, the leadership of President Lyndon Johnson, and the moral imperative of action on civil rights, Mansfield's democratized Senate met the challenge of history. In the summer of 1964, with the country and the rest of the world watching, the Senate broke the filibuster of the southern bloc to enact what is generally regarded as the most important piece of legislation in history—the Civil Rights Act of 1964.

Mansfield demonstrated his unique leadership style in the months long battle to break the southern filibuster. President Johnson, who knew the senators and the Senate intimately, advised Mansfield to exhaust the southerners with round-the-clock sessions, noting that "Richard Russell was old, Alan Ellender had cancer." Mansfield would have no part of it, and told the president so. He went to Russell, the unquestioned leader of the southerners, and told him that he was committed to overcoming the filibuster, which at that time required the vote of sixty-seven senators. He promised Russell a hard fight, but a clean fight, with full communication, no exhausting tactics, and no tricks. Mansfield designated Hubert Humphrey to lead the Democratic effort because of Humphrey's unmatched credibility with the broad liberal coalition supporting the legislation. Recognizing that breaking the filibuster would require the support of three-quarters of the Republican senators, Mansfield ensured that Everett Dirksen (R-IL), the Republican leader, could be the pivotal figure in the legislative battle, which reflected the political realities and gave the vain Dirksen the visibility and power that he enjoyed.

Under Mansfield's leadership, the Senate would no longer be the grid-locked graveyard of progressive dreams. It became the place where those hopes and dreams were translated into legislation, moved forward with presidents where possible, and where necessary, despite them.

Respectful of all senators, whether Democratic or Republican, senior or freshman, without flamboyance, letting others take the lead and the credit, Mansfield exercised his quiet brand of leadership as the Senate provided gravitas and ballast for our country during crisis times. He combined what his principal aide and biographer Francis Valeo called "awesome patience" with utter honesty and straight dealing.

Mansfield gave private advice to presidents Kennedy, Johnson, and Nixon about Vietnam. His numerous memos were heartbreakingly prescient about the folly of escalation. It was Mansfield who gave up on Nixon's commitment to ending the Vietnam War after the invasion of Cambodia, and encouraged senators, on a bipartisan basis, to finally cut off funding for the war. He had extraordinary influence because he was a true Asia expert and because he had tried to offer private counsel and to give Nixon the benefit of the doubt.

In October 1972, angered by evidence of "dirty tricks" and possibly il-legal practices in Nixon's reelection campaign, Mansfield announced that the Senate would investigate these abuses. In November 1972, Richard Nixon won forty-nine states and was reelected by the greatest margin in American politi-cal history. Yet so great was Mansfield's stature and credibility that two months after Nixon's landslide victory, the Senate unanimously approved the creation of the Select Committee on Presidential Campaign Activities, which quickly became universally known as the Watergate Committee. Then in a deft politi-cal move, Mansfield opted for a select committee to avoid Judiciary Chairman James Eastland (D-MS), a strong Nixon supporter, picking instead Sam Ervin (D-NC) for chairman, a folksy former state supreme court justice who had already emerged as one of Nixon's fiercest opponents.

Mansfield ate breakfast almost every morning with his closest friend, Republican senator George Aiken (R-VT). Mansfield's Senate was bipartisan to the core. Everyone—senators and staff—knew that it was impossible to get anything done on a partisan basis. When a Democratic staff member would propose a new initiative to his boss, the first response would always be: "Get a Republican cosponsor."

During most of the 1960s and 1970s, the Senate, although a political in-stitution, was surprisingly free from partisanship. The herculean effort to give civil rights to black Americans, the tragedy of Vietnam, the crisis of Watergate, checking the "imperial presidency" of Johnson and Nixon—these were not partisan issues, and the Senate responded in a bipartisan way. Thanks to Dirksen's leadership, the 1964 Civil Rights Act passed with the support of twenty-five out of thirty-three Republican senators. Democratic senators—Eugene McCarthy (D-MN), Robert Kennedy (D-NY), George McGovern (D-SD), William Fulbright (D-AR), Frank Church (D-ID)—were joined by Republican senators—Aiken (R-VT), John Sherman Cooper (R-KY), Mark Hatfield (R-OR), Charles Goodell (R-NY)—in opposing the Vietnam War during both the Johnson and Nixon administrations. Watergate had the potential to divide on partisan lines, but Sam Ervin and Howard Baker, the committee chairman and vice chairman, understood that a partisan breakdown would destroy the committee, and they worked closely together to avoid it. The great issues that threatened the country's stability were too important; the senators understood the stakes.

Of course, elections came every two years, and political campaigns went on around the country, but the Senate stayed somewhat separate, almost a demilitarized zone where partisan politics was concerned. More than forty years later, Birch Bayh, an Indiana Democrat, recalled his amazement during his first year in the Senate when Everett Dirksen, the Republican leader from the neighboring state of Illinois, spent an hour on the presidential yacht, *Sequoia*, telling Bayh what he had to do to get reelected.[13]

Things began to change in the late 1970s with the rise of the New Right and single-issue politics, marked by negative advertising and fiery grassroots campaigns around emotional issues such as abortion, guns, and the Panama Canal.[14] But even then, the Republicans elected to the Senate in 1976 and 1978 included distinguished moderates such as John Heinz (R-PA), Richard Lugar (R-IND), John Danforth (R-MO), William Cohen (R-ME), John Chafee (R-RI), John Warner (R-VA), and Alan Simpson (R-WY). The high walls that separated the Senate from the "permanent campaign" of raw, endless partisan politics would come down, but for several years, Mansfield's great Senate held together, still capable of subordinating partisanship to accomplishing the nation's business.

Mansfield's decision to retire, announced without fanfare on March 4, 1976, was typical of the man: "There is a time to stay and a time to go," Mansfield told a stunned Senate. "Thirty-four years in the House and Senate is not a long time" —to a scholar of Asian history—"but it is long enough."

The Senate that I chronicled in *The Last Great Senate* is the Senate from 1977 through 1980, the four-year period right after Mansfield's departure. The new leaders, Robert Byrd (D-WV) and Howard Baker (R-TN), had their own distinctive styles, and they confronted a changing and newly challenging political climate. But the Senate they led, which compiled an extraordinary record of accomplishment, was very much a continuation of Mansfield's Senate.

LESSONS LEARNED FROM MANSFIELD'S SENATE

Beyond Mansfield's distinctive leadership style, there are important lessons to be learned from his Senate.

Members of Mansfield's Senate shared a concept of what it meant to be a senator. Senators take an oath to preserve, protect, and defend the Constitution. But there is also an unspoken oath that many senators come to understand. The people of their states had given them the incredible privilege and honor of being U.S. senators. They had received the most venerable of titles that a Republic can bestow and a six-year term (usually leading to multiple terms) to serve. They would have the opportunity to deal with the full spectrum of issues, domestic and foreign, and they would develop unique expertise, valuable to the Senate and the country. In exchange, when they sorted out the competing, cascading pressures on them, they would serve their states and they would never forget their party allegiance, but the national interest would come first. They would bring their wisdom and independent judgment to bear to determine what is best for national interest.

Every senator was committed to the interests of his or her state. They served constituents from Washington and a network of offices throughout the state, and they considered the impact on their state of every piece of legislation that comes before them. But every state has many officials, at every level of government, working to protect and advance its interests. Each state only has two U.S. senators, who have a unique responsibility. The best senators never lost sight of the fact that their overriding commitment was to the nation.

Robert Byrd (D-WV), the longest-serving senator, became legendary for the federal funds and projects that he delivered to West Virginia over his fifty-year service in the Senate. Byrd turnpikes, bridges, buildings, and science centers appeared all over the state. But he became a great senator when he grew in office, taking on national responsibilities and becoming a leading defender of the Senate and its constitutional role. Byrd threw himself into foreign policy issues and became a leader in the historic fight for Senate ratification of the Panama Canal treaties in 1978. A quarter century later, Byrd became a hero to many Americans with his eloquent opposition to the invasion of Iraq, and in his book titled *Losing America*. He started his career as a pork-barrel senator, and ended it as, what David Corbin, his biographer, aptly called "the last great senator," who was admired for his commitment to the Senate, the Constitution, and the nation, as well as his wise judgment.[15]

The best senators not only understood that they had national responsibilities but also they developed deep substantive knowledge. Executive branch officials in every administration, whether Democratic or Republican, quickly came to realize that the senators knew an extraordinary amount about the areas in which they specialized. Secretaries of state and defense came and went, but no one knew more than Henry Jackson (D-WA) about the Soviet Union, America's nuclear arsenal, and conventional defenses. In Mansfield's Senate, Jackson had counterparts in virtually every substantive area.

The second part of the senators' unspoken oath was an obligation to help make the Senate work. As Mansfield memorably noted: "In the end, it is not the individuals of the Senate who are important. It is the institution of the Senate." The senators understood that the nation relied on the Senate to take collective action. Understanding that brought about a commitment to passionate, but not unlimited, debate; tolerance of opposing views; principled compromise; and senators' willingness to end debate and vote up or down, even if it sometimes meant losing.

These qualities characterized the great Senate and its members. Hubert Humphrey and Barry Goldwater (R-AZ) were poles apart politically, but no one doubted that they were both committed to the national interest and to the Senate as an institution. Because of those overriding commitments, in Mansfield's Senate, the members competed and cooperated, clashed and compromised, and then went out to dinner together. That Senate worked because of mutual respect, tolerance of opposing views, and openness to persuasion in the search for solutions that would command sufficiently broad support. And, of course, given the Senate rules and practices and the perpetual possibility of extended debate—a filibuster or the threat thereof—those solutions always had to be bipartisan.

The Senate always included members with strong views ranging across the political spectrum. But when a senator had views on the end of the political spectrum—left or right—the key question became whether that person understood that they served in an institution that needed to take collective action. Many Democratic senators deeply disagreed with the harshly conservative views of Jesse Helms (R-NC). But Helms posed a problem for the Senate (just as Ted Cruz does to today's Senate), not because of his extreme views, but because he was committed to his individual agenda to the exclusion of the Senate's responsibility to take collective action. That was the essence of Mansfield's wisdom: the agendas of individual senators did not ultimately matter; it was the Senate, and the country, that mattered.

When senators see the Senate as simply a forum for their own talents, interests, or advancement, when they see their views as so important or divinely inspired that compromise becomes unacceptable, or when they regard the Senate as merely an extension of the battle between the political parties, the Senate can become polarized and paralyzed, on the way to irrelevance and decline.[16]

The Senate in its best times unflinchingly faced up to these issues of the day. In 1977, the Senate convened with two new leaders: Democrat Robert

Byrd and Republican Howard Baker. Americans had elected a new, outsider president, Jimmy Carter, the former governor of Georgia. In the aftermath of Watergate, Carter had ridden to the White House as a contrast to Richard Nixon, an outsider who promised to restore ethics in government. It became clear quickly that Carter disliked political small talk, disliked politicians, and liked politics least of all.[17] Carter had hated the Georgia legislature, and he saw members of Congress as either captives of the interest groups or too quick to bend to their views. His concept of the presidency was as a trusteeship, where he had a special obligation to the country because he was the only person elected by the whole nation. Carter's training as an engineer, coupled with his inordinate self-confidence, convinced him that if he studied a problem closely enough, he could find the best answer, decide what was in the national interest, and pursue a solution, irrespective of political fallout. Compromise was the lifeblood of politics on Capitol Hill, and Jimmy Carter did not believe in compromise. He had a very ambitious agenda, and he expected the Democratic Congress to move it.

Obviously, the Senate and Jimmy Carter were not a match made in heaven, and they went through very rough times. But the Senate, on both sides of the aisle, worked with him, and helped him. They rejected his proposal for a $50 tax refund for every American, which they thought was ludicrous. They dove into his astonishingly complex proposal for a national energy policy, broke it into pieces, and passed it, piecemeal and with great pain, during the time he was president. The Senate killed his proposals for labor law reform but worked with him on imaginative legislation to rescue New York City in 1978 and Chrysler in 1979. The Senate supported his proposal to sell F-15 jet fighters to Saudi Arabia even though Israel and AIPAC were fiercely opposed to it.

When Jimmy Carter faced up to a challenge that five presidents going back to Eisenhower had avoided—the necessity of a new arrangement governing the Panama Canal—the Senate stepped up to that responsibility too, even though the potential political consequences were unmistakably clear. Howard Baker, the new Republican leader, recalled thinking: "Why now? Why me?"[18] Yet after careful study, Baker became convinced that a new treaty was in the national interest, and his leadership made the difference in its narrow approval. He exercised that leadership with full knowledge that Republicans around the country hated the treaty and that it would likely end his chances of ever becoming president. Frank Church was a leading liberal from the conservative state of Idaho, where opposition to the treaty was overwhelming. The handwriting was on the wall; Church knew that a vote for the treaty was likely to end his distinguished career. But he had favored a new Panama Canal treaty for many years; he was the Senate's most eloquent critic of "Yankee Imperialism" in Latin America. Church took on the key role of floor leader, and two years later, his Senate career ended after four terms.

In 1979, Carter's highest priority—the SALT II nuclear treaty with the Soviet Union—went down in flames as relations with the Soviets—already bad—were poisoned by their invasion of Afghanistan. Henry "Scoop" Jackson (D-WA), who deeply distrusted the Soviet Union, thought Carter did not understand the Soviet threat, and worked systematically and with great effect to defeat the treaty. The personal chemistry between Jackson and Carter was terrible; Carter had crushed his dreams of being the Democratic nominee in 1976. Jackson also disliked Carter's penchant for wearing religion on his sleeve, and he maintained grave doubts about his ability to govern. Yet Jackson, as chairman of the Energy Committee, would work to the point of exhaustion for several years to bring Carter's national energy program into law.

The New York City ("New York") rescue in 1978 provided a vivid example of the Senate at its best. In 1975, after an acrimonious debate. New York had been given a financial lifeline by Congress, which took the form of a three-year program of seasonal loans to be paid back in full, with interest, at the end of the year. As a condition of receiving the loans, New York went into virtual receivership, with a state-established Emergency Financial Control Board making its fiscal decisions.

By 1978, even New York's most severe critics acknowledged that the city had made progress in improving its financial management and getting on a more sustainable track. New York's advocates believed that with another round of loans, the city would not only survive but also prosper. However, the Senate Banking Committee, led by its brilliant, maverick chairman William Proxmire (D-WI), which had had engineered the 1975 rescue, had vowed "never again" to provide a federal bailout. In February 1978, the Banking Committee issued a unanimous report on the city's financial condition, which concluded that if interested local parties—city and state pension funds and financial institutions—would agree to provide reasonable amounts of aid to the city, there would be no need for continued federal assistance.

Nevertheless, the Carter administration saw the need to help New York, and Proxmire convened the committee to consider New York's request. No one doubted that the chairman, a severe critic of wasteful federal spending, was adamantly opposed, and a formidable adversary. But Proxmire did not use his power to block or duck consideration of the problem. In a series of remarkably searching hearings, New York and its advocates convinced the Banking Committee to reverse its position and support federal relief. With the help of freshman senator Richard Lugar, the Republican former mayor of Indianapolis, the committee fashioned a relief package, but with conditions so severe as to

deter other cities from requesting help. Proxmire insisted on managing the legislation on the Senate floor, where he took the position that although he was
still opposed, if the Senate was going to bail out New York, this legislation did
it in the best way possible. The legislation approving federal loan guarantees to
New York was approved 53–27, just weeks after any federal help had appeared
to be a lost cause.[19]

There are so many aspects to the story that are gratifying to those who
believe in government and the Senate. At a time when a tax revolt was sweeping the country, federal relief for New York required real political courage. But
the city, New York State, and the Carter administration made a strong case.
New York benefited from the great advocacy and stature of senators Jacob
Javits (R-NY) and Daniel Patrick Moynihan (D-NY). The Banking Committee changed its collective mind in response to compelling evidence. The
committee crafted a creative legislative solution, and Proxmire did not use his
position to block action. In the 1980s and 1990s, New York experienced the
renaissance that Mayor Ed Koch, Governor Hugh Carey, and other advocates
for the city had predicted. Many factors contributed to New York City's resurgence, including the strong national economy of the 1990s and the vibrant
(if oversized) financial sector centered on Wall Street. But there is little doubt
that the foundation of New York's revival was laid when the Senate showed the
courage to provide relief and the wisdom to design the right package.

*Individual acts of political courage and a sense of collective responsibility, leading to
creative legislative solutions, principled compromise, and timely action*—that was how
the senators saw their jobs, and that was how the Senate worked.

Readers may be understandably skeptical of my objectivity about Mansfield's Senate, since working there was an important part of my life, and I
returned to that era decades later in writing about it. But many observers of,
and participants in, politics share my perspective. The most telling endorsement comes from Senate Majority Leader Mitch McConnell, who got his
start in politics working as a legislative assistant to Kentucky senator Marlow Cooke. McConnell knows Senate history as well as anyone, with the
exception of Robert Byrd, and he has repeatedly expressed his admiration
for Mansfield's leadership and the Senate that he built. In McConnell's 2016
memoir, he wrote:

> As I looked at what the Senate could be, Mansfield's example offered a clue.
> His even-handedness and respect for every senator, regardless of political
> affiliation, made him popular not only among his Democratic colleagues,
> but among most members of the Republican minority as well. . . . There are
> many well-known stories of Mansfield's fairness and equanimity as a leader.
> But they all seem to come down to one thing, and that was his unbending
> belief that every senator should be treated equally.[20]

Obviously, despite the sentiments that Senator McConnell expressed, "Mansfield's Senate" bears no resemblance to any Senate that America has seen for a long time. The Senate has been in serious decline for at least twenty-five years. To be sure, today's vitriolic political culture makes being a senator harder than ever before. The endless demands of fundraising required for increasingly expensive campaigns drain the time and energy of senators and expose them to ceaseless demands of a vast corps of organized interests and lobbyists. The air travel that makes regular trips to their home states routinely possible diminishes the time that senators, and their families, once spent together. The impact of the twenty-four-hour news cycles, the blogosphere, and the tendency of Americans to choose only the news they want to hear, or follow on Facebook and Twitter, have changed the public debate profoundly.

But these changes in our political culture make it even more important that we have a Senate of wise men and women, bringing experience, wisdom, and independent judgment to their collective responsibility to determine the national interest. The political atmosphere is poisonous, and the political culture degraded. Neither of those factors have stopped Chuck Schumer (D-NY), Richard Durbin (D-IL), Patty Murray (D-WA), Dianne Feinstein (D-CA), Ben Cardin (D-MD), Jack Reed (D-RI), Ron Wyden (D-OR), Susan Collins (R-ME), John McCain (R-AZ), Lamar Alexander (R-TN), Lindsey Graham (R-NC), Jeff Flake (R-AZ), and others from behaving the way the best senators always have. Every two years, even as the Senate has declined, certain pieces of major legislation get written, debated, and enacted in the bipartisan fashion that was once commonplace.

What is most urgently needed is for senators to act like senators, not partisan operatives. They should not mirror, or even exacerbate, the nation's divisions. They were sent to Washington to overcome them. The arrival in the White House of Donald J. Trump, our first real insurgent president, presented an unprecedented challenge to the Senate but could also be the catalyst for its resurgence. But it is first necessary to understand what happened to Mansfield's Senate.

· 3 ·

From the Reagan Revolution
to the Clinton Impeachment

$\mathscr{R}$onald Reagan's landslide victory over President Jimmy Carter in 1980 was one of those unmistakable political watersheds that occur once every thirty or fifty years. Winning the popular vote by 10 percent (51–41), carrying forty-four states with 489 electoral votes, including every one of the ten largest states in the country, Reagan's victory signaled the end of the largely Democratic era that had begun with Franklin D. Roosevelt's victory in 1932.

Moreover, Reagan's sweeping victory produced an unexpected landslide in the Senate, where thirteen seats changed hands. Many of the Senate's most accomplished legislators and stalwart liberals, including George McGovern (D-SD), Birch Bayh (D-IN), Warren Magnuson (D-WA), Gaylord Nelson (D-WI), Frank Church (D-ID), John Culver (D-IA), and Jacob Javits (R-NY) were swept away. Against all odds, the Republicans gained majority control of the Senate for the first time since 1955. *Washington Post* columnist David Broder captured the moment with a column titled "A Sharp Right Turn": "Not only did Reagan hand Carter the first defeat an elected president has suffered in a reelection bid since Herbert Hoover went down in 1932, but a host of Senate Democratic invincibles joined him. . . . It certainly had the appearance of an era ending—and a new one beginning."

Coming after two consecutive elections, 1976 and 1978, in which thirty-seven new senators had been elected, the 1980 tsunami essentially shattered the Senate ecosystem. When the new Senate convened in January 1981, fifty-five of the hundred senators had been there six years or less. The stalwart veterans—colleagues that Senator Don Riegle (D-MI) recalled as "the tall trees"—were gone: retired or defeated. In their place stood what may have been the weakest group of first-termers ever to walk on the Senate floor, including Paula Hawkins (R-FL), Jeremiah Denton (R-AL), Mack Mattingly

(R–GA), John East (R–NC), and James Abdnor (R–SD). Many of the new arrivals combined a lack of political experience with a New Right ideology, an aversion to compromise, and, for some, a lack of interest in, or contempt for, the institution they were joining. John Sears, the respected Republican consultant, spoke for many Republicans when he quipped several years later: "If we had known that we were going to win the Senate, we would have found some better candidates."

The new Senate differed from its twentieth-century predecessors in another way. Traditionally, the House of Representatives reflects the popular passions and political swings of the moment. In the 1980 election, however, the House remained strongly Democratic; the Senate reflected the Reagan landslide. Senators would be the "foot soldiers in the Reagan revolution." Bipartisan comity and considered judgment counted for less than driving the Reagan program, particularly in the early 1980s.[1]

In September 1982, less than two years after the Republican takeover, a major article in *Congressional Quarterly* captured a new and dispirited mood. "In the Senate of the 1980's, team spirit has given way to the rule of individuals," journalist Alan Ehrenhalt wrote. "Every man is an island."

The article includes a famous 1954 photo of senators Jack Kennedy, Scoop Jackson, and Mike Mansfield playing softball. "[The picture] seems to stand for a Senate that has disappeared in the years since," Ehrenhalt wrote. "One whose members knew each other well, worked and played together and thought of politics as a team game. Today's Senate, many of its own members complain, is nothing like that. It is seen from within as a place where there is very little time to think, close personal relationships are rare, and individual rights, not community feeling, is the most precious commodity." John Tower commented: "Every year the Senate seems to be a less congenial place. The professionalism and dedication that once had been characteristic of the institution were ebbing away."

HOWARD BAKER: THE NATURAL

Still, it was not unreasonable to expect that the Senate could rebuild and recover from its 1980 shattering. There were plenty of strong senators in both parties. The very weakest fell by the wayside very quickly, soon to be replaced by promising new additions. The Senate also benefited greatly from having Howard Baker as majority leader. The son-in-law of Everett Dirksen, Baker had become minority leader in 1977, and quickly demonstrated that he was, to borrow the title of Bernard Malamud's novel, "the natural." Baker proved his character and independence as the vice chairman of the Watergate Committee, and he showed the Senate an ability as a leader and conciliator that rivaled even Mansfield's. Trained as an engineer as well as lawyer, Baker combined a superb intellect with a disarming, down-home style. An avid and skilled photographer, he managed to somehow be at the center of political action and still removed enough to be observing it. "Friendly and unfailingly courteous," the *New York Times* wrote, "he was popular with lawmakers in both parties, a kind of figure almost unrecognizable on Capitol Hill today." As his stepmother, a gifted politician in her own right, once said: "Howard is like the Tennessee River. He goes right down the middle." But as Tom Daschle (D-SD) and Trent Lott (R-MS) observed: "He was no softie. Baker was known to lock competing sides in an office or conference room and refuse to release them until a compromise was reached."[2]

Baker studied the way that politicians of the past managed to prevent their policy differences, even when severe, from spilling over into personal animosity.[3] He was fond of recalling the rivalry of two nineteenth-century Senate giants, John C. Calhoun (N/D-SC) and Henry Clay (R-KY):

> Calhoun and Clay worked together because they knew they had to. The business of their young nation was too important—and their role in that business was too central—to allow them the luxury of petulance.

Baker expanded on that theme further in a 1998 lecture to the Senate:

> People may think our debates are fraudulent if we can put our passion aside so quickly and embrace our adversaries so readily. But we aren't crazy and we aren't frauds. The ritual is as natural as breathing here in the Senate, and it is as important as anything that happens in Washington or in the country we serve.
>
> It's what makes us America and not Bosnia. It is what makes us the most stable government on earth, and not another civil war waiting to happen.
>
> We are doing the business of the American people. We do it every day. We have to do it with the same people every day. And if we cannot be civil to one another, and if we stop dealing with those with whom we disagree, or that we don't like, we would soon stop functioning altogether.

It was often observed that if the senators could have voted by secret ballot for president, Baker would have won overwhelmingly.[4] As Senate majority leader, working with other experienced legislators who were now committee chairmen, such as Tower, Bob Dole (R-KS), and Bob Packwood (R-OR), Baker made the Senate a vehicle for enacting the Reagan tax cuts and defense buildup and stabilized the Senate despite its drastic change in membership. At the end of 1984, Baker, who had long believed that senators should be "citizen legislators," carried out his pledge to retire after three terms, much to the regret of virtually anyone who dealt with the Senate.

THE EVOLUTION OF BOB DOLE

But the Senate continued to make a solid comeback under the leadership of Bob Dole. Dole had been elected to the Senate in 1968; despite his obvious talents, he had not been a major figure in the Senate of the 1970s. Rather, he rose rapidly within the party and became visible in the country by being chairman of the Republican National Committee. He operated through acerbic speeches, "gotcha" amendments, and slashing partisanship rather than through constructive deal making. There were notable exceptions to his partisanship, such as the start of his historic alliance with George McGovern to combat hunger, but those were exceptions.[5]

But Dole changed his approach in 1981 when he became chairman of the Finance Committee. He put together an impressive staff headed by Sheila Burke, who had been handling healthcare issues for him. Burke was a nurse who had moved from caring for patients to advocacy on health policy. When Dole interviewed Burke, she told him that she was a Democrat from California from a union family. Dole responded that her political background did not matter to him; what mattered was that she understood patient care.

As Finance Committee chairman, Dole threw his talents and energy into heavy legislative lifting, helping to engineer the historic Reagan tax cuts of 1981. But the enormous tax cuts, premised on the magic of "supply-side economics," which Baker candidly termed a "riverboat gamble," spooked Wall Street. The prospect of huge deficits, worsening inflation, and high interest rates caused the stock market to plunge as soon as Reagan signed the legislation. By September, blue chip stocks had dropped 20 percent; other economic indicators were equally bad. Purchases of new cars hit a twenty-year low; housing starts declined sharply; business bankruptcies increased 42 percent in one year. By January 1982, the economy was in recession, and the recession deepened as the year went on.

As future presidents and congresses would demonstrate, tax cuts were politically easy; tax increases, political poison. In 1982, Dole demonstrated his leadership and political skill as he played a central role in scaling back the 1981 tax cut by negotiating the Tax Equity and Fiscal Responsibility Act (TEFRA).[6] Combined with an increase in the federal gas tax, TEFRA represented "the single biggest tax hike in American history." But the enactment of TEFRA, with bipartisan support, allowed Federal Reserve chairman Paul Volcker to ease up on the money supply, and the economy surged in 1983 and 1984. Dole would later play a political price within his party when Newt Gingrich, the rising congressional firebrand, labeled him "the tax collector for the welfare state." But facing the possibility of a deep and continuing recession, Dole and the Reagan White House showed political courage, statesmanship, and imagination.

The next year, Dole again stepped up to a major challenge, working to put the Social Security system on a healthier footing.[7] Social security payments had increased by over 500 percent during the 1970s, thanks to a greater number of recipients and cost of living adjustments (COLA) tied to soaring inflation rates. The system faced the real possibility of collapse. In May 1981, Richard Schweiker, the secretary of Health and Human Services, proposed immediately reducing Social Security payments for anyone who retired before age sixty-five. The proposal caused an immediate firestorm from angry seniors, and the Reagan White House, stung by the backlash, moved quickly to establish a bipartisan, public-private commission chaired by Alan Greenspan, with members chosen in part by House Speaker Tip O'Neill (D-MA), to find a way to shore up the system. The Commission, with Dole playing a pivotal role, produced a far-reaching compromise that put the troubled Social Security system on a sound fiscal footing.

"The bipartisan compromise on social security stands in hindsight as about as striking a breakthrough imaginable in the deeply polarized and political environment of Reagan's first term," journalist Matthew Dallek wrote. "Bipartisan action can happen in swift and surprising terms on the thorniest and most insoluble issues."

When Howard Baker announced his intention to retire, Dole, benefiting from a series of huge legislative accomplishments, defeated four other contenders to become majority leader. Dole had come to relish legislating and deal making; he also thought that, despite Baker's defeat when he sought the Republican nomination in 1980, that a successful record as Senate leader could be a good springboard to the White House in 1988.

Working with a more experienced and less ideological White House in Reagan's second term, Dole's Senate helped bring about major legislative accomplishments. Packwood, now chairman of the Finance Committee, worked with Bill Bradley (D-NJ) on far-reaching tax reform, enacted in 1986. Alan Simpson (R-WY) worked with Ted Kennedy (D-MA) to fashion a landmark immigration bill, granting amnesty for five million illegal immigrants and making it unlawful for an employer to hire illegal immigrants. Barry Goldwater (R-AZ) and Sam Nunn (D-GA) championed a historic reform of the Joint Chiefs of Staff, the most significant change in the organization of the armed services since World War II. Conservative senator Orrin Hatch (R-UT) had just completed his collaboration with Henry Waxman (D-CA), one of the most liberal House Democrats, to give patent protection to research pharmaceutical companies while speeding the process of making generic drugs available—legislation still known as "Hatch-Waxman."

Sheila Burke remembered Dole constantly in motion, never happier than when he was moving from meeting to meeting, making deals, or creating the environment for other senators to complete them.[8] He turned his scintillating humor on himself and the frequent absurdities of the Senate. "If you're hanging around with nothing to do and the zoo is closed," Dole remarked, "come over to the Senate. You'll get the same kind of feeling and you won't have to pay."

Overall, the Senate under the leadership of Baker and Dole functioned capably. It compiled a significant legislative record and served as a far-sighted and moderating influence on major challenging issues. Ronald Reagan was a very different president than Jimmy Carter, and the left-of-center Senate led by Democrats Mansfield and Byrd had given way to a right-of-center Senate. The locus of American politics shifted from one forty-yard line to the other, but the "nation's mediator" was still playing its important role.

Still, even as significant legislative accomplishments continued, many observers detected a deteriorating culture in the Senate. Thomas Eagleton (D-MO) was best known nationally because George McGovern dropped him from the Democratic ticket in 1972 after revelations that he had been treated for mental illness. But Eagleton recovered from that devastating incident to become one of the most respected senators. (In 1989, when the Senate celebrated the two-hundredth anniversary of the Constitution, two former senators were invited to address the Senate: Howard Baker and Tom Eagleton.) In 1985, Eagleton went to the Senate floor to unleash an extraordinary indictment of the Senate's condition. "The Senate is now in a state of incipient anarchy," Eagleton began. "The filibuster, once used, by and large, as an occasional exercise in civil rights matters, has now become a routine frolic in almost all matters. Whereas our rules were devised to guarantee full and free debate, they now guarantee unbridled chaos."[9] The other side of the coin from chaos was paralysis, and in later years, that would be the chief manifestation of the misuse of the filibuster. Eagleton, only fifty-six, passionately loved the Senate during his first two terms. Now he announced that he would not seek a fourth term, partly because of the Senate's procedural frustrations and gridlock: "We, the great deliberators, are deliberating ourselves into national ridicule and embarrassment."

IRAN-CONTRA: A CRISIS FOR THE REAGAN PRESIDENCY

In November 1986, Ronald Reagan was finishing his sixth year in the White House, traditionally a difficult time for the party in power. The Republicans also faced the challenge of defending seats held by the weak senators elected in 1980. When the votes were counted, the Democrats recaptured the Senate majority that they had lost in 1980.

But as the transition started in the Senate, in mid-November, the nation was stunned by the revelation that the Reagan administration had sold arms to Iran, despite the publicly stated policy against selling arms to either Iran or to its adversary Iraq. The Arms Export Control Act prohibited the sale of weapons to nations that sponsored repeated acts of terrorism, and the secretary of state had designated Iran a terrorist state in 1984.

President Reagan defended the sales as an effort to provide the "bona fides" necessary to explore a diplomatic opening to Iran. Most observers concluded that the president was motivated by a desire to free U.S. hostages still held by Iran, although it was long-standing U.S. policy not to deal with hostage takers. It became clear that the administration had approved shipments of U.S. arms from Israel to Iran, without providing the required notification to Congress.

As Congress, the press, and the public clamored for answers, on November 25, Attorney General Ed Meese announced that the proceeds from the arms sales were being used to fund the Nicaraguan resistance, known as "the contras," at a time when U.S. law prohibited military assistance to them. The "diversion," as it was termed by Meese, was plainly intended to evade the strictures of law and congressional oversight, although defenders of the administration could note that Congress had several times modified the limitations on aid to the Contras. Indeed, some members of Congress suspected that the administration was continuing some forms of assistance regardless of the strictures in place, but there had been no concrete evidence to confirm it.

On January 6, 1987, the first day of the new Congress, the Senate moved quickly to establish the Select Committee on Secret Military Assistance to Iran and the Nicaraguan Opposition.[10] The House appointed its own select committee the next day. Byrd chose Daniel Inouye (D-HA), a respected senior senator who had served on the Watergate Committee, to be chairman. Inouye, a Japanese American, who had lost an arm in World War II combat, inspired many by his character and quiet courage. Dole selected Warren Rudman (R-NH), who had just been elected for his second term, to lead the committee Republicans. Rudman, a Korean war veteran and a highly regarded trial lawyer and state attorney general, nicknamed "Sledgehammer," was known to be fair and fearless. Inouye quickly designated Rudman as the committee's vice chairman, which meant he would preside over the committee hearings in Inouye's absence, a responsibility that would have ordinarily gone to the second-ranking Democrat. This move conveyed to the Republicans that they would be full partners in the investigation; Inouye reinforced that message by opting for a unitary staff rather than create two separate staffs, risking polarization and discord.

The House committee, led by Lee Hamilton (D-IN), one of the most distinguished Democratic members, and Richard Cheney (R-WY), a former White House chief of staff and rising Republican star, decided on separate staffs, increasing the likelihood that their investigation would be hampered by partisan disputes. In March, however, the two committees surprised congressional observers by agreeing to hold joint hearings. This virtually unprecedented move presented obvious advantages by avoiding duplicative testimony, but managing hearings with a twenty-six-member committee and keeping partisanship from flaring up would prove to pose daunting challenges.

After three months of investigation and 250 hours of testimony from twenty-eight witnesses, the committees presented the major elements of the program run by White House National Security Council director Robert "Bud" McFarlane, his successor, Vice Admiral John Poindexter, and his deputy, Lieutenant Colonel Oliver North. The investigation also illuminated the role of Defense Secretary Caspar Weinberger, who was later indicted by Special Prosecutor Lawrence Walsh. Oliver North, unapologetic and charismatic, ran roughshod over Chief Counsel Arthur Liman, a brilliant lawyer who was not a great television performer. To the disappointment of many observers, the Iran-Contra committee was not able to ascertain the scope of President Reagan's involvement. Despite that, however, the Committee's work gave Congress and the public a solid understanding of the ill-conceived program and the dangers it presented.

Senators George Mitchell (D-ME) and William Cohen (R-ME), who served with distinction on the committee, would go on to write *Men of Zeal: A Candid Inside Story of the Iran-Contra Hearings*, an insightful and fascinating book. Their conclusions deserve to be quoted at length:

> Prior to the Committee's hearings, the sale of weapons to Iran had been described as an act of folly and the diversion of profits to the Contras an aberrational by-product of President Reagan's loose management style.
>
> The facts that emerged from our investigation revealed a more complicated set of circumstances and an insidious chain of events. The sale of weapons to Iran was confirmed to be a foreign policy fiasco. But the establishment of a secret, off-the-shelf capability to fund and carry out future covert activities was a calculated deceit of immense consequence to our democratic form of government. . . . The selected use of "non-appropriated" funds to carry out undisclosed activities struck at the very core of government accountability, one of the fundamental tenets of the Constitution. . . .
>
> There is no doubt that President Reagan was motivated by a sincere desire to free our hostages in Lebanon. More than any other factor, particularly that of establishing an improved relationship with Iran, this desire became the driving force behind the arms sale to Iran. The nobility of one's motives, however, cannot obscure the folly of one's actions. To carry out a highly complex

mission of dealing with unidentifiable elements in Iran, the President turned to a private, amateur network of international operatives. In so doing, he displaced the institutional mechanisms designed to provide checks and balances against rash and impetuous conduct. These foreign-policy free-lancers drew a noose like circle of suspicion and secrecy around the White House. While carrying out one misguided initiative, they conceived another—the diversion of profits to the Nicaraguan Contras, a separate covert program that was of equal importance to the President. In the name of national security, lies were permitted to masquerade as truths before Cabinet officials, congressional committees, and ultimately before the American people.[11]

The insights of senators Mitchell and Cohen remind us of what the Senate can do to keep the constitutional balance in our system. America benefited from President Reagan surviving the Iran-Contra scandal and finishing his second term strongly. But the nation also benefited from fully airing the dangers of Iran-Contra. Richard Nixon's forty-nine-state landslide in 1972 did not insulate him from being investigated for the abuses of power now known as Watergate. Ronald Reagan's forty-nine-state landslide twelve years later did not protect him from a searching investigation of the Iran-Contra scandal. Our system depends on holding presidents accountable where necessary, and putting country over party to do so.

THE NOMINATION OF ROBERT BORK

In June 1987, as the investigation of Iran-Contra moved forward, President Reagan nominated Judge Robert Bork of the D.C. Court of Appeals to fill a vacancy on the Supreme Court created by the retirement of Lewis Powell.[12] Bork's nomination continued a period of intense activity with respect to Supreme Court nominations. The Senate had confirmed Sandra Day O'Connor, the first woman nominated to the Supreme Court, in 1981, and Antonin Scalia, the first Italian nominated to the Court, in 1986, both by unanimous votes. Also in 1986, the Senate had confirmed Reagan's decision to elevate Associate Justice William Rehnquist to be chief justice, replacing Warren Burger.

Ronald Reagan had pledged to remake the Supreme Court, and the White House saw replacing the respected conservative Powell with Bork as the way to do it. Just five days after Powell announced his retirement, Reagan brought Bork to the White House briefing room and announced his nomination: "Judge Bork, widely regarded as the most prominent and intellectually powerful advocate of judicial restraint, shares my view that judges' personal preferences and values should not be part of their constitutional interpretations."

Judge Bork, who had been a respected Yale Law professor specializing in antitrust law before going on the bench, was unquestionably the intellectual hero of the right-wing legal community that had strong influence in Republican circles. As a professor and as a judge, Bork had spoken out strongly against one major Supreme Court decision after another, from *Shelley v. Kramer*, a ruling outlawing racial covenants, to *Brown v. Board of Education*, which ended legal segregation in public schools, to *Harper v. Board of Elections*, banning the poll tax, to the one-man, one-vote ruling of *Reynolds v. Sims*, to *Griswold v. Connecticut*, which threw out a statute that prohibited the purchase of contraceptives, and to *Roe v. Wade*, legalizing abortion. Judge Bork was beloved by the right-wing legal community for good reason; his legal opinions could be fairly construed to be extreme.

Bork also carried unusually serious political baggage. In October 1973, when President Nixon ordered Watergate Special Prosecutor Archibald Cox to be fired, it was Robert Bork, then solicitor general, who carried out the order after Attorney General Elliott Richardson and Deputy Attorney General William Ruckelshaus refused to do so. The Senate Democrats had anticipated Bork's nomination and prepared for an enormous fight.

Hours after the White House announced Bork's nomination, Ted Kennedy, who had endured the assassination of his brothers, the tragic accident at Chappaquiddick, and a failed presidential bid to become the Senate's liberal lion, gave one of the most famous, and controversial, speeches in Senate history.[13] In just three minutes, he called on the Senate to reject Bork's nomination. He began by noting that "the man who fired Archibald Cox does not deserve to sit on the Supreme Court of the United States." Recalling the Saturday Night Massacre, Kennedy praised Richardson and Ruckelshaus, "who refused to do Richard Nixon's dirty work and obey his order to fire Special Prosecutor Archibald Cox. The deed devolved on Solicitor General Robert Bork, who executed the unconscionable assignment that has become one of the darkest chapters for the rule of law in American history."

Then Kennedy turned his fire on Bork's legal philosophy:

> Mr. Bork should also be rejected by the Senate because he stands for an extremist view of the Constitution and the role of the Supreme Court that would have placed him outside the mainstream of American constitutional jurisprudence in the 1960's, let alone the 1980's. He opposed the public accommodations provisions of the Civil Rights Act of 1964 and the one-man, one-vote decision of the Supreme Court the same year. He has said that the First Amendment applies only to political speech, not literature or words of art or scientific expression.
>
> Under the two pressures of academic rejection and the prospect of Senate rejection, Mr. Bork subsequently retracted the most Neanderthal of these

views on civil rights and the First Amendment, but his mind-set is no less ominous today.

Robert Bork's America is a land in which women would be forced into back alley abortions, blacks would sit at segregated lunch counters, rogue police could break down citizens' door in midnight raids, and schoolchildren could not be taught about evolution, writers and artists could be censored at the whim of the government, and the doors of the federal courts would be shut on the fingers of millions of citizens for whom the judiciary is—and is often the only—protector of the individual rights that are at the heart of our democracy.

Kennedy's fierce speech ignited the opposition against Bork. While Bork's supporters found Kennedy's characterizations unfair, since Bork pledged not to reverse established Supreme Court precedents, his views were certainly fair game. President Reagan chose him for his extreme conservative judicial philosophy, and Bork's elevation would further Reagan's social agenda, enhance the power of state governments, weaken protections for minorities and women, and likely provide the deciding vote to reverse *Roe v. Wade*.

In five days of memorable hearings chaired by Judiciary Committee Chairman Joseph Biden (D-DE), Bork had difficulty maintaining a consistent tone. While attempting to mollify the committee by saying that he would respect established precedents, he refused to back away from many of his extreme positions. Patrick Leahy (D-VT) labeled Bork's answers about respecting precedent as "a confirmation conversion."[14] Bearded (long before it was fashionable) and humorless, Bork generally came across to the Judiciary Committee and to the national audience as an arrogant intellectual, discussing vital constitutional matters in a detached, technical, and bloodless way. Alan Simpson (R-WY) asked the last question: "Why do you want to be an Associate Justice of the Supreme Court?" Judge Bork responded: "I think it would be an intellectual feast, just to be there and to read the briefs and discuss things with counsel and my colleagues." He left the clear impression that he wanted to be on the Supreme Court for the intellectual experience, rather than deciding cases in a way that provided justice for real people consistent with the constitution. A *Washington Post-ABC News* poll showed that public opinion shifted sharply against Bork during the days of his testimony.[15]

The Bork hearings are generally regarded as the high point of Joe Biden's thirty-five-year Senate career. "Biden ran the hearings elegantly," wrote Adam Clymer, a *New York Times* reporter and biographer of Ted Kennedy.[16] He never interrupted or berated Judge Bork, giving him full time to elaborate on his answers. But Biden was knowledgeable and frequently eloquent, starting with his opening statement when he invoked the language of the Declaration of Independence: "I believe that all Americans are born with certain inalienable rights. As a child of God, I believe that my rights are not derived from any government. My rights are not derived from any majority. My rights are because I exist." Biden, and other committee members, engaged in searching exchanges with Bork on the right to privacy, the First Amendment, and other vital legal issues. Frequently, the hearings reached the level of "profound constitutional debate," wrote Linda Greenhouse, the Pulitzer Prize–winning Supreme Court reporter for the *New York Times*.[17]

It was both an extraordinary constitutional debate and an absolute political war. From the Senate, Kennedy spearheaded an unprecedented coalition effort to defeat Bork.[18] Civil rights groups, unions, and other liberal groups took the anti-Bork message to their members, and to the country, going into churches and issuing anti-Bork radio spots. The Reagan White House, exhausted from the long Iran-Contra investigation, could not match the intensity of the opponents. And the strategy of making Bork pretend to be a moderate angered his conservative supporters without convincing anyone else.

On October 6, the Senate Judiciary Committee voted 9–5 against Judge Bork's nomination. Although this could have ended the nomination fight, the Senate acceded to the White House's request to allow the full Senate to debate and vote on the nomination. On October 23, the Senate rejected the nomination of Judge Robert Bork by a vote of 58–42.

Many Republicans commentators have always believed that the rejection of Judge Bork's nomination represented a seminal moment when American politics changed for the worst and was a major step downward in the standing of the Senate. These views, while deeply held, seem off base. Among advanced nations, America has the only Supreme Court that gives its justices essentially lifetime appointments. "Every place else in the world they have age limits or term limits," notes Paul Carrington, a law professor at Duke University.[19] We also have an unusually small high Court.

These facts combine to ensure that the Senate would take its "advise and consent" responsibility on Supreme Court nominations very seriously. In the two decades before the Bork nomination, the Senate had rejected Lyndon Johnson's effort to elevate Associate Justice Abe Fortas to chief justice (1968), and rejected Richard Nixon's nominations of Judge Clement Haynsworth (1969) and Judge G. Harrold Carswell (1970). The Senate had vigorously debated Nixon's nomination of William Rehnquist before confirming him to the Court in 1971, and did so again fifteen years later when Reagan chose to elevate him to chief justice. These confirmations also involved many outside combatants on both sides, although not at the level of the Bork fight. But the Senate had also overwhelmingly confirmed a series of Republican Supreme Court appointments: Warren Burger, Harry Blackmun, and Lewis Powell, nominated by Nixon; John Paul Stevens, nominated by Gerald Ford;

and O'Connor and Scalia, nominated by Reagan, as well as Anthony Kennedy, whose nomination followed Bork's rejection.

The truth is that in making the most ideological nomination possible, Reagan placated his extreme base. But he either overreached at a moment of political weakness or deliberately chose to provoke a fight with the Senate Democrats. Many Republicans, including Howard Baker, who had just signed on as Reagan's chief of staff, were not enthusiastic about pressing for Bork.[20] Judge Bork, despite his great intellect, proved to be a disastrous witness on his own behalf.

Despite the protests of Bork's supporters, the Senate's handling of his nomination received broad support around the country. The *Los Angeles Times* editorialized that "the Bork hearings were an extraordinary lesson; it was a celebration of Republican democracy at its best."[21] The *St. Petersburg Times* editorialized:

> The struggle over the Robert Bork nomination will be remembered as one of the great events of American history—not for the way it is about to end but for the reasons why. What the Senate majority has done is to say that the Supreme Court was correct when it declared that privacy is a fundamental right inherently protected by the Constitution. It has reaffirmed freedom of speech and equal protection of the laws as rights that belong to all Americans. It believes in access to the courts. It has chosen the concept of a living Constitution over the sterile philosophy of "originalism."

In his memoir, Biden recalls that several weeks later, he was invited to the White House to confer with President Reagan on possible Supreme Court nominees who could win Senate approval. Reagan, always affable, said: "Congratulations on Bork." Biden responded: "There's no cause for congratulations. I feel bad for Judge Bork. He was a good man."

To which Reagan responded: "Ah, he wasn't all that much."[22]

Like President Reagan, the Senate recovered quickly from the Bork fight. "Congress regained its voice in the 1987–88 session," the *New York Times* opined as the Congress adjourned "enacting groundbreaking legislation in areas as diverse as trade policy, welfare reform, civil rights and arms control."[23]

A BREAKTHROUGH IN TRADE POLICY

The Senate's role in forging a new U.S. trade policy warrants particular attention. Throughout most of the 1980s, even as the economy performed strongly, Congress was intensely focused on, and divided over, trade policy. This was the period of Japan's extraordinary economic rise, famously described in Ezra Vogel's *Japan as Number One* and Clyde Prestowitz's *Trading Places.*[24] A massive bilateral trade deficit, the surge of Japanese automobile and semiconductor imports, as well as Japanese purchases of Rockefeller Center and other prestige properties signaled that the United States was facing a serious competitive challenge. Frustrated autoworkers took a sledgehammer to an imported Toyota. Election-year politics turned up the heat on the trade debate as House Majority Leader Richard Gephardt (D-MO) sought the Democratic nomination for president with a tough, protectionist message.[25] Donald Trump entered public life in 1987 by placing several newspaper ads criticizing Japan's unfair tactics and America's hapless trade negotiators.[26] Nearly thirty years before Trump's presidential campaign, economic nationalism seemed to be sweeping the country.

For several years, the Reagan administration and Capitol Hill fought over the terms of a tougher trade policy and which branch would control it. Ultimately, however, the Reagan administration and Congress negotiated the Omnibus Trade and Competitiveness Act of 1988, a major bipartisan collaboration that committed the United States to a harder-edged, reciprocity-based trade policy, without the requirements for mandatory retaliation that Gephardt and other trade hawks favored.[27] The Senate, led by Lloyd Bentsen (D-TX) and John Danforth (R-MO), the chairman and ranking member of the Finance Committee, played a central role in the key compromises that made the legislative effort successful. The legislation sought greater reciprocity through both carrots and sticks: new authority for the president to negotiate with trading partners, and tougher statutes to pressure other nations to open their markets or risk U.S. retaliation.[28] The administration and Congress defied expectations: overcoming heated politics to find consensus in an election year.

THE DEFEAT OF JOHN TOWER'S NOMINATION

The good times would not last. In retrospect, the spiral downward for the Senate arguably began in January 1989, as President George H. W. Bush came into office and Senator George Mitchell succeeded Robert Byrd as majority leader. Having lost the White House for the third straight time, after a particularly vicious campaign waged against Michael Dukakis, the Democrats were ready for a more partisan edge. Mitchell, a respected former judge who had distinguished himself during the Iran–Contra investigation, combined a keen intellect, a judicious manner, and tough partisan instincts.

During the transition, president-elect Bush nominated John Tower to be secretary of defense. The Senate had never rejected a cabinet nomination made by a new president, and Tower, the former chairman of the Armed Services Committee and Reagan administration arms negotiator, had defense credentials that were long and strong. But Sam Nunn (D-GA), the new chairman of the Armed Services Committee, had concerns about what he believed to be Tower's alcoholism and womanizing.[29] Other senators, notably Carl Levin (D-MI), focused on possible conflicts of interest arising from Tower's representation of defense contractors after he had left the Senate.[30] The investigation of the nomination became protracted and ugly as Democratic opponents in the Senate derived further support from right-wing conservative activist Paul Weyrich, who hated Tower for being a defender of abortion rights.[31]

On the floor of the Senate, Rudman, a respected former prosecutor, launched a powerful critique of the Armed Services Committee report against Tower, saying that he had tried hundreds of cases and had never seen anyone "trashed on such flimsy evidence in my entire life."[32] Dole accused the Democrats of using the nomination to bloody the Bush administration in its infancy.[33] John McCain (R-AR), recently elected, and William Cohen both argued passionately on Tower's behalf. Mitchell made the vote a test of party solidarity, and Tower's nomination was rejected 53–47, virtually along party lines.

The bitter battle was not quickly forgotten. Twenty-five years later, Cohen still expressed outrage at the treatment that Tower received. The fratricidal fight caused more damage to the Senate's comity. It also had other lasting consequences, catapulting to national prominence Wyoming congressman Dick Cheney, whom Bush nominated to be secretary of defense.

THE RISE OF TRENT LOTT

The arrival of Trent Lott in the Senate in January 1989, after an impressive sixteen-year career in the House, understandably received less attention than the Tower fight, but ultimately, it would prove to be even more consequential for the Senate. The son of a shipyard worker, Lott attended college and law school at the University of Mississippi. After a brief stint in private practice, Lott came to Capitol Hill in 1968 to work for Congressman William Colmer (D-MS), an extremely conservative Democrat who chaired the House Rules Committee. When Colmer announced his retirement in 1972, Lott, understanding the way the political winds were blowing in the South, ran for Colmer's seat as a Republican and won handily, aided by the strength of Richard Nixon's landslide reelection.

In the House, Lott rose to become Republican whip. His influence increased after the 1980 election, as he proved extremely effective in helping the

Reagan administration get its tax and budget cuts through the House. Lott allied himself with Newt Gingrich and other young House Republicans who resented the high-handed treatment they had received from House Democrats and disliked the "get along, go along" attitude of the House Republican leaders. Lott was deeply involved in Gingrich's successful effort to bring down House Speaker Jim Wright on ethics charges. In 1988, when a Senate seat came open in Mississippi, Lott was easily elected.

Most newly elected senators come to the institution with a sense of deep respect, if not awe. Lott was an exception. As he describes in his candid memoir, *Herding Cats*, he hated the place from the moment he arrived.[34] "After giving up real national power in the House, after winning a score of victories for Ronald Reagan," Lott wrote, "I expected a warm welcome in the Senate." Instead, Lott and the other freshmen "found themselves in 'storage' as the Senate machinery creaked to life." Lott viewed many of his fellow senators as "distant, impossible to befriend." The Senate itself was a "confused and disorganized institution," with chaotic and unpredictable hours. Revealing an attitude shaped by his House experience, Lott also concluded that "the Democrats had been in power so long they had adopted bullyboy tactics to enforce their power," ignoring the fact that the Republicans had just recently been the Senate majority for six years.

Lott started making lists of things that he would change if he ever got the chance. He decided that he could rely on a "tight conservative clique of young senators," some who had recently arrived and some who would soon follow: "We were conservative, we were hungry, we intended to make a difference and eventually capture the leadership."[35] The goals would be to make the Republicans both more right wing and more unified and to remake the Senate in the House's image—efficient, driven by the leaders, and deeply partisan. Lott made it into the Republican leadership after the 1992 election on the bottom rung, and he started looking upward immediately.

AUTHORIZING THE GULF WAR

The year 1991 proved to be a Dickensian moment for the Senate: "the best of times, the worst of times." On August 2, 1990, Iraq's dictator Saddam Hussein had sent his forces to invade Kuwait. This unprovoked attack, which brought Saddam's armies close to the border of Saudi Arabia and seemed to threaten the flow of Saudi oil, shook the region and the world. President George H. W. Bush, vowing that Saddam's invasion "would not stand," assembled an extraordinary international coalition for military action to eject the Iraqi army from Kuwait. While Bush, like his predecessors, took the position that neither the Constitution nor the War Powers Act required him to seek congressional approval, he understood the wisdom of obtaining congressional approval and sought to demonstrate broad national support for the war effort.

While the Gulf War proved to be a swift victory for the U.S.-led international coalition, with strikingly few casualties, before the "shock and awe" invasion, it was by no means clear that it would be fast or easy. Several think tank reports, as well as Texas businessman Ross Perot, predicted that the coalition could suffer as many as twenty thousand deaths; Iraq had built, by some measures, the fourth largest military in the world, spearheaded by the vaunted Revolutionary Guards. Many military authorities counseled against invading, arguing that the economic sanctions imposed on Iraq were having effect. Nunn, the Armed Services Committee chairman, argued: "We are playing a winning hand. I see no compelling reason to rush to military action."[36] On January 12, 1991, after a three-day debate in which ninety-three senators spoke, the Senate approved the authorization to conduct military action by a narrow vote of 52–47. The House conducted a similarly searching debate and approved the authorization, by a vote of 250–183. Not since the war of 1812 had Congress approved military action by such a divided vote. But the debate, which the *New York Times* described as "remarkably full and thoughtful," contributed to public confidence and support for President Bush's action.[37]

CLARENCE THOMAS AND ANITA HILL

On July 1, 1991, President Bush, whose popularity had soared after the Gulf War victory, nominated Judge Clarence Thomas of the D.C. Circuit Court of Appeals to fill the vacancy on the Supreme Court created by the retirement of Justice Thurgood Marshall, the first African American to have served on the Supreme Court.[38] Marshall had served on the Court since 1967; before that, he had been the architect of the legal strategy pursued by the civil rights movement in *Brown v. Board Education* and other landmark cases. Judge Thomas, only forty-three years old, had been on the Court of Appeals only nineteen months, after serving as chairman of the Equal Employment Opportunity Commission (EEOC). He was the youngest nominee in Supreme Court history. Although also African American, Thomas shared none of Marshall's liberal views. He was as severely conservative in his legal views as Justice Scalia, and he particularly detested the concept of affirmative action, which raised questions about his record as EEOC chair.

The full spectrum of liberal organizations quickly opposed Thomas's nomination, making it clear that he would not get a free pass simply because he would be replacing the only African American justice on the Court. Although President Bush described him as the "best qualified nominee" available, no member of the American Bar Association committee on judicial appointments rated Judge Thomas "well qualified." Judge Thomas had one great asset in his favor. He had worked on the staff of John Danforth, one of the most respected senators.[39] Danforth regarded Thomas as virtually a member of his family and would not hesitate to lobby every senator on his behalf.

As the hearing started, early vote counts predicted a very close outcome along party lines. Judge Thomas declined to answer many questions about his legal philosophy, relying on his powerful life story rising from poverty. Then, on October 11, Anita Hill, a law professor at the University of Oklahoma, who had worked for Thomas at the EEOC, came forward and accused him of sexual harassment.[40] Ms. Hill's detailed, graphic description of Thomas's overtures to her rocked the Senate and the nation. Thomas denied every charge made by Hill and refused to acknowledge the possibility of a misunderstanding. Instead, he attacked the Judiciary Committee for a "high-tech lynching." Republican senators, particularly Arlen Specter (R-PA), Alan Simpson, and Orrin Hatch, savaged Hill.[41] Pointing out that she had continued to work at the EEOC and had subsequently stayed in touch with her former employer, they accused Hill of lying and fantasizing. When two other witnesses sought to testify that Hill had told them of Thomas's advances contemporaneously, Chairman Biden stunned the Democrats and the country by denying their request, despite the obvious relevance of the testimony being proffered. The Senate voted to confirm Thomas 52–48. Exactly one vote changed in response to Anita Hill's testimony. Robert Byrd, the longest serving senator, who had previously stated his intention to support Thomas, found Hill to be completely credible.[42]

Nina Totenberg, veteran legal affairs correspondent for National Public Radio (NPR), would later recall: "Despite the fact that Hill had passed a lie detector test, the two sides were no match for each other. The Thomas forces, frantic but unified, marched together to a strategic tune composed by Thomas and Danforth and orchestrated by the White House. Hill's forces, inexperienced, in disarray, and with little or no support from Senate Democrats, were left to flounder."[43]

Hill's accusation and Thomas's denial created an extraordinarily difficult "he said; she said" situation to be essentially adjudicated by the Senate and a rapt national audience. But the Judiciary Committee's handling of the situation made it even more ugly. The brutal treatment of Hill by the Republican senators was as much of a departure from normal as Donald Trump's presidential campaign would be a quarter century later. It diminished the Senate in the eyes of the nation.[44] The inability to bridge the partisan divide was complete; the Senate was riven along party lines. Before Anita Hill appeared, not one

Senate Republican had opposed Thomas's nomination despite his meager qualifications, and then, not one Senate Republican believed Hill. Women in the Congress and around the country were outraged by the treatment that Hill received. The year 1992 would be remembered as "the year of the woman" as six women senators were elected, led by Carol Moseley Braun (D-IL), who became the first African American woman senator.[45] Across the country, women provided substantial energy for the presidential candidate Bill Clinton, despite his acknowledgment of marital infidelity.

BILL CLINTON'S FIRST TERM

Bill Clinton was the first Democrat elected president since Jimmy Carter in 1976. Republican presidents had led the country for twelve years. Clinton would have the opportunity to govern with a Democratic Congress. Like Barack Obama sixteen years later, he would find that was no guarantee of political success.

From the beginning, the Senate Republicans' attitude was: "You have the reins of power. You're on your own. Don't count on Republicans for support or votes." None of Clinton's recent predecessors had faced a unified opposition party on the issues most central to their agendas. After a remarkable series of legislative achievements, culminating in the landmark Americans with Disabilities Act in 1990, Bob Dole warned the new president that he was reclaiming his earlier identity as a slashing partisan. "The good news is that he's getting a honeymoon in Washington," Dole wisecracked. "The bad news is that Bob Dole is going to be his chaperone."[46]

Dole justified his approach by claiming that Clinton lacked a mandate since he had fallen short of a majority of the popular vote, winning 43 percent. However, Clinton had decisively defeated President Bush, 43 to 38 percent, earning an overwhelming 370 electoral votes. He was held to 43 percent of the vote only because of Ross Perot's strong showing as a third-party candidate. Moreover, Dole's argument had no basis in history, as he surely knew. In 1968, Richard Nixon came to the presidency having very narrowly defeated Hubert Humphrey, winning exactly 43 percent of the vote, and no one questioned his legitimacy. Dole, elected to the Senate that year, was very familiar with the precedent.

According to Richard A. Baker, the long-time Senate historian, and Neil MacNeil, coauthors of *The American Senate*: "For this strident opposition, Dole would rely primarily on the filibuster, an extraordinary elevation of this dilatory tactic. . . . Dole now commanded great power. Part of it stemmed from his parliamentary skills and political nerve, but principally it flowed from his willingness to use the filibuster to carry out his purposes. *Never before had the Senate's minority party as a matter of party policy chosen to depend on the filibuster*" (italics added).[47]

"Dole didn't really dislike Clinton," former Clinton aide and author Sidney Blumenthal observed. "But when the whole Republican Party swiveled against Clinton to deny him any victory, Dole rushed to get to its head. He had prided himself on being a master of the Senate and now he turned his legislative skills to the purpose of blocking everything."[48] Dole moved to the right, trying to placate the increasingly extreme conservatism in his caucus while maintaining control. Twenty years later, in much more difficult political times, Republican leaders Mitch McConnell and John Boehner would confront the same challenge, with differing degrees of success.

The centerpiece of Clinton's agenda in 1993 was his economic and budget legislation, combining deficit reduction and new investments in education, training, research, technology, and environment while raising the top tax bracket from 31 to 36 percent and making a long overdue increase in the gasoline tax. The legislation traveled a perilous course, requiring Vice President Gore to break a 50–50 tie vote in the Senate after the House had passed it by a two-vote margin. Not a single Republican supported the legislation, branding it as a tax increase, a "job killer," and a one-way ticket to recession.[49] The years 1993 and 1994 featured fierce Republican opposition to Clinton's effort to bring about universal health insurance, which went down to resounding defeat. Interestingly, bipartisan cooperation prevailed on an issue of great controversy: trade. The Republicans in both houses provided most of the votes needed to give Clinton an extraordinary uphill victory on the North American Free Trade Agreement (NAFTA) in November 1993.[50]

Moderate Republicans felt the Senate change significantly. Warren Rudman had chosen to retire after two terms at the end of 1992, uncomfortable with "the confrontational, take-no-prisoners attitude" that the new Republicans brought to the Senate.[51] In 1994, Danforth, just months from retirement, joined Democrats in voting for cloture to pass Clinton's crime bill. When Danforth joined Republican colleagues at lunch, he was met with silence. "It was as though someone had pushed a mute button," he recalled. "It was devastating."[52] At the end of an eighteen-year career, Danforth found himself being treated like a pariah.

A year later, Republican leaders relentlessly pressured Mark Hatfield (R-OR) to support legislation for a constitutional amendment to balance the budget. The Republican caucus, fired up by Rick Santorum (R-PA) and others from the New Right, virtually ostracized Hatfield when he refused to go along. Hatfield, who had a strong moral streak, finally told Dole that he would resign if that was what the caucus wanted, but that he would not vote for the constitutional amendment.[53] It ultimately failed to get the requisite two-thirds of the Senate by one vote.

There had certainly been countless times in the past where Senate leaders had urged members of their caucus to vote with them on key issues. But if senators told the leader they could not do so, that traditionally ended the matter. Such decisions were regarded as being motivated by the senator's sincere judgment on the merits, or the senator's perception of political imperatives. Putting the screws to senators and treating them like outcasts if they refused to go along—this was a dramatic departure from the way Mansfield's Senate had always worked.

The most shocking retirement came on the Democratic side, when Majority Leader George Mitchell, whose performance had earned general admiration, announced on March 5, 1994, that he would not be seeking reelection.[54] Fifteen years in the Senate was enough; Mitchell wanted to consider "other challenges in public or private life." After turning down a Supreme Court seat when President Clinton offered it, Mitchell would render extraordinary service as a meditator and peacemaker in Northern Ireland, and to baseball in investigating its steroid problems. In the Senate, events would soon vindicate the wisdom of Mitchell's decision to serve in other ways.

LOTT AND GINGRICH COME TO POWER

In the autumn of 1994, a political tsunami gathered force. The Republicans, led by Newt Gingrich, offering a "Contract for America," succeeded in nationalizing the elections, blasting the Clinton administration for liberal policies and the House Democrats for ethical lapses. On election night 1994, the Republicans took control of both the House and Senate in a shattering rout reminiscent of 1980, defeating House Speaker Tom Foley and leaving President Clinton plaintively asserting that he was still "relevant." The Democrats chose Tom Daschle of South Dakota to succeed George Mitchell as their leader. Soft-spoken and still boyish looking at 47, Daschle had already served eight years and eight years in the Senate, after serving as an Air Force Intelligence officer, and working as a Senate staffer. He was a Midwest, farm state liberal in the tradition of Hubert Humphrey and George McGovern. While Daschle expected to work closely with the White House in the Democrats struggle to adjust to the new world in Washington, he made it clear: "We want to work with the White House, not for them."[55]

When the Senate convened in January 1995, Trent Lott, who had risen to number three on the Republican leadership ladder, challenged Alan Simpson, the popular Republican who held the number-two slot. Although Simpson had Dole's strong endorsement, Lott had been building support almost from the day he reached the Senate. When the Republican caucus met to decide, Connie Mack (R-FL), a former House member and one of the most conservative senators, spoke for Lott, arguing that his long friendship with Gingrich would give Republicans a more unified front in their battles against Clinton.[56] That type of argument would have cut no ice in the Senate just a few years before—senators Mitchell and Cohen compared relations between the Senate and House to relations between the Sunnis and the Shiites—but the mood of the Senate Republicans had changed dramatically.[57] One senator previously pledged to Simpson—Mitch McConnell—changed his mind and gave Lott a narrow margin of victory.

Because Dole was already focused on the presidential campaign, Lott made his impact felt almost immediately. He ordered the comfortable but casual Republican cloakroom redecorated in a much more formal way. He established a strong whip system to ensure Republican Party discipline. "To bring order to the chaos," Lott wrote, "I commanded the divided Senate through a team of six or seven Republican members."[58] The panel was nicknamed "The Council of Trent."[59] In June 1996, when Dole resigned from the Senate to run full time for president, Lott became majority leader. As Lott noted proudly, for the first time both the Republican Senate and the House had leaders from the South, the culmination of the GOP transformation that began with Barry Goldwater's opposition to the Civil Rights Act of 1964 three decades earlier.

Few Republican moderates remained in the Senate, and Simpson, Hatfield, Cohen, and Nancy Kassebaum (R-KS), finding the place much less congenial, decided to retire at the end of 1996. With increasing frequency, the new Republican senators came from the House, bringing hard-edged, right-wing credentials. Political scientist Sean Therault described the "Gingrich senators" as a principal cause of partisan warfare.[60] Dan Quayle (R-IN), the former vice president, had advanced to the Senate from the House in the 1980 election. "The House is the worst training ground in the world for bipartisanship," Quayle observed. "If anything, you come out of the House filled with hatred—with venom." In his characteristically outspoken way, Alan Simpson would later say: "The Senate changed when the battered children from the House arrived, led by Trent Lott."[61]

AMERICAN POLITICS BECOMES UNCIVIL AND UNHINGED

In 1996, the American people, enjoying an uncommon period of peace and prosperity, emphatically reelected Bill Clinton to a second term as president.

House Speaker Newt Gingrich overplayed his hand, causing a government shutdown that allowed Clinton to stand strongly for education, environment, Social Security, and Medicare and against Republican extremism.

Clinton carried the increasingly Democratic state of Maine by more than twenty points over Bob Dole. Maine voters, however, are notoriously independent, even contrarian. Despite Clinton's landslide, the Republican Senate nominee, Susan Collins, forty-two years old, who had never held elective office and had been crushed two years before when she ran for governor, won an upset victory over former Congressman Joseph Brennan.

Collins had been serving the people of Maine since she graduated college, first on Capitol Hill working for Bill Cohen in the House and the Senate, and then returning home to join the cabinet of Governor Jock McKernan. After her defeat in the race for governor, Collins went to work at a small college and seemed to be well out of politics. But when her mentor, Senator Cohen, surprised everyone by announcing that he would not seek a fourth term, Collins seized the opportunity, ran an impressive campaign, and won handily, thanks to the ticket splitters of Maine who valued her independence.

Susan Collins quickly discovered that the Senate she would enter was much different from the Senate she had left ten years earlier. The bonds of civility and mutual respect and trust had significantly eroded, and the partisanship resembled the House more than the Senate that she recalled.

The evidence of change for the worst was inescapable. Between 1946 and 1994, the number of senators retiring averaged between five and six. In 1996, fourteen senators, including some of the most respected members of each party, had chosen to retire.[62] The common thread that ran through their farewell speeches was a deep dismay about the condition and direction of America's politics.[63]

Jim Exon (D–NE), who served more than a quarter century as Nebraska's state governor and senator, put it eloquently in terms that the other departing senators could relate to:

> Our political process must be "re-civilized." What I have called the ever-increasing vicious polarization of the electorate, the us-against-them mentality, has all but swept aside the former preponderance of reasonable discussion of the pros and cons of many legitimate issues. Unfortunately, the traditional art of workable compromise for the ultimate good of the nation, heretofore the essence of democracy, is demonstrably eroded.

Exon focused on the phenomenon increasingly described as "the permanent campaign": "Much to the detriment of our nation, the political season no longer ends on Election Day. In fact, lately, it never ends. The late level of each campaign not only feeds the next campaign, but distorts the once respected legislative procedures that get trapped in the brief intervals between campaigns."

Bill Bradley, perhaps the most familiar name of the departing senators because of his basketball fame, spoke plaintively: "The political process is paralyzed. Democracy is at a standstill. The budget stalemate is only the latest headline. The federal government has not been able to act decisively, and with public consensus behind it, in years. On health care, on taxes, on creating jobs, on reforming welfare, we have been at continual deadlock." Bradley spoke urgently about the power of money in politics and the increasing domination of interest groups that "increasingly act almost like political parties themselves, dominating the information that flows between government and citizens, controlling perception, and taking over the grassroots of politics through direct mail, talk radio, and phone and fax networks."

Puzzling over why Americans had not derived more satisfaction from the end of the Cold War, Howell Heflin (D-AL) focused on the deterioration of the political process:

> It is supremely ironic that as we foster democratic principles throughout the rest of the world and have seen democracy make great strides in many areas, we seem to face our strongest threat from within. Some elected officials, media personalities, extreme elements within political parties, and single-issue organizations strive to pit one group of Americans against another. The focus on divisive issues has increased the alienation and driven us further and further apart.

Heflin suggested that the antidote was "compassionate moderation," and that the hallmarks of moderation were compromise and negotiation and the conscious pursuit of bipartisanship. Plainly worried that the Senate was losing its capacity to produce such results, Heflin advocated more informal gatherings that would help senators form and keep the friendships across party lines that "promote the identification of common ground."

Bill Cohen was a prolific author and a poet, as gifted a writer and thinker as he was a politician. Recalling the public anger about Washington at the time he began his service in Congress during the Vietnam War, Watergate, and stagflation, Cohen expressed puzzlement about the current national mood:

> Regrettably, contempt for government seems even more dangerous today. . . . Unlike the mid-seventies, the cause of today's anger and resentment is less apparent. . . . The country is at peace, employment is high, and inflation is low. We have preserved our original constitutional freedoms, and indeed, have enlarged them, particularly in the field of civil rights; we are as a nation more prosperous, better educated, and have at our finger tips and disposal more information than at any time in the history of humankind. Yet there

is a wave of unease and negativity surging throughout the society, a debasement of both language and conduct that threatens to shred the fabric that binds us together as a nation.

After reviewing the major policy issues facing the country, Cohen closed with the same theme that the other retirees had emphasized:

> Congress is an institution designed to permit ideas and interests to compete passionately for public approbation and support. It was never intended to be a rose garden where intellectual felicities could be exchanged with polite gentility. Life in politics is intended to be "a roar of bargain and battle." But enmity in recent times has become so intense that some members of Congress have resorted to shoving matches in hallways adjacent to hearing rooms. The Russian Duma, it seems, has been slouching its way toward the Potomac as debate has yielded to diatribe. . . . If, however, we permit the art of compromise to be viewed as abject surrender, then we should not lament that our system has become sclerotic or dysfunctional.

As Clinton began his second term, a booming economy improved the country's mood, and increased tax revenues dramatically reduced the deficit. Clinton's popularity and good-natured willingness to compromise brought Republican leaders to the table for serious bargaining. On May 2, Clinton and the congressional leaders announced an agreement to produce the first balanced budget since 1969.[64] The agreement extended the life of the Medicare program for an additional five years; offered health insurance to five million children; contained the largest increase in education spending in thirty years; gave incentives to businesses to hire welfare recipients; funded the cleanup of five hundred additional toxic waste sites; and provided significant tax relief for most Americans. Because both sides realized their major objectives, when the Budget Act reached the floor of the Senate, it received support from 82 percent of the Senate Democrats and 74 percent of the Senate Republicans, and comparable support in the House. It was a welcome reminder that America's political leaders were still capable of bargaining in good faith, without the threat of a government shutdown, and reach principled, bipartisan compromises in the national interest.

But the passions blazing through the Republican Party could not be contained for very long. In 1998, after the stunning revelation of President Clinton's affair with White House intern Monica Lewinsky, House Republicans moved aggressively to consider impeachment. Clinton's egregious bad judgment and behavior hardly seemed to reach the constitutionally mandated impeachment threshold of "high crimes and misdemeanors," but Republicans plowed ahead, even after polls showed 70 percent of the nation wanted Clinton to stay in office. Because of their overreach, the 1998 off-year elections went surprisingly well for the Democrats. Even after that, the House Republicans, virtually all serving in safe seats, went forward to impeach Clinton.

THE IMPEACHMENT TRIAL OF PRESIDENT CLINTON

It would fall to the Senate to conduct the second impeachment trial of a president in United States history, and the first of the twentieth century. Richard Nixon had spared the Senate, and the country, the agony of an impeachment trial when he resigned from the presidency in August 1974 before the House of Representatives voted to impeach him. The Senate would be in uncharted waters, establishing the rules for a Senate trial in a television age, acting as judge and jurors in a legal proceeding that was also the ultimate political act set forth in the Constitution.

The relationship between President Bill Clinton and White House intern Monica Lewinsky had enthralled and disgusted America since it exploded in January 1998 with Clinton's now famous denial—"I did not have sexual relations with that woman, Ms. Lewinsky." Clinton's admission in a grand jury proceeding in August 1998 that his denial was untrue sparked universal condemnation of the president's behavior and his lying about it. But the November Congressional elections inflicted such a clear loss on the Republicans that it forced House Speaker Newt Gingrich to resign his position and leave Congress. All evidence suggested that most Americans did not want Clinton removed from office. On election night, elated by the returns, Bill Clinton hugged his close friend Terry McAuliffe and said: "We made it through."

Even most Republicans thought the drive to remove Clinton was over. But they underestimated the raging fire in the party's right wing, which found expression and leadership in Representative Tom DeLay of Texas, a former pest exterminator nicknamed "the Hammer," who hated Clinton. It soon became clear that Clinton's celebration had been premature. The House Republicans were hell bent on impeachment—period—irrespective of what the American people wanted. "The crazy right has them by the throat," said House Democratic Leader Richard Gephardt said ruefully. On December 17, 1998, less than six weeks after the election, the House of Representatives, in a party line vote, approved two articles of impeachment against President Clinton. The first article charged Clinton with perjury for misleading a federal grand jury about the nature of his relationship with Monica Lewinsky. The second charged him with obstruction of justice for inducing others to lie in order to conceal his affair with Ms. Lewinsky.

Trent Lott and Tom Daschle would face the challenge of leading the Senate through a historic impeachment trial. Although far apart ideologically, Lott and Daschle had formed a good working relationship, reflecting a shared commitment to the importance of the Senate. Daschle started his career as a staffer in Mansfield's Senate. Lott appreciated the Senate much differently than when he had arrived in 1989. They enjoyed some early legislative success, being involved in the negotiations that produced the balanced budget legislation in 1997. They shared a determination to avoid the ugliness and partisanship of the House proceeding, and agreed "to co-pilot the plane" to a safe landing.

Lott and Daschle could count on several potential factors to mitigate partisanship as they embarked on their difficult course. Democratic senators deplored Clinton's behavior as much as their Republican counterparts. Some of the most heart-felt and eloquent criticisms of the president came from Democrats who were friends of Clinton and felt personally betrayed, such as Joseph Lieberman and Patrick Leahy. Both sides could count votes, and neither believed that the House managers presenting the case could convince the required two-thirds of the Senate to remove Clinton. No one wanted to replicate the frenzy of the House jihad; they also recognized the dangers that the salacious details of the case could pose. They all remembered how the Senate had discredited itself by its ugly and inept response to Anita Hill's allegations of sexual harassment by Judge Clarence Thomas. The members wanted the Senate to rise to the historic challenge, discharging their responsibilities in a way that reassured the American people.

But party differences were still cut deeply. While the Senate Republicans were moderate compared to their rabid House colleagues, most of them wanted Clinton removed from office. They had been quietly supportive of the 4½ year long march by Independent Counsel Kenneth Starr, as he turned his initial fruitless investigation of Whitewater, an Arkansas real estate deal, into an investigation of the president's involvement with Lewinsky, as well as allegations of previous sexual misconduct. While the Senate Democrats were angry about what Clinton had done, they hated the Starr investigation, which they saw as witch hunt. Removing Clinton from office might be a "national nightmare," to borrow President Gerald Ford's famous phrase, but it would also be a Republican victory and a Democratic defeat. There was no escaping the fact that impeachment was a political, as well as legal, proceeding.

The leaders committed to starting the trail just three weeks after the House decision to impeach. As they struggled to agree on rules, two overriding issues presented themselves. First, would the proceeding be structured like a real trial with witnesses, direct examination and cross examination? Or would it resemble an extended appellate argument, based of briefs, lawyers' presentations and questions and answers from the senators? Second, would the proceeding have to run its full course, ending only with a vote on the impeachment articles, or could it somehow be abbreviated, and be completed in some alternate fashion? The team of House managers wanted a full trial, with as many as fifteen or twenty live witnesses, including Clinton and virtually every White House staffer to whom he had spoken about Lewinsky. Lott was under pressure from his caucus to give the House managers latitude to present their case but was horrified when Senate lawyers estimated that that the trial could drag on more than four months. Lott wanted a trial that was fair, but expeditious. In contrast, Daschle knew that the White House wanted to avoid a trial entirely, perhaps through a compromise to reprimand or censure Clinton. On the day before the trial was scheduled to begin, all the key issues remained unresolved.

Lott and Daschle consulted, and decided to appoint a small group to wade through the difficult issues. Lott chose three of his most experienced, tough-minded senators: Appropriations Committee chairman Ted Stevens of Alaska, Budget Committee Chairman Pete Domenici of New Mexico and Watergate veteran and television star Fred Thompson of Tennessee. Daschle made three equally strong selections: Joseph Lieberman of Connecticut, Joseph Biden of Delaware, and Carl Levin of Michigan. Lieberman and Biden had been among Clinton's harshest critics and Levin was probably the Senate's most meticulous lawyer. This new group, quickly dubbed "the Gang of Six," decided to meet with the House managers to discuss the case.

The tense meeting started poorly. Biden told the managers that they had no chance of winning so a long trial was just a "self-indulgent process." Stevens added his assessment: "The president isn't going to be removed. I can produce 34 affidavits of senators tomorrow that would show they won't vote for conviction." The House managers reacted strongly, furious that the senators had decided the case before hearing a word of evidence. But when they outlined their order of proof, to show how the case was put together, the "Gang of Six" was impressed. The House managers were serious and well-prepared; the senators came away thinking, for the first time, that the case was more than a political jihad, and needed to be taken seriously.

On January 7, 1999, all one hundred senators took their seats in the Senate chamber to begin the historic trial. Chief Justice William Rehnquist presided, to add to the solemnity of the occasion, but his role was ceremonial. Responsibility for all the key decisions about how the trial would proceed rested with the Senate.

Lott and Daschle had formulated competing proposals for abbreviating the trial. Don Nickles of Oklahoma, a respected conservative, suggested that the senators meet privately in an unusual joint caucus. When Daschle did not respond immediately to Nickles' idea, Lott, impatient for a resolution on the path forward, made a rare misstep. He told his caucus that he would put the two competing plans to Senate votes, which he expected to win. Several Republican moderates, led by first-term senators Susan Collins and Olympia Snowe from Maine, pushed back strongly, arguing that forcing a partisan vote would push the Senate down the same road the House had followed. A group of Republicans pressed Lott to give the joint caucus another chance. Lott, reading the sentiments in the caucus, approached Daschle, and they agreed to hold a joint caucus the next morning.

On January 8, the hundred senators gathered in the historic Old Senate Chamber, the Senate met from 1810 to 1859. Lott and Daschle had agreed to start with statements by three senators from each party. Former Majority Leader Robert Byrd, 81 years old and the longest serving senator, spoke first. All senators saw Byrd as the keeper of the Senate flame; a master of the Senate rules and traditions, he had authored a four-volume history of the Senate. Byrd detested what Clinton had done, but he focused, as always, on the Senate's responsibilities.

"The White House has sullied itself," Byrd told his colleagues. "The House has fallen into the black pit of partisan self-indulgence. The Senate is teetering on the brink of the same black pit. We look very bad." He urged the Senate "to come together in a dignified and orderly way . . . to salvage a bit of trust from the American people for all of us, for the Senate and for their institutions of government."

The historic responsibility that the senators felt, and the intimate nature of the meeting without television, sound system or press, led to a candid and searching discussion of the procedural morass. Republican Phil Gramm of Texas, usually a hard-edged conservative and partisan, observed that the two sides were not that far apart. He suggested throwing out the Democratic and Republican resolutions, and writing one together. Democrat Ted Kennedy, perhaps the most liberal senator, said he agreed with Gramm. The witness question did not have to be resolved at that time; they could proceed with opening arguments and resolve the witness question later. Other senators sought to speak, but Lott jumped in: "If we have an agreement between Gramm and Kennedy, we ought to be able to wrap this up. Let's not talk ourselves out of something."

The few staff members in the room, listening intently, could not find any substantive agreement that had been reached, but the senators ended the extraordinary two-hour meeting in a good mood. They avoided a potential partisan breakdown, built camaraderie, and were facing the issues together.

The weeks that followed were an emotional roller coaster. On January 14, a compelling presentation by House manager Asa Hutchinson left Senate Democrats surprised and despondent about the strength of the case against the president on obstruction of justice. Russ Feingold waled out of the chamber thinking there might actually be a case here. Dick Durbin considered for the first time that he might have to vote for conviction. Another House manager, Lindsey Graham, effectively compared Clinton's behavior to federal judges who had been impeached and convicted for perjury and similar charges. "You could not live with yourself knowing that you were going to leave a perjurer on the bench," Graham implored. "Ladies and gentlemen, hard as it may be, for the same reasons, cleanse this office."

But on January 20, the formidable team of White House lawyers shifted the mood back. Charles Ruff, the distinguished White House counsel who worked from a wheel chair, punched holes in Hutchinson's presentation, citing several examples of "prosecutorial fudging." Cheryl Mills, a young (33) African-American lawyer, skillfully rebutted the obstruction of justice charges. She then compared Clinton to Thomas Jefferson, John F. Kennedy, and Martin Luther King, all of whom had strayed sexually. "We revere these men. We should. But they are not perfect men. They made human errors, but they struggled do humanity good. I am not worried about civil rights, because this president's record on civil rights, on women's rights, on all our rights, is unimpeachable." Mills' eloquence evoked an enormous reaction; she became a national celebrity overnight.

The White House had convinced Dale Bumpers, former Arkansas governor and four -term senator, to join the legal team. Just retired from the Senate, Bumpers, long known as the Senate's best orator, addressed his audience as colleagues friends, citing a number by name.

"The charge and the punishment are totally out of sync," Bumpers said. "When you hear somebody say, 'This is not about sex,' it's about sex." And he drove home the personal dimension of the case.

"You pick your own adjective to describe the president's conduct. Here are some that I would use: indefensible, outrageous, unforgivable, shameless. I promise you the president would not contest any of those or any others," Bumpers declared. "But there is a human element in this case that has not even been mentioned. . . . The relationship between husband and wife, father and child, has been incredibly strained, if not destroyed. . . ."

Bumpers reached his conclusion: "We are none of us perfect. Sure, you say, he should have thought of all that beforehand. And indeed, he should, just as Adam and Eve should have." Pointing to the senators, he added, "Just as you and you and you and millions of other who have been caught in similar circumstances should have thought of it before As I say, none of us is perfect."

On January 22, Republican senators showed increasing anxiety about where the trial was going. "We've got to get out of here," said Bob Bennett from Utah. "The horse is stinking up the room." But as the trial proceeded to the next phase—questions and answers rather than prepared statements—

the House managers regained their footing in vigorous exchanges with the White House lawyers.

Throughout the case, the Senate leaders, and the lawyers on both sides, had focused special attention on Robert Byrd. Besides being the great Senate institutionalist, Byrd detested Clinton's behavior, and he had the independence and stature to stand against the president if he chose to do so. To Byrd, there was no question about what Clinton had done to avoid having his infidelity discovered; the question was whether it warranted removing him from office. Now Byrd submitted a question which went to the central issue. He quoted *Federalist* No. 65, where Alexander Hamilton wrote that impeachment stemmed from 'the misconduct of public men or, in other words, from the abuse or violation of some public trust."

"Putting aside specific legal questions concerning perjury and obstruction of justice," Byrd asked, "how does the president defend against the charge that, by giving false and misleading statements under oath, such 'misconduct' abused or violated 'some public trust'?"

Charles Ruff responded that even if Clinton had committed perjury and obstruction of justice, it did not threaten the country. That was the conduct the framers sought to address through the impeachment clause.

"If we have not convinced you on the facts," Ruff continued, "I hope we will convince you that the framers would have asked: is our system so endangered that we must not only turn the president over to the same rule of law that any other citizen would be put under, after he leaves office, but must we cut short his term and overturn the will of the nation? And in our view, in that worst case scenario you can find, the answer to that question must still be no."

Byrd listened intently to Ruff's response, his face and reaction inscrutable. But barely two hours into the question-and-answer session, a Byrd press release was circulated on the floor. It was headlined "Statement by Robert C. Byrd— A Call for Dismissal of the Charges and an End of the Trial." In the statement, Byrd said he would introduce a motion to dismiss the case at the beginning of next week.

"I plan to make this motion not because I believe that the President did no wrong," Byrd said in the statement. "In fact, I think he has caused his family, his friends and this nation great pain. I believe he has weakened the already fragile public trust that has been placed in his care. But I am convinced that the necessary two-thirds for conviction are not there and that they are not likely to develop. I have also become convinced that lengthening this trial will only prolong and deepen the divisive, bitter, and polarizing effect that this sorry affair has visited upon our nation." The proceedings would go on for another three weeks, but Byrd's statement had sealed the outcome. If Byrd was not going to break with Clinton, none of the Democrats would.

But the Senate still faced the challenge of ending the trial in a way that satisfied the country, to the maximum extent possible, that the proceedings had fair and the result was right. When the Democrats met on January 25, Byrd's proposed motion to dismiss shocked them. His preamble included several paragraphs that paralleled the Articles of Impeachment, condemning Clinton's behavior so harshly that it seemed to point to conviction. It justified dismissal only because the two-thirds needed to convict was not there.

"How can you vote for that and then vote to acquit?" asked Pat Leahy. "With all due respect, Bob, I know you're our historian, but I've done as much work as anybody, and more than most, and there's no way I'm going to say he's guilty and then vote to dismiss."

"I'm not comfortable with saying we're dismissing because there aren't enough votes," said Chris Dodd.

The senators suggested various amendments, none of which earned consensus support. Finally, Byrd stood up and said: "Let's take it all out." The motion would be one sentence: "The Senator from West Virginia, Mr. Byrd, moves that the impeachment proceedings against William Jefferson Clinton, President of the United States, be, and the same are, dismissed." The Democrats applauded their approval.

At the same time, the Republicans were considering an offer from Daschle that the Democrats would drop the motion to dismiss if the Republicans would agree that no witnesses would be called. The trial would move immediately to closing arguments, followed by up-or-down votes on the articles of impeachment. Several Republicans expressed support.

"We have to get this over," Mitch McConnell said.

Susan Collins had been considering possible alternatives to simply voting up or down on the articles of impeachment. Now, she and Pete Domenici put forth the idea that the Senate should make "findings of fact," by which Clinton could be found guilty by a majority vote before the conclusion of the trial, even if there was not two-thirds to remove him from office on the final vote. This appealed to several Republicans who wanted to make sure that Clinton's acquittal could not be portrayed as vindication, and Collins thought it might also get traction with a group of Democrats most angry about Clinton's conduct.

Phil Gramm argued that they had to be fair to the House managers; "we must have a vote on witnesses," Gramm said. Jeff Sessions of Alabama said they should stick to procedures, call a small number of witnesses, "and we will have done our duty."

Ultimately the Senate split along partisan lines, 56-44, in rejecting the motion to dismiss, and allowing managers to call three witnesses: Vernon Jordan, the esteemed lawyer and civil rights leader, who was probably Clinton's closest friend and confidante; Sidney Blumenthal, the noted journalist and author who had become a trusted adviser to both Clintons, in part because the right wing despised him; and Monica Lewinsky, the central player in the drama who had not yet been heard from. But the House managers made no significant headway with Jordan or Blumenthal. And Lewinsky, deposed in a formal setting at a conference room in the Mayflower Hotel, proved to be a superb witness: intelligent, forthright, humorous, unshakable—and nobody's victim. Tom Griffith, the chief Senate lawyer, expressed his admiration to one of Lewinsky's lawyers: "She's the best witness I ever saw. She could go into business teaching people how to testify."

The Republicans had hoped to seize victory from the jaws of defeat by having Monica Lewinsky testify in the well of the Senate. But support for that idea vanished when senators watched videotaped excerpts of her testimony. "You can't get any worse than the video," Rick Santorum argued. "Things are getting worse," Slade Gorton retorted. "We've got to finish this next week," Don Nickels added. "It can get worse." There was "an ocean of downside" in going forward with witnesses, Fred Thompson warned. "Get out of Dodge," urged Sam Brownback.

Collins and Domenici continued to press for findings of fact. Collins had identified Democrats that she thought would be supportive. But the White House had pushed back hard against the idea; Clinton himself had called Tom Harkin to attack the proposal. The Republicans were trying to do with 51 votes what they could not obtain 67 votes for, the president argued. Findings would amount to a criminal indictment without any of the customary protections of law.

Harkin needed no persuasion. He had already consulted with leading constitutional scholars, including Laurence Tribe at Harvard and Bruce Ackerman at Yale. They were emphatic that the impeachment clause left no room for a two-tier process. A finding of guilt required a two-thirds vote and resulted in automatic expulsion from office. As the White House and Harkin pushed back against the idea, Collins and Domenici found no Democrats that would join them.

At the same time, Dianne Feinstein's effort, along with Bob Bennett, the Utah Republican, to censure Clinton, rather than vote on the articles of impeachment, failed even after they tried twenty different formulations. Liberals did not want to beat up Clinton anymore; conservatives wanted nothing short of removal; and institutionalists doubted that censure was constitutional. Countless hours and great creativity had gone into possible ways to avoid voting on the articles of impeachment, or find a way that Clinton could be judged guilty even if not removed from office. None of them had worked. It was time to vote.

Recognizing Clinton would not be removed from office, the Republicans desperately wanted to get 51 votes on at least one of the articles of impeachment. On the day of the vote, Collins found herself being lobbied by Nickels, Gramm, Santorum, McConnell, even Gordon Smith, the low-key senator from Oregon. When a staffer told Collins that Lott wanted to speak to her privately in the Republican cloakroom, Collins marched in, furious. Before Lott could say a word, Collins said angrily: "Look, my vote is not in play; I've got to do what I think is right." Lott tried to placate her by agreeing that the lobbying was totally inappropriate. But he still pushed gently, saying he needed to know what she was going to do. If she could support Article II, he would give her one of the two coveted speaking slots just before the vote. Collins said that he should find another senator.

Later that day, when Collins spoke, the agony that she felt about the case was clear. After reviewing the evidence, deploring Clinton's conduct, and concluding that he had obstructed justice, Collins went on: "As much as it troubles me to acquit this president, I cannot do otherwise and remain true to my role as a senator. To remove a popularly-elected president for the first time in our nation's history is an extraordinary action that should be undertaken only when the president's misconduct so injures the fabric of democracy that the Senate is left with no option but to oust the offender from the office the people have entrusted to him."

Leaders Daschle and Lott would speak last. Tom Daschle had done a superb job of balancing the competing pressures on him: working closely with Lott; holding his caucus together; and pushing back on the White House when its demands became excessive. Now, in his closing statement, Daschle criticized the Independent Counsel for crossing the line of propriety, the House Judiciary Committee for adopting Starr's report without doing its own investigation, and the House for degenerating into a partisan bloodbath. But he was most disappointed with the president. "Maybe it is because he holds so many dreams and aspirations that I hold about our country. Maybe it is because he is my friend. I have never been, nor ever expect to be, so bitterly disappointed again," Daschle somberly said.

He said that all those disappointments had made him determined that the Senate would not follow down the same trail. "The Senate has served the country well these past two months, and I have no doubt that history will so record," he noted. He praised Lott for his "steadfast commitment to a trial conducted with dignity, and in the national interest."

Trent Lott, who rose to power as a hard-edged, right-wing lieutenant to Newt Gingrich, had evolved to be an effective Senate leader. The new generation of right-wing Republicans in the Senate and the House had put significant pressure on Lott, but he had been willing to disappoint them when needed as he pursued the overriding objectives of ensuring that the trial was fair, and that the Senate discharged its responsibilities well. In his closing statement, Lott showed his partisan side, defending the House managers, recalling that the Democrats had enacted the Independent Counsel Act which had unleashed Ken Starr, and saying that Clinton should have been removed from office. But Lott also extended his appreciation to Daschle and recalled the moment in the Old Senate Chamber when the parties agreed to work together. "We tried to do impartial justice—honest, fair and quick," Lott said.

Chief Justice Rehnquist called the question on the first article of impeachment. The vote was 55-45, with ten Republicans joining all forty-five Democrats in pronouncing Clinton not guilty of perjury. On the second article of impeachment, the vote was 50-50, with five Republicans joining the forty-five Democrats in finding Clinton not guilty of obstruction of justice. The Republican effort to get a majority fell one vote short. The Senate had finally brought an end to this particular national nightmare.

The pride expressed by Trent Lott and Tom Daschle was justified. Facing an extraordinary historic challenge—the first impeachment trial in 130 years—the Senate came through for the nation. Realistically, the senators could not extinguish partisanship, but they did minimize it by working together forthrightly to resolve contentious and novel issues. They understood that Clinton's behavior was deplorable, but they understood that the American people did not want him removed from office for disgraceful private conduct. They gave the House managers the opportunity to present their full case, but refused to allow the trial to become a salacious embarrassment. They considered, and rejected, several thoughtful efforts to abbreviate the trial, although sorely tempted to do so. A critic might say, as Arlen Specter, the Pennsylvania Republican did, that having the Republicans and Democrats caucus separately conflicted with their responsibilities as impartial jurors. But impeachment of a president will always be a political matter, as much as a legal one. In this case, the hundred men and women of the Senate brought their intelligence, experience, judgment, respect for the Senate, and love of the country to a daunting task. It was reminiscent of Mansfield's Senate, which in crisis times functioned as a team and put country first. Clinton would finish his second term, and leave office a popular president, just as Reagan had after the Iran-Contra investigation.

"Ironically, having been through this crisis may make it easier, not harder, to work together," Susan Collins wrote in her diary that night. This experience has changed each of us individually, and as a Senate, forever." Time would tell if the fires of partisanship could be contained. In a period of peace and prosperity, American politics had become unhinged from the realities in the country. It was sobering to consider what our politics might be if the country faced a genuine crisis.

Bipartisanship Tried, Lost, and Found

$\mathcal{T}$he 2000 presidential election produced a virtual dead heat between Republican George W. Bush and Vice President Al Gore, the Democratic nominee. The outcome, which depended on the results in Florida, where Bush's brother Jeb was the governor, hung in the balance for thirty-six tense days of legal and political maneuvering. In the end, the Supreme Court, by a 5–4 vote, called a halt to the legislative and judicial processes in Florida, awarding the presidency to Bush. For many Americans, the Court's decision, which found the majority to be all Republican appointees and the minority mostly Democratic appointees, seemed political, rather than judicial, causing damage to the credibility and standing of the Court.[1] But Gore gracefully accepted the decision; Bush expressed his commitment to bringing the country together and began his presidency with a 57 percent approval rating.[2]

Bush came to the White House with a sharply Republican House and a Senate that was divided 50–50, although still with a Republican majority because Vice President Cheney had the deciding vote. The Senate seemed well positioned to be the balance wheel in the political system. In the early months of 2001, the Senate Democrats, led by Ted Kennedy and Max Baucus, moved quickly to work on Bush's top priorities: education reform legislation known as "No Child Left Behind" and major tax cuts, which would be known, in perpetuity, by the name of the president who pressed for them.

NO CHILD LEFT BEHIND

Ted Kennedy had come to the Senate in 1963, at the age of thirty, with absolutely no credentials beyond his name and riding the coattails of his brother the president, whose seat he would fill. The warmest personality in his family, accustomed to deferring to his seniors, Kennedy loved the Senate from day one, embraced it in a way that John and Robert Kennedy never did, and he quickly began mastering the legislative process. Of course, tragedy repeatedly struck Ted Kennedy: the assassination of his brother Jack, the assassination of his brother Bobby, his son's cancer, and the car accident at the bridge in Chappaquiddick, which caused the death of Mary Jo Kopechne, one of Robert Kennedy's former staffers. At every crisis point, Kennedy's work in the Senate, and his love for the place, helped sustain him. Kennedy took one shot at the presidency, losing the Democratic nomination to President Jimmy Carter in 1980 in a race that seemed ill prepared and unfocused. Despite being a young man, he never reached for the White House again. He settled back into the Senate and became, in the assessment of most experienced observers, one of the greatest legislators of his era—or any era. By 2001, Kennedy was respected and admired both as a liberal lion and as a superb legislator.

Kennedy's greatness as a senator stemmed from his ability to combine his deep-seated liberal views with an ability to work with people in the other party, even those on the opposite end of the political spectrum. Kennedy stood strongly for certain beliefs, and he knew how and when to compromise. This was more than natural talent or inclination; it was his inheritance from the great Senate in which he grew up. All the best senators had that ability, but by 2001 it had become a rare commodity.

After almost four decades in the Senate, Kennedy had earned the complete trust of Democratic constituencies. They knew he stood with them, and he knew how to work closely with them. When he chose to compromise with the Republicans, the constituencies understood why, and they supported him, even if they disagreed. Those strengths helped Kennedy immeasurably as he negotiated with the Bush administration on education reform.

Bush moved quickly to establish a rapport with Kennedy through an early invitation to the White House where they and their wives watched a screening of *Thirteen Days*, which depicted President Kennedy's handling of the Cuban missile crisis.[3] Mostly, however, Kennedy's approach to education reform reflected his enthusiasm that Bush supported a continuing federal role in education at a time when many Republicans favored abolishing the Department of Education.

Kennedy expressed a more basic reason for working with Bush: "We were elected to do something."[4] If there was an opportunity for real education reform, Kennedy "was going to try to seize it." Kennedy and his House counterpart George Miller (D-CA) spent most of the year in negotiations with the administration, reaching important compromises that achieved Democratic goals of a massive $4 billion increase in federal spending for education, which could make possible reduced class size and improved teacher training, in exchange for the White House getting the tough standards and accountability through student testing that they sought. At the time, Kennedy saw No Child Left Behind as "the most significant advance in public education of the past quarter century."[5] Unfortunately, the increase in federal funding promised by Bush and key to the compromise was never forthcoming—sacrificed to the need for additional homeland security and defense expenditures in the aftermath of 9/11. Kennedy later described No Child Left Behind as "underfunded, mismanaged and poorly implemented . . . a spectacular broken promise of the Republican administration and Congress."[6]

THE BUSH TAX CUTS

During the campaign, Bush made tax cuts the centerpiece of his economic policy. Once elected, taking a page out of Ronald Reagan's playbook, he proposed a massive tax cut of $1.6 trillion, phased in over ten years, in all tax brackets. Interestingly, after the prosperity of the Clinton years and the recent accumulation of the first budget surpluses in decades, the American people were not clamoring for a tax cut. However, the new administration could justify its request on the fact that the economy was slowing and that there was a budget surplus, not a deficit. Federal Reserve Chairman Alan Greenspan, at the peak of his influence and credibility, weighed in favoring the tax cut, which made front-page news everywhere.[7]

Kent Conrad (D-ND), the Budget Committee's ranking Democrat, and a champion of budget discipline, quickly grasped the impact of Greenspan's testimony. "Why are you backing the Bush tax cut? You're going to create a feeding frenzy."[8] Greenspan responded that the economic conditions and the budget surplus justified a tax cut, but that it would be wise to include triggers that would reduce or rescind the tax cuts if certain conditions were met. He noted that his testimony had included a cautionary statement: "We need to resist those policies that could resurrect the deficits and the fiscal imbalances that followed in their wake."

Most Senate Democrats shared Conrad's view. "You're going to start a stampede," said Ernest "Fritz" Hollings (D-SC), a deficit hawk.[9] "It wouldn't be far off the mark for the press to carry the story 'Greenspan Takes the Lid off the Punch Bowl,'" said Paul Sarbanes (D-MD). Minority leader Tom Daschle, who had made stopping a huge Bush tax cut his highest priority, observed: "You wouldn't need triggers if you had a smaller tax cut." Bush's political adviser Karl Rove called the trigger concept "dead on arrival with the president."[10] The White House wanted the $1.6 trillion tax cut, period.

The White House could count on an important Democratic ally. The retirement of Daniel Patrick Moynihan had made Max Baucus (D-MT) the ranking Democratic member on the Finance Committee. Despite having been in the Senate since his election in 1978, and having plenty of legislative accomplishments, Baucus lacked the standing and bulletproof credibility of Kennedy and several other veteran Democrats.[11] He faced election in 2002, and every senator treads carefully when they are up for reelection. Montana had gone for George W. Bush by a lopsided margin, and polls showed that 61 percent of Montanans favored a tax cut, with 57 percent saying the issue would be an important factor in determining how they voted in the Senate race.[12] Baucus decided early that he would play a key role in shaping the tax cut, and he approached Charles Grassley, the Iowa Republican who chaired the Finance Committee, suggesting that they work together.[13] Weeks of quiet negotiation followed.

Baucus knew that Daschle and most of the Democratic caucus opposed the tax cuts, but he pressed on. He believed that "politics should favor action and achievement rather than ideological combat. I'm not a bomb-thrower, not a demagogue; I just want to advance the ball." He was not completely isolated; other centrists, led by John Breaux (D-LA), favored the tax cut, and generally relished their magnified influence in a closely divided Senate where every senator's vote was critical. While Daschle and other liberal Democrats put pressure on Baucus, Grassley was under the gun from many conservative Republicans for conceding too much to Baucus by slowing down the tax cuts, making the $500 per child tax credit refundable and for failing to insist that the top rate be lowered from 39 percent to 33 percent.[14]

On May 10, Daschle and several other Democrats visited Baucus's office to check on the status of the talks with Grassley. After Baucus summarized the state of play, his colleagues ripped into him: either Baucus was being disloyal or he was naïve. The tax cut would help the rich while hobbling the government, and the surpluses that supposedly justified the cuts would disappear as the economy cooled. Baucus protested that his negotiations were making the tax cut more progressive. John Kerry (D-MA) told him that he was "being had"; the Republicans were getting everything they wanted in exchange for a few crumbs for the Democrats.

As the tough meeting closed, Daschle told Baucus that he was not empowered to reach a deal with Grassley. Baucus, stunned, repeated the message: "I don't have the authority to negotiate?" "That's right," Daschle said.[15]

Baucus brooded over his options, and the next day he decided to try to keep negotiating. Baucus and Grassley met again, showed each other their bottom lines, and reached agreement. They went before the press to announce their deal. Baucus had gained more relief for lower-class taxpayers than the House bill, which reflected Bush's proposed tax cut.

On May 11, Daschle was heading out the door for root canal surgery. He would soon have more pain. For months, Daschle had been mobilizing Democrats to oppose the largest tax cut in twenty years. Now, Baucus called to advise him that he had just cut a deal with Grassley and they would be working together to push through a major tax cut. Incensed, Daschle, always soft-spoken, told Baucus that he had "abandoned his colleagues" and "people would remember his breach for a long time."[16]

Baucus sensed, correctly, that several of his Democratic colleagues did not want the party to be portrayed as pro-tax; they also appreciated Baucus's efforts and some progressive features in the tax cut. The Finance Committee approved the Grassley-Baucus compromise, with Baucus and three other Democrats joining the ten Republicans to produce a 14–6 committee result. While the White House tried in conference to retain some of the provisions in the House-passed bill, most of the Senate provisions prevailed, including the expansion of the childcare tax credit that was important to many Democrats and Olympia Snowe (R-ME).

On May 24, Jim Jeffords (R-VT) stunned the Republicans by defecting from their caucus, shifting the balance in the Senate and making Daschle the majority leader. Nonetheless, Daschle was despondent about the long-term consequences of the tax bill, and the haste with which it had passed. He noted that the Senate had spent more time debating the issue of renaming National Airport after Ronald Reagan. But he recognized the limits of his leadership.[17] "Regardless of what the circumstances are, you have to accept the fact that I'm not a Lyndon Johnson," Daschle observed, a touch ruefully. "I can't intimidate someone into doing what I want them to do. I have to accept what comes and move on to the next issue."

Robert Byrd (D-WV), the former majority leader, now close to eighty-five, was already extremely critical of the new president and his team. He regarded Bush as someone who had become president only because of his family name.[18] Byrd also saw in the administration a penchant for arrogance and a willingness to disregard Congress that he had not seen since the Nixon administration. He ripped the tax cut as exorbitant, weighted toward the rich, and squandering the $2.5 trillion surplus that the Clinton administration had left thanks to increased tax revenues from a booming economy.[19] Byrd angrily wrote:

> Two and a half trillion dollars could have bought a lot of good things for the country. We could have paid down the publicly-held national debt. We could have funded education programs, financed a prescription drug benefit, and helped shore up Medicare to deal with the huge demands bearing down

on the nation with the beginning of the retirement of the baby boomers. The funds were available to meet future demands and challenges, but those opportunities were relegated to the back burner.[20]

The leading defender of congressional prerogatives, and a proud author of the Budget Act in 1974, Byrd expressed outrage at the Republicans' use of the reconciliation process to ram through the tax cuts with a fifty-one-vote majority and limited debate.[21] Byrd pointed out that reconciliation was intended as an expedited process to bring about needed budget cuts; it was improper to use it to accelerate passage of a massive tax cut without amendments or debate. In 1981, President Reagan had proposed the largest tax cuts in American history. "In stark contrast to the Bush tactics, Reagan's tax cuts were fully debated as a free-standing bill, the Economic Recovery Tax Act. There were twelve days of debate and 118 amendments before the Reagan tax cut finally passed the Senate," Byrd recalled. "No one could claim that the Reagan proposal, radical as it was, had not been fully aired."[22] To Byrd, the stakes were higher this time around. If the Reagan tax cut failed, there would still be time to correct course before the fiscal tsunami caused by the retirements of the "baby boom" generation. No similar latitude existed for the Bush tax cuts, which would still be in effect when the first baby boomers were starting to retire.

Byrd expressed puzzlement, and despair: "I have never understood why senators of long experience, men and women who well grasp a core duty to assert the Senate's constitutional powers, to provide an effective check on the executive branch, will topple and fade away when a president of their own party snaps his fingers."[23]

President Bush signed the tax cuts into law on June 7, less than five months after taking office. They rocketed through Congress even faster than Reagan's tax cuts twenty years earlier, even though Reagan was enormously popular, having been first elected overwhelmingly and then earning the admiration of all Americans by his courage in handling an assassination attempt. Even before the Bush rebate checks went out, the rosy ten-year scenarios about a budget surplus had disappeared. Greenspan would write in his memoir: "Suddenly and inexplicably, federal revenues plunged. The flow of personal income tax payments to the Treasury . . . started to come up billions of dollars short. The vaunted surplus, still going strong when Bush signed the tax cut in June and foreseen to continue for many years, was effectively wiped out overnight. Starting in July, red ink was back to stay."[24]

Greenspan and the Federal Reserve economists finally concluded that just as the stock market rise from the "dot.com" boom had sent tax receipts soaring in the late 1990s, the losses in the "dot.com" crash that started in 2000 had transformed the fiscal picture, virtually overnight—exactly as many Democrats had feared.

Ted Kennedy's experience with education reform provides a sobering reminder that even the most skillful legislator cannot guarantee that bipartisanship and principled compromise will bring about the results hoped for. Max Baucus's experience shows that when tax cuts are involved, a deliberative legislation process can disappear quite quickly. The Senate acted unwisely and much too rapidly. The long-term consequences for the revenue base were devastating. Unsurprisingly, tax cuts given could not easily be taken away.

IN THE SHOCKED AFTERMATH OF 9/11

Of course, American politics—and our country—changed dramatically on September 11, when the horrific terrorist attacks on the World Trade Center and the Pentagon killed nearly three thousand Americans. In the painful aftermath of the attack, George W. Bush found the central focus of his presidency. Until 9/11, "Bush lacked a big organizing idea," said David Frum, his speechwriter. Now, his mission was defined: the war on terrorism, starting in Afghanistan with the search for Osama bin Laden, and the rapid ramping up of intelligence capabilities to deal with the threat to our homeland. The Senate also found its mission: essentially, letting the president do whatever he wanted.

The heartfelt unity between the administration and Congress, across party lines, initially served the shocked nation well in responding to this unprecedented crisis. Congress quickly authorized the president to wage war in Afghanistan to find bin Laden. However, on October 26, Congress hurriedly passed the Patriot Act, a sweeping expansion of the powers of the intelligence and law enforcement agencies, by an overwhelming vote of 96–1 in the Senate.[25] The Patriot Act contained many provisions that would have to be revisited and revised in calmer times. Later the Bush administration would also move rapidly to create the Department of Homeland Security (DHS), the most massive reorganization of the federal government since the creation of the national security apparatus after World War II, merging twenty-two government agencies and 170,000 employees into one agency.[26] In the summer of 2002, the White House demanded that the Senate pass the legislation before the August recess, which meant no hearings and very limited debate. Daschle agreed to work to get quick Senate approval, a decision that Byrd sharply criticized.

"Have we all completely taken leave of our senses? The president is shouting 'pass the bill, pass the bill.' The administration's cabinet secretaries are urging adoption of the president's proposal without any changes, but that is not the way of the Senate," Byrd argued. "If there was ever a time for the Senate to throw a bucket of cold water on an overheated legislative process, it is now."[27]

Byrd's opposition prevented the passage of the DHS legislation before the August recess. He delayed it again the next month, when the White House called for its passage by the anniversary of 9/11. The *New York Times* called Byrd the "brakeman" on the Bush administration's homeland security "juggernaut." But despite the delays, the Senate would still pass the bill without a hearing, and with less than thirty hours of debate.

"We stand passively mute in the Senate today, paralyzed by our own uncertainty," Byrd chastised his colleagues. "We are truly sleepwalking through history. I have been amazed at the cowardice on the part of some of our members—well-intentioned—but they are just cowed."

"Standing up for the Constitution is a lonely ordeal these days," Byrd told a reporter. "All that matters is politics. When you talk about the Constitution, the eyes of Washington glaze over. . . . It isn't a fight for principles anymore. It's damn the Constitution, full speed ahead."

The Senate's worst abdication was yet to come.

THE RUSH TO WAR IN IRAQ

On September 12, 2001, President Bush asked Richard Clarke, his counterterrorism chief, whether there was any evidence that Saddam Hussein, the Iraqi dictator, had been involved in the 9/11 attacks.[28] "I know you have a lot to do and all . . . but I want you, as soon as you can, to go back over everything, everything. See if Saddam did this. See if he's linked in any way."

Clarke, incredulous, responded: "But Mr. President, al-Qaeda did this."

"I know, I know," the president responded. "But . . . see if Saddam was involved. Just look. I want to know any shred."

Clarke found no such evidence. But at a Camp David retreat of the group that was becoming Bush's war cabinet, Secretary of Defense Donald Rumsfeld called on Paul Wolfowitz, the deputy secretary, to outline the case for moving against Saddam.[29] Wolfowitz, a leading neoconservative foreign policy thinker, believed fervently that U.S. military action could transform the Middle East. He stated that there was a "10–50% percent chance" that Saddam had been involved, although he cited no evidence to support the imprecise claim. He went on to say that Afghanistan was a very difficult place to wage war, but that Iraq presented many good targets; military action there would demonstrate that the United States would not stand by and let a dictator like Saddam operate with impunity.

Wolfowitz's argument sounded crazy to most of Bush's senior advisers.[30] "No one will understand us doing anything but going after those who attacked us," Secretary of State Colin Powell said. Powell, who had been assembling an international coalition to wage war against bin Laden, thought that going after Iraq would shatter any coalition effort.

General Hugh Shelton, the chairman of the Joint Chiefs of Staff, laid out the military options for Afghanistan. But Wolfowitz interrupted: "But we really need to think broader than that right now," he said. "That's not big enough. We've got to make sure to go ahead and get Saddam out at the same time—it's a perfect opportunity."

General Shelton would later recall that Bush got angry. "How many times do I have to tell you that we are not going after Iraq right this minute?" he snapped at Wolfowitz. "We're going to go after the people we know did this to us. Do you understand me?"

Later in the afternoon, Cheney agreed that this was not the right time to go after Iraq: "If we go after Saddam Hussein, we lose our rightful place as good guy."

Nevertheless, Iraq remained a topic of conversation within the administration. By December, "while Bin-Laden was escaping in the mountains, Bush and Cheney were focusing on Iraq . . . From the start, they had seen Iraq as the nation's central threat," Peter Baker wrote in *Days of Fire: Bush and Cheney in the White House*.[31] On January 29, 2002, in his State of the Union address, Bush coined the most memorable phrase of his presidency, calling Iraq, Iran, and North Korea the "axis of evil." An earlier draft of the speech targeted only Iraq, but the president decided he also wanted to call out Tehran and Pyongyang. The "axis of evil" phrase upset U.S. coalition partners, particularly in Europe; they deplored saber rattling and feared the prospect of a war beyond Afghanistan.

But Bush and Cheney were on the course that would lead inexorably to war. "Every meeting on Iraq through the spring and summer had focused on *how* to attack Iraq—where they would send troops, who would be with them, and how long it would take," Baker wrote.[32] By July, Bush had decided to seek to resume the Six Party negotiations with North Korea that he had broken off when he took office. But with Iraq, he had no interest in talking.

On August 5, Secretary Powell, disturbed by the movement toward war, met one on one with the president in the Treaty Room.[33] Powell went through the consequences of the invasion: the loss of the coalition unity; the possible effect on oil prices; and potential destabilization of Saudi Arabia and other countries in the region. He made a prescient point: Bush and the United States would be responsible for a shattered country.

"If you break it, you're going to own it," Powell said, in what would become famously known as his Pottery Barn rule. "It isn't getting to Baghdad. It's what happens after you get to Baghdad. And it ain't going to be easy."

Bush asked what course Powell was recommending.

"We should take the problem to the U.N.," Powell said. "Iraq is in violation of multiple U.N. resolutions. The U.N. is the legally-aggrieved party." Powell went on to say that if Saddam stiffed the UN, then U.S. allies would be more supportive of military action. Alternatively, Saddam might acquiesce.

Bush was impressed by Powell's intensity. "Colin was more passionate than I'd seen him at any NSC meeting," Bush recalled.

On August 15, Brent Scowcroft, the universally respected National Security Adviser in President George H. W. Bush's White House, wrote an op-ed in the *Wall Street Journal* titled "Don't Attack Saddam."[34] Scowcroft argued that the war in Iraq would distract from the war against terrorism. It could also destabilize the Middle East and require a long-term military occupation by the United States.

The article incensed Bush. He saw it as a betrayal, given Scowcroft's ties to his family. He may have also have seen it as Scowcroft defending the decision by Bush's father (and Scowcroft) not to continue to Baghdad after dislodging Saddam and his army from Kuwait, and a not very subtle message from his father. But Bush and Cheney also knew that the article would be persuasive given Scowcroft's stature and experience. Cheney got a call from Trent Lott, the Senate Republican leader.[35]

"Dick, I think you may have a big problem here with public perception of a possible Iraq war," Lott advised. "The case hasn't been made as to why we should do it."

"Don't worry," Cheney responded. "We're about to fix all that."

The next day, Cheney delivered a tough speech to the Veterans of Foreign Wars in the Nashville convention center.[36] "Simply stated, there is no doubt that Saddam Hussein now has weapons of mass destruction," he said. "There is no doubt that he is amassing them to use against our friends, against our allies and against us." He went beyond saying that Saddam had chemical and biological weapons. "We now know that Saddam resumed his efforts to acquire nuclear weapons," Cheney said. "Many of us are convinced that Saddam will acquire nuclear weapons fairly soon."

Even though Bush was still considering the option of asking the U.N. to send in inspectors, Cheney ridiculed the idea. "Against that background," Cheney said, "a person would be right to question any suggestion that we should just get inspectors back into Iraq, and that our worries will be over. Saddam has perfected the art of cheat and retreat, and is very skilled at the art of denial and deception. A return of inspectors would provide no assurance whatsoever of his compliance with U.N. resolutions. On the contrary, there is a great danger that it would provide false comfort that Saddam was somehow back in his box."

The VFW speech outraged Powell, who demanded to know from National Security Adviser Condoleezza Rice whether it had been cleared as administration policy.[37] It had not, but both Cheney and Rumsfeld made a practice of routinely running over Rice. Bush was also angry, recognizing that his vice president was making administration policy and cutting off his options. Ultimately, Cheney's unilateralism may have contributed to Bush's gradual loss of confidence in his judgment. But in August 2002, Cheney had provided the ultimate justification for preemptive war: Saddam's weapons of mass destruction. No one in the administration challenged the core judgment that the threat posed by Saddam justified going to war. From that point on, the die was cast. The administration would seek congressional authorization to wage war against Iraq at a time of the president's choosing.

The next few weeks were a period of intense public activity as the administration tried to make its case that an invasion—even going it alone— could be necessary. Bush and other administration officials continued to emphasize the dangers of Saddam's WMD. But Bush also broadened his message, embracing the view of Wolfowitz and other neoconservatives. "I'm going to make a prediction," he told an audience of Republican governors at a private dinner. "Write this down. Afghanistan and Iraq will lead that part of the world to democracy. They are going to be the catalyst to change the Middle East and the world."

Congress faced one of the most momentous decisions in its history: whether to authorize the president to wage preemptive war against Iraq. The principal responsibility for the decision would inevitably fall to the Senate, which not only had a Democratic majority but also had traditionally played a much larger role in foreign policy than the House. The ninety-two-page National Intelligence Estimate (NIE) sent to Congress on October 1 leaned strongly toward the conclusion that Iraq had chemical and biological weapons and was reconstituting its nuclear weapons program. It did contain dissenting views, but mostly in the back of the document. Stunningly, although 71 Senators and 161 House members went to briefings by Bush, Cheney, and other administration officials, only six senators and a handful of representatives went to the secure room to read the entire NIE beyond the first five pages.[38] Given what was at stake, this lack of congressional interest in forming an independent judgment seems like prima facie evidence of dereliction of duty.

Three veteran Democratic senators strongly opposed giving the Bush administration the open-ended authorization he was seeking. Ted Kennedy, who had sat through the Armed Services Committee hearings, was struck by the testimony of several of America's foremost military leaders: General John Shalikashvili, former chairman of the Joint Chiefs of Staff; General Wesley Clark, former supreme allied commander, Europe; and Marine General Joseph Hoar, commander in chief of Central Command.[39] Kennedy questioned General Hoar about the potential for urban warfare. General Hoar said that Baghdad would resemble the last fifteen minutes of Stephen Spielberg's *Saving Private Ryan*.[40] General Clark expressed great confidence in our troops but opposed going to war because America would be mired in Iraq for ten years. Drawing on the teachings of St. Augustine and St. Thomas Aquinas, Kennedy concluded that the invasion of Iraq—a preventive war—was not a "just war."

Robert Byrd, whose anger toward the Bush administration had only continued to escalate, voiced the most forceful and constant opposition. He condemned the Bush administration for the rush to war and for forcing Congress to vote on the resolution a few weeks before the off-year elections. He reminded his colleagues that the first President Bush had delayed a vote on the Golf War authorization until after the 1990 elections to depoliticize it. Byrd thought the authorization resolution was too open ended, placing no constraints on the president's authority to wage war. He invited Walter Dellinger, who had been Clinton's solicitor general, to offer his opinion.[41] "If Congress passes this," Dellinger said, "you can just hang out a sign that says, 'Out of Business.' It's a complete grant of authority for the foreseeable future. The administration can take military action in Iraq, or anywhere else that it chooses as long as there is some connection to Iraq."

Carl Levin (D-MI), chairman of the Armed Services Committee, was probably motivated by a closed session exchange with John McLaughlin of the CIA. Levin had asked whether Saddam was likely to use chemical and biological weapons against the United States. McLaughlin had said it was unlikely unless he was attacked, in which case it would become very likely. Levin ultimately took the lead in preparing key amendments to the resolution.[42] He offered an alternative that would have authorized the president to go to war only if a new UN Security Council resolution was adopted first. Levin's approach urged the UN Security Council to demand unconditional access for UN inspectors; authorized the use of force by UN member states if Iraq refused to comply; authorized the use of U.S. armed forces if Iraq failed to comply with the UN resolution; affirmed the right of the United States to defend itself independent of UN resolutions; and prohibited the use of *sine die* adjournment, meaning that Congress would be able to reassemble quickly to consider other proposals if the UN did not adopt the suggested resolution.

It was a thoughtfully crafted amendment, but the arguments did not matter. The skids were greased; the outcome was preordained. Before the debate started, House Minority Leader Richard Gephardt (D-MO) and Senator Joseph Lieberman (D-CT) endorsed the authorization resolution, giving it a bipartisan stamp of approval.[43] Despite what was at stake, the debate had a desultory quality, lacking the urgency and focus that has characterized the

1991 debate on the Gulf War. The elections were only a few weeks away, and the Democrats were visibly anxious to get the vote done so they could move on to other issues, such as the economy or health care, that would favor them politically. The Senate leaders offered a cloture motion after only a few days to bring the debate to a close as soon as possible. Byrd recalled debates on education, trade, the farm bill, and energy that each lasted several weeks, as well as the two-and-one-half month debate on the Panama Canal treaties. Yet "we were only going to spend a week on whether to give this bellicose president unfettered authority to take us to war."

Byrd wrote bitterly:

> We were being stampeded, and anyone willing to look a fact in the eye knew it. We had been swept away by campaign fever. Some high-priced pollster had apparently convinced the Senate Democratic leadership that we could "get this war behind us" and change the subject to that of the flagging economy where the election prospects would appear to be more favorable to the Democrats. What nonsense. The White House war machine was in full gear. They would keep the focus on "terror." There would be no "getting it behind us."[44]

On October 11, the Senate voted 77–23 to give President Bush the grant of authority that he had requested. Byrd, the keeper of the Senate flame, would later reflect on this "terrible show of weakness. . . . Never in my half century of Congressional service had the United States Senate proven [so]unworthy of its great name. What would the Framers have thought?"[45]

The Senate had come through for the country three years earlier when it extinguished the flames of impeachment. Now, however, it had failed the nation by rushing to authorize a war that would have a devastating effect on Iraq, the Middle East, and America's standing in the world. "Divided among themselves, nervous about dissent in wartime, very much on the defensive against an aggressive executive with midterm elections approaching, the Democrats failed to muster effective opposition," historian George Herring observed.[46]

Despite putting politics first and foremost, the Democratic leaders miscalculated. At the same time as they were seeking and getting bipartisan support for the upcoming war, Bush and Cheney waged a tough and successful partisan campaign based on their leadership in the war on terror.[47] Republicans attacked Democrats for jeopardizing the nation's security because they had delayed the creation of the Department of Homeland Security. Senator Max Cleland (D-GA), who had lost three limbs as a soldier in Vietnam, lost his Senate seat to Saxby Chambliss because of outrageous paid media attacks on his patriotism. Bush, whose approval ratings were still in the midsixties, traveled to forty states and raised $200 million. Cheney campaigned almost as much. On election night, they celebrated a major victory. For the first time since 1934, the incumbent president's party gained seats in both houses of Congress.

The Senate Democrats made a concerted two-year effort to work with the White House, both before and after 9/11. It resulted in an education reform in which their priorities would be shortchanged, the unnecessary and exorbitant Bush tax cuts, and a collaboration in one of the worst congressional decisions in the history of our country. Plus, the Republicans recaptured the majority in the Senate. Given that track record, no one could blame the Democrats if they gave up on bipartisanship.

A RETURN TO PARTISANSHIP

George W. Bush, still benefiting from his image as a strong wartime leader, won reelection in 2004 by three million votes over Massachusetts senator John F. Kerry. Bush's public support declined dramatically after the tragically inept government response to Hurricane Katrina in August 2005, and it never recovered.

Partisan poison returned to the Senate during Bush's second term. Perhaps it was inevitable given how badly the Democrats' effort at bipartisanship had worked out. But certainly, the failed leadership of Senator Bill Frist (R-TN) played an important part in the Senate's performance. Frist had taken the majority leader's post in 2002 after Trent Lott was forced to resign as leader following racially insensitive remarks at Strom Thurmond's 100th birthday. For those who believe the Senate should include exceptional people from diverse walks of life, Frist represented a potentially exciting choice. He was one of the nation's leading heart surgeons who continued to make regular trips to Africa to perform heart and lung transplants.

Unfortunately, whether because of inexperience or presidential ambitions, the Senate leadership position did not bring out the best in Frist. It was an unwritten rule that senators did not campaign against their colleagues. Certainly, Senate leaders, responsible for working closely together every day, did not campaign against each other. Frist ignored that rule, going to South Dakota to campaign against Tom Daschle, the Democratic leader. Daschle lost narrowly, and one more tradition that contributed to Senate comity came to an end.

Many Americans were deeply troubled when the Senate intervened in the case of Terri Schiavo, a Florida woman who had been in a persistent vegetative state for fifteen years after suffering a loss of oxygen to the brain at the age of twenty-six. If there was ever a time for a wise and brave doctor to be the Senate majority leader, this was it. However, solely based on a videotape of Schiavo, Frist challenged the considered opinions of the Florida court that she was in a persistent vegetative state. Frist's opinion helped justify the congressional rush to action, which flew in the face of basic Republican principles about deference to states' rights.

John Danforth, an Episcopalian priest as well as a lawyer, now in private life, had watched the Republicans' march to the right with mounting concern. The Schiavo case pushed his concern over the edge. Danforth was appalled that his party would inject the federal government into the most personal and agonizing decision that a family could face. "This is not a coalition of traditional Republicans and a Christian right in the nature of a merger of equals," Danforth wrote in a book titled *Faith and Politics: How the "Moral Values" Debate Divides America.* "This is the takeover of the Republican Party by the Christian Right."[48] Danforth expressed contempt for Frist's role, saying that he could not "imagine a physician making a medical diagnosis without examining a patient unless he had a special need to appeal to the Christian Right."[49]

In 2005, the Democrats filibustered ten of President Bush's judicial nominees. Frist threatened to initiate a process to change the Senate rules to abolish the filibuster for judicial nominations, which became known, in a phrase coined by Senator Lott, as "the nuclear option." Cooler heads prevailed; a bipartisan "Gang of 14" defused the issue by agreeing that judicial nominations would not be filibustered except in "extraordinary circumstances," which were left undefined. In later years, when a similar eleventh-hour compromise was needed, Senate watchers would note sadly that there were no longer fourteen senators who shared the trust and mutual respect needed to reach such a compromise.

THE RISE OF HARRY REID AND MITCH McCONNELL

Frist proved to be a short-term leader. Following Howard Baker's Tennessee model of "citizen-legislator," Frist had pledged to serve only two terms in the Senate and did not seek reelection in 2006. Returned to private life, Frist was once again an extraordinary doctor and humanitarian. Yet Frist did shape the Senate's future in a unique and lasting way. Daschle's narrow defeat, at least partly attributable to Frist's campaigning, resulted in Harry Reid of Nevada, the Democratic whip, stepping up to be minority leader in 2005. Frist's retirement resulted in Mitch McConnell, the Republican whip, becoming minority leader in 2007. Together, Reid and McConnell would lead the Senate for the next decade—longer than any other pair of Senate leaders in history.

There was reason for cautious optimism about what the new leadership team could accomplish. Reid and McConnell were both veteran senators when they became leaders. Presumably, they revered the Senate, and having been party whips they knew how to count votes and "make the trains run on time." Their personal chemistry seemed good. Both men had come up the hard way. Reid, born in the small town of Searchlight, Nevada, grew up in abject poverty, in a shack with no water, toilet, or telephone. McConnell had been stricken with polio at the age of two and worked tirelessly to overcome the disease. Both men developed a passion for politics early; indeed, neither of them ever spent a day in the private sector. Both became lawyers, and each did an early stint on Capitol Hill—McConnell worked for Senator Marlow Cook and saw Kentucky's senior senator, John Sherman Cooper, as his idol.[50] Reid worked for the Capitol Police to put himself through law school.

Reid's political star rose first. His high school teacher and boxing coach, Mike O'Callaghan, ran for governor, and chose Reid, then city attorney for Las Vegas, to be his running mate. When O'Callaghan won in 1970, Reid became lieutenant governor at the age of thirty. He reached for the Senate in 1974 but was defeated by Republican Paul Laxalt. Reid then lost a race to be mayor of Las Vegas. But when the 1980 census gave Nevada a second congressional seat, Reid ran and won in 1982. Four years later, in 1986, a good year for Senate Democrats, Harry Reid was elected to the Senate.

McConnell went from his work on Capitol Hill to a brief stint as deputy assistant attorney general during the Ford administration, when his office mate was a young Italian lawyer, named Antonin Scalia. McConnell went back to Kentucky and jumped into a race for judge/executive of Jefferson County, the highest political post in Kentucky's largest county. His political consultants were struck by McConnell's lack of political appeal but were impressed by how well he took coaching, and that he would do anything to win, which he did.[51]

In 1984, McConnell challenged Walter "Dee" Huddleston, the Democratic incumbent senator. Huddleston, although not one of the Senate's bright stars, had performed respectably, and seemed on track to win despite the landslide victory that Ronald Reagan was building in his reelection race. But McConnell ran a television ad that would become an instant classic, showing bloodhounds looking for Huddleston who had missed many Senate votes while campaigning. On election night, Mitch McConnell won the Kentucky Senate seat by five thousand votes—four-tenths of a percentage point, or about one vote per precinct. Political careers—and McConnell's would be one of the most extraordinary in American history—often turn on small margins.

Reid and McConnell had many similar attributes. Both were fiercely hard workers, tough fighters, partisans to the core, dedicated politicians who were terrific tacticians. Each worked tirelessly to protect his state's unique special interests: McConnell championed tobacco and coal; Reid was backed by the gaming industry and protected Yucca Mountain against all efforts to store nuclear waste there. Neither man would ever demonstrate the substantive knowledge, constant intellectual growth, or broad-ranging intellect that characterized Mansfield, Byrd, or Baker. America's politics had diminished and coarsened over time, and with Reid and McConnell, the Senate probably found appropriate leaders for the times.

Yet no one could have predicted quite how badly the leadership combination of Harry Reid and Mitch McConnell would turn out. Where other leaders might have worked to rebuild a climate of trust and mutual respect in the Senate, McConnell and Reid deepened the partisan divide and the gridlock that resulted. They were destined to become, in the words of journalist Stephen Collinson, "the terrible twins of dysfunction in a gridlocked Senate, both using arcane procedures to slow and throttle the promise of the other's rule."[52] Their supporters would argue about who was worse—never who was better. Under their leadership, the Senate's long decline accelerated precipitously. Their joint legacy would be a broken Senate.

THE SURGE

When Congress convened in 2007, the Democrats, capitalizing on Bush's unpopularity and public fatigue with war in Iraq, had recaptured a majority of both houses. Democrats controlled the Senate by a paper-thin margin, 51–49.

In his 2016 memoir, widely praised for its candor, Mitch McConnell recalled his sharp disappointment at being deprived of his goal to be majority leader. McConnell expressed personal affection for Harry Reid. But he went on to state his full view:

> Harry is rhetorically challenged. If a scalpel works, he'll pick up a meat axe. He also has a Dr. Jekyll and Mr. Hyde personality. In person, Harry is thoughtful, friendly and funny. But as soon as the cameras turn on or he's offered a microphone, he becomes bombastic and unreasonable, spouting things that are both nasty and untrue, forcing him to later apologize. For example, a year earlier, he had called then–Federal Reserve Chairman Alan Greenspan a political hack and later decided to enlighten a group of sixty students by calling President Bush a loser during a speaking engagement at their high school.[53]

"This lack of restraint goes against what is expected from a party leader," McConnell observed, "and I was skeptical at best about the direction of the Senate under his leadership."

The Iraq war, which had become the quagmire predicted by General Wesley Clark, Ted Kennedy, and others, dominated the political debate. President Bush had developed private doubts about his stated commitment to "stay the course."[54] Support was eroding even among stalwart Republicans. Senator John Warner, the chairman of the Armed Services Committee, had returned from Iraq to report that "the situation is simply drifting sideways." Peter Baker wrote: "So Bush was now running from 'stay the course.' A phrase meant to convey steely resolve had become a symbol of out-of-touch rigidity and an attack line in Democratic commercials." Within a short time, Bush had clarified that "stay the course" meant "complete the mission": "We will do our job, and achieve our goal, but we're constantly adjusting our tactics. Constantly."

The day after the election, President Bush fired Secretary of Defense Donald Rumsfeld, one of the principal architects of the Iraq war, replacing him with Robert Gates, the former CIA director who had served four presidents. Strikingly, the president did not consult Vice President Cheney; rather, he informed him of the decision.[55] Bush also named David Petraeus as the new commanding general. The personnel changes were long overdue but did not reverse the tide running against the administration on the war. The president and his advisers went through a period of agonizing review of their options as political support for the war faded. Bush and his closest adviser, Condoleezza Rice, had a heated exchange about the prospects for the war, stunning the other advisers in the room. Bush's generals could not offer him a unified recommendation; some supported additional troops while others thought it was too late.

Senator Gordon Smith (R-OR), a moderate Republican, gave an emotional speech in which he said he had read John Keegan's *History of the First World War* and Thomas Ricks's *Fiasco*, about the first years of the Iraq war. "I for one am at the end of my rope when it comes to supporting a policy that has our soldiers patrolling the same streets in the same way, being blown up by the same bombs day after day," Smith said on the Senate floor. "It is absurd. It may be criminal. I cannot support that anymore."[56]

George W. Bush did not show the ravages of being a war president the way Lyndon Johnson had, yet now he was losing sleep and weight. But he received valuable advice from his former political rival John McCain. McCain had strongly supported the war but was a harsh critic of how it had been conducted. In a private three-page letter, McCain told the president that he would lose the war unless more forces were sent.[57] McCain said that the administration had its strategy backward: instead of working for a political settlement to reduce violence, the United States should work to establish a security to create space for political reconciliation.

On January 10, a week after Congress returned, Bush made one of the most dramatic decisions of his presidency. He spoke bluntly: "The situation in Iraq is unacceptable to the American people, and it is unacceptable to me."[58] He laid out a plan to send 21,500 more troops—it would later increase to 30,000— to carry out a strategy aimed at protecting the civilian population. He stated candidly that he had considered the option of withdrawing, and rejected it:

> We concluded that the step back now would force a collapse of the Iraqi government, tear the country apart, and result in mass killings on an unimaginable scale. Such a scenario would result in our troops being forced to stay in Iraq even longer, and confront an enemy that is even more lethal. If we increase our support at this crucial moment and help the Iraqis break the current cycle of violence, we can hasten the day our troops begin coming home.

Bush's courageous decision initially received very little support. The Democrats uniformly condemned it, and maverick Republican senator Chuck Hagel (R–NE) called it "the most dangerous foreign policy blunder in this country since Vietnam."[59] Bush hoped to buy some time for the surge by making it "the Petraeus plan," since the Senate had voted 81–0 to give General Petraeus his fourth star needed for his command. But Petraeus advised the president that he would need until September to show some results, and it was not clear that Bush could give him that time. Debating Bush's decision on "the surge," as it was uniformly known, became the central preoccupation of Congress.

McConnell, the new Senate Republican leader, recognized the unpopularity of the war but was strongly committed to leading the fight to give the plan enough time to work.[60] In February, the House, led by Nancy Pelosi, the first woman speaker, passed a resolution disapproving the decision to send additional troops to Iraq, but McConnell managed to prevent the Senate from considering such a resolution. He invited General Petraeus to brief Senate Republicans, and his presentation convinced wavering senators to give the surge a chance.[61]

On April 23, Majority Leader Reid made national headlines with a statement that the war was lost. McConnell would later write:

> Once again, Harry had done it. But of all the insensitive and regrettable things that had come out of Harry's mouth, this had to be at the top of the list. Saying the war was lost—when we had thousands of troops in the field, fighting every day for our country—only conveyed the impression that he was pulling for us to lose. . . . When we heard Reid make this statement, we pounced on it.[62]

McConnell and the Republicans also pounced quickly on a full-page ad by MoveOn.org, which appeared in the *New York Times* labeling General Petraeus as "General Betray Us."[63] Given General Petraeus's distinguished record and his stature in the country, the ad triggered a significant backlash against the opponents to the war. The stridency of the antiwar movement helped McConnell keep his Republicans unified, and they defeated or deflected a series of efforts to defund the surge or compel the withdrawal of troops.

In May, the Congress passed a $120 billion measure to fund the strategy, which included eighteen benchmarks that the Iraqis had to meet for funding to continue. By July the buildup was complete, and the surge began to show immediate results.[64] When Petraeus and Ambassador Ryan Crocker came to Capitol Hill on September 10, they were able to report indicators of real progress. Attacks on U.S. troops were down. Casualties in and around Baghdad were dramatically reduced. Refugees were returning to their homes. By the end of the year, U.S. and Iraqi units were conducting sweeps through once-violent Sunni neighborhoods with little resistance.

The surge had proven successful. McConnell took understandable pride in the leadership he had provided in blocking Democratic efforts to undercut it. President Bush, General Petraeus, Secretary Gates, and John McCain deserved enormous credit for formulating and executing a strategy that rescued the failing war effort. Reid's choice of words had been inept, but the bottom line was more fundamental. Democrats had relearned a lesson taught during Vietnam. However misguided the decision to invade Iraq had been, it was very hard to admit defeat and unacceptable to cut off funding for a war when our troops are in the field.

THE ECONOMIC CRISIS OF OUR LIFETIMES

As 2008 began, the success of the surge had eased the public concern about the war. However, the economy, which had grown steadily since the recession of 2001 to 2002, began to show signs of strain. On January 2, Treasury Secretary Henry Paulson advised the president that the economy was weakening significantly and that a stimulus package was required. The idea of a stimulus in an election year had bipartisan appeal. Bush proposed a $145 billion package on January 18, including a $600 tax credit for individuals, childcare credits, and other business tax relief. The legislation raced through the Congress in record time. It was a credible package, but of course, nowhere near enough for the one-hundred-year storm that was coming.

By the beginning of 2008, the housing bubble, fueled by cheap mortgages and lax lending standards, was unmistakable. But the ripple effect of securitized subprime mortgages, while not yet fully evident, soon would be. On March 12, Bush was scheduled to speak at the Economic Club on Wall Street amid the collapse of the housing market and fears about the cash flow of leading investment banks. Paulson noticed that Bush's text included an assurance that no investment banks would be bailed out.[65]

"Don't say that," Paulson cautioned.

Bush asked, "We're not going to do a bailout, are we?"[66]

"Mr. President, the fact is the whole system is so fragile," Paulson responded, "we don't know what we might have to do."

Just two days later, Bear Stearns, one of Wall Street's oldest firms, was about to go under as the subprime mortgage market began to melt down. Paulson organized the acquisition of Bear Stearns by JPMorgan Chase, with the help of a $29 billion credit line from the Federal Reserve. The venerable firm vanished, but Paulson's quick action prevented wider damage.

Not for long. On September 7, Bush had to give Paulson permission to seize Fannie Mae and Freddie Mac, the two government-chartered private corporations that funded two-thirds of home mortgages in the United States.[67] Days afterward, Lehman Brothers, another leading investment bank, had hit the wall. Paulson and Timothy Geithner, then president of the New York Fed, searched frantically for a bank to buy Lehman, but their best prospects decided against it. Lehman went under, sending shockwaves through financial markets. Even as they tried to deal with Lehman, Paulson had to inject the astonishing sum of $85 billion into American Insurance Group (AIG) in exchange for 80 percent control. The giant insurer had ties into every major bank; it was too big and too interconnected to be allowed to fail.

The bailouts of Bear Stearns and AIG, despite their astonishing costs, were only stopgap measures. Only a comprehensive legislative bailout might be enough to stop the collapse of the financial system. On September 18, Paulson, Geithner, and Federal Reserve chairman Ben Bernanke met with the eight congressional leaders in Speaker Nancy Pelosi's conference room. "Let me say it one more time," Bernanke said. "If we don't act now, we won't have an economy by Monday."[68]

Reid expressed doubt that Congress could ever act that fast, but McConnell said that immediate action was possible given the magnitude of this emergency.[69] Despite the anger at the financial institutions whose practices had produced this crisis, the congressional leaders and the Treasury officials began marathon sessions to produce legislation they could agree on. The leaders all knew the stakes and understood that the legislation could only pass if both parties supported it. They worked in a truly bicameral and bipartisan way, around the clock, and fast.

They produced the Troubled Assets Relief Program (TARP), which provided the authority that Paulson had requested to acquire $700 billion of mortgage-backed securities that were worthless. While the legislation received quick support from the Senate Republicans and Democrats and the House Democrats, John Boehner, the House Republican leader, said that he could not guarantee the support of his caucus. With the nation's attention riveted by the crisis, senators Barack Obama and John McCain, the presidential candidates, suspended their campaigns to come to the White House to join what was hoped to be the final meeting.

When President Bush called on House Speaker Nancy Pelosi, she said that Senator Obama would be speaking for the Democrats. Obama showed an impressive understanding of the problem and the legislative response.[70] He endorsed it, showing that the Democrats were united in their support. McCain, showing little grasp of the substance, said that House Republicans had some legitimate concerns that needed to be addressed without outlining the concerns or saying whether he agreed with them.

Bush, unimpressed, leaned over to Pelosi and said, "I told you that you'd miss me when I'm gone."[71]

Three days later, in an act of indefensible recklessness, the House of Representatives rejected the legislation that the administration and congressional leaders had prepared. The House action shocked the country and sent the stock market plunging 777 points, the largest single-day drop in history.

McConnell was as angry as anyone, but reassuring the country took priority. He went to the Senate floor and, speaking off the cuff, promised that Congress would act swiftly and decisively to protect millions of ordinary Americans who had played no part in the financial crisis that now threatened every household.[72] He said that the congressional leadership was assessing a legislative path forward and guaranteed that a bipartisan solution would be found. He was pleased when his staff member told him that the markets were rebounding after his speech.

The White House negotiated some minor changes in the legislation to provide cover for House members who wanted to switch their votes. This time, the Senate took up the legislation first, and on October 1, they passed it by a resounding 74–25 vote. On October 3, the House followed suit, approving it by a 263–171 vote as twenty-six Republicans switched to support the legislation.

McConnell and Reid were proud about what the Senate had done, and their work together. The House had reminded Americans why they needed a Senate. The Senate had stepped forward to act decisively at a time of national crisis. Other tests would come soon enough.

• 5 •

Obama's First Term

Strict Obstructionism[1]

$\mathcal{O}$n November 4, 2008, Barack Obama won a decisive victory over John McCain to become the forty-fourth president of the United States. Obama's nomination by the Democrats had already excited the country and captivated the world, and his victory—the election of the first African American president—was an extraordinary moment where hope seemed justified and change—uniting the country for progress—seemed to be a very real possibility. Obama's transition began in Chicago, and the president and the president-elect, already working together because of the economic crisis, began a smooth and cooperative transfer of power.

The election result did not surprise McConnell. A political realist to his core, he recognized Obama's superb political talent. During the crucial meeting on TARP in Speaker Pelosi's conference room, Senator Obama had spoken for the Democrats. McConnell recalled: "Obama had masterfully shown how well he understood the issue—delivering what sounded like third draft prose without any notes. Everyone in the room was spellbound."[2] McConnell left the meeting with no doubt how the election would turn out.

Every year as Republican leader, McConnell brought his caucus together for a one-day retreat to plan strategy. On January 9, 2009, the Senate Republicans met in the Library of Congress. "The weather was perfect for the occasion: cold, dreary and rainy," McConnell recalled. "Nobody was in a good mood."[3]

McConnell knew that his caucus was shell-shocked by the election results. The Democrats held the White House and both houses of Congress, and Obama would be coming to the presidency in ten days with an approval rating close to 80 percent. McConnell harbored no doubt that the new president would press for a strong progressive agenda. He feared the combination of a troubled economy and one-party control would lead to "an explosion of legislation and government control, such as we saw in the New Deal and the Great Society."[4] He felt the need to rally his troops, and he saw a strategy for doing so.

McConnell told his colleagues first and foremost to have patience. Citing long experience going back to his early work on Capitol Hill in the 1960s and 1970s, he said that no majority was permanent. The American people, exhausted by eight years of the Bush presidency and two wars, had voted for change, but America was still a right-of-center country. Using one of his favorite lines, McConnell told his colleagues "we hadn't suddenly become France." There were still one hundred million Republicans counting on them for leadership.

He intended to provide it. A few days after the election, McConnell told columnist George Will: "Governing is a hazardous business for presidential parties."[5] Now, he sketched out a strategy of opposition. They would pick fights that they could win to show that Obama was not invulnerable.[6] They would obstruct and oppose him on virtually everything else, undercutting his basic promise to usher in a new era of postpartisan cooperation. The Republican senators left the caucus feeling energized, with a new sense of purpose and unity.

McConnell's political calculus would not be influenced by his personal feelings. However, it did not help that he disliked Obama. He resented him for using the Senate as a launch pad to the presidency. More fundamentally, McConnell thought of Obama as an arrogant "professor." "He's like the kid in your class who makes a hell of a lot of effort making sure that everyone knows he's the smartest one in the room. He talks down to people, whether in a meeting among colleagues in the White House or addressing the nation," McConnell would later write.[7]

PREVENTING A SECOND GREAT DEPRESSION

Missing from the Republican senators' retreat was any discussion of the economic crisis that was devastating the nation. In October, the TARP had rescued the banking system at a moment when it could have collapsed. But in 2008, Americans lost 16 percent of their net worth, far more than in any year of the Great Depression. By January 2009, the economic crisis that began on Wall Street had spread to every Main Street in the United States.[8] American workers and families, with the value of their houses and stocks sharply reduced, were cutting back on demand. Banks, traumatized by the Lehman shock and the rapidly sinking economy, hoarded their assets and credit dried up. Economic stress meant more delinquent mortgages, which meant more troubled securities weighing down banks, which meant less lending and more economic distress. Major companies—Boeing, Caterpillar, Pfizer, Corning—responded to the deteriorating climate with major layoffs. Circuit City and Sharper Image went into bankruptcy. In January, as Obama prepared to start his presidency, America lost 750,000 jobs—in one month. As Tim Geithner, about to become Obama's treasury secretary, recalled: "This vicious cycle of financial and economic traction was gaining momentum, and no one was sure how it would end."[9] When the president-elect held a conference call with his transition team to discuss what he should seek to accomplish in his first term, Geithner spoke first: "Your accomplishment will be to prevent the second Great Depression."[10]

A massive economic stimulus by the federal government was only thing that could combat the drastic loss of private demand. Republican and Democratic economists agreed on that basic truth. McConnell had taken rightful pride in his strong, calm leadership on TARP. He regarded the Senate's action as one of the Senate's finest moments. He had spoken forcefully about the need for national unity in response to the economic emergency. That, however, was before the presidential election. Now, as the economic crisis continued to rage and spread, the Republican leader condemned the proposed spending. Even as the White House offered to make tax cuts a part of the stimulus, McConnell pressed his caucus to be united in opposition.[11]

Maine's Republican senators, Olympia Snowe and Susan Collins, notoriously independent and moderate, could not go along with the strategy of opposition. Nor could Arlen Specter (R-PA), the gifted and cantankerous moderate from Pennsylvania. "This is the only option we have in the final analysis as a fiscal tool," Snowe said. "We have to get it right, and we have to make it work."[12] Collins said, "This crisis is extraordinary, and my constituents don't expect me to stay on the sidelines. People don't want us to be the party that just says no."[13] Collins took the lead in difficult negotiations, which almost broke down repeatedly when she and the administration were $200 billion apart. A pivotal meeting between the White House and Collins went forward only because of the presence of Joseph Lieberman (D-CT), a trusted friend of Collins. Eventually, they reached agreement on a $787 billion stimulus, considerably smaller than it probably should have been, and containing too many tax cuts.

McConnell was publicly diplomatic toward the three defectors.[14] "It is safe to say that Republicans in the Northeast are not exactly the same as Republicans in the Deep South," he observed. He said that he had no complaints about how Collins had handled the negotiations.

Other Republicans were outspoken in their frustration. John McCain, probably still smarting from his election defeat, said, "This is not a bipartisan agreement. This is three members of the Senate—none on the House side—

who have joined Democrats for a partisan agreement. . . . We are committing an act of intergenerational theft."[15]

Collins conceded that her role had taken a toll on some friendships. "It is very hard. These are my friends. I work with them every day. I believe I have done the right thing, but there is a cost, a definite cost."[16] A *New York Times* picture showing Collins walking up a staircase alone absolutely spoke volumes.

The pattern would recur repeatedly throughout the Obama presidency. In concept, everyone agrees that a bipartisan approach to major issues would produce legislation that would receive more public support. But how can bipartisanship be achieved if one party decides, in advance, irrespective of the legislation or the urgency of the times, to be in opposition? The Republican stonewall against the economic stimulus, whipped by McConnell at a moment of absolute economic emergency, has little, if any, precedent in our history. It was a shameful action.

THE WAR OVER "OBAMACARE"

For McConnell, the fight over the economic stimulus was a minor struggle compared to the titanic political battle over health care. Every Democratic president since Harry Truman had been committed to extending health care coverage to all Americans. Obama, and virtually all Democrats, were appalled that Americans spent twice as much per capita on health care than any other country, while more than forty million Americans were without insurance. Unjust and inefficient, our "health care system" exacerbated the growing in-equality that afflicted America. Obama felt this was the moment for action; as his Chief of Staff Rahm Emanuel would famously say: "It would be a shame to waste a crisis."

To McConnell, Obama's ideas about health care represented the classic illustration of his attempt "to Europeanize" America. McConnell understood that the country had health care problems: "Costs were out of control and too many people were being squeezed out of the market."[17] But he did not believe a "big government" solution would solve any of the problems. Because it was "the worst bill that had crossed his desk" in his Senate career, he did not want a single Republican to vote for it. "It had to be very obvious to the voters which party was responsible for this terrible policy," McConnell contended. "The best we could do was ensure that there was no confusion in the public's mind come the next election that this was in any way a bipartisan proposal. So, the strategy, simply stated, was to keep everybody together in opposition."[18]

Of course, that was the strategy on everything. McConnell's "Horatio at the Bridge" act would be more convincing if his opposition to Obamacare was any different than his opposition to any other Obama initiative. McConnell would repeatedly blast Obama and Majority Leader Harry Reid for trying to ram through health care on a strictly partisan basis.[19] But in his memoir, recounting the challenges he faced in maintaining unified opposition, McConnell noted that "early on, the Administration reached out to the members of our conference who were deeply involved in health care issues."[20]

In fact, the lessons of the last Democratic failure on health care were seared into the memories of the Obama team and its outside advisers. They were determined to avoid the mistakes that had doomed the 1993 to 1994 effort of the Clinton administration. Not only did they reach out early to the Senate Republicans but also they reached out to all the major players in the health care area, including the doctors and nurses, hospitals, the insurance and pharmaceutical industries, patient groups, and retirees.[21] Even more fundamentally, Obama embraced what was essentially a Republican template for health care.[22] He did not seriously consider a single payer model, favored by Senator Bernie Sanders and many progressives, and did not endorse its little brother, a public option as an alternative if the private insurance markets were failing. Instead, the Obama administration turned to a model endorsed by the conservative Heritage Foundation that had surfaced in 1993 to 1994 from former Republican senators John Chafee (R-RI) and David Durenberger (R-MN), with the endorsement of Charles Grassley (R-IA) and Orrin Hatch (R-UT), who were still key players in the Senate. "Obamacare," as it came to be known, most resembled the Massachusetts insurance framework championed by former Governor Mitt Romney, who would attack his own plan when he later became Obama's opponent in 2012.[23]

The Finance Committee and the Health, Education, Labor and Pensions Committee (HELP) shared jurisdiction over health care. Ted Kennedy, the chairman of the HELP committee, was in the final months of a valiant fight against brain cancer. Chris Dodd, next in seniority on the committee and Kennedy's best friend, understandably did not want to push himself into the lead, and was already focused on strengthening financial regulation. Finance chairman Max Baucus took the bit between his teeth.

In June 2009, a bipartisan Senate "Gang of Six" came together to see if a bipartisan health care bill could be negotiated.[24] Baucus, the chairman, was joined on the Democratic side by Kent Conrad (D-ND), the chairman of the Budget Committee and a leading deficit hawk, and Jeff Bingaman (D-NM), a more liberal Democrat who chaired the Energy Committee. The Republican trio included the veteran Grassley, now the ranking Republican on Finance, who had worked extensively with Baucus; Mike Enzi (R–WY), ranking on the HELP committee; and Olympia Snowe, Finance Committee member who often served as a moderate bridge between the parties. They met for the first time on June 17 in a conference room in Baucus's office, decorated with a large map of Montana and portraits of Baucus's political hero and Senate icon, Mike Mansfield.[25]

Many observers expressed frustration that the fate of health care in the Senate was being determined by six senators from small states that were mostly rural.[26] In fact, the "Gang of Six" was a pretty representative group of senators, all of whom came to the table with a good base of knowledge on health care issues. They plunged into the talks, meeting more than thirty times over the next four months, often meeting twice a day for several hours. The complexity of the legislation demanded such a commitment, if there was any possibility of an agreement being reached, and explained to the other senators and the public. "It was a compatible group, composed of senators who were all committed to upholding the integrity of the legislative process," Snowe observed.

McConnell let the talks go on, but his basic position remained unchanged. As described in his memoir, he had one-on-one meetings with Grassley, Enzi, and Snowe "to encourage them to stay with the party."[27] He also met every Wednesday with the entire Republican caucus, "trying to build on the view that we were all in this together." Every morning, he was on the Senate floor "pounding away at the bill." He gave 105 daily speeches, in all. If the Republican members of the "Gang of Six" were going to reach agreement with the Democrats, they would be taking a position completely contrary to what their leader was preaching. It was hard to envision that happening.

Nonetheless, Baucus expressed optimism in his public comments through July.[28] Bingaman observed that "we wouldn't be spending this much time in these many meetings if there wasn't a good chance of an agreement."[29] But when Congress recessed for August, the members in their districts encountered an angry and fearful reaction from many constituents. Whipped up by the right-wing media and the blogosphere, many people believed "Obamacare" was "socialized medicine," would take away their doctors, and would devastate the budget.[30] Talk grew that the legislation contained provisions establishing "death panels" to determine the fate of grandparents and parents. Obama's optimistic message of hope and change virtually disappeared as the Tea Party came of age as a political force. Jonathan Oberlander, a University of North Carolina political scientist, identified a historical pattern: all previous efforts to achieve comprehensive health care had failed, and every time scare tactics had been used. "The reasons people use fear again and again is that it's effective.... The opponents to health care have changed over time, but the tactic of relying on fear and scaring Americans has not," Oberlander concluded.[31]

On August 25, Ted Kennedy died after a valiant fight against incurable brain cancer. The loss of a great senator, a national icon, the last of the Kennedy brothers, and a tireless champion of health care for all Americans momentarily quieted the partisan rancor as Washington united to honor Kennedy's memory. But within days, the health care wars resumed.

By early September, the effort of the "Gang of Six" to reach a bipartisan agreement was on life support. Baucus's comments turned increasingly grim.[32] "They all want to do health care," Baucus asserted, "but they've been told by the Republican Party not to participate." Grassley, a principal target of the Tea Party, returned to the conference room saying that he could only support an agreement that could attract seventy-five senators—an impossibility.[33] Enzi assured hometown press that he was only working to change the bill but would never support it.[34]

When the September 15 deadline set by the "Gang of Six" passed, Baucus announced that he would be seeking an agreement with Snowe, the only Republican who remained interested in talking.[35] Snowe was gutsy, independent, and substantive. She joined the Democrats on the Finance Committee in reporting out legislation after a seven-day committee markup that considered more than 130 amendments. Expressing admiration for Baucus's leadership and the bipartisan effort focused on policy rather than politics, Snowe pledged to "collaborate with other centrists to advance improvements."[36]

It later became known that McConnell had told Chris Dodd that they might be able to negotiate something on financial reform, but never health care.[36] Norm Ornstein, probably the most respected observer of Congress, would write: "What became clear before September when the talks fell apart, is that [McConnell] warned Grassley and Enzi their futures in the Senate would be much dimmer if they moved toward a deal with the Democrats that would produce legislation that Barack Obama would sign. They both listened to their leader.[38]

The essence of the legislative process is good faith discussion of issues designed to build understanding needed to find common ground and reach compromises that can win broad support. In this case, as with the stimulus, McConnell had already decided a result that could command such support would not be tolerated. Even if the senators in the room were serious, they were participating in what Ornstein termed "a faux negotiation," whose failure had been planned long ago.[39]

For Obama and the overwhelming number of Hill Democrats, enacting health care legislation had become an almost existential priority. If it could not be done on a bipartisan basis, the Democrats would have to do it alone.

House Speaker Nancy Pelosi had a clear majority in favor of whatever health care legislation the president would sign, as well as the benefit of House rules that would ensure limited debate. Harry Reid faced a very different challenge in the Senate.[40] If the Republicans united in opposition, Reid would need to hold his sixty Democrats together to break any Republican filibuster. The Senate rules and traditions provided for extended debate and created numerous opportunities for obstruction that McConnell was skilled at exploiting. Moreover, the Democratic caucus might not hold together; the public anger toward "Obamacare" was not lost on Democratic senators facing election in 2010, particularly those in states that leaned Republican.

Reid rose to the challenge. Many observers cringed at Reid's style and his frequent verbal gaffes, like the time he praised Barack Obama for his lack of "negro dialect" or called President Bush "a loser." "You never know what might come out of his mouth on any given day," a former Reid staffer noted.[41] David Broder, Washington's most respected political columnist, called Reid "a continuing embarrassment thanks to his amateurish performance."[42] But no one questioned Reid's toughness and his absolute commitment to Obama's agenda and the Senate Democratic caucus. As a result, his caucus was fanatically loyal to him. "He was a crucial partner to the president," David Axelrod, Obama's chief political adviser, noted. "I love the guy. He's canny, relentless, and yet deeply committed to politics as something more than the acquisition of power."[43]

Reid worked tirelessly to hold together his caucus, which ranged from Bernie Sanders and Barbara Boxer (D-CA) on the left to moderate or conservative senators such as Blanche Lincoln (D-AR), Mark Pryor (D-AR), Mary Landrieu (D-LA), Bill Nelson (D-FL), and Ben Nelson (D-NE). Norm Ornstein would observe later: "When Republicans like Hatch and Grassley began to write op-eds and trash the individual mandate, which they had earlier championed, as unconstitutional and abominable, it convinced conservative Democrats in the Senate that every effort to engage Republicans in the reform effort had been tried and cynically rebuffed."[44]

McConnell spearheaded a fierce counterattack. Knowing that the Democrats had to keep their moderate or conservative wing on board, McConnell's team watched carefully for provisions that would be inserted in the bill to ensure support from wavering Democrats. When McConnell's policy people found such provisions, they relayed them to the Communications shop, which flooded the media and blogosphere with unforgettable names.[45] A provision addressing Landrieu's concerns became the "Louisiana Purchase" and Bill Nelson's "Gator Aid." Special treatment was reserved for the last wavering senator, Ben Nelson, after he traded his vote for increased Medicaid payments for his state. Josh Holmes, McConnell's communications director, dubbed it "the Cornhusker Kickback," and said, "We're going to make this bill as popular as an internment camp."

In fact, it is likely that every piece of major legislation ever enacted contains within it provisions designed to win over key votes. Mitch McConnell had excelled at inserting such provisions throughout his career, including decades on the Appropriations Committee. But political war was war, and there is no doubt that as McConnell would recall later: "Within hours, the Cornhusker Kickback took on a life of its own and became emblematic of an entire process that had made the American people absolutely disgusted."[46]

It was probably ironic that the American people expected Barack Obama to be above politics as usual, and would judge him harshly for doing what needed to be done to enact a historic piece of legislation. On December 24, the Senate, on a straight party line vote of 60–39 (Ted Kennedy's seat had not yet been filled), passed the Democrat's version of the health care bill.

In January 2010, Scott Brown, a Republican state legislator previously best known for his career as a male model, shook American politics by winning Ted Kennedy's Senate seat in a stunning upset over Democrat Martha Coakley. Massachusetts was one of the most Democratic states in the nation, and this Senate seat had been held by Ted Kennedy and his brother John for more than fifty years. Coakley proved to be a lackluster and overconfident candidate, but given the fact that the Democrats needed to hold the seat to ensure a filibuster-proof sixty-vote majority, the election became a referendum on "Obamacare," which the Republicans won emphatically.[47] Without the sixty votes, Majority Leader Reid was forced to resort to the reconciliation procedures, which allowed for a fifty-one-vote majority, further amplifying the Republican's message that budget-busting, socialist legislation was being rammed through by shady procedures.[48]

President Obama signed the Affordable Care Act into law on March 23, 2010. Mitch McConnell had lost the legislative fight but won the political war. "The narrative of Obama steamrolling over Republicans and enacting an unconstitutional bill that brought America much closer to socialism worked like a charm to stimulate conservative and Republican anger," Ornstein wrote later.[49] That anger would fuel a sweeping Republican victory in the 2010 election with huge gains across the country, reclaiming the House majority and narrowing the Democrats' majority in the Senate. McConnell's handling of the economic stimulus during the time of national emergency was virtually unpatriotic. His handling of the Affordable Care Act, while cynical, was strategically and tactically brilliant—political hardball on one of the most important issues facing the country.

REINING IN WALL STREET

One day, in the first half of 2009, with the health care debate heating up, Mc-Connell approached Chris Dodd, an old negotiating adversary, and told him: "I can't think of a formulation for health care that we're going to be able to support.[50] But with financial reform, there's space for agreement." McConnell's words were music to Dodd's ears. Chairman of the Banking Committee, Dodd was determined to enact far-reaching reforms of the financial regulatory system to ensure that the abuses of Wall Street, which had plunged the U.S. and world economy to the brink of depression, could never happen again.[51] Dodd also had powerful personal motivations. He had crashed and burned in his effort to win the Democratic presidential nomination in 2008, finishing dead last despite moving his family to Iowa. He had tarnished his reputation by accepting a mortgage at less than market rates from Countrywide, one of the lenders most deeply involved in subprime mortgages.[52] Chris Dodd understandably wanted to be remembered for his long record of domestic and foreign policy accomplishments, and he was looking for a legislative capstone to his career.

Dodd plunged into the complex world of federal financial regulation, and the enormous gaps that existed. He had a superb House collaborator in Barney Frank (D-MA), the brilliant, irreverent, and fearless Massachusetts congressman who had been chairman of the Banking Committee. But Dodd needed a Republican Senate collaborator to achieve bipartisan legislation that could generate broad public support. "I was determined to demonstrate how the Senate could work," Dodd said.[53]

The ground seemed fertile for major financial reform. Public outrage against the big banks and the government that failed to regulate them was running very high. The TARP legislation, completed in the closing weeks of the Bush administration, was intensely unpopular because it was seen as bailing out the banks that had been principal players in the subprime mortgage outrage. The Obama administration was being pounded for being more worried about propping up the big banks than helping Americans who had lost their homes and their jobs.[54] Dodd, a respected Senate insider, reached out to Richard Shelby (R-AL), who was the ranking member on the committee.

A central challenge was how to regulate the major financial institutions that had developed since the repeal of the Depression-era Glass-Steagall Act in 1999. Glass-Steagall had established a legal divide between commercial banking (the issuance of credit to households and firms) and investment banking (issuing and trading securities). Under Glass-Steagall, commercial banks received government protection in case things went wrong, while investment banks had freedom to take risks but would get no government protection if their investments went south. Glass-Steagall's repeal led to the emergence of massive financial institutions, like Sanford Weill's Citicorp—"supermarkets" that performed commercial and investment banking. It was no longer clear where the government safety net would end.[55] As the financial crisis had illustrated, several institutions—Citicorp, Morgan Stanley, Goldman Sachs, AIG, JPMorgan Chase—had become "too big to fail." Letting them go bankrupt would have catastrophic consequences for the whole financial system.

Essentially, there were three possible approaches to reform.[56] The Treasury and the Federal Reserve believed that reducing the leverage in the system was key. Requiring the banks to hold more capital was the most straightforward way to help them survive when they encountered sudden losses. The second approach, championed by former Fed chairman Paul Volcker, would tightly restrict the risky activities that banks could engage in by restoring a line between commercial and investment banks without going all the way back to Glass-Steagall. The third approach, supported by some independent economists, was that no financial firm should be so large or interconnected that it was too big to fail. The "big banks" should be broken up. Real-world politics, and the extraordinary lobbying power of the financial sector, quickly killed the third approach, leaving Dodd and his colleagues to struggle with the two other approaches.

Paul Volcker achieved iconic status by wringing inflation out of the economy as Fed chairman in the early 1980s. Volcker had always been skeptical about the bankers and other financiers; he had opposed the Reagan administration legislation that gave struggling savings and loans the right to make commercial loans.[57] During the go-go years of the 1990s, Volcker's skepticism about the practices of the big banks seemed old-fashioned, but the financial catastrophe of 2008 had vindicated his cautious views. Now serving as an adviser to the Obama administration, Volcker's unmatched stature and credibility seemed to make him the de facto arbitrator of what would be the right policy on how to rein in reckless bankers.

Volcker put forth a proposal to bar banks from speculating in the markets—a practice known as proprietary trading—and from operating and investing in hedge funds and private-equity funds. Volcker believed that commercial banks were deserving of government assistance, and even, in extreme cases, taxpayer bailouts, because firms and consumers depended on them for credit. In return for those enterprises being sheltered, they should refrain from risky activities such as propriety trading and sponsoring hedge funds. "If you're going to be a commercial bank, with all the protections that implies, you shouldn't be doing this stuff," Volcker said. "If you are doing this stuff, you shouldn't be a commercial bank."[58]

In the words of a *New Yorker* profile, "Volcker was driven by a sense of moral urgency. He had been appalled for years as financiers, dazzled by the prospect of short-term gains, had made fortunes through increasingly complex financial engineering, insisting they earned them by creating wealth for the clients and making the markets more efficient. In 2008, misguided financial engineering had virtually brought down the U.S. and world economy."[59]

Dodd's ambitious effort to bridge the partisan divide depended, first and foremost, on being able to collaborate with Shelby. It looked like an unlikely alliance.[60] Shelby had jumped parties in 1994, and had compiled one of the Senate's most conservative voting records. He had questioned Obama's citizenship, and criticized an early effort by the Treasury Department as based on "a grossly inflated view of the Fed's expertise." But Dodd and Shelby had collaborated successfully on a credit card reform bill that Obama had signed into law. "Odd couple" legislative efforts were often at the heart of successful legislating in the Senate. A senior Treasury official praised Shelby's staff for being deeply engaged, saying: "We share the view that he wants to get something done."

Recognizing both the complexity of the issues and the need to garner broad political support, Dodd and Shelby organized a process in which eight members of the Banking Committee took leadership roles on key issues. Mark Warner (D-VA) and Bob Corker (R-TN) took on the issue of which government agencies could dissolve and resell big banks that failed. Chuck Schumer (D-NY) and Mike Crapo (R-ID) focused on new provisions for corporate governance designed to rein in risk-taking CEOs and their boards. Jack Reed (D-RI) and Judd Gregg (R-NH) faced the daunting task of charting a course to handle complex derivatives that had gone unregulated and contributed to the economic wreckage in 2008. Dodd and Shelby began to debate a linchpin of the White House proposals: a new agency to protect consumers from the misleading and abusive lending practices that had become pervasive in the years leading to the crisis. "It's good politics for people to be invested in a major part of the legislation, in terms of having a sense of ownership," Dodd observed.[61]

On December 23, against the backdrop of an increasingly bitter divide on health care, Dodd and Shelby issued an uncommonly upbeat report on their progress.[62] "Our country needs financial regulatory reform and we are committed to working together on legislation to create a sound regulatory structure," the statement said. Dodd and Shelby noted that they shared many of the same goals: "We seek to end 'Too Big to Fail.' We need to protect Americans from future bailout by enhancing our resolution regime. We agree that consumer protections need to be strengthened. We believe that our regulatory system needs to be modernized and streamlined while preserving the dual banking system. We agree that the Federal Reserve should be more focused on its core responsibility—conducting monetary policy. Finally, we need to modernize regulations and oversight of the derivatives market." Describing the committee's negotiations as "extremely productive," Dodd and Shelby concluded: "We hope to resolve the remaining issues before we reconvene in January"— meaning, there would be no holiday season for the committee staff.[63]

This extremely optimistic statement soon proved to be wildly off base. Treasury Secretary Geithner would recall: "At times, Senator Shelby could seem genuinely interested in bipartisan reform. At one early dinner at Treasury, he expressed enthusiasm for higher capital requirements, central clearing of derivatives, and other administration priorities."[64] But as the political heat from the Tea Party intensified, Shelby found it harder to maintain his commitment. Geithner recalled one meeting in Dodd's Capitol hideaway: "Shelby was edging toward a compromise on some contentious issue, when he suddenly stopped in mid-sentence. He had caught the eye of one of his top aides, who was glaring and shaking his head. 'But, of course,' Shelby hastened to add. 'The outcome would depend on what my caucus is willing to do.'"[65]

In late January, Dodd and Shelby reached an impasse, and Shelby left the talks. Dodd, still seeking a bipartisan bill, reached out to Bob Corker as a possible negotiating partner. Corker slept on it, and in the morning advised Shelby and McConnell that he had decided to accept Dodd's entreaty. Corker, the feisty former builder and mayor of Chattanooga, saw himself as a deal maker and had become intrigued by the challenge of reforming financial regulation.[66]

But the Dodd-Corker effort lasted only a month. Although liberal Democrats already were criticizing Dodd for letting the banks get off scot-free, conservative Republicans were attacking Corker for seeking a deal with the socialist president. Critics blasted both the veteran senator Dodd and the freshman senator Corker for thinking that they could actually bridge the partisan divide at a time when the health care battle was tearing the Senate even further apart. Whether or not McConnell was sincere in his early statement to Dodd that bipartisan reform was possible, by early 2010, he had shifted to complete opposition. McConnell and Republican Whip John Cornyn (R-TX) traveled to Wall Street to raise campaign funds on the strength of Republican opposition to Dodd-Frank.[67] On March 10, Dodd announced that he would put forth his own bill, without a single Republican endorsement.

Anger at Wall Street provided the impetus for the White House and Dodd to move ahead. By the end of 2009, even as the real economy suffered, the firms that had been bailed out a year earlier were making big profits and paying big bonuses. Goldman Sachs granted its employees $16 billion in compensation and bonuses.[68] Despite its earlier reservations, Treasury offered strong backing to the Volcker rule separating investment banking, private equity, and proprietary trading (hedge funds) from commercial bank lending services.[69] In March, Volcker put his stamp of approval on an amendment by Carl Levin (D-MI) and Jeff Merkley (D-OR), which was an explicit statement of his rule. He then worked to defeat the efforts of Ted Kaufman (D-DE) and Sherrod Brown (D-OH) for size limits on banks, which would have forced many banks to break up.

As the full Senate took up the legislation, the Republican leadership pulled a parliamentary move that allowed a strict version of the Volcker bill to be deleted. "It got out-maneuvered," Volcker said. "I don't know how it happened."[70] Merkley put the responsibility squarely on the Republican leaders who wanted to protect the big banks, without a record vote showing they had done so.[71] Ultimately, the House-Senate conference agreed on legislation that included a watered-down version of Volcker's rule. "The banks own this place," Richard Durbin (D-IL), the Democratic whip, ruefully observed. Volcker's adviser, Anthony Dowd, said: "We both felt like we got kind of excluded at the very end. But there were fifty-four lobbying firms and $300 million spent against us. So, we didn't do too badly."

On July 15, 2010, Congress gave final approval to the Dodd-Frank legislation, the most ambitious overhaul of financial regulation in generations. The Senate passed the legislation by a now familiar vote of 60–39, with three Republicans—Susan Collins, Olympia Snowe, and Scott Brown—joining the Democrats. It was a major legislative victory for President Obama, who had pledged to rein in the reckless Wall Street behavior behind the crisis and to change the regulatory structure to prevent any recurrence.

The legislation gave the government new authority to seize and shut down large, troubled financial companies. It also set up a council of federal regulators to watch for threats to the financial system. The vast market for derivatives would be subject to government oversight. Shareholders would have a greater say in determining executive pay. The legislation established an independent consumer bureau within the Federal Reserve to protect borrowers against abuses in mortgage, credit card, and other forms of lending.

Chris Dodd, undoubtedly elated and exhausted, said the legislation would restore Americans' confidence in the financial system.[72] "My goal was, from the very beginning, to create a structure and an architecture reflective of the 21st century in which we live, but also one that would rebuild public trust and confidence." McConnell responded sourly: "The White House will call this a victory. But as credit tightens, regulations multiply, and job creation slows even further as a result of this bill, they'll have a very hard time convincing the American people that this is a victory for them."[73]

The titanic legislative battles were over. As the November off-year election approached, the Senate had come to an extraordinary juncture. Against the odds, it had passed three momentous pieces of legislation—the economic stimulus, the Affordable Care Act, and Dodd-Frank—and yet it was universally regarded as dysfunctional. Carl Levin, a thirty-two-year Senate veteran, was struck by the paradox.[74] "It's been the most productive Senate since I've been here in terms of major accomplishments," Levin said, "and by far the most frustrating. It's almost impossible day to day to get anything done. Routine bills and nominations get bottled up indefinitely. Everything is stopped by the threat of filibusters—not real filibusters, just the threat of filibusters." In his widely read *New Yorker* article titled "The Empty Chamber," George Packer noted that "the two lasting legislative achievements of this Senate, financial regulation and health care, required a year and a half of legislative warfare that nearly destroyed the body."[75] The battles of the past year had taken its toll on Obama's standing, but also on that of Congress. In March 2009, 50 percent of Americans had a favorable opinion of Congress. In March 2010, it was 26 percent.

Obama had won the legislative fights, but McConnell would claim political victory. In November, the Democrats suffered major losses across the country. Florida, Ohio, Pennsylvania, Michigan, Wisconsin, and Iowa—all states that Obama had carried easily in 2008—would now be controlled by Republican governors and state legislators. The Republicans gained sixty-three House seats and recaptured the majority in the House. They gained six Senate seats, which brought them within striking distance of the Senate majority. Jonathan Alter would write: "Less than two years after arriving in Washington as a historic figure heralding a new era, Barack Obama was a wounded president fighting for his political life."[76]

The Republican caucus included a significant number of senators who had been positive and constructive forces in the past, but at some point decided it was necessary to join a unified Republican minority. In the lame duck session of 2010, the Republican senators showed how quickly the Senate could change when they returned to exercising independent judgment—in essence, to being senators. The Senate enacted legislation to end the policy of "don't ask, don't tell" for gays and lesbians in the military because eight Republican senators refused to follow McConnell. The Senate ratified the START treaty limiting nuclear arms because thirteen Republican senators voted against the Republican leader. Lamar Alexander (R-TN) went into a confidential briefing on START opposed to the treaty, listened to the presentation, and came out convinced that he should support it.[77] His change of position was striking because it happened so rarely in 2010. But that type of thing was commonplace in Mansfield's Senate.

McConnell may have relaxed the pressure on his caucus to stay in line. He also may have been focused on negotiations with Vice President Biden about the Bush tax cuts that were finally due to expire after inflicting massive damage on the economy and ballooning the deficits. McConnell negotiated a two-year extension for all the Bush tax cuts, including those for the wealthiest Americans.[78] The White House got an extension of unemployment assistance and a temporary reduction of payroll taxes for millions of workers. McConnell judged it to be a Republican victory, and given the impact of keeping the Bush tax cuts, it was. But both the White House and the Republicans won important victories in the lame duck session.

Perhaps the productive lame duck session would pave the way to progress when the new Congress convened in January. With health care and financial regulation completed, the economy starting to recover, and with power now divided, there was reason to hope that the Senate could move in a more constructive fashion.

FLIRTING WITH DISASTER

Events in 2011 extinguished that hope rapidly. The House Republican sweep brought in about thirty new members whose principal commitment was to the Tea Party. John Boehner, an old-style conservative Republican from Ohio, now Speaker of the House, found himself dealing with a group of new forces, led by Majority Leader Eric Cantor (R-VA), Whip Kevin McCarthy (R-CA), and Budget Committee Chairman Paul Ryan (R-WI), the intellectual leader of the conservative Republicans. The "Young Guns," as they called themselves, were far to the right of Boehner and deeply disdainful of his inclination to traditional Capitol Hill deal making. "The parties often had young Turks rebelling against their leaders and pushing for bolder, simpler and more confrontational solutions or actions," Ornstein and Mann observed. "These young Turks were not outsiders, however, but core members of their own party establishment and key figures high up in the party leadership.[79] They had lofty ideological goals combined with fierce personal ambition." The "Young Guns" promptly concocted an audacious plan to use the debt ceiling bill to leverage major reductions in spending and changes in entitlement programs, while taking an absolute stand against additional revenues.[80]

In fact, since the debt ceiling was only raised to cover congressional commitments already made, it should have been perfunctory, or eliminated completely. Instead, legislation to raise the debt ceiling bill had become a traditional opportunity for mischief and pious rhetoric about the soaring national debt. The debt ceiling was raised seventy-eight times between January 1960 and August 2011, and the debates were often contentious, sometimes going on until the eleventh hour before the government's borrowing power would expire. But much of the sound and fury was kabuki; Congress knew that the debt ceiling had to be raised, and that it would be. No Congress would be crazy enough to call into question America's full faith and credit.

Until now. The "Young Guns," and their Tea Party followers, were willing to do exactly that. They wanted to make reductions in federal spending and entitlements, and felt that they could force the White House into accepting those changes by refusing to raise the debt ceiling, which would put the United States in the position of defaulting. "For the first time, major political figures, including top congressional leaders and serious presidential candidates, openly called for default or demanded dramatic and unilateral policy changes in return for preserving the full faith and credit of the United States," Ornstein and Mann noted. "The real threat of Armageddon was a way of spurning 'politics as usual,' of showing that they would operate outside the old-boy network of standard Washington practices."[81]

The division between House Republican leaders soon became apparent. Two weeks after the election, incoming Speaker Boehner told his large freshman class: "We're going to have to deal with [the debt limit] as adults. Whether we like it or not, the federal government has obligations, and we have obligations on our part." But at a January meeting of the newly installed Republicans, Cantor asked them to see "a potential increase in the debt limit as a leverage moment when the White House and President Obama will have to deal with us." He called for the House Republicans to stick together to seize the opportunity afforded by the debt ceiling bill.

Treasury Secretary Geithner reported on August 2 that the government would no longer have the funds to pay its obligations. In May, Obama administration officials and congressional leaders met to begin to negotiate the debt ceiling legislation. Cantor reported "good rapport" at the initial meeting where the discussion was on spending cuts.[82] But when the discussion turned to revenue increases as part of a comprehensive plan to reduce the long-term debt by $2 trillion, Cantor wanted no part of such a "grand bargain" and abruptly pulled out of the talks on June 23, leaving Boehner to deal with the impasse and with Cantor and the Tea Party sniping at him.[83]

The next month became a nightmare for those seeking to reach a balanced and fair-sighted compromise. Both the president and the speaker appeared to be seriously committed to reaching a "grand bargain." On July 17, secret negotiations moved the parties toward a deal that would have included $800 billion in new revenues through growth and closing tax loopholes, as well as $1.7 trillion in spending cuts, which included significant changes in entitlements, including raising the Medicare eligibility age to sixty-seven.[84] Obama's willingness to deal caused anger and chagrin among many of his strongest supporters who were opposed to any changes in entitlements unless much more could be raised on the revenue side. Obama called Boehner to tell him that he needed more revenue, and to make it clear that he would not give in to Cantor's demand to end the individual mandate in the Affordable Care Act.

After this, Boehner refused to return a series of calls from Obama. When they finally connected the next day, Boehner told the president that he was walking away from the negotiations.[85] "The near breakthrough would turn into a highly public breakup," Ornstein and Mann would write. "It seemed clear that a deal had been in sight, and Boehner blinked, again fearing a firestorm of criticism from his own colleagues and a lack of backup from the Young Guns in the leadership."[86]

With the August 2 deadline looming, Obama went on national television to explain his position. He underscored his commitment to the $4 trillion plan that he and Boehner had come close to securing. He reiterated his opposition to a plan that relied only on spending cuts, and expressed alarm at the possibility that America's AAA credit rating might, for the first time, be downgraded. "The American people may have voted for divided government, but they didn't vote for dysfunctional government," the president said, calling for compromise.[87]

Boehner responded with his own address from the Capitol, arguing that Obama had refused to accept the significant debt reduction that the Republicans had offered in what he called their "Cap, Cut and Balance" legislation. "I gave it my all," Boehner said. "Unfortunately, the president would not take yes for an answer. Even when we thought we might be close to an agreement, the president's demands changed."

While the negotiation between the White House and Boehner took center stage, a group of senators, anticipating a deadlock, had been working hard on their own plan. This "Gang of Six" had been meeting periodically since 2009 to try to fashion a bipartisan deficit reduction plan.[88] Briefly, they appeared to make a breakthrough, announcing an agreement on July 19. Obama called the plan "good news" and consistent with his own approach. But as Michael Allen of *Politico* revealed at the time: "A Senate Republican aid e-mails with the subject line 'Gang of Six': Background Guidance: The President killed any chance of its success by 1) Embracing it. 2) Hailing the fact that it increases taxes and 3) Saying it mirrors his own plan."[89] As Ornstein and Mann note: "In other words, anything that Barack Obama is for, Republicans reflexively oppose."

That pretty much reflected the view that Mitch McConnell had taken since Obama became president. But McConnell saw danger for the Republicans if the Young Guns' strategy caused a default. As he observed on July 13:

> I refuse to help Barack Obama get re-elected by marching Republicans into a position where we have co-ownership of a bad economy. . . . If we go into default, he will say that Republicans are making the economy worse and try to convince the public—maybe with some merit, if people stop getting their Social Security checks and military families start getting letters say-

ing service people overseas don't get paid. It's an argument he could have a good chance of winning, and all of a sudden we have co-ownership of a bad economy. . . . That is very bad positioning going into an election.[90]

McConnell was ready to make a deal, "not because he feared the economic consequences for the country, but because failing to do so might damage the Republican brand," Ornstein and Mann concluded.

As the deadline approached, McConnell and Reid joined the negotiation, and together with the White House and Boehner, they reached an agreement on July 31. The complex deal ultimately included no tax increases but raised the debt limit enough to get past the 2012 election, barring an unexpectedly sharp downturn. The deficit reduction would come in two tranches. The first tranche would be $900 billion, requiring offsetting cuts in discretionary spending over ten years, with $400 million coming immediately to avoid default. There would follow an additional $1.2 to $1.5 trillion increase in the debt limit, with a new "super committee" of twelve members, drawn equally from both houses and both parties, to recommend offsetting debt reductions that would receive up or down votes in both houses. If the committee could not attain a majority, or if Congress rejected the committee's plan, a set of across-the-board cuts, coming equally from defense and domestic spending, with a small amount from Medicare, would follow.

The congressional leaders congratulated themselves on the imaginative deal.[91] Almost no one else was impressed. They had driven too close to the edge, convincing the financial markets that the prospect of default was real and imminent. Four days later, Standard & Poor's (S&P), for the first time in history, downgraded the credit rating of the United States, pointing specifically to Washington's dysfunction.[92] Soon enough it would become clear that the White House and Congress had simply kicked the can down the road because the supercommittee, despite including some of Washington's savviest dealmakers, could no more transcend the ideological differences between the parties than the Congress as a whole. When the November 23 deadline arrived, the supercommittee acknowledged failure, meaning that in January 2013, the automatic cuts—the sequesters—would fall indiscriminately on domestic and defense spending. But that would be after the 2012 elections. An entire year would pass before any meaningful legislative action was considered, as a tight, fiercely contested campaign between President Obama and Mitt Romney, the former Massachusetts governor, took place.

· 6 ·

Obama's Second Term

The Fiscal Cliff and the Nuclear Option

$\mathcal{T}$here were no longer old-style landslides in American presidential elections; the electorate was too closely divided. But in the context of twenty-first-century American politics, Barack Obama decisively defeated former Massachusetts governor Mitt Romney, winning the popular vote 52–47 and the electoral vote by 332–203. Obama carried nine of the ten most hotly contested states. In the Senate, the Democrats ran the table and won twenty-five of the thirty-three races, including the ten most closely watched. The result gave the Democrats the opportunity to celebrate a major comeback from 2010, and shocked the Republicans, who had convinced themselves that the country shared their animosity to Obama.

The unexpected defeat seemed to have a sobering effect on the Republicans. As the inevitable postelection soul searching began, Jonathan Alter observed:

> Many prominent Republicans acknowledged that they had become the "stupid party," as Bobby Jindal, the Republican governor of Louisiana, put it. Senators took positions in support of comprehensive immigration reform that would have led them to be ostracized from the GOP a year earlier. Governors who had supported repeal of Obamacare changed their minds and supported it for their states. A long list of prominent conservatives signed a letter supporting same-sex marriage.

But on taxes and spending, the unrepentant Tea Party wing still had control of the House, and the country was facing what Federal Reserve chairman Bernanke had called "the fiscal cliff." The Bush tax cuts, which had been extended for two years by the agreement reached by McConnell and Vice President Biden, were now set to expire on January 1, which would

111

raise taxes by $500 billion. At the same time, because of the inability of the supercommittee to reach agreement, it would cause mandatory spending cuts—the sequester and budget reductions of $1.2 trillion—to take effect. The combination of major tax increases and spending cuts could easily throw the country into a deep recession.

The return to negotiations between Obama and Boehner quickly deteriorated into a Washington version of *Groundhog Day*, the Bill Murray movie in which every frustrating day is like the day before. Obama had run, and won, with the argument that the Bush tax cuts had to be rescinded for Americans with incomes over $250,000. Boehner, cowed by his Tea Party caucus, still refused to consider any changes in the Bush tax cuts. "Let me get this straight," Obama said at a December 4 meeting. "I won the election and you want Mitt Romney's tax cuts. Let's get serious." The stalemate continued; Christmas Day came and passed without an agreement. The Capitol was empty except for a handful of frustrated White House and congressional staff members.

On December 28, Obama called for a meeting of the congressional leaders in his office. In his memoir, McConnell would describe "the president's condescending attempts to lecture us about why everything we were negotiating was wrong." He also criticized Nancy Pelosi for "coming with one talking point and repeating it over and over again." On December 29, McConnell sent an offer to Harry Reid, who promised to respond by 10 a.m. When Reid had not responded by 2:00 p.m., McConnell left a message for Biden, his favorite (and only) Democratic negotiating partner.

"Is there anyone over there who knows how to make a deal?" McConnell asked. "I need you to get up to speed about this, Joe. Get off the plane, think about this, and call me in an hour." Biden did, and after multiple conversations, an agreement was reached. A news conference was held at 8:45 p.m. on New Year's Eve, and the Senate passed the bill at 2:00 a.m. on New Year's Day, the first time since 1948 that the Senate had been in session between Christmas and New Year's.

The agreement reached extended the Bush tax cuts for everyone except individuals making more than $400,000 a year, resolved the estate and other high-end tax breaks, ended the payroll tax holiday, and kicked the $1.2 trillion in "sequestration" budget cuts down the road. Boehner's caucus refused the deal; he needed Pelosi's Democrats to get the compromise through the House and avoid the fiscal cliff.

After the bitterly disappointing election results, McConnell plainly enjoyed being back in the role of responsible adult in the room. He praised himself for the agreement and for his political courage, noting that he would face some heat from the Republican Tea Party wing. He cited as his model Ronald Reagan, the conservative icon who had struck many deals, settling for

80 percent of what he sought: "[Reagan] knew when to hold firm, and when it was time to forge a compromise. In this moment, given the government we had—the Democrat-controlled government the American people had elected—we had done very well."

The truth was that McConnell had cut a good deal for the Republicans. Assessing the agreement, Jonathan Alter would write:

> In retrospect, it was a mistake for Obama to give up the leverage offered by the January 1 expiration of the Bush tax cuts. Doing so left him with no bargaining power to prevent what he called the "idiotic" sequestration cuts that began in March, when everything from critical scientific research to White House tours faced indiscriminate cuts.

But McConnell had played his own part in driving the country to the fiscal cliff. Weeks before the frenetic Christmas week negotiations, Obama had repeated his long-standing proposal for a "balanced approach," which would include $1.6 trillion over ten years in new tax revenues, as well as spending cuts and entitlement reforms. McConnell had dismissed the proposal as "laughable." His revealing memoir reflected his disdain for all the leaders involved, with the exception of Biden: Obama most of all, but also Pelosi, Reid, Boehner, and Cantor.

Former senator Bill Bradley, who was centrally involved in the landmark 1986 tax reform legislation and the 1993 approval of NAFTA, recently wrote: "Legislating is a very human experience in which trust and mutual respect play critical roles." McConnell did not share the ideological fervor of the House Republicans, and he understood the danger that the fiscal cliff posed to the party and the country. Nonetheless, his attitude toward other leaders and his willingness to misuse the Senate for his own ends had been a major factor in the paralysis that had gripped Capitol Hill. As 2013 started, the basic question was whether the election would help break gridlock, or whether every day would be Groundhog Day.

A CRY FOR "REGULAR ORDER"

Commentators quickly agreed that the 2012 elections would change nothing. A headline in *Politico* read: "New Congress, Same Old Problems." Fareed Zakaria described "America's Political Failure" and the specter of our political system "seizing up."[1] Ezra Klein went one step further, noting that "while the 112th Congress was surely one of the most incompetent in our history, the worst is possibly yet to come."[2]

Yet 2013 began on a more positive note for the Senate. The ice of grid-lock seemed to be thawing, replaced by a healthier and more normal form of politics.[3] Reid and McConnell announced an understanding on how executive and judicial nominations would be handled, defusing calls for the "nuclear option" by which Senate rules would be changed to prevent nominations from being filibustered.[4] Within the first few weeks of the session, the Senate had passed its first budget in four years.[5] Gratifying progress was being made on comprehensive immigration reform, spearheaded by a self-appointed "Gang of Eight," a bipartisan group of veteran and younger senators who shared a deep commitment to resolving the issue through legislation.[6] In the wake of the terrible massacre of schoolchildren in Newtown, Connecticut, the Judiciary Committee passed its first gun control legislation in twenty years.[7] Carl Levin and John McCain combined to issue a powerful report on the abusive trading practices of JPMorgan Chase.[8] Liberal Democrats Elizabeth Warren (D-MA) and Sherrod Brown (D-OH) joined with Republicans Bob Corker and Chuck Grassley to speak about the dangers of "too big to fail" banks.[9] Finance Chairman Max Baucus worked intensively with Republican House Ways and Means chairman Dave Camp (R-MI) to seek agreement on the first comprehensive tax reform since 1986.

With the rancorous presidential election over, the atmosphere seemed generally improved. Obama, despite his well-known distaste for schmoozing, embarked on something of a charm offensive.[10] Pat Roberts (R-KS), who had previously called Obama "thin-skinned" and suggested that he "take a Valium," now praised the president for his substantive meeting on the economy and the budget.[11] McConnell showed more graciousness, even punctuated by occasional humor.

Certainly, part of the improvement reflected the Republicans reassessing and repositioning themselves after the shellacking they had just received. The strategy of absolute obstruction seemed to have failed. In its postmortem review of the election results, the Republican National Committee concluded that the party needed to reach out to minorities, women, and millennials if it wanted to be successful.[12] Many Senate Republicans sensed that they should be looking for opportunities to cooperate with the White House.

But another powerful factor was at work. For many of the senators in both parties, dismay about the Senate had hardened into disgust and a determination to bring the institution back to respectability. They were fed up with lurching from crisis to crisis, enduring endless filibusters and "holds," leaving their offices only to make fundraising calls, and returning to line up with their leaders for straight party votes. Veteran senators and new arrivals understood what the Senate was supposed to be and how far short it was falling. Liberal Democrat Barbara Mikulski (D-MD), the longest-serving woman senator, pointed to the "zone of civility" that the growing group of women senators had created.[13] Conservative Republican Jeff Sessions (R-AL) likened the Senate to the "Russian Duma . . . an endless series of secret enclaves, with meetings everywhere but the committee room or the open air of the Senate floor."[14] Democrat Chuck Schumer (D-NY) wished for "the good old days when we had major legislation go through committees." From many senators, the demand came for "regular order"—the process of committee consideration of legislation, vigorous floor debate with the opportunity to offer amendments, and good faith negotiations to reach principled compromise.

The Senate's comeback produced a long-awaited legislative milestone. On June 26, 2013, the Senate, by a resounding 68–32 vote, passed the most monumental overhaul of immigration laws since 1986, establishing a thirteen-year path for millions of undocumented residents to gain citizenship, a guest worker program for low-skilled immigrants, an unprecedented commitment of $40 billion over the next decade to increased border security, including twenty thousand additional Customs's agents and seven hundred miles of fencing at places along the border.[15] The legislation reflected the successful efforts of a wide-ranging coalition: business groups and labor unions; farm workers and growers; Latino, gay rights, and immigration advocates; and religious groups. The hundred senators voted from the desks, which occurred only in cases of major historic legislation. It was a great triumph for the "Gang of Eight": Democrats Richard Durbin (D-IL), Chuck Schumer (D-NY), Bob Menendez (D-NJ), and Michael Bennet (D-CO), and Republicans John McCain (R-AZ), Marco Rubio (R-FL), Jeff Flake (R-AZ), and Lindsey Graham (R-NC). Obama praised the legislation as a compromise that reflected all the principles he had sought in immigration reform. Schumer exultantly said, "The strong bipartisan vote we took is going to send a message across the country and to the other end of the Capitol as well. The bill has generated a level of support we believe will be impossible for the House to ignore."[16]

To experienced political observers, Schumer seemed to be reading the tea leaves correctly. For the first time in nearly five years, President Obama and the Senate, on a strong bipartisan basis, had come together on a major legislative accomplishment. Surely this had to be the formula to breaking gridlock and making our government work. But even on the day of celebration, House Speaker John Boehner said that he would not take up the Senate bill, and that the House would not pass any immigration legislation unless it was supported by a majority of the House Republicans, which could never happen.[17] Nor did it matter that comprehensive immigration legislation had clear majority support in the House; Boehner would not ally himself with Nancy Pelosi and the House Democrats to defeat his Tea Party caucus. In retrospect, the immigration legislation was already doomed, even as its supporters celebrated their triumph.

The repercussions from the failure to achieve a legislative solution were far-reaching. Millions of undocumented workers would continue to live in fear for themselves and their families. Many progressives would become more deeply disillusioned with a political system that could not deliver results on a major issue facing the country. Republicans like Marco Rubio who had tried to bridge the gap between the parties on immigration would no longer have the courage to do so. In the absence of legislation, President Obama would be forced to address the nation's immigration challenge through executive actions, increasing his protection of the "dreamers," the children of undocumented workers who were born in the United States, while stepping up the pace of deportations of those illegals who had committed crimes. And of course, two years later, border security would become a central plank in the presidential campaign of Donald Trump.

UNLEASHING THE NUCLEAR OPTION

For the Senate, the immigration legislation represented the high-water mark of what had seemed to be a promising comeback. Within a few weeks, the Senate plunged into a bitter, continuing fight over the filibuster, what Senate experts Richard A. Arenberg and Robert B. Dove call "the soul of the Senate."[18]

The constant resort by the Republican minority to the filibuster had caused rising anger among Senate Democrats. It deeply frustrated the Democrats that they could win the White House and hold comfortable majorities in the House and Senate and yet have their legislative agenda blocked using the filibuster, or the threat of the filibuster. In addressing the problem, the Democratic senators agitating for reform, led by freshmen Tom Udall (D-NM) and Jeff Merkley (D-OR), faced two closely linked questions.[19] First, virtually all the senators understood that a decision to change the filibuster rule would be a fundamental transformation in the way the Senate operated, making it more closely resemble the majoritarian House. Second, they also understood that if the filibuster were to be fundamentally changed, such a change would likely occur only if the simple majority could change the Senate rules, rather than two-thirds required by the Senate rules. But if the majority could change the rules, then the rules could be altered virtually every time the majority changed.

These compelling considerations had traditionally caused cooler heads to prevail and compromises to be worked out. In 1979, Majority Leader Robert Byrd had used the threat of the "nuclear option" as a lever to produce a significant change in the Senate rules to put limits on the postcloture filibuster.[20] But the package of rules changes adopted was approved by a vote of 78–16.

In 2005, the bipartisan "Gang of Fourteen" had fashioned a compromise that stopped Majority Leader Bill Frist (R-TN) from detonating the "nuclear option" by pledging to filibuster judicial nominees only in "extraordinary circumstances."[21] Both Reid and McConnell were on record strongly opposing the nuclear option. In 2008, Reid had responded to the earlier threat by Frist to detonate the "nuclear option":

> What the Republicans came up with was a way to change our country forever. They made the decision that if they didn't get every judge they wanted, they were going to make the Senate just like the House of Representatives. We would in effect have a unicameral legislature where a simple majority would determine whatever happens. The Senate was set up to be different; that was the genius, the vision of our Founding Fathers that this bicameral legislature, which was unique would have two different duties. One was as Franklin [*sic*] said, was to pour the coffee into the saucer, and let it cool off.

Reid pledged that he would never invoke the nuclear option.[22]

In January 2011, Senator Udall (D-CO) wrote in the *Washington Post* that "the Senate was dysfunctional and broken."[23] He asserted that "on the first day of the new session, the rules can be changed under a simple, rather than two-thirds, majority." He asked his colleagues to "recognize the obstruction that has prevented us from doing our jobs and join me in reforming the Senate rules."

McConnell responded strongly to the idea of changing the rules by majority vote:

> What is being considered is unprecedented. No Senate majority has ever changed the rules except by following those rules that is, with the participation and the agreement of the minority. . . . The Founders crafted the Senate to be different. They crafted it to be a deliberate, thoughtful place. Changing the rules in the way that has been proposed would unalterably change the Senate itself. It will no longer be the place where the whole country is heard and could have its say, a place that encourages consensus and broad agreement.[24]

Reid and McConnell reached a bipartisan "gentleman's agreement" to support several rules changes to avoid the nuclear option.[25] On a series of agreed-upon votes, the Senate made two limited, but meaningful, changes to reduce obstruction: eliminating secret holds, and ending the delaying tactic of requiring that the full text of amendments be read on the floor. The leaders also allowed for roll call votes on more radical reforms.[26] Udall's proposal to eliminate filibusters on the motion to proceed, and guarantee amendments to the minority, was defeated 44–51; Merkley's attempt to establish a "talking filibuster," requiring those senators who were filibustering to stay on the floor and keep talking, lost narrowly, 46–49. Tom Harkin's (D-IA) proposal to eliminate the filibuster was crushed 84–12.

After two more years encountering obstruction, in January 2013 Harry Reid's patience had worn thin, and he was ready to consider the nuclear option to change the Senate rules by majority at the beginning of the session.[27] Although Reid claimed that he only wanted to make minor changes, the minority, unsurprisingly, strongly objected. A group of veteran senators, led by Levin and McCain, intervened to defuse the crisis with a compromise.[28] On January 24, with the blessing of Reid and McConnell, the changes suggested by the McCain-Levin group were approved by 78–16 (S.Res. 15) and 86–9 votes (S.Res.16). S.Res. 15 established an alternative path for the majority leader to call up legislation if he could not obtain unanimous consent. He could take up the bill after four hours of debate, with the proviso that four amendments would be in order, two for the majority and two for the minority. S.Res. 15 also reduced the amount of postcloture debate time on presidential nominations to eight hours on subcabinet appointments and two hours on district court judges, instead of permitting thirty hours after cloture was invoked. S.Res. 16 made two permanent changes in the Standing Rules of the Senate, which gave the leadership tools to accelerate cloture votes. One allowed for the expedited consideration of a cloture vote on a motion to proceed, if eight senators from each party, including the majority and minority leaders, filed the cloture motion. If cloture were invoked, there would be no postcloture debate on the motion. The tool gave the leadership the ability to cut off debate if a handful of senators were obstructing. S.Res. 16 also reduced the number of cloture votes needed to go to conference from three to one, and shortened the postcloture debate on that motion from fifteen hours to two.

Levin also concisely stated his fear of the nuclear option and his understanding of the essence of the Senate: "There have without question been times that a self-interested or hide-bound minority in the Senate has frustrated American progress. But there have also been times when a Senate majority has attempted to impose its will in ways that would have been harmful. Those instances resonate far less loudly when one is a supporter of a frustrated majority. But those of us who have served in the minority of this body, as I have for nearly half my time in the Senate, remember them well."[29]

"The bipartisan proposal before us holds the promise of restoring the Senate deliberative and legislative process, without going down a 'nuclear' path that might severely damage the Senate in an attempt to save it," Levin contended. "This proposal holds the promise of demonstrating to a nation hungering for bipartisan cooperation that we are capable of providing it." Tom Harkin, also a veteran senator, belittled the efforts of Levin and McCain: "This is not significant. It's a baby, baby step."[30]

The Levin-McCain reforms kept the peace only briefly. By May, Republican obstructions over Obama's executive and judicial nomination plunged the Senate back into crisis.[31] The Republicans hated the Consumer Financial Protection Bureau (CFPB), and blocked the nomination of Richard Cordray, Ohio's attorney general, to be its first director because they wanted changes in the structure of the agency. They blocked Obama's nominations to the National Labor Relations Board (NLRB) in order to prevent the Board from having the quorum required to do business. (This battle was particularly intense because Obama had exercised his authority to make recess appointments the year before, and the Republicans objected that the Senate had actually not been in recess.) These obstructionist moves outraged most Senate Democrats and a phalanx of progressive organizations.

Reid looked like he had been duped by McConnell's assurances of cooperation. This time, he appeared prepared to trigger the nuclear option. He consulted with President Obama, who said he would support the exercise of the nuclear option if Reid chose to do it. Reid's plan was to invoke the nuclear option to abolish the filibuster on executive appointments, but not judicial appointments, because a number of the Democratic senators wanted to retain the sixty-vote requirement for judges, who would be receiving lifetime appointments. As Arenberg and Dove would write:

> Gone was the elegant constitutional argument behind the ploy. No longer were the reformers claiming that the debate could be ended by a simple majority only at the outset of a new session of Congress. That had [always] been a central feature of the argument. . . . Now they threatened to use the nuclear option to overcome the Republicans' blockade of these nominations in the middle of the session.[32]

The group of veteran senators, led by McCain and Levin, tried again to avoid the detonation. On July 30, the full Senate held an extraordinary meeting in the ornate Old Senate Chamber where the Senate had met prior to 1859 when the Capitol was completed. More than thirty senators spoke in the three-hour meeting; no decision was made, but the emergency session seemed to have cleared the air. Reid told the waiting press: "We've had a very good conversation, which will continue tonight."[33] Within the next twenty-four hours, through a series of calls and meetings centering on McCain and Levin, an agreement was hammered out and several of Obama's nominees, including Cordray and two NLRB board members, were confirmed.

The possibility of future nominations being filibustered remained, but key senators were optimistic that they had finally turned the corner. "Many expressed the hope that the compromise would change the spirit in the Senate and lead to better behavior," Arenberg and Dove recalled. McCain observed: "We need to talk, we just proved that last night."[34]

The new era of good feelings lasted only three months. The D.C. Court of Appeals, the second most powerful court in the country, was divided 4–4 along ideological lines, and there were three vacancies for Obama to fill. He nominated three judges who were widely acknowledged to be highly qualified. The Republicans showed their determination to block the nominations, saying that the prestigious court had less of a workload than other circuits and therefore did not need the vacancies filled. They accused the president of seeking to pack the Court, drawing an outrageous analogy to President Franklin Roosevelt's 1937 failed effort to enlarge the Supreme Court to circumvent the Court's anti–New Deal majority.[35] McConnell stated that Obama was trying to "pack the D.C. Circuit so it can rubberstamp the president's big government agenda." It was clearly an ideological battle over three critical lifetime appointments on which the Republicans refused to move.

Reid could not accept this latest outrageous Republican maneuver. Senior members of his caucus, including Jay Rockefeller (D-WV), Max Baucus (D-MT), Barbara Boxer (D-CA), and Dianne Feinstein (D-CA), who had previously opposed the nuclear option, now shifted their views. Asked if she supported filibuster reform, Feinstein responded grimly: "I do now. We had a meeting in the Old Senate chamber, and everyone had a chance to express themselves. I thought it was going to bring about a new day. That new day lasted about one week, and then we're back to the usual politics."[36] Udall, the leading reformer, said, "The Senate needs to break this blockade one way or another if we have any hope of moving beyond government by dysfunction."[37]

On November 21, Harry Reid finally detonated the nuclear option.[38] On the Senate floor, Reid began: "The American people believe the Congress is broken. The American people believe the Senate is broken. And I believe the American people are right." He noted that in the history of the country, "half the filibusters of executive and judicial nominees had occurred during the Obama administration: so, 230 years, fifty percent; four and one half years, fifty percent. Is there anything fair about that?" Pushed beyond their limit, Reid and the Democrats were prepared do away with the filibuster for executive and judicial nominees, except for the Supreme Court.

McConnell responded, noting that the Democrats had begun the process of filibustering judicial nominees made by George W. Bush in 2005. He noted that prior to these three judicial nominees, the Senate had confirmed 215 Obama nominees while rejecting only two. "If you want to play games and set another precedent," McConnell warned, "I will say to my friends on the other side of the aisle, you'll regret this and you'll regret it sooner than you think."[39]

Reid led the Senate through the convoluted parliamentary moves leading to the reconsideration of a cloture vote on one of the nominations that had failed. He reached the point where the motion of the chair denying the appeal of a motion to reconsider the cloture vote was nonappealable. At that point, the Democrats, by a vote of 52–48, overturned the presiding officer's ruling by a simple majority and established a new standing order of the Senate that cloture on executive and judicial nominations, other than the Supreme Court, could be invoked by simple majority. This action also established that a simple majority could amend Senate rules, at virtually any time.

It was a major change in the way the Senate functioned, with repercussions that were incalculable but likely to be far-reaching. The *Washington Post* editorialized: "The Democratic majority was justified in its grievance, but not in its rash action."[40] Levin, one of only three Democrats who broke with Reid, prophesized: "Overruling the ruling of the Chair [as the Senate has done] is not a one-time action. If a Senate majority demonstrates that it can make such a change once, there are no rules which bind a majority, and all future majorities will feel free to exercise the same power—not just on judges and executive appointments, but on legislation."[41] Arenberg and Dove, among the most knowledgeable scholars on the history of the Senate and its procedures, would write: "To reach understandable ends, the Senate Democrats adopted tragically flawed means."[42] They predicted ominously: "Given the new precedent, majorities will do what majorities will do, that is—take control."

Their fears would be justified soon enough. In the off-year elections, Mitch McConnell achieved his thirty-year goal, becoming majority leader of the Senate. And of course, two years after that, America would have an insurgent president, coming to the White House as a Republican, with Republicans in control on both sides of Capitol Hill. The Senate had jeopardized its historic role as a protector of the rights of the minority party, and "majorities will do what majorities do."

Harry Reid had the responsibility of moving the agenda of a president who had been elected and reelected. Mitch McConnell only had to obstruct. As Sam Rayburn, the legendary Speaker of the House, once observed: "Any jackass can kick down a barn, but it takes a carpenter to build one."[43] The United States does not have a parliamentary system. Our system requires some degree of minority cooperation to function. No one can specify precisely what that degree of cooperation should be, but it must be greater than zero. Reid triggered the nuclear option because he saw no other option. Nearly all the Senate Democrats felt the same way. McConnell's unyielding obstruction had driven them all to an extreme response.

FILLING THE AMENDMENT TREE

The Senate descended to even deeper gridlock in 2014, as both parties jockeyed for position in the upcoming off-year elections. McConnell remained committed to blocking virtually every Obama initiative. Reid responded by resorting to one of the most powerful tools in the majority leader's arsenal. Using the majority leader's right to obtain recognition first, Reid could "fill up the amendment tree," which prevented the minority (and the majority) from offering amendments on the Senate floor. This tactic allowed Reid to control the amendments that could be offered, and particularly to prevent the minority from bringing up politically difficult amendments.

As minority leader, Reid had described filling the amendment tree as "a very bad practice. It runs against the basic nature of the Senate."[44] As majority leader, however, he resorted to the device more frequently than his predecessors. The cycle intensified: the minority would threaten to filibuster; the majority leader would file a cloture petition earlier—even before the debate would start—and the leader would then fill the amendment tree. This "tit for tat" formula for gridlock became known as "the Senate syndrome." In January 2014, McConnell took the floor to deliver a nearly hour-long speech, describing the Senate that Reid had created as "a post-apocalyptic wasteland ruled by a dictatorial autocrat despised by allies and foes alike," wrote Jonathan Weisman of the *New York Times*.[45]

In November 2014, the Republican Party, capitalizing on continuing public discontent about the performance of Washington, won a sweeping victory in the off-year elections, increasing their House majority and recapturing the Senate majority. Barack Obama, who had won reelection comfortably in 2012, would confront a Republican Congress for his last two years in office. Mitch McConnell, already the most influential Senate leader since Mike Mansfield, would attain his life goal of becoming majority leader. He would be rewarded with that extraordinary honor even though he had played the leading role in the obstruction and gridlock that had contributed substantially to the public's anger toward Washington. While exercising at home, Harry Reid would suffer a severe injury to his eyes and head, and shortly thereafter, he would announce his intention to retire rather than seek reelection in 2016.

McConnell would not only outlast his adversary; he would also benefit enormously from the Democrats' willingness to cooperate, and the Senate would begin to function respectably. Then, after the unexpected death of Justice Scalia, McConnell would administer the coup de grace by refusing to consider any nominee for the Supreme Court that President Obama would put forward in his last year as president. McConnell would not suffer adverse consequences in the election. Only time would tell the effects on the deeply divided Senate as it faced the historic challenge of dealing with America's first insurgent president.

Part II

THE POLARIZED SENATE MEETS
THE INSURGENT PRESIDENT

· 7 ·

Politics Upended

$\mathscr{D}$onald Trump's election victory represented the most shocking political moment in American history. No precedent existed for Trump, the billionaire celebrity and reality television host, without previous government or military experience, to run an outsider campaign, seize control of the Republican Party, and be elected president. The fact that he pulled off an upset, defying virtually every prediction and poll, compounded the shock. Many commentators would criticize the press for giving Trump so much "free media." But by any fair measure, this improbable and sensational story warranted as much coverage as it got. The morning after the election, every country in the world woke up to find that it had to recalculate its view of the United States and its global strategy. American politics was also upended. The polarized and shrunken Senate would face the challenge of dealing with America's first truly insurgent president.

Mitch McConnell found himself to be an enormous beneficiary of Trump's upset victory. While McConnell had not publicly agonized about Trump capturing the Republican nomination the way House Speaker Paul Ryan did, he clearly had no great enthusiasm for Trump.[1] He focused his efforts on minimizing what Trump's near-certain loss would do to Republican Senate candidates.[2] As Election Day drew near, McConnell faced the increasing likelihood that he would have to surrender his position as majority leader after just two years. His brazen effort to prevent a Democratic president from filling the Supreme Court vacancy created by Justice Scalia's death seemed likely to fail, given the near certainty of Hillary Clinton's election. But Trump's narrow margins of victory in Pennsylvania, Wisconsin, and North Carolina, coupled with massive infusions of outside "dark money" to senators Pat Toomey, Ron Johnson, and Richard Burr, were enough to keep those seats Republican, preserving McConnell's majority.[3]

When the votes were tallied, Mitch McConnell would remain Senate majority leader, and, for the first time, he would be working with (at least a nominally) Republican president. It was his second triumphant election in a row. Not only had McConnell retained his position as majority leader, he had also pulled off his theft of the Supreme Court seat. There would seemingly be no more carping from the right wing of the Republican Party about Mitch McConnell.

McConnell would face the same challenge that world leaders everywhere would have. He would have to understand Trump, figure out what mattered to him, whom he listened to, and whether he took advice and could grow in office. But McConnell would make his calculations from the most powerful position next to the presidency. Even after the 2012 election, when Obama's victory over Romney had shattered his hope of becoming majority leader, the game still had to come through McConnell, and he exercised his power with devastating effectiveness. With the Republicans controlling the White House and both houses of Congress, McConnell had a great opportunity to realize his highest priorities: confirming a conservative Supreme Court justice; repealing "Obamacare"; and reining in EPA and gutting Obama's climate policies. He would have to navigate between the inexperienced insurgent White House and the divided House Republicans while coping with the Senate Democrats likely to be shocked, angry, and driven by the passion of the party's progressive wing. But if the Senate was, in the words of *Hamilton* "the room where it happens," McConnell always relished his role as being the responsible adult in the room. With the unexpected help of Donald Trump, he had again come out a big winner.

In contrast, Chuck Schumer, replacing Harry Reid as Democratic leader, would take the reins in circumstances that were bittersweet. McConnell was not the only successful practitioner of the long game. Schumer came to his leadership position after eighteen years in the Senate, following eighteen in the House. Indeed, Schumer had never held a job other than as an elected official, having been elected to the New York state assembly right out of Harvard Law School. Schumer had been cautiously, but realistically, optimistic that the Democrats would gain the four seats needed to make him majority leader.[4] He was looking forward to being the legislative leader working with President Hillary Clinton. They had known each other for decades, having worked together to pass the Brady Bill in 1994, and they had formed a deep bond working to help New York City recover after 9/11.[5]

Schumer had invested time, some of his prodigious energy, and financial resources in the effort to return the Democrats to the majority. He had not hesitated to take strong positions; he had instructed the Senate Democratic Campaign Committee to intervene in the Democratic primary race in Pennsylvania, putting money and staff to support Katie McGinty over Joe Sestak, the former congressman who had disappointed Democrats by losing to Pat Toomey in 2010.[6] He had invested considerable hope in Russ Feingold's comeback attempt in Wisconsin, and the strong races by Deborah Ross in North Carolina and Jason Kander in Missouri. Now, Chuck Schumer would become the Senate minority leader. Unexpectedly, he would also become the most powerful Democrat in the country, carrying the responsibility of leading the opposition against Donald Trump.

Schumer had risen in the Senate Democratic ranks because of his relentless energy and his skill in combining policy and messaging. He had outhustled Dick Durbin, the popular Democratic whip, to become Reid's anointed successor without antagonizing Durbin's friends, which was certainly no mean trick in the intimate confines of the Democratic caucus.[7] It certainly helped that Schumer was the Senate's best fundraiser, tapping the New York financial community and channeling support to other Democrats.[8] The old joke about Schumer's insatiable desire for press—"the most dangerous place in Washington was between Chuck Schumer and a camera"—had given way to respect and admiration. There was a certain amount of affection as well; Schumer was a gym rat, and schmoozed with his colleagues tirelessly. He was known for being something of a matchmaker, bringing together staff members, who often ended up married.[9] But he was also a serious legislator, having most recently devoted time, energy, and ideas to the "Gang of Eight" immigration effort. Lindsey Graham, one of the gang members, admiring Schumer's ability to find bipartisan common ground, called him "a worthy successor to Ted Kennedy, and that's saying a lot."[10]

Schumer moved rapidly to assemble a broadly based leadership team. Patty Murray (D-WA) had become one of the Senate's most effective legislators, having managed to forge a major bipartisan education reform bill as well as the first budget in four years. Schumer made her the number-three Democrat and assistant minority leader. Debbie Stabenow (D-MI), able and popular, who represented the auto industry and agricultural interests with equal effectiveness, became the policy and communications director. Schumer expanded the group by adding Joe Manchin (D-WV), the most conservative Senate Democrat and a leading defender of the coal industry. His leadership team eventually grew to include thirteen of the forty-eight Senate Democrats.[11]

Notwithstanding his undeniable political skills, Schumer would face his own challenges, leading the opposition after the wreckage of the Democratic Party. Having failed to capture the majority in 2016 when the Republicans were defending twice as many seats as the Democrats in 2018, the Democrats would have to defend twenty-five seats, while the Republicans were defending only eight incumbents. Democrats such as Manchin, Heidi Heit-kamp (D-ND), Joe Donnelly (D-IN), Jon Tester (D-MT), and Claire Mc-Caskill (D-MO) would be seeking reelection in states that had strongly supported Trump, and Schumer would have to anticipate their need to protect themselves on certain issues.[12] At the same time, Schumer's close ties with Wall Street were troubling to the ascendant progressive wing of the Democratic Party.[13] He had made a well-publicized speech saying that Obama had put too much emphasis on health care; now he would have to lead the defense of "Obamacare."[14] His quick indication of a willingness to work with President Trump on infrastructure and tax reform where common ground could be found angered progressives.[15] He was known to be a close friend of Israel, but his opposition to the Iran nuclear pact surprised many Democrats.

American politics is notoriously volatile. Democrat Lyndon Johnson won a historic landslide over Barry Goldwater in 1964, but his presidency crumbled as the Vietnam War widened, and Republican Richard Nixon became president just four years later. Nixon carried forty-nine states in 1972, but after Watergate, four years later, Democrat Jimmy Carter, the original outsider, won the presidency. But even by historic standards, the Democrats' defeat was stunning in its suddenness and its magnitude. During the 2016 campaign, many serious commentators wondered if the Republican Party could survive its divisions over the rise of Donald Trump and his likely defeat. But with Trump's victory, the Republicans would control the White House and both houses of Congress. Moreover, while the Democrats had focused on the presidency and the Senate, the Republican Party and its Super PAC supporters had carried on a brilliant stealth campaign that had produced a virtual sweep at the state and local level. Suddenly, the Republicans now had thirty-three of the nation's governors and controlled both houses of the state legislature in thirty-two states, including seventeen with veto-proof majorities.

Ordinarily, the Democrats might have slowly begun the extended period of soul searching that losing parties go through. But the stunning election of Trump and the threat that his presidency posed short-circuited the normal process. The energy in the Democratic Party was coming from its angry liberal wing, which remained devoted to Bernie Sanders and adored Elizabeth Warren.[16] The Democrats' grass roots were on fire; they had no patience with the established leaders whom they saw as responsible for the electoral debacle.[17] Confronting the Trump administration became the order of the day. The resistance that sprang up across the country, manifesting itself in marches, protests, angry town meetings, mobilization of political candidates, and fundraising, was as unprecedented as the presidency it confronted. Schumer would have to tread carefully, and lead boldly, to keep up with Democrats across the nation.[18]

If there was ever a time that the American people needed a Senate at its best, it would be during the presidency of Donald Trump. Yet the Senate that would deal with President Donald Trump had not been at its best for decades. After a long period of decline, the Senate bore little resemblance to the institution that held presidents Johnson, Nixon, and Reagan accountable for their abuses of power. Nor did it bring back memories of the Senate that partnered with every president from Kennedy to Reagan in achieving their most significant legislative accomplishments.

Obviously, Donald Trump did not cause the Senate's long decline, but the Senate's downward spiral and its central role in the paralysis of our government opened the door of the White House to Donald Trump. America's ability to navigate the uncharted waters in the months ahead will very much depend on whether the diminished Senate can step up to the historic challenges facing it across the board.

In a letter to Thomas Jefferson, James Madison, the principal architect of the Constitution, referred to the Senate as "the great anchor of the government."[19] In Federalist paper #263, Madison wrote about the Senate: "Such an institution may sometimes be necessary as a defense to the people against their own temporary errors and delusions."[20] Madison and the other framers anticipated the possibility that someone like Donald Trump would become president. Now what remains to be seen is whether the Senate would play the role the framers envisioned for it. The Senate's record during the first nine months of the Trump administration has been decidedly mixed, but it does provide some encouraging news.

· 8 ·

Confirmation Battles
over the President's Team

The Senate's responsibility to "advise and consent" on cabinet appointees and other presidential nominations became the first opportunity for the Senate to deal with president-elect Donald Trump and key members of his administration. Everything pointed to an acrimonious confirmation process. Democrats across the nation remained in shock, depressed and angry about the bitter campaign and the stunning result. The president-elect preened over his victory, and, despite losing the popular vote by more than three million, did not make even a perfunctory effort to reach out to his opponents. No one expected Trump to strike a conciliatory note in putting together his cabinet.

Historically, the Senate had rejected very few cabinet nominations. The most recent one, in fact, was in 1989 when President George H. W. Bush nominated former senator John Tower to be secretary of defense.[1] Nonetheless, the confirmation process served a valuable function. It provided an early opportunity to get a sense of the new administration and its ability to handle relations with the Senate. It allowed the Senate and the nation to become acquainted with the cabinet nominees. It gave the senators a chance, in courtesy calls and then at the hearings, to convey to the incoming officials their priorities and concerns, which was a valuable form of communication.

Almost inevitably, the process produced unexpected bombshells that threatened nominations, testing the new administration's ability to handle unanticipated problems. President Jimmy Carter had to withdraw the nomination of Theodore Sorensen, President Kennedy's famous speechwriter and a distinguished lawyer, to be CIA director because of his dovish views on security matters.[2] President-elect Bill Clinton had to withdraw the nominations of Zoe Baird and Kimba Wood, his first two candidates to be attorney general, because they had not paid taxes for their housekeepers.[3] His nominee for secretary of defense, Bobby Ray Inman, a former CIA director, withdrew from consideration after accusing *New York Times* columnist William Safire of giving derogatory information to Senate Republican leader Bob Dole to defeat the nomination.[4] At the beginning of his second term, Clinton nominated Anthony Lake, his national security adviser, to be CIA director.[5] That nomination was also withdrawn.

President-elect Barack Obama had to withdraw two nominations for secretary of commerce: New Mexico governor Bill Richardson, because of irregularities involving some of his political donors, and New Hampshire Republican senator Judd Gregg, who dropped out because of policy differences with Obama.[6] Former Senate leader Tom Daschle, nominated by Obama to be secretary of health and human services, withdrew from consideration when reports surfaced that he had not paid all the federal taxes that he owed.[7] After Obama's reelection, he floated the name of Susan Rice, who had been UN ambassador, to be secretary of state.[8] When Rice encountered major Republican opposition, Obama nominated Senator John F. Kerry instead. Plainly, the fact that the Senate almost never voted to reject a cabinet nominee conveyed a deceptive calm. The confirmation process came with minefields to be navigated.

Trump's first major appointment, which did not require Senate confirmation, came on November 17 when he picked retired army lieutenant general Michael Flynn, former head of the Defense Intelligence Agency (DIA), to be his national security adviser.[9] This choice, which would soon prove to be utterly disastrous, sounded alarms from the moment it was made. General Flynn had an extraordinary record as a military leader conducting covert missions in Afghanistan. But he had been fired from DIA because of his rabid anti-Islamic views, an inability to manage the agency, and an absolute intolerance for dissenting views. During the campaign, Flynn had shown an unnerving pattern of spreading outrageous conspiracy theories and "fake news" about Hillary Clinton. "This is not typically the behavior of someone who has the necessary sobriety to advise the president on the most critical matters facing the nation," observed a former military colleague of General Flynn.[10] The national security adviser leads the National Security Council process, which brings all the relevant players together in the Situation Room to arrive at the best consensus advice for the president, or, if no consensus can be reached, a best possible statement of the president's options. General Flynn seemed particularly unsuited to the position for which he had been chosen, particularly given the fact that Trump, thin skinned, impulsive, and not committed to truth or facts, also had no national security experience. Knowledgeable observers predicted Flynn would not last a year.

President-elect Trump's second major selection, the day after Flynn, was more predictable but equally controversial. Senator Jeff Sessions of Alabama had been one of Donald Trump's earliest and strongest supporters when Trump was seeking the Republican nomination. Sessions had become one of Trump's senior advisers; his hard-line views on immigration and law enforcement issues generally closely mirrored Trump's. Sessions's nomination was the latest chapter in a remarkable political story. Thirty years earlier, when President Ronald Reagan nominated Sessions to be a federal district court judge, the Senate had rejected his nomination because of concerns that Sessions harbored racist views.[11] Sessions, then thirty-nine, had gone on to win a seat in the Senate that had rejected him. A former U.S. attorney, Sessions, sixty-nine years old, welcomed the chance to straighten out the Department of Justice, which in his view had moved dangerously to the left while he had been in the Senate.[12] Now his Senate colleagues would face the decision whether to make him the nation's chief law enforcement official.

On November 23, the president-elect selected Nikki Haley, the Republican governor of South Carolina, to be UN ambassador.[13] It was an inspired choice. The campaign had convinced most Americans that Trump was anti-woman and anti-immigrant, and Governor Haley, the Indian American daughter of immigrants, had become a powerful symbol of tolerance when she had ordered the Confederate flag to be removed from the grounds of the State Capitol after the mass killing in South Carolina. She had not been a Trump supporter, so the choice made Trump look like a bigger man. Also on November 23, Trump nominated Betsy DeVos to be secretary of education.[14] DeVos, a billionaire philanthropist, a leading Republican fundraiser, and a passionate champion of school choice, had no education background. She would, like Sessions, be controversial from day one.

The nominations accelerated the next week. On November 29, Congressman Tom Price of Georgia was chosen to be secretary of health and human Services (HHS).[15] Price, who had been a leading orthopedic surgeon before coming to Congress, had risen to become the House Republican leader in the endless effort to repeal Obamacare. He was a natural choice for the position, particularly as Chief of Staff Reince Priebus worked to strengthen the links between the insurgent Republican president and the harshly conservative House Republican caucus. On November 30, Trump nominated the two leaders of his economic team: Steven Mnuchin to be secretary of treasury and Wilbur Ross to be secretary of commerce.[16] Mnuchin had been Trump's chief fundraiser. He had spent seventeen years at Goldman Sachs, rising to become chief information officer, before leaving to start a hedge fund. He then became a movie producer and helped finance some of the most successful motion pictures, including *Avatar, Mad Max: Fury Road,* and *Wonder Woman.* Ross was one of America's most successful businessmen and investors, a billionaire who had built his fortune buying distressed companies and selling them for huge profits. Both choices reassured the business community but were disconcerting to those who had believed Trump's populist rhetoric that included harsh attacks on Wall Street and the business elite.

Filling out his economic team, Trump also nominated Elaine Chao to be secretary of transportation. Chao was the most experienced and familiar Washington hand, having already served as secretary of labor and deputy secretary of transportation.[17] She would assume responsibility for the nation's transportation and for most of Trump's infrastructure initiative. She was also the wife of Senate Majority Leader Mitch McConnell, which would likely be an additional asset in dealing with the Hill. The president filled out his domestic team on December 17 by nominating Mick Mulvaney (R-SC), who rode the Tea Party wave into the House in the 2010 election. A founding member of the House Freedom Caucus that had made Speaker Boehner's life unremitting hell, Mulvaney, who favored deep cuts in domestic spending, was a deficit hawk who had made his desire for the OMB job well known.[18]

As the nominations continued to roll out, Trump was plainly struggling with the premier cabinet post: secretary of state. Press reports indicated that the president-elect was considering two of his leading supporters, Newt Gingrich, the former speaker of the House, and Rudy Giuliani, the former New York mayor.[19] Both choices provoked widespread alarm. Gingrich had mellowed slightly over the years, but he remained the embodiment of the "politics of destruction" that was closely tied to his rise to power. Giuliani, who had been "America's mayor" for his stellar leadership of New York after 9/11, had become an increasingly erratic and vituperative figure, attacking Hillary Clinton by leading chants of "lock her up." The erratic, incendiary president-elect hardly needed his chief diplomat to be in the same mold.

Given those two unattractive options, Trump made headlines by meeting with Mitt Romney, the former Massachusetts governor and Republican presidential nominee.[20] Many mainstream Republicans were excited about the possibility of Romney as secretary of state, although the right wing of the Republican Party went ballistic at the thought. Ultimately none of their views mattered. Trump was happy to meet with Romney, but only to torture him. No one had attacked Trump more harshly or repeatedly than Mitt Romney. He had about as much chance of being secretary of state for President Trump as Hillary Clinton. By December 5, Trump was no closer to making his choice, and the White House made it known that he was expanding the list of possibilities.

Trump bought himself some time by turning to two more generals, who proved to be acclaimed choices.[21] On December 1, retired general James Mattis was chosen to be secretary of defense. General Mattis, who had served with distinction in Iraq and Afghanistan, had a superb reputation as a soldier, a military leader, and a strategic thinker. Given deep concerns about the president-elect and his national security adviser, General Mattis quickly became seen as the wise, strong, and stable figure that this new administration needed. On December 7, Trump nominated General John Kelly to become secretary of the Department of Homeland Security (DHS). General Kelly had been the commander in chief of "Southcom," the ranking officer in this hemisphere. He understood the complexities of the region and the U.S.-Mexico relationship. Kelly seemed to have a deep, sophisticated, and sympathetic understanding of the challenges of border security and immigration. On January 20, the Senate would confirm Mattis and Kelly, both by overwhelming votes.

On December 5, the press reported that Trump was considering five new additional potential choices to be secretary of state.[22] Of the new candidates, General David Petraeus stood out in terms of accomplishment, fame, and knowledge of Washington politics and government. But Petraeus's once-brilliant star had fallen when he accepted a guilty plea arising from his shocking decision to give classified information to his biographer Paula Broadwell, with whom he was having an extramarital affair. Jon Huntsman, the former Utah governor and ambassador to China, was a plausible candidate, but he was more likely to be offered a diplomatic post later. The list included a new name, a complete political unknown: Rex Tillerson, the chief executive officer of ExxonMobil Corporation, scheduled to retire after spending forty-three years at the company. Robert Gates and Condoleezza Rice, former secretaries of defense and state, had warmly recommended Tillerson, based on their experience serving on the Exxon board.[23]

On December 6, Donald Trump met Tillerson for the first time and asked him to be secretary of state.[24] The two men shared a total lack of government experience. But Tillerson had led Exxon, which employed seventy-five thousand people in two hundred countries, making it about the same size as the State Department and much more profitable, which probably impressed Trump more than the difference in the missions of ExxonMobil and the U.S. government. Tillerson, distinguished, silver haired, and a past national leader of the Boy Scouts looked like a secretary of state, as far as the president-elect was concerned. In fact, Tillerson bore some resemblance to John Connolly, the former Democratic governor of Texas who became Richard Nixon's secretary of treasury, beginning a long line of Texas dealmakers who worked at the intersection of government and business, including Robert Strauss, James Baker, and

Lloyd Bentsen. Each of them, however, had extensive government experience, which Tillerson did not.

Exxon's global business had left a trail of lawsuits related to environmental damage, worker safety, and other serious issues.[25] While under Tillerson's leadership, Exxon had acknowledged for the first time the dangers of climate change, but Exxon remained, along with the Koch brothers, the single largest funder of climate change deniers.[26] However, the most serious issue posed by Tillerson's nomination was his relationship to Russia. Rex Tillerson had spent more than a decade building ties to Rosneft, Russia's state-owned oil and gas company.[27] Between 2011 and 2013, he had successfully negotiated ten joint ventures between Exxon and Rosneft, including in the Arctic. "Russia was going to be Exxon's next mega-area, and the list of mega-areas in the world is very short," the *Financial Times* observed.[28] By 2015, Exxon's holdings in and with Russia totaled 63.7 acres, almost five times its second largest holdings, which was fourteen million acres in the United States.

Vladimir Putin had personally given Tillerson an award for his friendship to Russia.[29] The sanctions placed by the Obama administration on Russia after the invasion of Crimea stopped many of those joint ventures, not only halting them but also making it impossible to book the potentially enormous reserves. Many men and women who have been successful in the private sector have brought their talents to high levels of government and made notable contributions—that is how our system works. But there was no precedent for Rex Tillerson, whose entire career had been devoted to the interests of Exxon, a company that had enormous stakes in relationship between the United States and its leading adversary. Tillerson had been to the White House several times since 2014 to argue for easing the sanctions on Russia that were very damaging to Exxon.[30] As secretary of state, he would play a central part in determining the future of U.S. policy toward Russia, including the continuation, or not, of sanctions. The Senate would have to decide whether it was realistic to think Tillerson could view the situation from a perspective other than Exxon's.

The president-elect filled out his national security team by nominating Mike Pompeo (R-KS) to be the director of the Central Intelligence Agency (CIA).[31] A former tank commander who had graduated first in his class at West Point, Pompeo had come to Congress as part of the large group of Republicans elected in 2010, and he rapidly established himself as a formidable figure in the national security area. Pompeo would be quickly confirmed by a comfortable 66–32 vote, attesting to his credentials and the strong reputation he had already earned.[32]

The day after Trump's fateful meeting with Rex Tillerson, the White House announced that Scott Pruitt, Oklahoma's attorney general, would be nominated to head the Environmental Protection Agency.[33] Trump had years ago branded climate change "a hoax," conjured up by China to give it an advantage over U.S. manufacturers.[34] He had pledged to pull the United States out of the international climate change agreement reached in Paris in 2015 and scrap Obama's Clean Power Plan, the centerpiece of the effort to reduce carbon emissions.[35] Trump had also said: "We are going to get rid of it [EPA] in almost every form."[36] Scott Pruitt was a perfect choice to carry out that program. In his decade as Oklahoma attorney general, Pruitt had become the leading advocate in the legal and regulatory battles being waged by climate change deniers. Pruitt was a close ally of the fossil fuel industry, "a hero to conservative activists," and a major player in the lawsuit by twenty-eight states against the Obama clean power regulations.[37] Pruitt had sued EPA at least fourteen times. Pruitt was also a close ally of James Inhofe (R–OK), who was among a small handful of Senate climate change deniers.[38] Shortly after the election, Michael Mann, a prominent climate researcher, said, "A Trump presidency might be game over for the climate."[39] Would the Senate give Scott Pruitt the opportunity to accelerate that process?

Chuck Schumer, now the most powerful Democrat in the country, faced the challenge of Trump's cabinet appointments at an extraordinary juncture. The combination of fear and anger felt by Democrats around the country had only increased during the transition. Trump's inaugural address, which made no effort at outreach to those who had voted for other candidates, intensified the anger. The Women's March called for Washington, D.C., for January 21 grew into the largest protest in history, involving an estimated four million people across the United States and another million around the world.[40] A week later, the Trump administration issued its travel ban barring Muslims from seven nations, which created an unprecedented explosion of anger and demonstrations in the streets and airports all around the country. On January 30, Schumer, who had already announced his opposition to the nominations of Tillerson, Sessions, and DeVos, said that he would oppose five other Trump nominees.[41] Trump's unprecedented presidency had provoked an extraordinary resistance by Senate Democrats to his cabinet nominees.

McConnell had already complained about the pace of the confirmation process, pointing out that the Republicans had cooperated in the rapid confirmation of President Obama's first cabinet, including seven confirmations on the afternoon of January 20 following his inauguration.[42] Much of the delay reflected the disorganization in the Trump White House and the wealth of his nominees, which had caused a serious backlog in the reviews of the nominees' financial holdings.[43] McConnell and Schumer had already scuffled about the Republicans' decision to move ahead with some of the hearings even before the Office of Government Ethics could review the financial statements to air possible conflicts—another unprecedented development.[44]

But Schumer and his Democrats faced a much more fundamental problem. Several of Trump's nominees were unqualified or radical choices; others presented conflicts of interests much more serious than those that had doomed earlier nominees. However, the "nuclear option" triggered by Harry Reid in 2013 prevented the Democrats from filibustering the president's executive nominees.[45] If the fifty-two Senate Republicans stayed together, the Democrats would not be able to block any of the nominees. McConnell would point out that he had warned the Democrats in 2013 of precisely that possibility.[46] Their chance to prevent one or more of the Trump nominees from being confirmed depended on the willingness of several Republicans joining the opposition, not an easy step for Republican senators being asked to let the new president have his team.

The Senate quickly and by overwhelming votes confirmed generals Mattis and Kelly, Chao, and Governor Haley, who impressed senators with her intellect and humor despite her lack of international experience. But other nominations destined to be contentious became protracted, bitter contests. Jeff Sessions's confirmation became certain when Susan Collins, the most moderate and independent Republican, agreed to "introduce" and endorse Senator Sessions to the Judiciary Committee.[47] In testimony, Sessions received tough scrutiny from his Senate Democratic colleagues, who praised him for personal congeniality while blasting him for his lifelong regressive record on civil rights. Sessions's confirmation hearings took place against the backdrop of President Trump's continuing unfounded claims that voter fraud had accounted for his losing the popular vote.[48] The Obama Justice Department had vigorously opposed several state laws that would have restricted access to voting by requiring voters to have driver's licenses. Senator Sessions made no commitment to continue those appeals. Cory Booker (D-NJ) chose to oppose Sessions based on his decades-long opposition to civil rights.[49] Booker and other committee Democrats did not accept Sessions's characterization of himself as a civil rights supporter. Jonathan Turley, a respected George Washington law professor, commented: "The Justice Department is likely to be one of the most transformed departments in the cabinet in the Trump administration, and with an Attorney General Sessions, you'd probably see a strong law and order figure at the top."[50] That was Trump's intention and the Senate Democrats' fear. After the contentious hearings and Senate debate, charged by allegations of racial bias, the Senate confirmed Sessions along strict party lines by a vote of 52–47.[51]

Of the significant number of controversial cabinet nominees, Betsy DeVos provoked the most concerted opposition.[52] DeVos was a billionaire investor, education philanthropist, and a leading contributor to Republican candidates and causes. DeVos had spent her career championing pushing for controversial school choice programs. She was known as an opponent of public schools, and in her hearing she showed an absence of knowledge of any education issues beyond school choice. The nation's teachers, led by Randi Weingarten, the longtime president of the American Federation of Teachers (AFT), mobilized a national campaign against DeVos, including demonstrations around the country.[53] Phone calls from those opposing DeVos virtually overwhelmed the Capitol switchboard and Senate voice mail systems. The *Los Angeles Times* opposed DeVos's nomination in a scathing editorial: "Betsy DeVos' love of private school vouchers doesn't disqualify her for the role of U.S. education secretary, even though vouchers are a bad idea. Nor did her lack of experience in public schools. What did render her unacceptable was her abysmal performance in her confirmation hearing in which she displayed an astonishing ignorance about basic education issues, an extraordinary lack of thoughtfulness about ongoing debates in the field, and an unwillingness to respond to important questions."[54]

In contrast to DeVos, Congressman Tom Price, nominated to be Health and Human Services (HHS) secretary, had extensive experience in the health care issues that he would face if confirmed. He had become the Republican leader of the seven-year effort to repeal the Affordable Care Act.[55] During the campaign, Trump's health care views had been hard to track. While he frequently blasted "Obamacare," he promised to replace it with a cheaper and better plan, in which no one would lose their health care.[56] Price, however, had a long-established record of seeking to reduce costs by reducing the number of Americans that had access to health care. By nominating Price to be his HHS secretary, Trump had chosen to enlist in the obsessive Republican campaign to repeal the Affordable Care Act, without regard to the potential consequences for millions of Americans, many of whom voted for him.[57]

In addition to his hard-line views, Price had compiled a stunning record of investments in pharmaceutical and medical device companies within the jurisdiction of his committee. Price had invested specifically in companies that benefited from laws and regulations that he had introduced or endorsed.[58] In May 2016, he had invested in Zimmer Biomet just before introducing a law delaying Medicare valve purchasing rules that would have reduced payments to Zimmer.[59] Similarly, Price invested in six major pharmaceutical companies while cosponsoring a bill to block a proposed change in Medicare reimbursement rates that would have reduced returns to those companies. Leading companies in the life sciences sector comprised a part of most diversified stock portfolios, but none of these investments occurred through mutual funds. Price's broker decided, at his general direction, to pick these stocks based on information she had about their financial prospects.[60]

Even more inexplicable and questionable, Price invested between $50,000 to $100,000 in Innate Immunotherapeutics, an Australian company that had no approved drugs and no notable presence in biomedical markets but whose stock price had risen because of purchases by prominent Republicans, including Representative Chris Collins (R-NY), the company's largest shareholder and a board member.[61] "It shows a lack of judgment to be buying and selling health care company stocks if you are serving on a congressional committee that is making decisions that are going to impact the value of health care company stocks," Richard Painter, chief ethics lawyer for President George W. Bush, said. "In particular, if someone has access to confidential information, the SEC could investigate them."[62] Democrats, led by Ron Wyden and Patty Murray, expressed strong opposition to Price's nomination, in significant part because of his conflicts of interest.[63]

Against the backdrop of almost daily demonstrations across the country, the Senate Democrats mounted concerted opposition to Trump's cabinet nominations. Following the pattern of Donald Trump's campaign and election, the confirmation hearings and the Senate floor debates featured one unprecedented moment after another. When Elizabeth Warren (D-Mass.) read a 1986 letter from Coretta Scott King to Senator Ted Kennedy urging opposition to Jeff Sessions's nomination to be federal judge, Majority Leader McConnell silenced Warren by invoking the rarely used Senate Rule XIX, which prohibits senators from criticizing their colleagues on the Senate floor.[64] The *New York Times* described the "bitter and racially-charged nomination battle . . . [as] ferocious even by the standards of moldering decorum that have defined the body's recent years."[65] When Lamar Alexander, presiding over the DeVos nomination, refused to extend the hearing, committee Democrats decided to boycott the committee vote.[66] EPA employees, horrified at the prospect of the agency being led by one of its fiercest adversaries, called their senators, urging them to reject Pruitt's nomination.[67]

Ultimately, one nomination after another—Tillerson, Sessions, Mnuchin, Price, DeVos, Pruitt, Mulvaney—was opposed by more than forty senators, also unprecedented. But the Senate approved each of the nominations. DeVos faced the closest call; the Senate deadlocked 50–50, and Vice President Pence had to break the tie to confirm her: another first.[68]

No one needed any additional evidence as to how deep the divisions in the country were, or how bitter the election had been. But the polarization in the Senate was still striking. The Senate Republicans had remained virtually unified in support of several seriously flawed nominees. Relatively few senators shared Scott Pruitt's extreme views on climate change or his desire to dismantle EPA. Yet every Republican except one (Susan Collins) voted to allow him to swing his wrecking ball. No Republican voted against Price, despite an investment history that would have surely provoked Senate opposition in the past. The Republicans could justify their action by saying that the president was entitled to have his team. Time would tell whether the team members were capable, and whether the Senate would oversee the way they did their jobs.

Six months into the Trump administration, virtually all the cabinet members were working without a team of political appointees.[69] While the White House blamed the Senate for moving slowly on the president's nominees, in fact, Trump, by historical standards, had put forth very few appointees. As of June 30, 384 of the 564 high-level positions requiring Senate confirmation had no formal nominee.[70] Some 130 had been nominated but not confirmed. Deputy secretaries, assistant secretaries, and dozens of ambassadors had yet to be nominated. "The biggest obstacle [to filling the positions] is that the White House hasn't submitted nominations," said Darrell West, director of governance studies at the Brookings Institution.[71] The president had previously said, "In many cases, we don't want to fill those jobs."[72] But without political appointees in place, the Trump administration had to rely on career civil servants, whom Trump had repeatedly accused of seeking to undermine his agenda. "It really empowers the career bureaucracy," West observed. "If you don't have the senior political leadership within a particular agency, it's going to be the long-term staffers who make decisions. That's challenging for the administration because most people don't support the Trump agenda."[73]

· 9 ·

The Gorsuch Nomination

When No Compromise Is Possible

$\mathscr{A}$s Donald Trump entered the White House, the diminished and divided Senate, which had lost public confidence and self-confidence through its long decline, would face an agenda of historic magnitude. The Senate would confront the challenge of investigating Russia's involvement in the 2016 presidential election and assessing whether there had been any collusion by the Trump campaign and Russia. It would almost inevitably be called to decide whether the House Republican effort to repeal and replace the Affordable Care Act would prevail, be rejected, or be substantially modified. Plus the Senate would be asked to "advise and consent" on President Trump's first Supreme Court nomination. It would be hard to remember when the Senate confronted three such momentous issues at the same time. Moreover, in seeking solutions that commanded respect from a significant majority of the country, the senators would be working at a moment of extraordinarily deep and bitter political division in the country.

Of the three challenges, the Supreme Court nomination was the most familiar. Many of the current members had been in the Senate long enough to consider and vote on President George W. Bush's nominations of Chief Justice John Roberts and Associate Justice Samuel Alito and Barack Obama's nominations of associate justices Sonia Sotomayor and Elena Kagan. Nine senators had served more than twenty-four years, long enough to consider and vote on Bill Clinton's nominations of Ruth Bader Ginsburg and Stephen Breyer. The deans of the Senate, Patrick Leahy and Orrin Hatch, had been there for the confirmations of twelve and eleven justices respectively, including, of course, the entire current Court.

But if the process were familiar to the Senate and the public, this nomination would come up in an atmosphere more fraught than any other in American history. McConnell had prevailed in his effort to prevent President Obama from filling the vacancy left by the death of Antonin Scalia. His unprecedented action had damaged the Senate and enraged the Democrats. Any Supreme Court nominee put forth by President Trump would carry the additional burden left by the majority leader's gambit.

MOVING THE COURT TO THE RIGHT

Nothing mattered more to the moving forces in the Republican Party than the makeup of the Supreme Court—perhaps not even tax cuts. In 1968, a full half-century ago, the Republicans, angered by the decisions of the liberal Supreme Court led by Earl Warren, began a concerted effort to turn the Court in a conservative direction.[1] They got their first opportunity in 1968 when President Lyndon Johnson tried to elevate Justice Abe Fortas, his close friend and counselor, to replace Earl Warren as chief justice.[2] He also nominated a Texas friend, Judge Homer Thornberry, to take Fortas's seat as associate justice. Johnson was in his last year as president, and crippled by the Vietnam War, he had announced that he would not seek reelection. Warren, who had been a progressive governor of California, despised Richard Nixon, the Republican presidential nominee, who had been a California senator before becoming Dwight D. Eisenhower's vice president.[3] Nixon had leveled harsh attacks against the Warren Court, and Warren wanted to make sure that Nixon would not get the chance to name his successor.[4]

Johnson's bold plan failed badly.[5] The Republicans, led by Robert Griffin of Michigan, enlisted enough conservative southern Democratic allies to kill the nomination by filibustering it. Even while Nixon was campaigning, he took time to coordinate efforts with the Republican senators. He desperately wanted to appoint Warren's successor, and his narrow victory gave him the chance. In the first month of his presidency, Richard Nixon would nominate, and the Senate would confirm, Judge Warren Burger to be chief justice of the Supreme Court. Nixon would also get the priceless opportunity to send several other nominees to the Senate. After the Senate rejected his next two nominations—judges Clement Haynesworth and G. Harrold Carswell—it confirmed Judge Harry Blackmun, an old friend of Chief Justice Burger, and then corporate lawyer Lewis Powell and Assistant Attorney General William Rehnquist. A lasting pattern was set. The Supreme Court would become markedly more conservative than the Warren Court had been. Starting with Nixon, Republican presidents named ten consecutive Supreme Court justices. After Bill Clinton had two nominees confirmed, George W. Bush placed two of his nominees on the Court. At that point, in the forty-year period from 1969 to 2009, Republican presidents had chosen twelve out of the last fourteen Supreme Court justices.

But somehow, all those nominations were never enough to satisfy the "constitutionalists," as the Republican conservative legal community liked to call itself.[6] At different times, they would be enraged by what they saw as the betrayals of Harry Blackmun, John Paul Stevens, Sandra Day O'Connor, David Souter, and Anthony Kennedy. In 2012, the constitutionalists would even turn their wrath on Chief Justice John Roberts, whose nomination had thrilled them, because he had the temerity to conclude that the Affordable Care Act was constitutional.[7] Despite all the justices nominated by Republican presidents, the Republican legal right wing could not get everything they wanted because their reading of the Constitution was so extreme.

The right-wing legal community, which clustered in the Federalist Society and the Heritage Foundation, had no affinity for, or confidence in, Donald Trump.[8] He had been a Democrat much too recently, and they doubted that he shared their view of the Constitution. They were prominent among those Republicans most opposed to Trump as he made his astonishing run through the primaries. While Trump's campaign operation was somewhat chaotic, Senator Jeff Sessions, Trump's foremost advocate on Capitol Hill, had strong connections to the legal right wing. Sessions believed that it was important to win over this influential part of the Republican Party and that a commitment to appointing conservative Supreme Court justices was the only way to accomplish that. Given the skepticism about Trump, the commitment had to go beyond a general assertion. On May 18, the Trump campaign made an unprecedented move, announcing a list of eleven judges whom Mr. Trump would consider for the Supreme Court if he became president.[9] The list included six federal appellate judges and five state supreme court justices, all of whom were white, eight of whom were men, and all well qualified and proven to be extremely conservative judges. The list received a wholehearted endorsement from the Federalist Society and the Heritage Foundation, which was not surprising since they had supplied the list of judges.[10]

Nan Aron, president of the liberal Alliance for Justice, had been in the forefront of every Supreme Court battle since Robert Bork. "The list includes some of the most extreme conservatives on the federal bench today. Their opinions demonstrate open hostility to Americans' rights and liberties, including reproductive justice and environmental, consumer and worker protections," Aron stated. "They have ruled consistently in favor of the powerful over everyone else. They would move the needle even further to the right on the Supreme Court."[11] Subsequently, Trump announced a second list of ten additional possible nominees, giving him twenty-one possible choices.

Trump's decision to put forth a list of right-wing judges proved to be a brilliant political move. Nothing did more to unify Republicans behind Trump in November than the recognition that the future direction of the Court was at stake, and a strong sense that Trump would nominate someone who shared their constitutional principles.

DELIGHTING THE "CONSTITUTIONALISTS"

He did not disappoint them. On January 31, President Trump, on primetime television, introduced his nominee, Neil T. Gorsuch, judge on the Tenth Circuit Court of Appeals.[12] Judge Gorsuch had been in the second group of possible nominees but quickly rocketed to the top tier of possibilities. Despite Trump's antiestablishment campaign, he reached for a judge for superb establishment credentials. Only forty-nine years old, Gorsuch had already served ten years on the federal bench. Educated at Columbia and Harvard Law School (where he was a classmate of Barack Obama) and Oxford, Gorsuch had clerked for Supreme Court justice Anthony Kennedy after being hired by Justice Byron White, who chose to retire. He was respected for the clarity of his thinking, his lively writing, and his judicial demeanor.[13] He was also, by any measure, a judge with a very conservative philosophy—an originalist in the mold of Justice Scalia. One study concluded that he was more conservative than 87 percent of the federal judges.[14] Another called him more conservative than either Justice Alito or the late Justice Scalia, each of whom epitomized the conservative judicial philosophy.

Judge Gorsuch's nomination came at an extraordinary moment. Across the nation, widespread protests against President Trump's travel ban were continuing. The day before, Trump had fired acting attorney general Sally Yates when she refused to defend the travel ban, doubting its constitutionality.[15] Less than two weeks after his Inaugural, Donald Trump had become the first president since Abraham Lincoln to face active resistance.

Judge Gorsuch's extremely conservative record would have been anathema to many Democrats under the best of circumstances, and these were close to the worst of circumstances. Neil Gorsuch would have to overcome the fact that roughly half the nation would oppose any Supreme Court nomination that President Trump made. Both Senate Democrats and grassroots Democrats were still seething about Senator McConnell's treatment of President Obama and his nominee, Judge Merrick Garland. "This is the first time a Senate majority leader has stolen a seat," Senator Jeff Merkley (D-OR) said. "We will use everything in our power to stop this nomination."[16] Schumer said that "there would be no payback," but went on to note that Judge Gorsuch would bear a special burden in proving his views were in the judicial mainstream, as justices Sotomayor and Kagan had done. Nan Aron saw "no sign that [Judge Gorsuch] would offer an independent check on the dangerous impulses of this administration," a view that was widely shared in the progressive community.[17]

Judge Gorsuch began the important ritual of making courtesy calls on senators, accompanied by Kelly Ayotte, the popular and respected senator from New Hampshire who had been narrowly defeated by Governor Maggie Hassan. Press reports indicated that Gorsuch—intelligent, open, and well prepared to discuss issues of importance to each senator—came across impressively.

On February 5, President Trump vented his anger at federal judge James Robart, who had issued a nationwide injunction against his travel ban.[18] Calling Robart a "so-called judge," Trump said his opinion was "ridiculous and would be overturned." Three days later, in a speech to law enforcement officials, the president called on the appellate panel to review Judge Robart's decision to reinstate the travel ban on the grounds of national security. "A bad high school student would understand this," Trump said.

The next day, Richard Blumenthal (D-CT) announced that in his courtesy call, Judge Gorsuch had described the president's remarks as "demoralizing and disheartening."[19] Blumenthal called on Gorsuch to acknowledge publicly what he had said to Blumenthal privately. Judge Gorsuch declined to do so, but did not deny that he made that comment to the senator. President Trump fired back at Blumenthal, noting that he had made false statements about serving in Vietnam. On balance, Judge Gorsuch earned some admirers for his defense of an independent judiciary.

THE JUDICIARY COMMITTEE HEARINGS

Hearings on Judge Gorsuch's confirmation began on March 20. They would take place against the backdrop of continuing trouble for the Trump administration where justice issues were concerned. On March 1, Attorney General Jeff Sessions, who had been very narrowly confirmed by the Senate, admitted that he had testified inaccurately to the Judiciary Committee when he said that he had not met with any Russian officials. He recused himself from any investigation of Russia's interference in the presidential campaign.

Against the turbulent background roiled by a series of unpredictable events, one certainty remained. The Senate would take up the nomination of Judge Neil Gorsuch, and McConnell would do anything needed to get him confirmed.

Press reports had shed light on Gorsuch's personal background, and liberal opponents had compiled a thick dossier of his decisions in favor of corporations and against workers, consumers, and the disabled.[20] It fascinated veteran Washingtonians that Gorsuch's mother, Anne Gorsuch Burford, had been Ronald Reagan's administrator of the EPA and was forced to step down in the face of congressional anger about her antienvironment views. Even as a young man at Columbia and Harvard Law School, Gorsuch had shown a powerful intellect and a passion for taking on the prevailing liberal views on campus in vigorous essays in student publications, but without engendering personal acrimony. "There were conservatives who were provocateurs," said one of his Harvard Law classmates. "He wasn't anything like that."[21] Gorsuch had maintained that approach in his career on the bench. While unmistakably conservative, he had demonstrated enough judicious open-mindedness to attract some important liberal endorsements, including Neal K. Katyal, who had been the acting solicitor general in the Obama administration.[22] Judge Gorsuch lived in Boulder, Colorado, perhaps the most progressive city in the country. He taught at the University of Colorado Law School; one of his liberal students described him as "an eager mentor with a brilliant mind, always solicitous of student opinions . . . He's dedicated to the pursuit of truth in the justice system. I do take some comfort that he can be a Trump choice." The Trump administration was floundering in its early weeks, but in nominating Judge Gorsuch, the president had picked a strong, if extremely conservative, nominee.

Around the country, many angry progressives, still seething about the treatment of Judge Garland, were spoiling for a fight.[23] But the conservative groups that supported the nomination vastly outspent Gorsuch's opponents, by nearly twenty to one, targeting seven senators in states that Trump had won.[24] A proposal by Democratic campaign operatives for a $30 million effort directed at five Senate Republicans running in states where Obama had won twice failed to attract potential funders; those potentially persuadable Republican senators encountered no real pressure.[25] In North Dakota and Montana, where Democrats Heidi Heitkamp and Jon Tester faced tough reelection contests in strongly red states, 99.5 percent of the media money spent in the confirmation fight went to supporting Gorsuch.[26] "The resistance"—as the progressives had begun to call themselves—was intensely active, but fighting on several fronts, opposing the travel ban and the repeal of the Affordable Care Act. The Republicans, as always, had abundant funding and focused like a laser on the Supreme Court.

The Judiciary Committee hearings on Supreme Court nominees, occurring on the average every three or four years, had become a familiar ritual in Washington. In 2002, Judge Gorsuch, then still in private practice, wrote an article decrying the decline of the modern confirmation process, which he described as "an ideological food fight."[27] Fifteen years later, the process had deteriorated further into bitter partisanship. "The Senate confirmation process for Supreme Court justices has always been cabined by norms of behavior and unwritten rules," said Nathaniel Persily, a Stanford Law professor. "With the failure to even have a hearing on Garland, the norms have all gone out the window." He predicted that "the Democrats now feel emboldened to try anything."[28]

Indeed, the hearings never could escape the cloud created by McConnell's treatment of the Garland nomination. Virtually every judiciary committee Democrat touched on the "unprecedented treatment" of the Obama nominee, and outside the hearing room, even some Republicans acknowledged that the Democrats had good reason to be upset.[29] However, Judge Gorsuch was, as expected, well prepared, amicable, intelligent, and often folksy. In a sixteen-minute speech, he portrayed himself as a fair-minded judge, favoring no party above the law.[30] "I've ruled for disabled students, for prisoners, for the accused, for workers alleging civil rights violations, and for undocumented immigrants," Gorsuch stated. "Sometimes, too, I've ruled against such persons." He went on to observe that a judge who is pleased with every decision he reaches "is probably a pretty bad judge, stretching for policy results he prefers, rather than those the law compels." In the tradition of every nominee since Bork's disastrous confirmation hearings, Judge Gorsuch avoided commenting on any controversial legal issue or offering an opinion on decisions that the Supreme Court had previously rendered.

The Democratic committee staff and the liberal opponents to the nomination had surfaced some serious concerns about Judge Gorsuch's record. For example, he had expressed his opposition to the "Chevron doctrine," by which the Supreme Court had held that federal courts needed to defer to agency interpretations of regulations where they were implementing ambiguous legislative language.[31] In contrast, Judge Gorsuch had spoken approvingly of the 1935 case of *Schechter Poultry*, the cornerstone of the conservative Supreme Court's effort to block Franklin D. Roosevelt's New Deal.[32] Human rights and civil liberties activists expressed deep concern about Gorsuch's experience in the Bush Justice Department in 2005 and 2006 where he helped defend and advance the executive branch's positions on detainee treatment and surveillance.[33]

Despite the high stakes, by the third day, the hearings had taken on a predictable and perfunctory feel. The American Bar Association called Judge Gorsuch "well qualified," the group's highest rating.[34] Two of his former Tenth Circuit colleagues praised his intellect and temperament.[35] Most of the attention had shifted to the upcoming political fight. Schumer went to the Senate floor and announced that he would lead the Democrats in blocking an up-or-down vote on Judge Gorsuch. "After careful consideration, I have concluded that I cannot support Judge Neil Gorsuch's nomination to the Supreme Court,"

Schumer said, emphasizing concerns about Gorsuch's tilt toward companies and against workers. "His career and judicial record suggest not a neutral legal mind, but someone with a deep-seated conservative ideology. . . . My vote will be no, and I will urge my colleagues to do the same."[36]

Even if the fifty-two Republican senators all supported the nomination, McConnell would still have to attract eight Democrats to have the sixty votes needed to invoke cloture and defeat the filibuster. Several Democrats would likely support the nomination, but not eight. McConnell would face the choice of whether to trigger the nuclear option so that Gorsuch could be confirmed by a simple majority vote. McConnell had said that Gorsuch would be confirmed "no matter what."[37] No one doubted that, having brought the Senate to this point, he would finish what he had started.

CONFIRMATION AND FALLOUT

While quiet discussions about possible compromises had gone on for days, there was no way to bridge the chasm between the parties and the leaders. McConnell was committed to putting Gorsuch on the Court, and Schumer was committed to fighting the nomination with a filibuster. "The problem we have is finding a trustworthy, verifiable approach to an agreement," said Democratic whip Dick Durbin.[38] "The Senate has changed," said John McCain, who had helped broker previous deals to defuse crises. "You can't do what we used to do, what I did in the past. There is too much ill will."[39]

Weeks before, McConnell had promised that the Senate would confirm Judge Gorsuch before it recessed on Friday, April 7. On Thursday, April 6, with Democratic leader Schumer standing close by, McConnell made the series of statements needed to change the Senate rules to lower the threshold for advancing Supreme Court nominees from sixty votes to a simple majority. "When history weighs what happened, the responsibility for changing the rules will fall on the Republicans' and Leader McConnell's shoulders," said Schumer. "They have had other choices, and they have chosen this one."[40]

McConnell, unsurprisingly, saw the history quite differently. "This is the latest escalation in the left's never-ending judicial war, the most audacious yet," he responded to Schumer, after describing the Democratic opposition to the Bork and Thomas nominations. "And it cannot and it will not stand. There cannot be two sets of standards: one for the nominees of Democratic presidents and another for the nominees of Republican presidents."[41] He could be seen exchanging exuberant high-fives with colleagues and aides after the vote to change the Senate rules.[42]

The next morning the Senate confirmed Neil Gorsuch to the Supreme Court by a vote of 54–45. He would be sworn into the Court in time to participate in several of the most closely watched cases of the session. Only forty-nine years old, Justice Gorsuch would likely be deciding cases for the next thirty or forty years.

Many senators seemed stricken by what had just happened to the institution.[43] Susan Collins, the only Republican who had supported giving a hearing to Judge Garland, had worked hard to broker an agreement to head off the filibuster and the nuclear option but recognized that no deal had been possible. "There is such a profound lack of trust between the two parties," said Collins. "It's hard to know whether the polarization in the Senate reflects the country or whether the polarization and divisiveness in the Senate affects the country."[44] Ben Cardin asked, "Where do we go from here? Will there be further erosions?" Asked about the possibility that this could be a point for a new start, Cardin morosely responded, "We're pretty early in this Congress. So, there's plenty more time for more harm to be done."[45]

If the debate seemed somewhat mechanistic and predictable, it was because the outcome was preordained. If there ever was a situation in which a supermajority requirement seemed appropriate, it should be in the case of a lifetime appointment to the Supreme Court. But as soon as the minority moved to use the filibuster, the majority moved to abolish it. It is at least possible that the Democrats would have done the same if circumstances had been reversed. Republicans enjoyed pointing out that Joe Biden had suggested as much in a 1992 speech when he was Judiciary Committee chairman, contemplating the possibility that President George H. W. Bush might get to nominate a Supreme Court justice in the last year before an election.[46]

But while no one questioned the anger and anguish of the Democrats over the confirmation of Neal Gorsuch after the treatment of Merrick Garland, was it actually a body blow that would cause more lasting harm to the already diminished Senate? For most observers, the answer depended on whether the Senate was destined to become a purely majoritarian institution—the fear that Arenberg and Dove had expressed when Harry Reid detonated the nuclear option in 2013. McConnell and Schumer expressed confidence that the legislative filibuster would never be abolished.[47] Bob Corker (R-TN), often given to plain speaking, thought they were being naïve or disingenuous. Corker anticipated intense pressure to change the rules coming from conservative activists and the Trump administration when they could not secure sixty votes for a piece of high-priority legislation. He questioned whether either party would be strong enough to resist the demands of their base once they were in the majority. "Two years ago, there would not have been a single Republican in our caucus who would have even considered voting for the nuclear option,"

Corker contended. "As a matter of fact, we had discussions about changing it back. Then the elections occurred and we decided not to do that. . . . To say that we will never get to a point where we will not change a legislative piece . . . give me a break. Someone is not living in reality."[48]

Yet, legislation, inevitably the product of compromise and tradeoffs, offering numerous opportunities for senators to participate and buy in, does differ fundamentally from a judicial nomination, which poses a binary choice—yes or no. Certainly, as the Senate awaited the possibility that the House would pass legislation repealing the Affordable Care Act, many members were undoubtedly very grateful for the legislative process that the supermajority requirement would ensure. Collins circulated a letter committing senators to oppose any changes in the legislative filibuster; it quickly gathered more than sixty signatures.[49] When President Trump suggested that the Senate should change its rules to allow fifty-one senators to pass legislation, McConnell publicly rejected the suggestion within minutes.[50]

McConnell and Schumer had a large incentive to improve on the truly terrible start that they have made together. "If they were looking for ten different ways to get off to a bad start, this would be number 11," said Lamar Alexander, a close friend of both men.[51] "The nature of the Senate has become increasingly anchored around the two leaders," observed Paul Kane, the *Washington Post*'s veteran Senate reporter. "A generation of powerful committee chairmen from each party—whose stature equaled or even eclipsed the party leaders—have either died or retired, leaving behind a power vacuum that the floor leaders have consumed."[52] Kane offered the optimistic take that the Gorsuch showdown might well have been "the last act of the Reid-McConnell wars rather than the first showdown between McConnell and the new Democratic leader [Schumer]. It's possible that now that each side has changed rules on a party-line vote, the 'nuclear option,' a clean slate might finally appear and a new framework could be built."[53]

"Any relationship can be repaired," said Leahy, the longest-serving senator.[54] "This intensifies the commitment of the Senate to maintain the legislative margins that have always been a part of the Senate," said Roy Blunt, the Missouri Republican, who served in leadership roles in both houses of Congress. "I would hope we can start compartmentalizing and start to get things done."[55] Moreover, just as in 2013 and 2015, McConnell and Schumer could count on the support of most senators who desperately want to be part of a functioning Senate.

Even while fighting over Gorsuch, McConnell and Schumer began working on a deal to fund the government for the rest of the year.[56] There were tradeoffs to be made and compromises to be reached, and the budget deal reached a successful conclusion in late April.[57] Ultimately, the Senate's performance in the first year of the Trump presidency would be remembered and judged less by the Gorsuch fight than by how it dealt with the investigation into Russian interference in the 2016 presidential election and the biggest legislative issue facing the country: the future of the Affordable Care Act and the American health insurance system.

At a time of extraordinary anger and division in Washington, one person appeared to be supremely happy. Justice Neal Gorsuch stepped into the work of the Court with astonishing speed.[58] As Adam Liptak wrote in the *New York Times*, "His early opinions were remarkably self-assured. He tangled with his new colleagues, lectured them on the role of the institution he had just joined, and made broad jurisprudential pronouncements in minor cases."[59] Veteran observers of the Court recalled that justices Stephen Breyer and Clarence Thomas had said they needed several years to feel comfortable with their awesome responsibilities. "So extraordinary an intellect as Brandeis said it took him four to five years to feel that he understood the jurisprudential problems of the court," Justice Felix Frankfurter wrote of Justice Louis D. Brandeis. However, we live in what Thomas Friedman has called "the age of accelerations," and several weeks of involvement, rather than several years, apparently sufficed to acclimate Justice Gorsuch.[60] The constitutionalists and Senator McConnell were delighted by Gorsuch's swift adjustment, his lively pen, and—what mattered most—his extremely conservative opinions.

· *10* ·

Investigating the Russian Connection

$\mathcal{A}$s Election Day 2016 approached, Richard Burr, the two-term Republican senator from North Carolina, expected to coast to an easy reelection, suddenly faced a surprisingly stiff challenge from Deborah Ross, a liberal former state representative best known for her work as executive director of the state chapter of the American Civil Liberties Union in the 1990s.[1] A series of polls showed Burr only one or two points ahead of Ross.[2] North Carolina had become perhaps the hottest battleground state in the country.[3] In a state that Barack Obama had carried in 2008 but lost in 2012, Trump and Clinton were locked in a very close race, while the gubernatorial contest between Republican governor Pat McCrory and his Democratic challenger Roy Cooper, the state attorney general, had attracted national attention because of the highly charged debate over the state's "bathroom bill."[4] Burr received unfavorable press coverage when he jokingly expressed surprise that an anti-Hillary ad by the National Rifle Association "didn't have [Hillary] in the bullseye."[5]

Burr had previously announced that this would be his last term.[6] Now, in these turbulent waters, he suddenly confronted the serious possibility that he would be done six years earlier than expected. Even as Republicans privately criticized Burr for his overconfident and lethargic campaign, outside money poured into North Carolina to try to rescue the embattled incumbent.[7]

Neighboring Virginia was also a major presidential battleground. Obama had won Virginia twice, and Hillary Clinton was clearly favored there, having chosen Tim Kaine, the popular senator and former governor, as her running mate. Mark Warner, the senior senator from Virginia, was not on the ballot; he had barely survived an unexpectedly close race in 2014. Warner could be forgiven for wondering what, exactly, had happened to the seemingly unlimited potential of his career. Once touted as a likely presidential prospect, Warner had been generally ineffective and frustrated in the gridlocked Senate. Warner, a moderate, probusiness consensus builder given to working in a bipartisan basis, had channeled his energy and passion to the failed efforts to produce a "grand bargain" on spending and taxes.[8] Now he suffered the indignity of watching his former lieutenant governor be tapped to be Clinton's vice president. If the Democrats held the Senate, Warner could look forward to becoming the chairman of the Rules Committee, probably the least inspiring assignment that the Senate could offer. Mark Warner, who had given serious thought to quitting the Senate after one term, was probably considering what else he might want to do in life.

When the Senate convened in January 2017, just two months later, Richard Burr and Mark Warner found themselves in situations that had been stunningly transformed. Buoyed by the "dark money" that flooded the campaign, Burr had won a relatively comfortable victory over Ross, and returned to the Senate to chair the Intelligence Committee.[9] Warner had benefited from an improbable sequence of events, as Patrick Leahy, the longest serving senator, decided to give up his position as ranking Democrat on the Judiciary Committee to become ranking on Appropriations.[10] Dianne Feinstein chose to leave her position as ranking on the Intelligence Committee to take the ranking position on Judiciary. Suddenly, Mark Warner became the ranking member on the Intelligence Committee. Together, Burr and Warner would face the responsibility of leading the most important Senate investigation of a president since Watergate. Ultimately, history is likely to remember and judge the current Senate for how it faced the historic challenge of investigating Russia's interference with the presidential election of 2016.

DONALD TRUMP'S INEXPLICABLE
AFFECTION FOR RUSSIA AND PUTIN

During the campaign, Donald Trump's long-standing admiration for Russia and its strongman president Vladimir Putin had become unmistakably clear. As far back as June 2013, Trump expressed excitement about bringing the Miss Universe Pageant to Moscow, tweeting: "a big deal that will bring our countries together."[11] He wondered whether Putin would be going to the pageant, and "if so, will he become my new best friend?"[12] In an interview with David Letterman, Trump boasted that he has conducted "a lot of business with the Russians" and that they are "smart and tough."[13] Returning from the pageant,

Trump tweeted: "I just got back from Russia—learned lots & lots. Moscow is a very interesting and amazing place! U.S. MUST BE VERY SMART AND VERY STRATEGIC."[14]

Those statements could have reflected the good feelings surrounding the beauty pageant. But after Trump began campaigning, his rapid-fire praise of Russia and Putin accelerated. In October 2015, Trump expressed doubt about the intelligence community's assessment that Russian separatists were behind the downing of Malaysia Airlines Flight 17.[15] The next month, in a Republican presidential debate, Trump enthused that he and Putin were on *60 Minutes* together "and we had fantastic ratings."[16] In his end-of-the-year press conference, Putin praised Trump. Trump was evidently delighted; in a series of political events, Trump proudly noted that "Putin called me a genius."[17]

In his first major foreign policy speech, Trump made the aspirational and unobjectionable statements: "We are not bound to be adversaries. We should seek common ground based on shared interests. Russia, for instance, has also seen the horror of Islamic terrorism. I believe an easing of tensions and improved relations with Russia—from a position of strength—is possible. Common sense says this cycle of hostility must end."[18] But at a time when U.S.-Russia relations had spiraled downward because of the invasion of Crimea, the military pressure on Ukraine, and the murder of several leading Russian dissidents, including prominent opponents of Putin, Trump and his advisers repeatedly described Putin as a much stronger leader than President Obama and expressed no concerns about Russia's actions.[19] In contrast, Trump leveled his harshest foreign policy blasts at the NATO alliance, the central pillar of U.S. collective security policy for sixty years, without showing any recognition of Putin's long-standing interest in undermining NATO. "The idea of dismembering NATO would be the best possible thing for Putin," Lindsey Graham observed.[20]

Trump's seeming infatuation with Putin raised serious questions during the campaign. His lack of experience in the foreign policy realm presented only one possible explanation. His obvious admiration for Putin came at a time when Trump was showing increasing hostility toward the press and his political opponents, causing many observers to suggest that he had authoritarian tendencies. Trump also had significant business dealings in and with Russia, making it possible that criticizing Putin could cause him financial pain if Russian banks were to call in loans that they had made to the Trump family business.[21] It also troubled many observers that leading Trump advisers—retired Lt. General Michael Flynn, campaign chairman Paul Manafort, and senior adviser Carter Page—all had uncommonly strong ties to the Russian government and business communities.[22]

MOUNTING EVIDENCE OF RUSSIAN INTERFERENCE
IN THE PRESIDENTIAL ELECTION

Trump's inexplicable attitude toward Putin and Russia invited more scrutiny as evidence appeared that Russia was working to influence the presidential election. On May 18, Director of National Intelligence (DNI) James Clapper stated that there were "some indications" that cyber hackers, possibly working for foreign governments, tried to infiltrate the Democratic and Republican presidential campaigns.[23] On June 14, the Democratic National Committee (DNC) announced that it had been attacked by Russian hackers.[24] Guccifer 2.0, a hacker with ties to Russia, posted a document stolen from the DNC, which outlined a plan to attack Trump.[25] A week later, Guccifer 2.0 posted more documents stolen from the DNC, addressing Hillary Clinton's vulnerabilities and possible responses she could offer to Republican attacks.[26] On July 22, WikiLeaks published twenty-two thousand emails stolen from the DNC. The emails showed the DNC's strong preference for Hillary Clinton,[27] enraging the supporters of Bernie Sanders on the eve of the Democratic convention and prompting the resignation of Debbie Wasserman Schultz as chairman of the DNC.[28]

On July 25, the FBI announced that it would be investigating the DNC hack, and the *Daily Beast* reported that the FBI suspected Russia of doing the hacking.[29] Intelligence officials advised the White House that they had "high confidence" that Russia was responsible.[30] The next day, President Obama confirmed that intelligence experts had tied Russia to the DNC hacking.[31] On August 12, Guccifer 2.0, using documents stolen from the DNC, released the cell phone numbers and email addresses of almost all Democrats in the House.[32] The same day, the firm ThreatConnect announced that DCLeaks, which had been posting leaked documents primarily targeting Democrats (although they had also released emails targeting senators McCain and Graham) appeared to be linked to Russian intelligence.[33]

On August 17, Trump received his first private briefing by U.S. intelligence officials, who showed him the direct leak between Russia and the hacked emails.[34] On September 5, the *Washington Post* reported that U.S. intelligence officials are investigating "a broad covert Russian operation in the United States to sow public distrust in the upcoming presidential election and in U.S. political institutions."[35] At the G20 meeting, presidents Obama and Putin met for ninety minutes. After the meeting, Obama stated: "We've had problems with cyber intrusions from Russia and other countries in the past."[36]

On September 7, DNI Clapper reiterated that the intelligence experts believed that Russia was behind the DNC hacks.[37] Despite that further confirmation, during an NBC forum, Trump expressed admiration for Putin's 82 percent approval rating, noted again that Putin had complimented him, and repeated his view that "[Putin's] been a leader far more than our president has been a leader."[38] The next day, flying in the face of the consensus in the intelligence community, Trump gave an interview to *Russia Today* in which he stated that Russian interference in the presidential campaign is "probably unlikely."[39]

On October 7, while the Trump campaign reeled from the explosive revelations that Trump had discussed grabbing women by their genitals, WikiLeaks dumped emails hacked from John Podesta, Hillary Clinton's campaign chairman.[40] The Obama administration accused Russia of interfering in the election. On October 9, during the second presidential debate, Trump cited WikiLeaks to accuse the DNC of rigging the primaries in favor of Hillary Clinton and against Bernie Sanders.[41] Clinton responded heatedly: "We have never in the history of our country been in a situation where an adversary, a foreign power, is working so hard to influence the outcome of the election. And believe me, they're not doing it to get me elected. They're doing it to try to influence the election of Donald Trump."[42]

Trump responded defensively: "Maybe there is no hacking. But they always blame Russia, and the reason they blame Russia is because they think they're trying to tarnish me with Russia. I know nothing about Russia. I know—I know about Russia, but I know nothing about the inner workings of Russia. I don't deal there. I have no businesses there. I have no loans from Russia."[43] The following day, at a Pennsylvania campaign rally, Trump shouted: "I love WikiLeaks" and read several excerpts from Clinton's emails.[44]

On October 19, during the third and most combative presidential debate, Hillary Clinton stated that Putin backed Trump because he "would rather have a puppet as president of the United States."[45] She went on to say: "It's pretty clear you won't admit the Russians have engaged in cyberattacks against the United States of America, that you encouraged espionage against our people, that you are willing to spout the Putin line, sign up for his wish list, break up NATO, do whatever he wants to do, and that you continue to get help from him because he has a very clear favorite in this race."[46]

On November 9, the Russian lower house of parliament erupted into applause as Donald Trump was declared winner of the election.[47]

EXTENSIVE TIES BETWEEN TRUMP ADVISERS AND RUSSIA

Russia's unprecedented interference in our presidential election fully justi-fied a searching investigation under any circumstances. But as the campaign progressed, press reports cast a spotlight on suspicious ties between high-level Trump campaign advisers and Russia. The threat to our democracy from foreign interference in the presidential campaign became even graver as evidence mounted of possible collusion between the Trump presidential campaign and Russia.

During the campaign, retired Lieutenant General Michael Flynn, who had held the position of director of the Defense Intelligence Agency (DIA) until fired by President Obama, had emerged as Donald Trump's principal adviser on national security matters. On November 18, Trump confirmed General Flynn's status by naming him as his National Security Adviser; it was literally the first appointment that the president-elect made.[48] However, General Flynn's ties to Russia had already prompted increasing attention. On June 17, 2016, in an article on Trump's financial ties to Russia, the *Washington Post* reported that General Flynn had attended the tenth anniversary dinner of *RT* (Russian Television)[49] on December 10, 2015, at which he sat with President Putin and gave a speech for which he received an honorarium of $45,000.[50]

On March 21, in a press interview, Trump listed Carter Page, an American banker, as one of his foreign policy advisers.[51] Page lived and worked for three years in Moscow and had extensive ties there.[52] On March 28, Trump hired Paul Manafort, a veteran Republican lobbyist, to head his delegate selection efforts.[53] Manafort had previously worked for President Viktor F. Yanukovych, the Ukrainian president who was a virtual puppet of Russia and who was driven from power in 2014.[54]

Trump's advisers shared the candidate's outspoken enthusiasm for Putin's Russia. In June 2016, at a gathering of foreign policy experts meeting with India's prime minister Modi, Carter Page praised Putin as "stronger and more reliable than President Obama" and "touted the positive effect that a Trump presidency would have on U.S.-Russia relations." On July 7, in a speech in Moscow, Page criticized the United States and other western democracies.[55] Trump's campaign manager, Corey Lewandowski, had approved the trip.[56] During the week of the Republican National Convention, Page and several other Trump foreign policy advisers met with Russian ambassador Sergey Kislyak.[57] During the same period, the Trump campaign worked behind the scenes to remove the language in the Republican platform calling for providing weapons to Ukraine for resisting Russian aggression.[58]

Roger Stone, one of the most experienced Republican campaign veterans and a former partner with Manafort in a lobbying firm, was a long-time Trump friend and ally, dating back to when he worked to advance Trump's casino interests in New York. Stone was perhaps America's best-known practitioner of campaign dirty tricks, beginning with his time in the Nixon White House and continuing in virtually every election cycle. On August 8, Stone told a meeting of Florida Republicans: "I actually have communicated with [Julian] Assange (the head of WikiLeaks). . . . I believe the next tranche of documents pertain to the Clinton Foundation, but there's no telling what the October surprise may be."[59] On August 19, Manafort resigned from the campaign after a press report that $12.7 million in cash had been earmarked for him by the Russian-aligned Ukrainian Party of Regions.[60] Two days later, Stone tweeted: "Trust me, it will soon be Podesta's time in the barrel."[61] On October 3, Stone tweeted: "I have total confidence that @wikileaks and my hero Julian Assange will educate the American people soon."[62] The next day, Assange announced that new information would be published each week for the next ten weeks.[63] On October 7, Stone's prediction about Podesta became true as WikiLeaks published his emails.[64] Four days later, Podesta charged that there might be ties between the Trump campaign, especially Stone, and WikiLeaks.[65] The next day, Stone, never a shrinking violet, stated that he had a "back channel" connection with Assange.[66]

Evidence continued to mount showing a constant stream of contacts between Trump campaign advisers and Russian officials, particularly Ambassador Kislyak. In December, Jared Kushner, Trump's son-in-law, and General Flynn met with Ambassador Kislyak at Trump Tower.[67] Carter Page, who had resigned from the Trump campaign, showed up in Moscow to meet with "business and thought leaders."[68] The Trump team claimed that all these contacts were routine parts of ordinary Washington political life, and in fact, Ambassador Kislyak was only one of many ambassadors who attended the Republican convention and worked to build relationships with the incoming Trump administration. But Kislyak was no ordinary, hardworking ambassador. The relations between the United States and Russia had deteriorated to an atmosphere reminiscent of the Cold War. The intelligence community had provided their stunning judgment that Russia had conducted a concerted campaign to interfere in the presidential campaign. Senior Trump aides appeared to have warm relationships with the Russian government and business community, including beneficial financial ties. Stone openly flaunted his close relationship with Julian Assange, and WikiLeaks appeared to be working in league with Russia.

On November 28, in an interview with *Time*, president-elect Trump said: "I don't believe they interfered.[69] That became a laughing point—not a talking point, a laughing point. Any time I do something, they say, 'Oh, Russia interfered.'"

In fact, by late November, no one outside Moscow was laughing; Russia's interference in the presidential election had been clearly established and confirmed by the intelligence community. On December 29, in retaliation for the election interference, President Obama ordered the expulsion of thirty-five suspected Russian intelligence operatives from the United States and imposed sanctions of two Russian intelligence services.[70] Ambassador

Kislyak, when summoned to the State Department and informed, threatened a forceful Russian response.[71] After leaving the State Department, Kislyak called General Flynn, the first of a series of calls between the two of them over the next thirty-six hours.[72] On December 30, Putin announced that he would not retaliate against the U.S. expulsions.[73] Trump responded on Twitter: "Great move on delay [by V. Putin]—I always knew he was very smart!"[74] Intelligence officials attempted to understand why Putin had responded unpredictably. Their search turned up Kislyak's communications, which were subject to routine surveillance, and the phone calls with Flynn.[75] From that call and subsequent intercepts, FBI agents wrote a secret report summarizing Flynn's discussions with Kislyak.

PRESIDENT-ELECT CRITICIZES INTELLIGENCE COMMUNITY

On December 31, at Mar-a-Lago, president-elect Trump again expressed doubt about the Russian involvement. "Hacking is a hard thing to prove," he told reporters. "So, it could be somebody else."[76] On January 3, Trump tweeted that "the intelligence briefing on so-called 'Russian hacking' was delayed until Friday, perhaps more time needed to build a case. Very strange!"[77] On January 4, Trump tweeted: "Julian Assange said 'a 14-year-old could have hacked Podesta—why was the DNC so careless?' Also, said Russians did not give him the info."[78] Two weeks before his inaugural, the president-elect persisted in defending the Russians and disbelieving U.S. intelligence agencies while relying on Julian Assange as a validator.

On January 6, DNI Clapper met with president-elect Trump to deliver the conclusion reached by the CIA, FBI, and NSA that Vladimir Putin had directed a vast cyberattack with the intent of defeating Hillary Clinton and installing Donald Trump in the White House.[79] "Putin and the Russian government aspired to help President-elect Trump's election chances when possible by discrediting Secretary Clinton and publicly contrasting her unfavorably to him,"[80] the report asserted bluntly. This extraordinary report represented "a virtually unheard of real time revelation by the American intelligence agencies that undermined the legitimacy of the president who was about to direct them."[81] Trump told the *New York Times* that the Russia controversy is a "political witch hunt"[82] and released a statement asserting that the hacks had "absolutely no effect on the outcome of the election."[83]

The outcry from angry Democrats presented minimal problems for the president-elect. He could easily brand them as "cry babies" and rely on Republican control of both houses of Congress to prevent them from doing much damage. Choosing to pick a fight with the U.S. intelligence community was quite a different matter, and, on its face, clearly an unwise choice for someone who would be crucially dependent on their work for the duration of his presidency. But Trump would face immediate political problems if his Republican support fractured; given the nature of John McCain and Lindsey Graham, Trump would feel the heat within days, not months or years.

SENATORS McCAIN AND GRAHAM: PUTIN'S HARSHEST CRITICS

By 2017, John McCain occupied a special place in the Senate, in Washington, and in the hearts and minds of the American people. Universally admired for his extraordinary courage as a POW for five and half years during the Vietnam War,[84] McCain also had carved out a well-deserved reputation for straight talk and independence on a full range of national security and domestic issues.[85] In 2000, at the peak of his maverick appeal, McCain lost the Republican nomination to George W. Bush. Eight years later, when the Republicans finally nominated him, McCain had little chance against the charismatic newcomer Barack Obama, as the country reeled from the financial crisis and the effects of two long wars.[86] He inflicted serious damage on his reputation for good judgment and putting "country first" by his desperate choice of Alaska governor Sarah Palin to be his running mate.[87]

In 2016, approaching the age of eighty, McCain reached for one more Senate term. Donald Trump's extraordinary rise had made it a miserable campaign year for John McCain. Trump shocked everyone by denigrating McCain's patriotism and courage early in the campaign and then emerging unscathed from the controversy.[88] For long months, McCain, tight-lipped and obviously unhappy, refused to withdraw support from Trump despite the disrespect that the Republican nominee had shown him.[89] Ultimately, McCain's independent brand remained strong enough to carry him through to a comfortable victory. He returned to Washington to start his sixth Senate term, with no affection or respect for Donald Trump and with a strong incentive to finish his career by continuing to put "country first."

John McCain's stature as a great senator stemmed from a combination of independent judgment and deep substantive knowledge. Chairman of the Senate Armed Services Committee, McCain had a lifetime of experience in foreign policy and national security. It was no accident that Senator McCain had helped George W. Bush with his crucial decision to send additional troops to Iraq for the "surge."[90] Like Henry "Scoop" Jackson four decades earlier,

John McCain had made himself an independent force to be reckoned with in American national security policy. And just as Jackson had distrusted and despised the Soviet Union and its leaders, McCain distrusted and despised Russia and Vladimir Putin.[91]

McCain had taken the lead in Congress in imposing sanctions on Russia after the invasion of Crimea.[92] Now the evidence that Putin orchestrated the systematic interference into the presidential election outraged him.[93] On January 27, a week after Donald Trump's inauguration, McCain offered a slashing comment about a phone call that Trump was scheduled to have with Putin.[94] Noting the "widespread speculation that the White House is considering lifting sanctions against Russia,"[95] McCain urged the president to "reject that reckless course":

> In the most flagrant demonstration of Putin's disdain and disrespect for our nation, Russia deliberately interfered in our recent election with cyberattacks and a disinformation campaign designed to weaken America and discredit Western values. . . .
>
> Putin wants to be our enemy. . . . He will never be our partner, including in fighting ISIL. He believes that strengthening Russia means weakening America. President Trump . . . should remember that the man on the other end of the line is a murderer and a thug who seeks to undermine American national security interests at every turn.[96]

Lindsey Graham, first elected to the Senate in 2002, had served six years in the Air Force as a lawyer[97] and combined hawkish views of foreign policy and defense[98] with a moderate and independent streak on other issues, including global warming[99] and foreign aid.[100] He had joined the "Gang of Eight" that produced the Senate's comprehensive immigration legislation in 2013.[101] He had been one of the House prosecutors of Bill Clinton during his impeachment trial but later established a good working relationship with Hillary Clinton in the Senate.[102] Graham became perhaps best known in the Senate as one of the "three amigos," joining with McCain and Democrat Joseph Lieberman (D-CT) in championing the Iraq war.[103] After Lieberman retired from the Senate, Graham and McCain continued in lockstep on virtually all national security issues, particularly opposition to Putin's Russia. In 2015, Graham joined the race for the Republican presidential nomination,[104] to which he added his characteristic candor and humor. He fell out of the race early, endorsing Jeb Bush and then Ted Cruz. He never endorsed Donald Trump, becoming one of his most caustic critics.[105]

Now as Trump began his presidency, Graham, like McCain, fiercely attacked Russia for interfering in the presidential election. As chairman of the Judiciary Subcommittee on Crime and Terrorism, Graham and Sheldon

Whitehouse (D-RI), the ranking Democrat, pressed forward with their own investigation of Russia's hacking.[106] "I will never be satisfied until the Congress and the White House work together to punish Russia for trying to interfere with our election," Graham told CNN.[107] "If Donald Trump forgives Putin for what he tried to do to our election, that will scream weakness and the world will get a lot more unstable. . . . An attack on one party by a foreign entity is an attack on all parties. We're all in this together."[108]

MICHAEL FLYNN'S UNDISCLOSED DEALINGS WITH RUSSIA

On January 10, ten days before Trump's inauguration, Senator Jeff Sessions, nominated to be attorney general, told the Judiciary Committee under oath that he "did not have any communications with the Russians."[109] On January 15, in an interview, Vice President Pence stated, based on a conversation with Flynn, that Flynn and Kislyak "did not discuss anything having to do with the United States' decision to expel diplomats or impose censure against Russia."[110]

These two statements would soon prove false, blowing up with major harm to the new president. On February 9, the *Washington Post* reported that Flynn had in fact discussed the sanctions issue with Ambassador Kislyak.[111] It soon became clear that Flynn had misled Vice President Pence, and on February 13, Flynn resigned.[112] A drumbeat of revelations accelerated. The *New York Times* and CNN reported that members of Trump's campaign and other Trump associates were in constant contact with suspected Russian intelligence operatives in the year before the election. On March 1, the *Washington Post* reported that Sessions, recently confirmed by the Senate to be attorney general, met with the Russian ambassador during the campaign.[113] Congressional Democrats, led by Schumer, called on Sessions to resign.[114] Sessions proved adept at damage control: acknowledging that he had testified inaccurately to the committee, correcting the record, and saying that he would recuse himself from any investigation of connections between Russia and the Trump campaign.[115] In a press conference, Trump labeled "the whole Russian thing . . . a ruse."[116] But the president looked increasingly isolated in his view.

THE SENATE INVESTIGATION BEGINS

Leading members of the Senate had begun discussing the best way to investigate the Russia connection in December. The incoming Democratic leader

Chuck Schumer and Jack Reed (D-RI), the ranking Democrat on the Armed Services Committee, joined McCain and Graham in a bipartisan letter to Majority Leader McConnell, calling for the appointment of a Select Senate Committee on cybersecurity to investigate Russian hacking and interference in the campaign. Noting that the issue cut across the jurisdiction of several committees, based on the experience of Watergate and Iran-Contra, the senators contended that "only a select committee that is time-limited, cross-jurisdictional and purpose-driven can address the challenges of cyber."[117]

In his separate remarks, Schumer added: "We want to find out what the Russians are doing to our political system and what other foreign governments might do to our political system. And then figure out a way to stop it. Only a select committee can do it. To send it to just one committee or a multiplicity of committees will leave things out, won't reconcile contradictory information, and because the existing committees are so busy in the new administration it won't get the focus that it needs."[118]

The senators recommended the right course of action; a select committee was, far and away, the best way to investigate the Russian interference in the campaign.[119] But Schumer had made a serious error by joining the letter. The involvement of the Democratic leader inevitably gave the letter a partisan cast; it also empowered McConnell, as the sole recipient of the letter, to reject the request. McConnell had already expressed his view that Russia's interference in the election demanded a serious investigation. But he opposed appointing a select committee, saying that the Intelligence Committee, which had already begun its investigation, was the proper place for the investigation.[120] To skeptical observers, McConnell's preference for "regular order" represented his way of keeping tighter control over the investigation. McCain and Graham were independent bomb throwers; Burr seemed likely to be more malleable. It was also disconcerting because bipartisan cooperation, which had once characterized the work of the Intelligence Committee, had frayed considerably during the probes during the Bush administration interrogation techniques of enemy combatants and the incomplete intelligence leading up to the Iraq war.

The Intelligence Committee probe started poorly with Democrats threatening to boycott until Burr agreed to include the possibility of collusion between Moscow and the Trump campaign.[121] Burr made a serious—potentially fatal—mistake by calling reporters at the request of the White House to refute allegations of frequent communications between Trump aides and Russian officials, causing Warner to express "grave concern."[122]

But this type of investigation into the presidency, requiring some senators to take on a president of their own party, can take some time to get on track. Even Howard Baker, remembered for his independence and role in bringing down Richard Nixon, over Watergate, initially provoked concern among Democrats that he was communicating too closely with the Nixon White House. Baker grew into his role as an independent seeker of truth as he came to understand the full seriousness of Watergate. Burr would right himself soon enough.

In any event, Burr's initial misstep was overshadowed by the erratic and often outrageous behavior of House Intelligence Committee chairman Devin Nunes (R-CA). Nunes's position as a Trump transition adviser had raised concerns about whether he could chair a serious investigation into the possible collusion of the Trump campaign with Russia.[123] However, he surprised skeptics by chairing the first major hearing on the issue, in which FBI director James Comey publicly confirmed that the Bureau was investigating Russian interference into the presidential campaign and whether associates of the president were in contact with Moscow.[124] Immediately thereafter, however, Nunes was found to have briefed the White House on information that his investigation had turned up without sharing the information with Adam Schiff, the ranking Democrat, or other committee members.[125] The plot thickened when it became known that Nunes had actually held a secret meeting on White House grounds with an unnamed source who provided what Nunes claimed to be evidence that Trump transition aides had been improperly monitored.[126] Graham spoke for many when he described Nunes's probe as "sort of an Inspector Clouseau investigation."[127] Under pressure from House Speaker Paul Ryan, Nunes subsequently stepped aside to allow Representative Mike Conaway to chair the Russia probe.[128]

On March 28, recognizing that Nunes's bizarre behavior could undermine public confidence in both congressional investigations and public confidence, senators Burr and Warner stepped forward to reassure the public with a "deliberate bipartisan show of force." In a joint news conference, Burr and Warner complimented each other and vowed to bridge over their political differences to lead an investigation that resolved the major issues: Why and how Russia interfered in the election and whether there was any collusion with the Trump campaign. Burr said that the committee staffers were receiving access to information previously available only to the congressional leaders and the heads of the Intelligence panels. He also said that the committee had scheduled five private witness interviews and was working to set up fifteen more.[129]

Expectations about the Senate had sunk so low, with partisanship so all consuming, that senators Burr and Warner could receive accolades for simply having a joint press conference and pledging to work together. But it was also an important reminder of the impact that senators still have if they are willing to work together. One Republican standing up with one Democrat provided reassurance that a full and credible investigation was possible. That is the power of bipartisanship. Moreover, senators Burr and Warner came to the job with a close personal friendship, brought together by a mutual friend, former

Georgia senator Saxby Chambliss. Warner, a multimillionaire, jokes with Burr for wearing Kirkland Signature shirts from Costco. In March 2016, they were leading a delegation through Europe when terrorists struck at Brussels. In 2014, Burr contributed generously to Senate Republican candidates but refrained from helping Ed Gillespie, who was running against Warner. Two years later, Warner reciprocated by declining to help Burr's opponent.[130] In short, they have the kind of real friendship that was common in Mansfield's Senate but is all too rare today.

THE FIRING OF FBI DIRECTOR JAMES COMEY

The Trump presidency often reminded people of a political novel, and the "seven days in May" beginning with the firing of FBI director James Comey on May 10 transformed the investigation of Russian interference from a serious problem for the president into a raging firestorm that threatened to consume his presidency. One bombshell revelation followed another. The White House claimed that the president had acted at the recommendation of Deputy Attorney General Rod Rosenstein.[131] The next day, the president bluntly admitted that he had already decided to fire Comey before hearing from Rosenstein because "of the Russia thing."[132] The firing came shortly after Comey had requested more resources to pursue the investigation.[133] Trump met in the Oval Office with Sergey V. Lavrov, Russia's foreign minister, and Ambassador Kislyak, excluding American press but allowing *Tass*, the Russian state newspaper, into the White House.[134] It soon came out that Trump had revealed some of America's most sensitive intelligence to the Russians, shocking even Trump administration officials, and putting General McMaster, his national security adviser, in the position of having to defend the indefensible.[135] Subsequently, it was also reported that Trump had told Lavrov and Kislyak that he called Comey a "nut job" and that firing him had eased the pressure on him because of the Russia probe.[136] But Trump had expressed his hope to Comey that he could go easy on Michael Flynn, who was "a good guy."[137]

The firing of Comey raised questions of whether the president had committed obstruction of justice, given Trump's admission that he had acted because of "the Russia thing."[138] Rosenstein, under stinging criticism from Capitol Hill for being used by Trump, appointed Robert Mueller, the distinguished former director of the FBI, to serve as independent counsel supervising the investigation into the Russia connection.[139] Mueller's appointment produced a rare moment of universal agreement that Rosenstein had made a superb choice, erasing any doubts that the investigation would be conducted with

absolute integrity with "the chips falling as they may." It also should have provided a respite for Trump as he embarked on his first foreign trip as president.

But even as the president made headlines from successful visits to Saudi
Arabia and Israel, the *Washington Post* reported that Trump had separately called
Dan Coats, the director of National Intelligence, and Admiral Michael Rogers,
the head of the National Security Agency (NSA), and asked each man if he could
get the FBI to stop its investigation.[140] As Jeffrey Smith, former general counsel to
the CIA, quickly noted, Trump's action mirrored precisely what Richard Nixon
had done on June 23, 1972, when he asked the CIA to turn off the FBI investigation into the break-in at the Democratic National Committee headquarters in
the Watergate.[141] The tape recording of Nixon's statement became the "smoking
gun"—clear evidence of obstruction of justice—that led to the final crumbling
of Republican support for Nixon, followed by his resignation.

Russian interference into the presidential campaign, with an intent to
undermine our institutions and affect the outcome, posed an unprecedented
challenge to American democracy. The possibility of Russian collusion with
the Trump presidential campaign made the situation far more ominous. Douglas Brinkley, one of America's most prominent historians, sensed "a whiff of
treason in the air."[142] Now a series of blatant actions by and statements by
Trump raised the clear possibility of obstruction of justice and witness tamper-
ing. Mueller's appointment removed any doubt that the Justice Department/
FBI investigation would be full and fair.

But the shocking events also erased any lingering doubt about the seriousness of the Senate Intelligence Committee's investigation led by Burr and
Warner. Immediately after Comey's firing, the Committee ordered its first sub-
poena, ordering Michael Flynn to hand over records of any emails, phone calls,
meetings, and financial dealings with the Russians.[143] Soon after, the Committee requested documents from the Treasury Department's office of Financial
Crimes, which could shed light on financial transactions between the Trump
campaign and Russia, as well as possible transactions by the Trump family or
the president himself.[144] McConnell, who had initially mocked the Democrats
for "complaining about the removal of an FBI director whom they themselves
had repeatedly and sharply criticized,"[145] now said that the Senate needed to
hear from Comey in public, as soon as possible.[146]

At the same time, the Judiciary Committee, which had jurisdiction over
the FBI and criminal justice generally, stepped forward to launch a separate
investigation into Comey's firing and the possibility of obstruction of justice.[147] By mid-May, the committees were competing over where Comey
should testify publicly. "Lawmakers can barely hide their ambition at landing
what would be a grand media spectacle," *Washington Post* congressional correspondent Paul Kane wrote.[148]

While there was no denying that senators were known to enjoy the spotlight, President Trump's extraordinary actions and statements had provoked another group of senators who subscribed to McCain's famous guideline: "country first."[149] Chuck Grassley, the Judiciary Committee chairman, was a strong partisan Republican who had angered Democrats in the Senate and the country by refusing to consider Obama's nomination of Judge Garland to the Supreme Court.[150] But Grassley was also extremely hardworking and notoriously independent; he had compiled a long record of very tough oversight of the FBI and a willingness to assert Congress's prerogatives vis-à-vis the Executive branch.[151] Similarly, Dianne Feinstein, the ranking Democrat on Judiciary,[152] had shown her independence and backbone in a long series of clashes with the Bush and Obama administrations during her tenure as chairman of the Intelligence Committee.[153]

Grassley and Feinstein were both eighty-three and recognized that this investigation could be the capstone of their distinguished careers. They also had very powerful support from Graham and Sheldon Whitehouse (D-RI), the leaders of the subcommittee on criminal justice, which had already launched its own investigation.[154] Within a short time, quiet conversations with Comey, and between senators, produced a consensus road forward. Comey would testify first before the Intelligence Committee,[155] with which he had been working closely, and that committee had the overall lead on Russian interference in the presidential election.[156] But the Judiciary Committee would proceed with its investigation of possible obstruction of justice, including any interference with the FBI's investigation.[157]

THE COMEY HEARING

Since the advent of television, many of America's most dramatic political moments had taken place in Senate committee hearings. Comey's appearance on June 8 seemed destined to be another moment in that great tradition. But on June 7, the Intelligence Committee had another, less publicized hearing, which also proved to be very important. Dan Coats, the Director of National Intelligence (DNI) and Michael Rogers, the director of the National Security Agency (NSA), had the misfortune of testifying before the committee about the operation of the Foreign Intelligence Surveillance Act (FISA) hours after a *Washington Post* front-page story that Trump had pressured them to turn off the FBI investigation into possible collusion.[158]

Facing persistent questioning from Democratic and Republican senators, Coats and Rogers repeatedly refused to discuss the specifics of any conversation with the president. While they appeared to base their refusals at least in part on the doctrine of executive privilege, Rogers admitted that the White House had not told him to assert executive privilege. This produced a heated exchange with Angus King, the independent senator from Maine who caucuses with the Democrats.[159]

"Is there any invocation of executive privilege? If there is, let us know about it. If there isn't, then let's answer the question," King said.[160]

Coats also indicated concerns about discussing conversations with the president due to Mueller's investigation.[161]

"When there is an ongoing investigation, I think it's inappropriate," Coats said. But he subsequently acknowledged: "I'm not sure I have a legal basis," further angering King. "The special counsel is entitled to ask you questions about this, but not an oversight committee of the United States Congress?" King asked rhetorically.

"It just shows the kind of Orwellian existence we live in," McCain said, pointing out that Coats was refusing to discuss interactions with Trump that had been reported in the *Washington Post* that morning. He called the report "more than disturbing."[162]

Ultimately, Coats and Rogers got through the senators' grilling by promising to tell the lawmakers as much as possible behind closed doors. "Just because it's been published in the *Washington Post* doesn't mean it's unclassified," Coats noted. But the senators were not buying the witnesses' shifting rationales. Coats's admission—"I'm not sure I have a legal basis"—spoke volumes.[163] What exactly was the justification for not confirming or denying that the president had pressured them to stifle the FBI investigation? The blood was in the water, even a day before Comey's testimony.

On June 8, "Washingtonians were working from home, taking the day off or otherwise mentally playing hooky to bear witness to the big hearing,"[164] the *New York Times* reported. James Comey, an experienced witness at ease in the hot seat, electrified the nation with his detailed depiction of five instances in which Donald Trump had demanded "loyalty" and pressured him to "let Mike Flynn go."[165] He said that the president had lied, "pure and simple," when he claimed that the FBI was in disarray and that agents had lost confidence in Mr. Comey.[166] He said that he had prepared contemporaneous memos of each conversation, and that he had never felt the need do so with presidents Bush or Obama. He acknowledged turning over memos about his meetings and calls with Mr. Trump to Mueller, raising the possibility that the Special Counsel would investigate possible obstruction of justice by the president. Comey also acknowledged leaking his memos through an intermediary in response to the president's tweet that Comey "better hope there were no tapes of their discussion."[167]

Comey had ensured that he would get his story out by releasing his full testimony the previous day. The senators questioned him for nearly four hours, covering a broad range of issues. Chairman Burr asked a central question: Did the president try to obstruct justice or was he just seeking a way for Mike Flynn to save face? Mark Warner called Comey's firing "shocking" and suggested that the fact that he was leading an investigation into possible collusion "might explain why you're now sitting here as a private citizen." James Risch (R-ID) emphasized Comey's acknowledgment that President Trump was not personally under investigation (at that time). Risch also noted that the president had expressed his "hope" rather than order Comey to drop the investigation. Marco Rubio (R-FL) pointed out that while Trump pressed Comey to say that he was not under investigation, at no time did he ask Comey to drop the whole Russia investigation. Ron Wyden questioned whether Attorney General Sessions had violated his recusal from the Russia investigation by being involved in firing the person who was heading up the investigation. Susan Collins got Comey to acknowledge that his "intermediary" was a professor at Columbia University; David Richman, a Columbia law professor, confirmed that he was a close friend of Comey's and the intermediary in leaking the memos.[168]

In one pivotal moment, Tom Cotton (R-AR) asked: "Do you believe Donald Trump colluded with Russia?" If Senator Cotton was expecting a flat denial, Comey did not give him one. Instead he responded: "That's a question that I don't think I should answer in an open session. When I left, we didn't have an open investigation into President Trump."[169] Of course, that was then. Trump's firing of Comey and his candid admission that it was because of "the Russia thing" virtually ensured that Special Counsel Mueller would add possible obstruction of justice to the other issues that he was investigating.

In the aftermath of Comey's dramatic testimony, events continued to move rapidly. Intelligence committee members—Democrats and Republicans—pressed for the attorney general to testify about the Trump campaign's ties to Russia, as well as his role, if any, in firing the FBI director.[170] Remarkably, a day before the hearing, the committee had not yet decided whether the attorney general would testify in an open or closed session. In a letter to Burr and Warner, Wyden said: "These matters, which are directly related to our democratic institutions, are of the utmost public interest. I believe we owe the American people transparency."[171] Pat Leahy, angry that Sessions had canceled an appearance before the Appropriations Committee for the second time, tweeted: "You need to testify before both (committees) in public. You can't run forever."[172]

On June 13, only five days after Comey's appearance, Attorney General Sessions testified in public before the Senate Intelligence Committee. He angrily dismissed any suggestion that he had colluded with the Russians as "an appalling and detestable lie."[173] He professed not to recall the substance of any conversation with Russian ambassador Kislyak, and he attributed his earlier failure to recall a meeting with Kislyak to being flustered by Senator Al Franken's question after having testified for hours.[174] Sessions confirmed that Comey had expressed concern to him about being left alone to meet with President Trump. He defended his role in Comey's firing as being consistent with his recusal from the Russia investigation: "The recusal involved one case in the Department of Justice and the FBI. . . . I do not believe it is a sound position that if you recuse from a single case, you can't make a decision about the leadership of the agency."[175] He steadfastly refused to answer any questions about his private conversations with Trump, including whether he spoke to the president about Comey's handling of the investigation into Russian collusion.[176] Like Coats and Rogers the week before, Sessions referenced the concept of "executive privilege," without actually claiming to invoke it since President Trump had not done so. Sessions said he would not respond to the questions to preserve the president's right to invoke executive privilege if he chose to do so.[177]

This evasive performance by their long-time colleague angered several senators. Wyden sharply criticized Sessions for ducking key questions: "I believe the American people have had it with stonewalling. Americans don't want to hear that answers to relevant questions are privileged or off limits. We are talking about an attack on our democratic institutions, and stonewalling of any kind is unacceptable."[178]

Trump continued to administer an unprecedented series of shocks to the political system. Having referred ominously to the possibility that there might be tapes of his conversations with Comey, the president waited nearly six weeks before admitting that no such tapes existed, raising the possibility that he had tried to influence Comey's testimony.[179] One of his closest friends,[180] Chris Reddy, said that the president was giving serious thought to firing Mueller because of the Special Counsel's friendship with Comey and because he was hiring lawyers with ties to Hillary Clinton. Bluffs, threats, and other hardball tactics may work in the real estate business, but in the world of politics and government, they prompted Comey to disclose his memos and undoubtedly strengthened Mueller's implacable resolve to see the investigation to a full and fair conclusion.

COORDINATING INVESTIGATIONS

By late May, the American people had strong assurances that there would be two thorough investigations, neither of which would be a whitewash or a witch hunt. However, Mueller and the senators faced the challenge of ensuring that the investigations did not interfere with each other. Both investigations were probing Russia's interference in the presidential election, as well as possible collusion between the Trump campaign and Russia. But Mueller was investigating possible criminal activities. His team included prosecutors who were receiving information gathered by the FBI and presenting evidence to grand juries, under strict rules of confidentiality. In contrast, the Senate committee sought to produce a full understanding of Russian interference as well as possible collusion. Its investigation was not tethered to criminal activities, and the committee could easily reach the conclusion that public hearings were necessary to educate the public to what had occurred. At the most obvious level of conflict, Burr and Warner's committee might want to hear from a witness who would only testify if given immunity from prosecution, which Mueller might well oppose.

Previous investigations of the presidency had shown that these conflicts were not theoretical. During Watergate, although the Senate Select Committee, the House Judiciary Committee, and special prosecutors Archibald Cox and Leon Jaworski and U.S. attorney Earl Silbert all comported themselves with distinction, they clashed at key junctures, particularly over whether the Select Committee should grant immunity to White House counsel John Dean. The grant of limited immunity opened the door to Dean's testimony, which paved the way to Nixon's eventual resignation.

In Iran-Contra, the Senate Select Committee reached an early agreement with Lawrence Walsh, the independent counsel, in which the committee agreed to delay granting immunity to Oliver North, a central actor in the complex plot, to give Walsh several months to gather evidence. But the committee did not accede to Walsh's request to delay granting immunity until after the special prosecutor reached his conclusion as to whether North had committed an indictable offense. "By deferring its grant of immunity to North for a reasonable period, the Committee altered the timing of North's testimony and the degree of his cooperation," senators George Mitchell and William Cohen would later write.[181] "It may have been a mistake to do so . . . but the fact remains that North's testimony was crucial, if only because he disclosed the existence of the so-called off-the-shelf covert capability that is so inimicable to our concept of democracy. Future congressional investigatory committees will be faced with similar choices for which there are no fixed rules."

But experienced prosecutors and investigators working in good faith can handle these challenges. Burr and Warner were likely to benefit greatly from Mueller's broad experience; the former FBI director who served through the most difficult period after 9/11 will understand that ultimately the American people need the full picture of the Russian interference into the election and the possible collusion more than the indictment and convictions of what may be a few bad actors.

On July 8, the *New York Times* reported that in June 2016, Donald Trump Jr., Jared Kushner, and Paul Manafort[182] had met with Natalia Veselnitskaya, a Russian lawyer with close ties to the Kremlin in response to an offer of information damaging to Hillary Clinton. The shifting explanations about the meeting, with its growing cast of memorable characters, did not alter the fact that Trump Jr. had enthusiastically accepted the meeting and immediately invited two of the people closest to the president and the campaign. No longer could President Trump brush off the idea of collusion as "fake news" from Democrats making excuses for losing the election. Instead, the White House shifted to contending that anyone would have taken the meeting, and that Veselnitskaya provided no important information. After the bombshell disclosure, the president and his closest advisers were unmistakably in much graver jeopardy as the investigations by Mueller and the Senate committees continued.

But long before the disclosure of the meeting with Veselnitskaya, President Trump had driven the Senate past the tipping point. There was no convincing explanation for his actions and statements with respect to Comey other than the obvious intention to derail the investigation into the possibility that his campaign colluded with Russia to affect the 2016 presidential campaign, and/ or into whatever financial connections the Trump family empire might have with Russia. It is safe to assume that virtually every senator was dismayed, angered, or sickened by Trump meeting jovially with Lavrov and Kislyak in the Oval Office the day after firing Comey, bragging about getting rid of the "nut job," while also giving the Russians sensitive intelligence information. Senate Republicans and Democrats remain deeply divided over many issues, but where Russia, and Russian intentions toward the United States, are involved, it is "country first."

The Senate demonstrated both its implacable anger toward Putin's Russia and its deep distrust of President Trump when on June 13, it passed, by a 98–2 vote, legislation strengthening sanctions on Russia, and making it impossible for Trump to weaken them without congressional approval.[183] The measure directed sanctions toward Russia's intelligence and defense apparatus, as well as parts of its energy, mining, railways, and shipping economy. It aimed to punish Russia not only for interference in our presidential election but also for its annexation of Crimea, continuing military activity in eastern Ukraine, and human rights abuses. The legislation represented the close collaboration of Bob Corker and Ben Cardin, chairman and ranking member of the Foreign Relations Committee, Mike Crapo (R-ID) and Sherrod Brown (D-OH), chairman and ranking member of the Banking Committee, and leaders McConnell and Schumer. McCain and Graham, the most intense Russia critics, also played a part in the discussions. Schumer said in a statement that the legislation will "send a powerful and bipartisan statement to Russia and any other country who might try to interfere in our elections that they will be punished."[184]

The Senate-passed legislation, which also extended sanctions on North Korea and Iran, encountered some delay in the House, but on July 21, congressional leaders reached agreement on the sweeping package. The legislation passed both the Senate and House with near-unanimous votes (98–2; 419–3). On August 2, President Trump signed the legislation, asserting that the measure included "clearly unconstitutional provisions" that encroached on the ability of the executive branch to conduct foreign policy.[185] "Yet despite its problems," Trump noted, "I am signing the bill for the sake of national unity. It represents the will of the American people to see Russia take steps to improve relations with the United States. We hope there will be cooperation between our countries on major global issues so that these sanctions will no longer be necessary."

Sanctions are a frequently used tool of American foreign policy, and often a source of contention between Congress and the president. Trump's objections to Congress intruding on his ability to conduct foreign policy were quite consistent with positions taken by previous presidents. In fact, limiting the president's ability to suspend or terminate the sanctions was a striking departure from normal practice, reflecting the widely shared fear in Congress about Trump's attitude toward Putin and Russia. David Ignatius, probably the most respected commentator on national security issues, suggested that the near-unanimous vote reflected "an unthinking herd mentality. . . . This legislation limits presidential flexibility at the very time it may be most needed to conduct delicate negotiations with those adversaries."[186] Ignatius went on to observe: "If this were any president other than Trump, and any other antagonist but Russia," Trump's argument would have received more support.

But of course, it was Trump and Russia. Even as the president grudgingly signed the sanctions legislation, he reinforced congressional and public concern by thanking Vladimir Putin for expelling 755 Americans who had been serving in the U.S. embassy in Moscow. Trump may well have been joking when he said that Putin's action would help him reduce the size and cost of government, but it was a shocking response, particularly from a president with an established pattern of refraining from ever criticizing Putin.[187]

By the summer of 2017, the American public could be confident that Special Counsel Mueller will pursue a full and fair investigation. They can also count on the Senate. The Intelligence and Judiciary Committees have leaders, plus numerous other members, who will not back off. The overwhelming vote on the sanctions legislation makes it increasingly clear that they will have the support of the full Senate. This commitment provides additional reassurance if President Trump decides to fire Mueller. The truth will come out, and the chips will fall where they may.

• *11* •

Catastrophic Health Care

*D*onald Trump's presidency provided virtual assurance that there would be many unexpected developments ahead. But in addition to the early consideration of a Supreme Court nomination, one more certainty existed. The year 2017 would witness a titanic fight over the Affordable Care Act (ACA) and the future of the American health care system, and the Senate would take center stage as "the nation's mediator."

The Republican Party, led by Mitch McConnell, had waged a fierce battle against President Obama's signature initiative. After its passage on March 23, 2010,[1] the Senate moved on. McConnell focused on opposing Obama's financial regulation[2] and climate change initiatives,[3] and walking along "the fiscal cliff" until such moments when he saw compromises that would be advantageous.[4] The House, however, never overcame its obsession with Obamacare. As the Freedom Caucus[5] and the Koch brothers tightened their grip on the House,[6] and the "Young Guns" arose to challenge House Speaker John Boehner,[7] the Republicans voted more than fifty times to repeal Obamacare.[8] It was the central plank in their platform, and it provided the energy needed to regain a Republican majority in 2010[9] and then expand it in 2014.[10]

With Trump's victory giving the Republicans control of both ends of Pennsylvania Avenue, the Republicans faced the challenge of meeting their promise to end what they saw as the nightmare of "Obamacare." Many observers, led by *New York Times* columnist Paul Krugman, noted that the Republicans had never offered an alternative to the ACA.[11] They would soon find out that governing required vastly different skills than giving vent to their rage and whipping up their troops.

THE ACA'S TROUBLED START

The Patient Protection and Affordable Care Act (ACA) was one of the largest legislative undertakings of all time. The actual legislation was 906 pages[12]; the regulations implementing it nearly 11,000 pages more.[13] The Obama administration failed miserably in explaining the benefits of the Act.[14] Ezekiel Emanuel, one of the nation's leading doctors and an Obama adviser, graded the communications efforts as "F-," including those of his brother Rahm, the president's chief of staff.[15]

As Jonathan Alter would write:

> For years, Democrats had mindlessly framed the debate as a struggle for "universal coverage," a technical term that meant nothing to the public. When Americans finally learned what it meant, they didn't much like it. Polls showed that more than 90 percent of people that vote already had health insurance . . . This meant that liberal politicians were asking voters to support benefits for someone else, not themselves, which is the hardest thing to do in politics.[16]

Obama compounded the problem by telling the public that if they were happy with their doctors, they could keep them, which, in fact, was not always the case.[17] The state insurance exchanges rolled out slowly and proved difficult to navigate.[18] The federal website crashed after its rollout, further undermining public confidence.[19]

The legality of ACA was clouded for two years by a major challenge that reached the Supreme Court. On June 28, 2012, the Court by a 5–4 decision written by Chief Justice Roberts held that the requirement that most Americans obtain insurance or pay a penalty was constitutional because of Congress' right to levy taxes.[20] Even then, the Court's decision created further uncertainty and confusion by ruling that Congress had overstepped by coercing states to expand their Medicaid programs under the threat to eliminate their existing federal payments.[21] Seven justices agreed on this issue, effectively rewriting the law to permit states to choose between accepting federal funds for expansion of their Medicaid programs or refusing to accept the funds while continuing to receive their existing payments.[22]

The complexity and confusion, rising costs of premiums and deductibles, and the Democrats' communications failures gave the Republicans ammunition for their endless attacks on the ACA. "In war and peace, the side that seizes the initiative often keeps it, especially when the opposition refuses to see it for what it is," Alter observed.[23]

THE LOGIC AND APPEAL OF THE ACA

In fact, despite the sound and fury, the basic architecture of the ACA was sound. Insurance companies were regulated, preventing them from denying coverage or charging higher prices to Americans with preexisting conditions.[24] To reduce the number of uninsured Americans, it was necessary to require people to purchase insurance[25]; this was the "individual mandate." To enforce that requirement, so that the system would include young, healthy people as well as those who were old and sick, penalties would be imposed on those who did not buy insurance. Recognizing that many people would still not be able to afford insurance, families received subsidies linked to both income and premiums.[26] To cover more Americans, Medicaid would have to be expanded.[27] To incentivize the states already struggling with increased Medicaid costs, the federal government would have to bear the cost of the expansion—100 percent for the first three years, and 90 percent thereafter.[28]

"In drafting his health care plan, Barack Obama chose a moderate, market-based approach," David Leonhardt noted in his *New York Times* column.[29] "It was to the right of Bill Clinton's and Richard Nixon's plans and way to the right of Harry Truman's—and yet Republicans still wouldn't support it. . . . The version that did pass doesn't leave the Republicans much room to maneuver."[30]

The Republicans also confronted the fact that key features of the ACA were very popular. Requiring insurance companies to cover people with preexisting conditions was a godsend to millions of Americans. Allowing parents to keep their adult children on their insurance until age twenty-six constituted a meaningful benefit for millions of others.[31] Making health insurance portable so that people could choose to leave their jobs while still having health care provided an enormous relief to individuals and their families and contributed to making the economy more dynamic.[32]

While the Obama administration had failed in the challenge of educating the general public, they had very effectively mobilized support for the legislation from a full range of affected constituencies. The ACA received the support of the insurance industry, the hospitals, the doctors, the nurses, the pharmaceutical companies, consumer groups, and senior citizens. They were invested in it, and they would oppose its repeal or significant changes. They would also oppose a process in which they were not serious participants.

Some Democrats, including Chuck Schumer, would criticize Obama for having shifted his focus from the economy to health care in 2009 after the initial economic stimulus. That argument seems to rest on the assumption that the Republicans would have supported a further economic stimulus,[33] which, given their obstruction from day one, seems demonstrably false. But it also fails to recognize the true impact of expanding health insurance coverage to the economy, and to the American people. By 2008, inequality in the United States had soared, having risen astronomically since 1980.[34] American exceptionalism now extended to the sorry reality that we were the advanced economy with the most inequality. It would take a major revamp of the tax structure to reverse that situation, and realistically, that was not going to happen. The single most important thing that President Obama could have done to reverse the inexorable rise of inequality was provide health care to millions of additional Americans, and he did.

With Donald Trump, rather than Hillary Clinton, in the White House, the Republicans would now get their chance to repeal Obamacare. As more than one commentator wryly noted, they were like the dog that had caught the truck.[35] They confronted the painful reality that once people faced the stark possibility of losing their benefits, Obamacare became more and more popular.[36]

A month after the election, liberal groups had already mounted a significant campaign to save Obamacare based on devastating stories of what people would face if their health care was taken away. "The huge number of people who would lose coverage, there is no way anyone would not have empathy [for their] plight," said Ron Pollack, executive director of Families USA.[37] "It is really irresponsible to pass a repeal at a point where nobody understands what will take its place."[38] Rob Restuccia, the executive director of Community Catalyst, a national health advocacy organization, stated: "It's a very cynical strategy that puts at risk millions of people and potentially not just people who are currently uninsured, but the whole health care system."[39] An Urban Institute report predicted that the number of uninsured Americans would rise from twenty-nine million to nearly fifty-nine million by 2019.[40] "This scenario does not just move the country back to the situation before the ACA," the report noted.[41] "It moves the country to a situation with higher uninsurance rates than was the case before the ACA reforms."[42]

INITIAL SENATE REACTIONS

When Congress reconvened in January, McConnell promised that repealing the ACA would be the first item that the Senate would consider.[43] Although he had allowed the House Republicans to do the bomb throwing after 2010, McConnell took a back seat to no one in his vehement opposition to Obamacare. In the early morning hours of January 11, just a week after Congress convened, the Senate by a vote of 51–48 had passed a budget resolution, which would be the vehicle to accomplish the repeal of the ACA.[44] In an emotional end to the debate, Senate Democrats kept speaking, one after another, during the roll call. "Ripping apart our health care system—with no plan to replace it—will create chaos," said Patty Murray (D-WA), the senior Democrat on the Health, Education, Labor and Pensions Committee.[45] "If Republicans repeal the Affordable Care Act, it's women, kids, seniors, patients with serious illnesses, and people with disabilities who will bear the burden."[46]

On January 17, the Congressional Budget Office (CBO) estimated that at least eighteen million people would lose their health insurance in the first year if Republicans moved ahead to repeal the ACA without a replacement.[47] Senate Finance Committee chairman Orrin Hatch and House Speaker Paul Ryan each blasted the CBO report as one-sided because it could not calculate the impact of any transitional policies or replacement measures, which did not yet exist.[48]

Several Republicans, led by Susan Collins, who had been a state insurance commissioner, and Bill Cassidy (R-LA), a new senator who was a physician,[49] quickly recognized that "repeal" without "replacement" would outrage and frighten the public, while sending the insurance markets into a "death spiral."[50] But they were nowhere near having a replacement, and the multiple challenges facing them were becoming more evident. Medicaid posed perhaps the knottiest problem. Conservatives had long wanted to turn Medicaid into a block grant, which would cap spending and give states direct control over the program.[51] It was generally understood that the block grants would not be sufficient to cover all those receiving Medicaid at their present level; large cost savings at the expense of the poorest Americans—estimated at $1 to $2 trillion over ten years—were an essential part of the Republican plan to insure other Americans. Steve Daines (R-MT), whose sparsely populated state had sixty thousand new Medicaid recipients because of the ACA, said, "We've got to take care of these folks who have expanded Medicaid."[52]

One of the most striking outcomes of the ACA had been the split between the states over whether to accept the offer of federal funding for those covered by the expansion of Medicaid.[53] Some thirty-one states, including a number with Republican governors, had accepted the ACA offer, while nineteen, largely Republican, had declined to do so.[54] Medicaid had become the nation's largest insurance program, covering sixty-nine million people,[55] or more than one in five Americans. Now the Congress, and particularly the Senate, would face the challenge of finding a way to be fair to both the states that took the expansion and those that decided not to do so.

Former House Speaker John Boehner, driven to retirement by the relentless pressure of the right-wing Freedom Caucus,[56] enjoyed the luxury of speaking his mind. "In the 25 years that I served in the United States Congress, the

Republicans never, ever, one time agreed on what a health care proposal should look like. Not once," Boehner said on February 23.[57] "And all this happy talk about repeal, repeal, repeal . . . if you pass repeal without replace, anything that happens is your fault. You broke it."[58]

THE TORTURED HOUSE CONSIDERATION

Most observers had always assumed that some repeal of the ACA would rocket through the House, and then slow down sharply in the Senate, where a contingent of Republicans would insist on a comprehensive replacement plan before agreeing to repeal. The flurry of Senate Republican meetings, statements, and press releases seemed to confirm that impression. But even House passage had started to look difficult. The relatively few remaining House Republican moderates were opposed to any change that would reduce benefits that their constituents were receiving. Town meetings where angry constituents protested the threat to their health care had left a strong impression on members, just as the Tea Party–dominated town meetings had done in 2010.[59] At the same time, many Freedom Caucus Republicans just favored flat-out repeal, blowing up the system, saving billions of dollars, and forcing people to resort to health spending accounts.[60] The more heated the debate, and the more imminent the threat of repeal, the more popular Obamacare seemed to become. By mid-February, a Pew Research Center poll showed 54 percent approval of the Affordable Care Act, with 43 percent disapproving, a clear shift from just two months before.[61]

By early March, the right-wing forces that had passionately opposed Obamacare for eight years grew tired of waiting. The conservative activist groups founded by the billionaire Koch brothers feared that the Republicans, now controlling all branches of government, were welching on the pledge to repeal Obamacare. "We've been patient this year, but it is past time to act and act decisively," said Tim Phillips, the president of Americans for Prosperity, which took the lead in coordinating the groups across the Koch brothers' political network.[62] "Our network has spent more money, more time and more years fighting Obamacare than anything else. And now with the finish line in sight, we cannot allow some folks to pull up and give up."[63]

Phillips and other group leaders warned that they would rally near the Capitol and send activists to the members' offices. They would track down Republican members and confront them with their quotes calling for repeal. A nationwide digital advertising campaign would begin.[64] They would give failing marks on their influential scorecards to members that opposed them.

They would directly confront Republican leaders Mitch McConnell and Paul Ryan.[65] "This is existential for Republicans," said David McIntosh, the president of the Club for Growth.[66] "If they don't repeal Obamacare and replace it, I don't think they'll stay in the majority in the next election."[67] The Koch brothers called their campaign "You Promised."[68] But it might have also been called "You Owe Us," and "If you don't deliver, we'll get you in the primaries."

The House Republican leaders got the message. Just days later, with great fanfare, the Republican alternative, titled "American Health Care Act," was introduced.[69] The AHCA, as it would be known, bore somewhat more resemblance to Obamacare than expected. Although it eliminated the penalty for people not buying insurance, it substituted a penalty for those who gave up insurance that they had.[70] While eliminating the subsidies to lower-middle-class people for out-of-pocket expenses such as premiums and deductibles, it offered a refundable tax credit to the same people.[71] It would phase out Medicaid expansion starting in 2020,[72] seemingly removing millions of people from the rolls and substituting block grants to the states while allowing them more flexibility in managing the program.[73] The legislation eliminated virtually every tax that had been used to raise the funds needed to pay the benefits, starting with the taxes on medical devices, health insurance premiums, tanning salons, and prescription medicines,[74] but also the 3.8 percent tax on the investment income of high-wealth individuals. It would also delay the tax scheduled to be imposed on high-cost employer-provided insurance, known as "Cadillac plans," until 2025.[75]

Speaker Paul Ryan unveiled the bill in an unusual news conference on cable television, speaking for twenty-three minutes.[76] He said that Republicans faced a "binary choice"—they could vote for the House bill, or they could let the ACA survive.[77] "We have been waiting seven years to do this. This is the closest we will ever come to replacing and repealing Obamacare," Ryan intoned. "The time is here; the time is now. This is the moment."[78]

The House Freedom Caucus was unimpressed. Their leaders quickly leveled three fundamental objections to the bill: that the tax credits it created represented a new government entitlement; that it did not do enough to curtail the ACA's Medicaid expansion; and that it largely left the ACA's insurance coverage mandates intact.[79] The bottom line from the Freedom Caucus to the president, stated with unaccustomed politeness, was: "If you want to reduce costs, this may not do it."[80]

Ryan was obviously seeking to thread the needle; he wanted to produce a bill that would meet his commitment to repeal Obamacare without going so far that he would sacrifice the support of Republican moderates in the Senate and the House. But he also had to satisfy the Koch brothers, the Heritage Foundation, and the right-wing talk radio hosts who had combined to bring down John Boehner and made Ryan's tenure a miserable experience. It quickly became evident that he had failed to do it. The powerful network of right-wing political groups spoke in one harsh voice, condemning Ryan's effort. They threatened to punish Republicans politically for abandoning their repeated promise to repeal Obamacare, root and branch.

Mitch McConnell was probably unsurprised by these developments. He had seen Boehner and Ryan unable to control the Freedom Caucus at virtually every key juncture, no matter how high the stakes. McConnell seemed momentarily unsteady himself, pledging to put the House bill on the Senate floor without any hearings, which angered many members of his own caucus while defeating the purpose of having a Senate.[81] But he recovered quickly, saying that the lawmakers needed to get the CBO estimate of the budgetary impact and the number of insured people that would result.

The Republicans also faced the problem of knowing where President Trump stood. Repealing Obamacare was an obsession of the congressional Republicans; it was not central to Trump's populist campaign based on economic nationalism and border security. Trump had worried Ryan and other repeal advocates with periodic statements that he would not let anyone lose their health care.[82] In a rare admission, Trump, to his credit, acknowledged that health care was an extraordinarily complex subject.[83] Even when Ryan introduced the Republican alternative, fundamental differences seemed to continue. "What we hear from the White House is, this is a work in progress," said Representative Mark Sanford (R–SC). "What we hear from the leadership is, take it or leave it."[84]

But the president and the speaker bridged their differences quickly. Within forty-eight hours, White House press secretary Sean Spicer announced that President Trump supported the American Health Care Act as Speaker Ryan had introduced it—without changes.[85] Faced with an important political decision, Trump had chosen to go with Ryan rather than the Freedom Caucus wing of the party and their financial backers, led by the Koch brothers. They had already taken to mocking the legislation with the harshest description possible, calling it "Ryancare." They were incensed, and particularly upset, that the AHCA phased out the Medicaid expansion beginning in 2020 rather than 2018.

With the president's support and the speaker's control over the House agenda, the House seemed certain to pass the AHCA within a relatively short time. Ryan scheduled a vote for March 24. He faced unanimous Democratic opposition but felt confident that he could win the vote by limiting Republican defections.[86] Stunningly, Ryan's assessment proved incorrect. The thirty members of the Freedom Caucus refused to accept the bill,[87] and Ryan could not move toward their position without losing some Republican moderates.

The day before the scheduled vote, Ryan, knowing that he did not have the votes, shocked Washington and the country by announcing that the AHCA would not come to the floor.[88] The stinging defeat for Ryan also constituted a major blow to Trump, who had lobbied intensively for the bill. The failure undercut his claims to be a great negotiator and closer.[89]

Experienced political observers could not recall a similarly embarrassing debacle. When Ryan pulled the bill, polls showed that it had the support of 17 percent of Americans.[90] Many predicted that the president and the speaker would move on to other potentially more popular parts of their agenda, such as tax reform and infrastructure.[91] But the Republicans had made repeal of the ACA the rallying cry for their base for seven long years. Now controlling all branches of government, the Republicans faced significant risk if they could not deliver on their central promise. Ryan and the White House went back to work and made the bill more attractive to the Freedom Caucus, despite the risk that it would cost them the support of the dwindling number of House Republican moderates.[92]

On May 4, by a vote of 217–213, the House resurrected the AHCA, taking the first step to redeem the pledge to remake the American health care system without mandated insurance coverage.[93] The far-reaching legislation, as promised, abolished the individual mandate requiring Americans to purchase insurance or pay a penalty.[94] It allowed insurers to offer health plans with higher deductibles and copayments.[95] Customers in states that waived benefit rules could buy plans that covered fewer medical services. Insurers could price their products to provide lower prices to younger people without preexisting conditions. But the bill imposed significant additional costs on the insurance for older customers—a sixty-four-year-old might have to pay five times the cost of what an eighteen-year-old was paying.

The bill would also cut back substantially on federal funding for state Medicaid programs while giving the states only limited flexibility in how they managed them. Many states would be expected to roll back the expansion of Medicaid to cover childless adults without disabilities, and the bill would reduce subsidies to those Americans just over the poverty line, the group that benefited most from Obamacare's subsidies. In perhaps the most controversial provisions, the bill would allow states to waive rules requiring plans to have minimum essential benefits and rules that prohibit insurance companies from charging higher prices for customers who have major preexisting illnesses—or even minor diseases. According to the Congressional Budget Office (CBO), poor Americans were much more likely to become uninsured under the bill, and those who retained coverage would pay more in premiums and deductibles.

The House Republicans and the Trump administration had given new meaning to the words *catastrophic health care*. Empowered by President Trump's election, the House Republicans went beyond their irresponsible demagoguery about the ACA to reckless action. The extreme nature of the legislation produced what the *New York Times* called "a rare unifying moment" as doctors, hospitals, insurers, and consumer groups all expressed immediate, vehement opposition.[96] "It raises the specter that the sickest and neediest among us will be disproportionately hit in losing access," said Paul Markovich, the CEO of Blue Cross of California.[97] "This is not a reform," said Michael J. Dowling, chief executive of Northwell Health, a large health system in New York. "This is just a debacle."[98]

The AHCA richly deserved to be buried, and never seen again. But inaction was not an acceptable option. Premiums and deductibles under the ACA were rising.[99] Uncertainty about the ACA's future was causing insurers to abandon the marketplace, leaving some communities with only one insurance option and others with none.[100] Moreover, the success of the ACA depended on good faith implementation, including a strong effort by HHS to advertise and attract new subscribers. Trump and HHS Secretary Price seemed to relish the fact that they had the power to undermine the ACA and try to blame its failure on Obama.[101] The ACA's "death spiral," which House Republicans loved to portray, was not yet happening, and was by no means inevitable, but ACA's diehard opponents could produce it.[102]

BALL IN THE SENATE'S COURT

The Senate would face the challenge of shaping America's health care landscape for the foreseeable future. Some of the country's savviest politicians are in the Senate; even before the House vote, the questions of what to do about Obamacare had already brought the Senate Republicans to life. A complex policy issue, of great consequence to millions of Americans, with potentially dramatic political impact—it was hard to remember an issue that quickly engaged so many senators. Susan Collins, Bill Cassidy, Lisa Murkowski, Rob Portman, Corey Gardner, Chuck Grassley, Orrin Hatch, and Lamar Alexander floated alternative bills and ideas. Tom Cotton of Arkansas, extremely conservative on national security issues, showed a more liberal side as he critiqued the House product. In the style of the times, Cotton tweeted: "Start over. Get it right. Don't get it fast."[103]

The Senate Republicans responded immediately to the House vote. A group of senators, led by Lamar Alexander, chairman of the aptly named HELP committee (Health, Education, Labor and Pensions), quickly expressed the view that the Senate would write its own legislation, and would take the time needed to do it well.[104] Senators always enjoy being the responsible adults in the room compared to the rambunctious lower House, and certainly, Speaker Ryan and his colleagues had made that conceit easy enough to maintain in this case.

Collins and Cassidy quickly launched a bipartisan effort. In mid-May, half a dozen Republicans, including Graham, Dean Heller (R-NV), Dan Sullivan (R-AK), and Shelley Moore Capito (R-WV) sat down for an initial meeting with three moderate Democrats—Joe Manchin (D-WV), Heidi Heitkamp (D-ND), and Joe Donnelly (D-IN).[105] The senators expressed their understanding that a strictly partisan solution would not work. "I don't think there's a Democrat that would vote for any type of repeal," said Manchin.[106] "But I think there would be forty-eight Democrats who are willing to work on some repairing or fixing."[107] Heitkamp noted: "The [GOP] language is: This is spiraling out of control. I don't believe that. But I came here to repair the health care law and make it more workable, and that's my job."[108]

The senators were cautiously, even somewhat impishly, aware that they were acting independently, and perhaps at cross purposes, from their more partisan leaders. "I am complimented that you think Cassidy-Collins can rival Mitch McConnell in terms of political oomph," Cassidy said with a grin.[109] "But I think the leader is the guy who has most of the cards here."[110] A GOP leadership aide said that "senators don't need permission slips to meet on this subject or any subject."[111] But there were plenty of Republican senators who remembered that when their colleagues had cautiously stepped forward to explore bipartisanship on health care and financial regulation, McConnell had, not so subtly, cut them off at the knees. They also knew that McConnell hated the ACA, and left to his own devices he would favor full repeal. For their part, the Democrats understood that Schumer wanted a caucus united against repeal of the ACA and would look skeptically at any bipartisan agreement that compromised that position.[112]

Despite the public backlash against the House-passed legislation, the Trump administration escalated its war on the health care of Americans. The Trump budget, released on May 23, carried forward the massive Medicaid cuts—$800 billion over ten years—originally found in the House health care bill.[113] The budget, prepared by OMB director Mick Mulvaney, a leading deficit hawk, clearly rejected the urging by some Senate Republicans to avoid major Medicaid cuts.[114] The budget also included significant cuts in the Children's Health Insurance Program (CHIP), legislation with enormous bipartisan support on the Hill, prompting an immediate objection from Finance Committee chairman Orrin Hatch.[115] At the same time, the administration, led by HHS Secretary Price, continued to do nothing that would reduce uncertainty in the insurance markets, which were causing insurers to leave many markets or raise premiums and deductibles significantly.[116]

The fate of the health care system touched countless millions of Americans and affected one-sixth of the American economy. The complexity of the health care issues cried out for a serious legislative process, starting with hearings that allowed a broad range of affected interests to express their views on the successes and failings of the ACA and the wisdom of possible approaches to repealing or fixing the system. The House-passed legislation was deeply unpopular across the country, potentially posing enormous political risks to Republicans in the 2018 elections. It seemed obvious that only a bipartisan approach to the issue could produce a successful legislative result and minimize the political danger to the Republicans.

McCONNELL'S FATEFUL DECISION

McConnell took the opposite course. He decided that the Senate would act on a strictly partisan basis. Recognizing the unpopularity of the House legislation, he would seek to fashion a somewhat better bill that could unite the Senate Republican caucus. He had even less room to work than Ryan had, because he would need fifty of the fifty-two Senate Republicans to pass the legislation by using the reconciliation process.[117] Yet he needed legislation that could bridge the divide within the caucus to command the support of moderates like Susan Collins, Lisa Murkowski, Rob Portman, and Shelley Moore Capito, as well as his "Freedom Caucus" faction—Rand Paul, Ted Cruz, Mike Lee, and Ron Johnson. He would also be trying to find a consensus on an issue that was frightening and angering much of the country.

McConnell formed a task force of thirteen Republican senators to produce a Senate bill. He chose to exclude all five women in the Republican caucus, even though three of them—Collins, Murkowski, and Capito—had already shown deep interest in the health issue.[118] "The leaders have a right to choose whoever they wish," Collins said stiffly. "It doesn't mean that I'm not going to work on health care."[119] McConnell's process envisioned no hearings, no committee action, and in fact, very little public exposure of the legislation being cobbled together.[120] Speed and stealth were of the essence, making it clear that the majority leader hoped to ram the legislation through before affected constituencies could review it and rally against it.[121]

It was an astonishing approach. Experienced observers could think of no case when the Senate had dispensed with hearings on a major issue, and no issue affected more Americans than this one. Republican senators had sometimes chafed at McConnell's discipline before but ultimately had gone along. They understood the need for a strong leader in an intensely partisan period.

They recognized McConnell's political ability, and they owed their subcommittee and committee chairmanships in large part to his legislative victories and political strategies. But it was one thing to follow the leader in a partisan fight; here he was asking his caucus to fall in line to support legislation that would do grave harm to millions of their constituents.

McConnell promised a discussion draft would be released on June 22, and he expressed his intention to have the Senate vote before the July 4 recess, giving senators just a few days to assess the bill that he produced.[122] "If the Republicans continue down this path, ignoring the principles of transparency and open debate that define this legislative body, we Democrats will continue to do everything we can to shine a light on what our Republican friends are doing," Chuck Schumer said on the Senate floor.[123]

But increasingly, Republican senators were also pushing back, going public with their concerns and anger about the process and the substance of the legislation. "Do you know what the health care bill looks like?" Murkowski asked reporters.[124] "Because I don't." John McCain criticized the "terrible process" every chance he got. Mike Lee, part of the thirteen-man task force, said that he did not know what was in it. "It's not been written by us," Senator Lee noted. "It's apparently been written by a small handful of staffers in the Republican leadership."[125]

The discussion "draft," released on June 22, satisfied virtually no one's concerns. Compared to the House bill, it did delay the phase-out of the expansion of Medicaid and preserved protections for patients with preexisting conditions. But to mollify the conservatives, McConnell had made even deeper cuts in the growth of Medicaid spending and generally followed the broad outline of the House bill by ending the individual mandate.[126] The bill's prospects, already dim, worsened when the CBO estimated that twenty-two million more people would be uninsured over a decade than under the current law.[127]

Collins was the first and most vocal dissenter: she opposed the bill, continued her outreach to Democrats, and noted that she was sure that Mitch had "done his best" but that she would have handled it differently.[128] Dean Heller (R-NV), probably the Republican most vulnerable in 2018, joined with Nevada's Republican governor Brian Sandoval in denouncing the bill for the harm it would inflict on Nevadans.[129] Portman and Capito expressed deep concern about the massive cuts in Medicaid spending.[130] At the same time, Rand Paul and Ron Johnson opposed the bill as containing too little reform; Paul called it "Obamacare-lite."[131]

With pressure building, McConnell, always tough and unflappable, startled his caucus by dressing down Rob Portman, chiding him for abandoning the commitment to entitlement reform that he had shown as OMB director for George W. Bush.[132] While McConnell's working group labored unsuccessfully, countless patient groups, health care providers, and retirees mobilized furiously against the bill. Key Republican governors, led by Sandoval and John Kasich, nationally known from his presidential campaign, joined their Democrat counterparts in opposing drastic changes in Medicaid.[133] Although Republican whip Cornyn tried to impose discipline by saying that there would be a vote before recess,[134] McConnell, recognizing the number of defections he was facing, wisely decided not to move forward.[135]

The July 4 recess produced widespread press coverage about Republican senators opting out of traditional holiday events to avoid enraged constituents.[136] Jerry Moran (R–KS), a mainstream Republican loyalist, braved a town meeting and announced that he could not support the legislation as written.[137] He called for "a national debate that includes legislative hearings. . . . It needs to be less politics and more policy."[138] John Hoeven (R–ND) made a similar statement.[139] Each time a senator went public with a statement of nonsupport or opposition, it emboldened others. Ten Republican senators wrote to McConnell, asking him to shorten the August recess to give the Senate time to accomplish something.[140] When the Senate returned to Washington on July 11, press reports speculated whether McConnell could hold the last few votes he needed. In fact, he did not seem to be within shouting distance of fifty votes. Relatively few Republicans had declared themselves in favor of the bill.

Assessing the debacle, political reporters mused that McConnell had no real background in major policy; his formidable streak of victories took the form of obstructing Democratic initiatives, or engineering eleventh-hour, "split the difference" compromises to avert disaster.[141] It was certainly true that health care was extraordinarily complex, and that McConnell received little help from an erratic, uninformed president who celebrated the passage of the House bill but later called it "mean."[142]

But the blame for this legislative malpractice fell squarely on the majority leader. McConnell, the supposed institutionalist, disregarded every traditional aspect of legislating in the Senate, and every commitment he had made about restoring "regular order." He railed against Obamacare for being done on a partisan basis, but Obama had reached out to key Republicans before McConnell made it plain that cooperation was verboten. The Affordable Care Act was the product of thirty-six hearings where two hundred witnesses, representing every conceivable interest, had testified.[143] McConnell's obsession with repealing Obamacare and his desire for a Republican victory seemingly blinded him to the magnitude of the issue and the threat posed to Republican senators. During his long reign as leader, McConnell had routinely sacrificed the Senate to accomplish his partisan objectives. But previously, he never had sacrificed Republican senators.

Even as he continued the seemingly futile quest of looking for a bill that could unite Senate Republicans, McConnell searched for a workable "Plan

B." He startled observers with a frank admission that it might be necessary to "shore up" the ACA.[144] "If my side is unable to agree on an adequate replacement, then some kind of action with regard to the private insurance market must occur," McConnell said in a speech in Kentucky.[145] "No action is not an alternative. We've got the insurance markets imploding all over the country."[146] Minority leader Schumer quickly called McConnell's statement "encouraging" and said his caucus "is eager to work with Republicans to stabilize the markets and improve the law. At the top of the list should be ensuring cost-sharing payments are permanent, which will protect health care for millions."[147]

On July 11, McConnell announced that the Senate would be giving up two weeks of its August recess, which would provide more time to work on legislation and save his members from having to face their angry constituents.[148] Refusing to admit defeat, McConnell found an improbable ally—Ted Cruz. They had crossed swords repeatedly since Cruz came to the Senate,[149] and McConnell did not forget that Cruz had accused him of "lying" on the Senate floor.[150] But Cruz had devised a new amendment that would allow insurers to offer plans that do not comply with the requirements of the ACA as long as they offered one plan that did.[151] Cruz had credibility with the right wing, and his amendment would satisfy a central demand from conservatives to increase consumer choice.[152] But Douglas Holtz-Eakin, a respected former CBO director and a Republican, predicted that the Cruz amendment would send the young, healthy people who are cheaper to cover into one insurance pool, and leave sicker, older people "in a glorified high-risk pool. . . . If the public policy goal is to give people access to affordable insurance options, there's a set of people who would just not have access to that."[153]

It was difficult to envision the Cruz amendment persuading any of the Republican moderates to drop their opposition to McConnell's bill, but it offered the possibility of new life to McConnell's effort. At the same time, Cornyn announced that two of the tax increases on wealthy individuals, which had been used to pay for the ACA but had been eliminated by the House bill, would be restored in the Senate bill.[154] McConnell continued to tinker with his bill, twisting the dials to see if he could put together fifty votes, which still seemed like an unattainable goal. He again stated his intention to put his bill before the Senate, in essence forcing his Republican senators to a "binary choice"—pass our bill, or be forced to work with Democrats.

COLLAPSE OF McCONNELL'S EFFORT

The thin ice on which McConnell skated, melting for weeks, broke in mid-July when Jerry Moran and Mike Lee joined Collins and Paul in opposing the legislation. On July 17, McConnell conceded that "the effort to repeal and immediately replace[155] the failure of Obamacare will not be successful." He said that he would ask the Senate to vote on repealing the ACA now and work on a replacement over the next two years. That course of action seemed surprising; McConnell would never compound his failure by forcing his caucus to cast a vote that would be so damaging to so many members. Of course, it was possible that he would bring up the bill knowing it would lose, allowing each Republican senator to vote as he or she judged it in their best interest.

Republican senators continued to express anger about the process. McCain, in Arizona recovering from serious surgery on a blood clot above his eye, soon to be diagnosed as brain cancer, called for a "return to regular order," to craft a health care bill by holding hearings and working with Democrats. "We should not be making fundamental changes[156] in a vital safety net program which has been on the books for 50 years without having a single hearing to evaluate what the consequences are going to be," Collins said. Jennifer Steinhauer of the *New York Times* observed: "Without hearings, committee work or a public drafting of the bill[157]—all marks of the original health care law—members on both sides of the [Republican] divide felt bruised and left out."

ONE LAST ATTEMPT

Having seemingly admitted defeat, within days McConnell surprisingly regrouped to mount an enormous, all-out effort. He probably concluded that he had no alternative. President Trump was goading Senate Republicans to step up and repeal the ACA. Paul Ryan, hardly a strong leader, had managed to get a bill through the House. And of course, McConnell himself deeply opposed the ACA and understood that powerful forces in the Republican Party detested it. No one could have fully predicted the drama of the days that would follow.

On Tuesday, July 25, John McCain, whose surgery to remove a blood clot above the eye had led to a diagnosis of incurable brain cancer, returned to the Senate to participate in the health care issue. It was a moment of wrenching emotion on the Senate floor when the senators from both parties greeted their returning colleague. It reminded many senators of a similar experience when they greeted Ted Kennedy, the last Senate giant, who returned to the chamber after a similar diagnosis.

With almost every senator in the chamber, McCain challenged his colleagues to return the Senate[158] to what it had been in its better days. Having repeatedly criticized the "terrible" process that McConnell had imposed to produce his health care bill, McCain broadened his comments, reflecting on the increasingly partisan, tribal, and fractured nature of the Senate. Noting that the Senate was once routinely described as the "greatest deliberative body in the world," McCain observed that Senate "has not been overwhelmed by greatness lately . . . We've been spinning our wheels on too many important issues because we keep trying to win without help from across the aisle," McCain said. "We're getting nothing done, my friends. . . . Both sides have let this happen." He cited the vital importance of the Senate to the country and the need for bipartisan cooperation. Describing the challenges of governing our country, McCain talked about the importance of things other than winning: "incremental progress," "compromise," and "just muddling through" to solve problems. Returning to the health care debate, he predicted that the current effort would fail, and after it did, he hoped for a return to "regular order"—legislating through hearings and a thoughtful committee progress. Describing the bill that would be coming before the Senate, McCain said, in a staccato fashion: "I will not vote for this legislation as it is today."

It was a moving and thoughtful speech about the Senate, at an emotional moment. Nevertheless, later that evening, McConnell managed to persuade fifty out of fifty-two Republican senators,[159] losing only Susan Collins and Lisa Murkowski, to support a motion to proceed to consider health care legislation. When Vice President Mike Pence, sitting in the chair of the Senate, broke the tie, McConnell won a major victory, and the Senate would finally move to debate the merits of health care legislation. McCain surprised many observers by voting for the motion to proceed, having so sharply condemned the process and the legislation. He would contend, however, that he was only allowing debate to begin, and a vigorous amendment process to begin. The Republican effort to repeal the ACA, and the threat to the health care of millions of Americans, was still very much alive.

Later that evening, McConnell brought to the floor his most complete version of a plan[160] to repeal and replace the Affordable Care Act. Worked out behind closed doors, the new bill would dismantle major parts of the ACA, including the requirement that most people have health insurance. It offered concession to the conservatives by including the Cruz amendment and one to the moderates by including $100 billion to help pay out-of-pocket medical costs for low-income people, as a partial offset to the drastic reductions in Medicaid. Because the Congressional Budget Office had not yet assessed the bill, it needed sixty votes to overcome a Democratic objection that it violated Senate rules. It received only forty-three votes, as nine Republicans opposed it. Even after weeks of work, McConnell was not close to holding his caucus together.

On Wednesday, the majority leader tried again,[161] this time offering a measure to repeal major parts of the Affordable Care Act without offering a replacement. The Senate approved this approach in 2015, when everyone knew that President Obama would veto the legislation. Now, however, with President Trump ready to sign such a bill, many Senate Republicans justifiably feared that they would be leaving millions of Americans without any certainty that their health care would continue. Repeal without replacement garnered only forty-five votes, with seven Republicans voting against it.

The stakes could not have been larger, and emotions were running high. Many progressives, led by Paul Krugman,[162] castigated McCain for supporting the motion to proceed, and McConnell's first two bills, despite his memorable speech the previous day. Senator Murkowski denounced a heavy-handed effort by the Interior Secretary Ryan Zinke to pressure her by threatening to withhold Interior Department funds that would ordinarily go to Alaska.

McConnell had one more arrow in his legislative quiver. With the Senate having twice rejected large-scale repeal, McConnell cobbled together a "skinny repeal," an eight-page piece of legislation that abolished the mandates for individuals and employers to buy insurance, as well as some of the taxes that funded the ACA. The "skinny repeal" immediately drew scathing criticism[163] from McCain, Lindsey Graham, and Ron Johnson. Graham called it a "disaster" and a "fraud" and said he could only vote for it if Speaker Ryan guaranteed that the House would not approve it and that much different legislation would emerge from conference. The Republican health care drive had come full circle, with the original plan—the Senate somehow improving the disastrous House bill—a distant memory. Ryan hesitated, then offered the requisite assurance, giving McConnell the votes of Graham and Johnson.

Events conspired to make Thursday, July 27,[164] one of the most memorable nights in Senate history, when a decision of great political consequence combined with a moment of extraordinary emotional impact. Earlier in the day, McConnell and the Republican leadership team believed that they could count on McCain's vote for the "skinny repeal." But at lunchtime, McCain came into McConnell's office in the Capitol and warned Cornyn: "Don't count on me as a yes." McCain later received calls from two of his closest Democratic friends: former senator Joseph Lieberman and former vice president Joe Biden, urging him to oppose the bill. Throughout the day, the Republican leaders received varying reports about McCain's intentions, leaving them genuinely uncertain about where he would come down.

The Senate worked late into the night. Around midnight, McCain came to the floor and had a brief conversation with Chuck Schumer that left the Democratic leader smiling. "I knew it when he came on the floor," Schumer later recounted, saying that McCain had called earlier to share his plans. McCain took a seat next to Graham, and when Murkowski walked up, he gave her a "thumbs down," signaling his intention. McConnell dispatched Jeff Flake, Arizona's junior senator, to try to persuade his senior colleague, but McCain continued to confer with Collins and Murkowski. At that point, Vice President Pence left the chair to talk to McCain, Collins, and Murkowski. Pence's effort to persuade went on for more than twenty minutes.

"You could see the body language in the entire chamber change in two hours," David Perdue (R-GA) said. "One side was kind of ebullient, moving around and talking, and the other side was subdued, and all of a sudden it began to change. There was an instinctive reaction that maybe this thing wasn't going to pass. Nobody knew for sure."

At 1:10 a.m., McCain finally brought an end to the uncertainty. He crossed the chamber to talk to several Democrats. Fully aware that he was the center of attention, McCain told them he was afraid the press watching from the gallery could read his lips. He looked up and shouted "no," as the senators and reporters laughed.

The vote started at 1:24 a.m. McCain was out in the lobby, again conferring with Pence. At 1:29 a.m, he returned to the floor, approached the desk, and gave a thumbs down, providing the decisive third vote, making the final vote 51–49 against the "skinny repeal." McConnell, tight lipped and face flushed, took the floor to offer an understated observation: "This is clearly a disappointing moment." He then criticized the Democrats for not participating in a process from which they had been completely excluded.

THE AFTERMATH

Actually, it was a seismic moment, with political and policy repercussions that were incalculable but likely to be enormous. The Republicans' seven-year campaign to repeal the Affordable Care Act had finally failed. Although President Trump immediately began pressing the Senate to try again, Senator McConnell made it clear that he planned to move on to other issues, such as the urgent need to raise the debt ceiling and working on tax reform, which was a Trump administration priority. In fact, McConnell would try once more in September, but the Graham-Cassidy bill did not come to vote after many Republicans expressed opposition.[165]

Within days, Lamar Alexander and Patty Murray, the chairman and ranking member of the Senate HELP committee, announced their plan[166] for a series of hearings in early September to produce legislation to "stabilize and strengthen" the individual insurance markets. Alexander emphasized that the work would be bipartisan, and that the hearings would feature a broad range of health policy experts, including state insurance commissioners, patient groups, and insurance industry representatives. He also noted that he had urged President Trump to continue paying for the ACA's cost-sharing subsidies through

September to give Congress time to fashion a stabilization plan that would include one year of funding for the payments. These suggestions responded directly to Trump's threats to end the cost-sharing subsidy, which would drive up premiums and could prompt insurers to flee many markets entirely.

In short, Chairman Alexander proposed to do what the Senate should have done in the beginning of the year: hold hearings to identify the positive features and the shortcomings of the ACA, and craft bipartisan legislation to stabilize the insurance markets, safeguarding and improving health care for millions of Americans. The Republican obsession with repealing the ACA made that approach unacceptable to Speaker Ryan and Majority Leader McConnell, who were deeply invested in the issue, and President Trump, who had not been. Together, they wasted months, inflamed and paralyzed the Congress, and put the country through an unnecessary ordeal. How many Americans found themselves living in fear, confronting what seemed to be the imminent threat of losing their health care?

The "blame game" for the Republican debacle began quickly. On August 7, McConnell made a speech in Louisville[167] in which he observed that President Trump, who "has not been in this line of work," had "excessive expectations" about the speed with which Congress could pass major legislation. This matter-of-fact observation enraged the thin-skinned president. In a series of tweets and press statements, Trump lashed out at McConnell[168] for his failure, even suggesting that if he could not deliver on major issues, he should step down as leader. Trump's extraordinary attack on his most important legislative ally probably pleased many of his supporters, who thought that the Republican congressional leaders were part of the "swamp" that needed to be "drained." But it was a strikingly shortsighted move by the president who would need all of McConnell's experience and good will if he was to accomplish anything legislatively and hope to contain the impact of the Russia investigations. Trump's intemperate words undoubtedly strengthened McConnell in the Senate Republican caucus, where nearly twenty Republican senators quickly leaped to his defense.[169] Orrin Hatch, the longest-serving Republican, outdid his colleagues[170] by praising McConnell as the most effective leader with whom he had ever served, breaking with the conventional wisdom about Howard Baker and Bob Dole.

In fact, there was blame enough for both the president and the majority leader. McConnell surely believed, accurately, that Trump—unfocused and ignorant about the substance of health care issues—failed to provide any useful help in a major political battle where presidential leadership was essential. Trump's failure to engage contrasted starkly from the energy and commitment that Obama showed in fighting for the Affordable Care Act, and Obama was no Lyndon Johnson when it came to legislative battles. Every congressional Republican watched with chagrin as Trump celebrated the passage of the House health care bill in May only to turn around and pronounce it "mean" in June.

But McConnell failed Trump in a very fundamental way. The neophyte president needed the wise counsel of the veteran majority leader, particularly given the inexperience and chaos of the Trump White House. McConnell should have understood that it is much more difficult to take away a benefit once given (not unlike a tax cut, as the Democrats had repeatedly discovered). He should have known very early on that it would not be possible to hold fifty of his fifty-two Republican senators together to repeal and replace the Affordable Care Act. McConnell could have counseled Trump, who came to office as a populist insurgent who did not emphasize health care, to find a different road forward. One of McConnell's guiding principles, which he demonstrated brilliantly during the Obama years, is that the party in power gets blamed for things that go wrong. Consequently, he should have been looking for a bipartisan approach. If an Obamacare fix proved popular, the Republicans could claim the credit. If it proved unpopular because of increased premiums and deductibles, or the insurance markets crashed anyway, the Democrats would share the blame. Trump did not get the caliber of advice from McConnell that Jimmy Carter received from Robert Byrd, or Ronald Reagan got from Howard Baker. McConnell's fixation with repealing the ACA blinded him to the political realities and the human costs and caused him to overreach.

McConnell was straightforward about his principal objective: "My view is that the Medicaid per capita cap with a reasonable growth rate that is sustainable for taxpayers is the most important long-term reform in the bill. That is why it has been in each draft of the bill that we have released." The growth of federal spending on health care is unsustainable. In 2016, federal health care spending totaled $1.2 trillion, which was 31 percent of the federal budget of $3.85 trillion—twice as much as defense spending ($593 billion) and significantly more than Social Security outlays ($913 billion). Our country is still at the front end of the "baby boom" retirements, with longevity continuing to increase. Very hard policy choices remain ahead. But Congress will make those choices, if at all, only through a process where all interests are fully and fairly considered—the exact opposite of the process that McConnell had inflicted on the Senate and the country.

Senator McConnell understands how the Senate, at its best, is supposed to work. Speaking on January 8, 2014, with the memory of Harry Reid's use of the "nuclear option" still fresh, McConnell described how he would work to restore the Senate if he was fortunate enough to become majority leader. "The best mechanism we have for working through our differences and arriving at a durable consensus is the Senate," McConnell stated. "An executive order can't do it. The fiat of a nine-person court can't do it. A raucous and precarious partisan majority in the House can't do it. . . . This is what the Senate is supposed to be all about, and almost always has been."

In McConnell's view, the Senate had lost a "vigorous committee process" and a "robust amendment process" that was central to its operation. The committees had traditionally provided substantive expertise, and "the committees have served as a school for bipartisanship. By the time a bill got through committee, you could expect it to come in a form that was acceptable to both sides." Sharply criticizing Reid and the "activist president," McConnell decried the fact that "major legislation is now routinely drafted not in committee but in the majority leader's conference room and then dropped on the floor with little or no opportunity for members to participate in the amendment process."

Reviewing the history of enormous legislative accomplishments, including Medicare and Medicaid, he noted that they had received, and earned, bipartisan support. "None of this happened by throwing these bills together in the backroom and then dropping them on the floor with a stopwatch running," he caustically observed. "The real problem is an attitude that views the Senate as an assembly line for one party's partisan agenda. . . . Without meaningful buy-in, you guarantee a food fight. You guarantee instability and strife."

McConnell invoked Mike Mansfield as the Senate leader he most admired; and he condemned Lyndon Johnson for his "heavy-handedness" and his "iron-fisted rule"; and he concluded, mixing humility and plain speaking: "Both sides will have to work to get us back to where we should be. It won't happen overnight. We're all out of practice. . . . But restoring this institution is the only way we'll ever solve the challenges we face. That's the lesson of history and experience."

It was a terrific speech, given at a time when the Senate, and the country, needed to hear it. But in preparing the "Better Care Reconciliation Act," which would affect the health and security of millions of Americans, McConnell disregarded everything that he had said, and that he knew, about how the Senate should work.

Mitch McConnell's effort to write a bill radically revamping the health care system and ram it through the Senate without hearings or committee consideration showed just how far the leader-driven Senate had degenerated. Fortunately, his effort failed, thanks to the steadfastness of Susan Collins and Lisa Murkowski and the ultimately decisive vote of Senator McCain. But it is deeply disturbing that McConnell came very close to pulling it off. In mid-July, when McConnell seemed to acknowledge defeat, the Senate appeared to be performing admirably. Many Republican senators were dismayed and angry about both the legislative process and the legislative product. McConnell faced defections from both his moderates and his Freedom Caucus wing. The senators were pushing back, exercising independent judgment; it seemed to mark the moment at which the Senate began to reset the balance between the leader and the other senators. What appeared to be the emphatic rejection of an indefensible bill and an indefensible process augured well for the future of the Senate.

Just ten days later, the picture looked much different. Senator McConnell asked the members of his caucus to fall on a grenade, and all but three of them did. Notwithstanding the disgraceful process and the deeply unpopular product, the Senate came within a vote of passing legislation that would have gone to conference with the House, where almost anything would have been possible. Under the circumstances, it is possible to feel grateful for the outcome but still be troubled about how the Senate had performed. Hopefully, the bipartisan efforts led by senators Alexander and Murray will allow the Senate to redeem itself.

· 12 ·

America versus the World

$\mathcal{O}$n the July 4th weekend, while most senators were home for holiday events or hiding from constituents enraged about McConnell's health care bill, senators John McCain, Lindsey Graham, Elizabeth Warren, Sheldon Whitehouse, and David Perdue were in Afghanistan, eating dinner with our troops and meeting with Afghan civilian and military leaders. From Kabul, they issued a call for President Trump to fill vacant embassy and State Department positions to help Afghanistan meet its mounting military and political challenges.[1] It was a powerful reminder that senators, and the Senate, have played a vital role in America's foreign policy and national security.

For the Senate, the bitter debate over the Gorsuch nomination, the ramping up of the Senate Intelligence Committee's investigation into Russia's interference in the presidential election, and the pitched battle over the Affordable Care Act were destined to take center stage for most of 2017. But the Trump presidency presented a more basic, fundamental challenge to the Senate and the country. Donald Trump came to office with a commitment to change America's relationship to the world that had developed since World War II. If the president meant what he said and got his way, America would no longer be open to immigrants, would no longer champion open trade, and would walk away from our international environmental commitments.

"America First," a phrase with an unfortunate history, melding isolationism, protectionism, nationalism, and a whiff of fascism, provided the connecting thread to Trump's approach to many international issues. Trump's first nine months in office showed that it was not just campaign rhetoric. The Senate faced the question of whether it would allow the president to single-handedly remake America's place in the world.

The modern Senate has played a strong role in America's foreign policy. The senators considered themselves powerful voices on both America's policies and America's values.[2] The Senate's record had many blemishes, from the Tonkin Gulf resolution in 1964, which President Lyndon Johnson misused to escalate the Vietnam War, to authorizing the invasion of Iraq in 2002. But the Senate pushed back against the Vietnam policies of Johnson and Richard Nixon and held Ronald Reagan accountable for selling arms to Iran and using the proceeds to fund the Nicaraguan contras. The Senate played an important role in the legislative efforts to sanction apartheid in South Africa and account for loose nuclear weapons after the fall of the Soviet empire. The Senate approved the Panama Canal treaties, and found a way to establish relations between the United States and China while still maintaining our friendship with Taiwan.

Even though the Senate had slipped far from its peak of influence, Americans would expect the Senate not to allow a new president to redefine America's relationship with the world unilaterally. That applied to any president, but it applied in spades to a president who had no relevant experience that provided grounding for his often radical and always shifting views. In the early months of the Trump presidency, the Senate, and the individual senators, were outspoken about Trump's punitive travel ban and immigration policies; they were low key but influential in reacting to Trump's protectionist trade policy and were largely missing in action on Trump's historic decision to withdraw the United States from the Paris Agreement on climate change.

IMMIGRATION AND BORDER SECURITY

Although immigrants built America, the assimilation process has never been easy. Our history is marked by periods of fear, and even hatred, for people who are different from the majority population. Donald Trump tapped into those emotions and exacerbated them when he described illegal immigrants from Mexico as criminals, rapists, and drug dealers.[3] No campaign pledge of Donald Trump's resonated more loudly than his pledge to "build a beautiful wall" on the southern border and have Mexico pay for it.[4] Trump also capitalized on the fear of terrorist attacks on the homeland to support a ban on immigrants and refugees from primarily Muslim countries.[5] Trump reinforced his commitment to tough action when he chose Jeff Sessions, the fiercest opponent of immigration in the Senate, to be his attorney general. No one doubted that a harsh policy would be forthcoming.[6]

In declaring this two-front war, Trump ignored the facts that: the number of immigrants crossing the border from Mexico had declined sharply[7]; the

Obama administration had deported approximately four hundred thousand illegal immigrants who had committed crimes[8]; and the number of refugees from the Middle East entering the United States was negligible, and overwhelmingly mothers and children.[9]

On Friday, January 27, just one week after taking the oath of office, President Trump signed an executive order to block entry from seven Muslim-majority nations—Syria, Iraq, Iran, Sudan, Libya, Somalia, and Yemen—and restrict travel by legal U.S. permanent residents and citizens with dual nationalities.[10] The executive order banned refugees from resettling in the United States for 120 days, and those from Syria indefinitely.

To a nation already divided, angry and fearful because of Trump's campaign and his dark and uncompromising inaugural address, the travel ban hit with stunning force. The badly implemented executive order caused passenger chaos at airports[11]; protests from many citizens, the Council on American-Islamic Relations, the American Civil Liberties Union, and religious organizations; and dissent from nearly one thousand State Department diplomats. Many Americans were appalled that the travel ban targeted one religious group, raising fundamental constitutional questions. The travel ban faced immediate legal challenges across the country and received intense public attention.

While the Senate took no immediate legislative action, many senators spoke out quickly against the executive order. Democrats were united in their condemnation; many joined their angry constituents in demonstrations around the country. Tom Carper (D-DE), a usually low-key progressive who served on the Homeland Security and Governmental Affairs Committee, ripped Trump for executive action to "deny refuge to thousands of Syrians seeking asylum from the hellacious conditions of civil war. . . . I believe these actions wrongfully vilify a group of people on the basis of their religion and nationality, and jeopardize our nation's ability to lead the world with moral clarity."[12]

However, many Republicans were also dismayed and angry. John McCain and Lindsey Graham, working together as they frequently do, stated: "Our government has a responsibility to defend our borders, but we must do so in a way that makes us safer and upholds all that is decent and exceptional about our nation." Noting that the executive order was not properly vetted, they went on forcefully:

> We should not stop green-card holders from returning to the country they call home. We should not stop those who have served as interpreters for our military and diplomats from seeking refuge in the country they risked their lives to help. And we should not turn our backs on those refugees who have shown through extensive vetting to have done no demonstrable harm to our nation, and who have suffered unspeakable horrors, most of them women and children.[13]

The feisty Republican mavericks were not alone. Jeff Flake protested that the order was "unacceptable" as written.[14] Orrin Hatch wanted the ban to be much narrower[15]; Ben Sasse thought the overly broad order would help terrorist recruiters.[16] Rob Portman, the moderate conservative who had served in the Bush administration as director of the Office of Management and Budget (OMB) and United States Trade Representative (USTR), criticized the executive order for insufficient vetting, saying "it needs to be consistent with our values."[17] Portman's home city, Cincinnati, generally moderately conservative as well, declared itself a sanctuary city.[18] Lamar Alexander observed that "while it is not explicitly a religious test,it comes close to one which is inconsistent with our American character."[19] McConnell had been working hard to be supportive of the new president, but he quickly said that he considered a Muslim ban to be "completely and totally inconsistent with American values.[20] . . .We don't have religious tests in this country."[21]

Across the nation, federal courts responded quickly to legal challenges brought against the travel ban. On February 4, U.S. District Court judge James Robart granted a temporary restraining order to block its enforcement.[22] President Trump lashed out against the "so-called judge" who was endangering national security. But when the administration appealed Judge Robart's order, a three-judge panel of the Ninth Circuit Court of Appeals quickly affirmed his ruling, suspending the executive order and thus allowing refugees and citizens from the seven predominantly Muslim countries to continue to enter the United States.[23] Rejecting the Trump administration's national security argument, the panel said: "The government has pointed to no evidence that any alien from any of the countries named in the Order has perpetrated a terrorist attack in the United States." The panel was unimpressed by Trump's claim that the president's broad power over immigration made his determinations essentially unreviewable.

The administration came back with a revised executive order on March 6.[24] The revised order stopped all refugee resettlement in the United States for 120 days and blocked citizens from six Muslim-majority countries (Iraq was removed from the list) from entering the United States for ninety days. Once the suspension was lifted, there would be a cap of fifty thousand refugees that would be allowed into the United States in fiscal year 2017. The new order also removed a preference for refugees who belong to a religious minority and gave exemptions to green-card holders and individuals who already had valid visas. The ban would give the Trump administration time to develop more stringent vetting requirements and give the six targeted countries fifty days after a Department of Homeland Security review to comply with U.S. government requests to update or improve information used by the United States for visa and immigration decisions.

Despite the revisions, federal judges in Hawaii and Maryland quickly blocked the new executive order.[25] Although the ban's stated purpose was protecting national security, the continued focus on banning individuals from six Muslim-majority countries left the appearance that the order was still a "Muslim ban." Hawaii's state attorney general Douglas Chin persuasively argued that "Trump's own words acted against him."[26] Litigation would continue for months. Losing in courts around the nation gave the Trump administration the chance to forum shop, and it appealed to the Fourth Circuit, which it believed to be more sympathetic than the Ninth Circuit had been.[27]

The federal courts had given a shaken nation, and the aggressive new president, reassuring lessons about the Constitution. In fact, Trump's mean-spirited and badly executed travel ban had brought much of the country together in unified opposition. State attorneys general had taken the lead in the litigation.[28] The American Civil Liberties Union and religious organizations played a prominent role.[29] Major U.S. corporations, particularly the high-tech community, denounced the ban as contrary to their values and damaging to their ability to attract and retain foreign talent.[30] Universities and state colleges expressed their fears that talented foreign students would end up in Canada, Europe, or Australia as applications for 2018 declined.[31] The tourism industry reported large decreases in bookings from foreign visitors.[32] But above and beyond the interests of the particular groups, the travel ban provoked widespread condemnation because it simply seemed un-American, contrary to our commitment to religious freedom and our tradition of welcoming immigrants and refugees.

The nationwide resistance to the proposed travel ban may have pushed the Trump administration in a more moderate direction. The president's foreign policy briefings may have also convinced him that indiscriminate attacks on all Muslims jeopardized any chance of finding allies for the United States in waging war against ISIS and limiting the influence of Iran in the Middle East. Even as the Trump administration continued to litigate the constitutionality of the travel ban, the president's rhetoric toward the Islamic world changed dramatically when he made his first foreign trip to Saudi Arabia.[33]

But the travel ban was only half of the Trump administration's offensive on border security. President Trump signed two other executive orders on January 27. The first directed federal agencies to start building a wall on the U.S.-Mexico border.[34] Part of the estimated $8 to $25 billion needed to construct the wall would come from the 2006 Secure Fence Act signed by President Bush, and on March 27, Trump requested $1 billion in funding to cover forty-eight miles of the wall and fourteen miles of existing fence updates along the border. However, more funding would be needed from Congress if Trump's fantasy wall were going to be built. No one believed his claim that Mexico was going to pay for it.

The second order was designed to boost the number of immigration agents and to end the "catch and release" policy that had border enforcement agents quickly return border crossers to Mexico rather than processing and deporting them.[35] Detention facilities to hold undocumented immigrants would be built along the two-thousand-mile border to allow faster and cheaper deportations. The order would also allow the United States to withhold visas from countries that refuse to take back illegal immigrants. It would remove federal grants from "sanctuary" cities and states that choose not to enforce immigration laws.

Most of the Senate Democrats responded quickly and strongly. "We already have 650 miles of fencing along our southern border with Mexico in the areas where it is most effective, and the Obama administration has made tremendous progress securing the border with smart investments in advanced surveillance technologies," Carper stated.[36] "Net migration from Mexico is less than zero.[37] In fact, many experts agree that the border is more secure than it has been in years. . . . Building a new wall is an expensive and ineffective substitute for comprehensive immigration reform, and it will show little return on investment if we don't work with our neighbors in Central America to address root causes of migration."

On March 16, Carper, joined by more than twenty of his Democratic colleagues, introduced legislation to rescind Trump's executive order to construct the border wall and ramp up deportations and detentions. He reiterated his view that smart and effective investments in border security were needed and had been made before Trump's executive order. Focusing on the $21 billion estimated price tag for the wall, Carper noted that the DHS budget included substantial and unwise reductions for the Coast Guard and the Transportation Security Administration. On April 28, congressional leaders and Trump administration officials reached a compromise on spending legislation that would fund the government through September 30. The agreement included a flat rejection of Trump's request for funds to build the wall.[38] The administration received $1.5 billion for border security, but with strict limitations specifying that the funds could be used only for technology investments and repair of existing fences and infrastructure.

Congress had the power of the purse; it could prevent the funding of the wall. But it could not solve the underlying problem of eleven million illegal immigrants living and working in the shadows. Led by the "Gang of Eight," the Senate had passed a comprehensive immigration bill in 2013 by an overwhelming vote, only to have that effort quashed by the House Republicans. Now Congress and the country would face the consequences of that failure.

On February 21, Dianne Feinstein issued a sharp attack on the guidance released by the Department of Homeland Security (DHS), charging that it creates an unprecedented situation for undocumented immigrants living, working, and paying taxes in the United States, as well as Homeland Security, which is now charged with picking up otherwise law-abiding people in their homes and places of work. Up until this point, the priority for removal has been dangerous criminals. But under this new guidance, eleven million undocumented immigrants are now priorities for deportation.[39]

The "Dreamers," the young people brought to the United States illegally as children, posed the most emotional aspect of the deportation issue. President Obama had established the Deferred Action for Childhood Arrivals (DACA) in 2012 to give this group a two-year reprieve from being deported.[40] Obama assumed that Congress, in its wisdom, would resolve the problem in the comprehensive legislation being considered at that time. Some 750,000 people were issued work permits and temporary protection against deportation under the program. With the legislative effort having failed, the Dreamers were again at risk.

During the campaign, Trump said he would kill the program.[41] Once in office, however, Trump indicated a desire to find a solution for these individuals who had known only the United States most of their lives.[42] Senators Dick Durbin and Lindsey Graham introduced the Bridge Act in December 2016 and then reintroduced it in January 2017 to allow young people currently protected from deportation to stay in the country for three years while Congress decides how to handle the immigration issue. Senator Cornyn, the Republican whip, expressed his view that the legislation did not go far enough to protect the Dreamers. McConnell also showed sympathy for the young people.[43] He felt the president would have some latitude in Congress to address their plight in a positive manner if he chooses to do so. However, mistakes in the enforcement of Trump's executive order, which was supposed to leave DACA recipients alone while rounding up criminal immigrants for deportation, created a wave of fear in many communities.[44] One month into the Trump presidency, fearful Hispanics rushed to Mexican consulates seeking dual citizenship Mexican passports for their children or guidance to avoid deportation. Some families went into hiding,[45] kept their children home from school, quit their jobs, or moved into "sanctuary" homes, churches, and hospitals in the hope of resisting deportation.

Trump's executive orders had provoked national resistance, and senators from both parties had been sharply critical. Senate Republicans, however, refrained from joining any of the Democratic legislative initiatives, other than the Bridge Act. Understandably, they were willing to hope that their criticism of the executive orders would push Trump in a more moderate direction. On March 1, President Trump left the door open for a compromise immigration bill.[46] However, his statements were met with skepticism. If he was truly open to a compromise immigration bill that offered a path for eleven million un-documented immigrants to become citizens, that would be a dramatic change of position, even for a president who was showing that his views were infinitely flexible. It was also unclear why he would be willing to deport so many immigrants if a legislative solution could be devised.

On April 11, Attorney General Sessions directed federal prosecutors across the country to give higher priority to immigration cases and look for opportunities to bring serious felony charges against those crossing the border illegally.[47] He urged prosecutors to consider whether they could bring felony charges against those who had entered the United States illegally multiple times and to evaluate whether they could charge illegal immigrants with aggravated identity theft, which carried a mandatory two-year prison sentence. He also said law enforcement would no longer catch and release undocumented immigrants taken into custody at the border.

"Which prosecutors and agents does he want to divert from the growing threats like terrorism, cybercrime, the opioid and heroin trade, organized crime and cartel activity?"[48] asked Jenny Durkan, who served as U.S. attorney for the Western District of Washington from 2009 to 2014. "The 'surge' philosophy always requires taking agents, money and prosecutors from other priorities."

The previous month, Sessions had threatened to strip federal funding from cities that did not communicate with Immigration and Customs Enforcement (ICE) and cosigned a letter with Homeland Security secretary John Kelly endorsing the practice of arresting undocumented immigrants at court-houses. "This is a new era," said Sessions, "the Trump era."[49]

On May 25, the Fourth Circuit Court of Appeals, by an emphatic 10-3 vote, refused to reinstate the president's temporary travel ban.[50] The majority said that the travel ban looked less like a national security measure and more like a Muslim ban. Citing the president's campaign rhetoric, the court said that the executive order "drips with religious intolerance, animus and discrimination." The court found that the challenges were likely to suffer "irreparable harm" if the ban was implemented and that it might violate the Constitution.

On June 26, on the last day of its term, the Supreme Court agreed to hear arguments in October on the constitutionality of the travel ban.[51] In a unanimous decision, the Court allowed parts of the travel ban to go into effect to permit the Trump administration to enforce the ban on "foreign nationals who lack any bona fide relationship with a person or entity in the United States." President Trump welcomed the decision, and the Department of Homeland Security said it would begin enforcing the ban after reviewing the ruling with the Justice and State departments.

The Supreme Court's decision to hear the case makes it likely that a major decision on the scope of the president's national security powers will be forthcoming. Opponents of the ban contend that it violates the fundamental constitutional principle that government cannot favor or disfavor any one religion. At the same time, the Constitution and previous Supreme Court rulings give the president broad power in the area of immigration. Conservative legal scholars contended that the appellate courts, objecting to the ban, had intruded on the president's authority and gone too far in speculating about his motives based on his campaign statements. No one can confidently predict the outcome with a Supreme Court closely divided between liberals and conservatives.

The courts play a vital role in our system, and have responded to the travel ban with independence and integrity. But ultimately, comprehensive immigration policy will require the Senate to step up again, as it did in 2013 when it passed the "Gang of Eight" legislation. Any legislative effort would undo the focus on protecting the /sreamers, whose situation evoken concern and empathy that seemed to cross party lines.

DEBATING ECONOMIC NATIONALISM

During the campaign, Donald Trump positioned himself, with great effectiveness, as an insurgent. Although seeking the Republican nomination, he seemed to view both parties in equal contempt as coconspirators in an elite establishment that had failed the American people. This was particularly true with respect to trade, and Trump won because there was a diamond-hard, substantive core to his message: economic nationalism. When the Democratic "blue wall" states of Pennsylvania, Michigan, and Wisconsin each narrowly went to Trump, giving him the election, everyone understood that anger about trade and globalization, a strong undercurrent in American politics for forty years, had finally become a decisive electoral issue.

As a candidate, Donald Trump minced no words about what he saw as the devastating impact of trade on America and American workers. In Trump's view, the North American Free Trade Agreement (NAFTA) was "the worst trade deal" ever reached.[52] He promised to renegotiate NAFTA or impose 35 percent tariffs on Mexican imports.[53] He vowed to withdraw the United States from the Trans-Pacific Partnership (TPP), the regional trade agreement with twelve nations completed in August 2015 and being prepared for congressional approval.[54] Trump described U.S. trade negotiators as "political hacks" and promised to replace them with some of America's greatest businessmen (including himself) who knew how to negotiate.[55] He threatened China with 45 percent tariffs to reduce the bilateral trade deficit and to make up for their subsidies, dumping, currency manipulation, and ripping off American intellectual property.[56] As Trump biographers Michael Kranish and Marc Fisher wrote in *Trump Revealed*: "The image of the rest of the world laughing at U.S. leaders would become an enduring theme in Trump's political rhetoric."[57]

Ironically, the very week in June 2015 that Donald Trump came down the escalator in Trump Tower to launch his extraordinary presidential campaign, the Senate was engaged in an intense debate over whether to grant President Obama the negotiating authority required, known as Trade Promotion Authority (TPA), to complete the TPP agreement.[58] It appeared to be a defining moment in U.S. trade policy, when the Senate, and the House, would have to choose between the clashing viewpoints over trade that had divided America for twenty-five years since NAFTA had first made trade into a fiercely controversial public issue.

On June 23, the Senate granted President Obama the negotiating authority to complete the TPP negotiation by a 60–38 vote.[59] At a time when Washington was deeply polarized and virtually dysfunctional, the debate over trade promotion authority was the rarest of all things: a real clash of opposing worldviews, characterized by cross-party alliances and a series of principled compromises that created a solid majority in the Senate and a narrow majority in the House. Interestingly, Trade Promotion Authority prevailed because TPP was the only issue in eight years on which Barack Obama, Mitch McConnell, and Paul Ryan would agree and collaborate. McConnell, with wry humor, called working with the president "something of an out-of-body experience."[60]

Since 1945, every American president—in good times and bad—had adhered to the view that the United States was the leader of an international system based on free trade and open markets.[61] Trade stands uniquely at the intersection of foreign and domestic policy. It affects America's relationships with other countries, but it also impacts the domestic economy and jobs. In our political system, Article I of the Constitution assigns Congress the power over interstate and foreign commerce. But Article II makes the president the commander in chief, which includes the authority to reach executive agreements with other nations. Over time, an uneasy accommodation had been reached[62]: Congress would define the objectives for U.S. trade policy, and the president, through his trade representative, would negotiate trade agreements, which would then be submitted to Congress for approval on an up or down basis, without amendment, within a certain time. Over time, another reality emerged. Presidents favored trade agreements because they amplified America's place in the world. Members of Congress were often more skeptical of trade because they had to deal, up close and personal, with the adverse effects of trade, such as the closing of a plant in their district. President Trump's populist stance set him apart from all his modern predecessors.

Of all the issues where the Senate might play the role of "national mediator," trade was probably the most natural fit. For the past thirty years, the

Senate had been a moderate, constructive, and deeply engaged force on trade. Senators developed a deep and granular understanding of the impact of trade on the economy, developed through careful study and endless lobbying connected with a long series of intense debates on controversial trade agreements. There was a great advantage to representing states, which usually had a broad range of diverse economic interests in play. Most senators had to take account of manufacturers who were hurt by rising import competition and agricultural interests whose livelihoods depended on open foreign markets. Consequently, the number of pure free traders in the Senate was relatively small; so was the contingent of hard-core protectionists. The business community and the labor unions might hold diametrically opposed views on trade, but most senators, balancing many constituencies and interests, held more nuanced views. Often, they ended up being what might be described as 60–40 free traders—tough on our trading partners and unfair trade practices, but generally in favor of trade agreements that increased market access in countries that had traditionally been more closed than the United States. The senators also knew their history and remembered that one of the few pieces of legislation whose sponsors' names would live forever was Smoot-Hawley, the protectionist tariff that helped bring on the Great Depression.

The Senate was long accustomed to give and take with pro-trade presidents and their trade officials. In the 1980s, Senator Lloyd Bentsen (D-TX) and John Danforth (R-MO) took the lead in pushing the Reagan administration to a tougher trade policy toward Japan.[63] In the 1990s, senators Daniel Patrick Moynihan (D-NY) and Bob Packwood (R-OR) made it clear to President Bill Clinton that he would get no further negotiating authority for free trade deals after NAFTA.[64] In 2000, the Senate reached an early consensus that it was time to bring China into the WTO, and strongly supported Clinton in granting permanent normal trade relations to China. Dealing with Trump, an aggressive economic nationalist with an "America First" trade policy, posed a completely different challenge.

Barack Obama came to the White House skeptical of trade and understandably focused on preventing a second Great Depression. By 2011, with economic disaster averted, Obama looked forward and recognized that the Asia-Pacific region was rapidly integrating as countries made bilateral and regional trade agreements with their preferred partners. Obama saw the clear danger that the Asia-Pacific region would integrate without the United States, leaving China likely to dominate the region and write the trade rules to favor their state capitalist model to our further disadvantage. He also contended that the United States, with 5 percent of the world's people, would build its future prosperity only by doing business with the other 95 percent, particularly in the Asia-Pacific, which was building the largest middle class in the world.

With these concerns in mind, Obama doubled down on the U.S. effort to exert economic leadership in the region.[65] The TPP, a modest regional negotiation, had been moving along slowly, but as Obama intensified the U.S. commitment, Canada and Mexico joined in 2011, greatly expanding its size. In 2012, Japan became part of the negotiation. This was big news: the third-largest economy in the world, historically disposed to being closed, was now open to trade and economic liberalization to jar its economy out of long-term stagnation.[66] The TPP negotiation picked up steam and became the most important trade negotiation since the Uruguay Round.

Congress affirmed its importance by giving Obama the negotiating authority to complete it. Orrin Hatch and Ron Wyden, chairman and ranking member of the Finance Committee, had worked tirelessly in the battle for TPA. Because Congress had acted, the United States and eleven other nations successfully completed the TPP negotiation. Now the new president would abandon the centerpiece of American trade policy on which the previous president and Congress had collaborated. America's trading partners viewed Trump's election with great trepidation and wondered whether their concerns, the American business community, Congress, or anything, could moderate Trump's views on trade.

During the transition, president-elect Trump moved quickly to put pressure on major U.S. companies to keep jobs in the United States. On the campaign trail, Trump had repeatedly called out Carrier, the Indiana manufacturer of air conditioners, for its announced plan to move 1,100 jobs to Mexico. On November 29, Trump announced that Carrier had agreed to keep nearly one thousand jobs in Indiana. While it later became clear that only seven hundred jobs would stay, Trump got plaudits for moving rapidly to carry out his campaign promise. A rapid series of announcements about investments made, or jobs retained, in the United States by other leading companies followed.[67] Trump clearly enjoyed pressuring companies; the companies seemed quite willing to cooperate, even though many of the announcements reflected plans made before the election.

After being inaugurated, President Trump turned immediately to his trade agenda. Mexico was the top priority for Trump—the place where his two leading promises, building the wall and renegotiating, or withdrawing, from NAFTA, came together. In his first week of office, Trump threatened to impose a 20 percent tariff on imports from Mexico. Despite its constant efforts to diversify its trade, Mexican still sent 80 percent of its exports to the United States.[68] Moreover, Mexico depended on NAFTA to draw in foreign investment by ensuring multinational companies of stable access to the U.S. market and the safety of their investment. Trump's threats quickly caused the Mexican peso to drop sharply.[69]

Mexican president Enrique Pena Nieto had good reasons to seek a positive relationship with any president of the United States, but his decision to invite Trump to Mexico during the campaign had made him look even weaker than his bad poll numbers.[70] Foreign leaders had their own politics to worry about; Trump could not pressure them as if they were American CEOs. Pena Nieto stiffened his spine and made it explicit that discussions with the United States would not be limited to President Trump's agenda. "We will bring to the table all themes," he said in a speech.[71] "Trade, yes, but also migration and the themes of security, including border security, terrorist threats and traffic of illegal drugs, weapons and cash." Jorge Castaneda Gutman, the former Mexican foreign minister, put it succinctly: "Mexico has a lot of chips to play," including noncooperation at the border, which would open the floodgates to thousands, if not millions, of people trying to escape cartels and failing governments in Central America.[72]

In the early weeks of his presidency, in addition to constant pressure on Mexico, Trump continued to threaten trade action against China, although he did not fulfill his promise to label China a "currency manipulator" on his first day in office.[73] He lashed out unexpectedly against Germany[74] for its trade surplus, and against Canada, where the traditional tough issues of lumber and dairy had heated up again.[75] The president redeemed his pledge to withdraw America from the TPP, a decision made easier by the opposition expressed by Hillary Clinton, Bernie Sanders, most congressional Democrats, and progressive NGOs.[76] The Trump administration made it clear that it had no enthusiasm for the World Trade Organization (WTO) and would not hesitate to disregard its decisions and to pursue unilateral trade measures. Having abandoned the TPP, Trump endorsed bilateral agreements as preferable, including with the countries of the European Union, which had always negotiated through the EU.[77] Some of the talk could simply be hardball, an opening negotiating position. But taken together, Trump's statements represented a dramatic break with the trade views of presidents going back to FDR. If Trump's goal was to shake the world, he was achieving it.

The threat of trade war with Mexico drew immediate attention. There was a consensus among expert trade lawyers that President Trump had the legal authority to withdraw the United States from NAFTA without the approval of Congress. Given that possibility, starting in February, Republican senators began pushing back against Trump's views on NAFTA. John Cornyn, party whip and chairman of the Finance Subcommittee on Trade, praised NAFTA, noting that it had helped make Texas the nation's top exporting state. Cornyn acknowledged that the twenty-year-old NAFTA could be improved, but added: "I want to make it clear that the United States is not retreating from the world economy." Charles Grassley, the long-time champion of the corn, beef, and pork industries, warned: "There will be real and immediate economic consequences[78] for farmers if we lose exports." Ben Sasse noted that Mexico was exploring other sources for imported corn. He urged the Trump administration to reassure Mexico that it would "continue to be a valued trading partner" lest Nebraska become "collateral damage in trade war."[79]

The Republican senators found strong allies in the American business community. For a broad range of U.S. industries, threatening the disruption of trade between the United States and Mexico constituted the greatest danger posed by the new president. While NAFTA had long been a dirty word for Democrats in Congress and during presidential primaries, it had been in effect since 1995.[80] Many U.S. manufacturing industries, starting with the "Big Three" auto companies, had built North American supply chains in which Mexico provided cheap labor while design, engineering, and advanced manufacturing took place in the United States and Canada. The U.S. business community could certainly support modernization of the NAFTA (which, in fact, had largely been accomplished in the Trans-Pacific Partnership agreement). But business leaders thought Trump's view that he could unilaterally disrupt NAFTA and somehow rebalance it to add benefits for the United States was naïve and dangerous.[81]

During the transition, U.S. Chamber of Commerce CEO Tom Donohue reassured business executives[82] from the three countries that the Chamber would defend NAFTA if it became necessary. When Trump, in office, showed no signs of moderating, Donohue vigorously defended NAFTA. In a February 6 speech, Donohue said: "Withdrawing from NAFTA would be devastating for workers, businesses, and economies of our countries."[83] The twenty-three-year-old trade pact could benefit from modernization, but dismantling it would be a grave mistake.

Despite this first round of lobbying, in late April Trump contemplated issuing an executive order withdrawing the United States from NAFTA.[84] Republican senators and their business allies pushed back quickly, in unified opposition. Withdrawal would have "the worst possible impact" on my state, said John McCain. "I'd be glad to have a renegotiation of some of the terms, because a lot of time has passed," but withdrawal would be "disgraceful" and "a disaster."[85] Cornyn warned that "we'd better be careful about unintended consequences."[86] Lindsey Graham said that he had been skeptical of NAFTA initially but that the pact had produced real benefits for the country and his state. "Trying to renegotiate it makes sense; withdrawing from it doesn't," Graham added.[87] In Mexico City, Donohue invoked the Hippocratic oath: "First and foremost, do no harm."[88] A unified business community stressed that the NAFTA should be "amended, rather than ended."

Senators laid down other markers. Trump favored quick action on NAFTA, but the senators reminded him that the TPA law set out the process that he would have to follow. "We have these provisions where you have to wait long periods of time.[89] You have to notify Congress, and after you notify Congress, you have to get certified," Trump sputtered in frustration. "The whole thing is ridiculous."

Trump has chosen Robert Lighthizer to be his trade representative.[90] Lighthizer was a trade lawyer who represented the steel industry fighting imports; he shared the president's hard-line views and bristled with the same sense of grievance about foreign unfair practices. But he also had been Deputy U.S. Trade Representative during the Reagan years and was well connected in the business trade community. USTR had a special relationship to the Hill trade committees that created it, and Lighthizer, who had served as chief trade counsel of the Finance Committee, understood the nature of that relationship very well.

During the Reagan and George W. Bush administrations, the Finance Committee had buried initiatives to merge USTR into the Commerce Department. They feared that the elite agency of career negotiators would be lost in the huge Commerce Department, and, more parochially, that they would lose jurisdiction over trade negotiations. Now, President Trump wanted Commerce Secretary Ross to take the lead on NAFTA renegotiation, but Finance Committee chairman Orrin Hatch made it clear that the U.S. Trade Representative was the chief negotiator for the United States.[91] The Finance Committee would support Lighthizer as he worked to establish his leadership on trade within Trump's chaotic administration. But the committee members would also expect him to be keenly aware of their concerns and priorities. At his confirmation hearing, Lighthizer repeatedly reassured the agriculture state senators[92] that despite his background as a steel industry lawyer, he understood the overriding importance of agricultural exports. The committee Democrats were happy to let the Republicans warn Trump not to harm NAFTA. They took the opportunity to poke at Trump, saying that, despite his rhetoric, he was weak on trade. Maria Cantwell (D-WA), a strong supporter of the Export-Import Bank, whose loan portfolio helped major U.S. exporters compete internationally, criticized Trump for his refusal to fully fund the bank. "You can't go and stand in front of a Boeing plane in South Carolina and not have a fully functioning Export-Import Bank," Cantwell commented.[93] Ron Wyden (D-OR), a strong defender of the U.S. lumber industry in its endless battle with Canada, chastised Trump for suggesting that the NAFTA agreement with Canada needed only "tweaking."[94] Debbie Stabenow (D-MI) ridiculed Trump's promised review of "Buy America" laws. "There's $70 billion in the last five years spent on foreign products with American taxpayer dollars on federal procurement, so we need to fix that," Stabenow contended. "We don't need more studies.[95] We don't need more talking. What we need is more action."

On May 18, the administration gave the formal notice to Congress needed to begin the long-promised renegotiation of the NAFTA.[96] The letter, signed by Lighthizer, specified that the administration's primary goal was updating the twenty-three-year-old pact by adding provisions on digital trade, intellectual property rights, and labor and environmental standards, which had been "an afterthought" in NAFTA. Lighthizer acknowledged that NAFTA had been successful for several U.S. sectors, including agriculture, investment services, and energy, but noted that other sectors, namely, manufacturing—"particularly with regard to Mexico, have fallen behind." He emphasized that in seeking gains for manufacturers, the United States would not take steps to hurt other export industries that were benefiting from NAFTA.

The letter marked a clear retreat, not only from the incendiary language of Trump's campaign but also from the more detailed draft notice in late March in which the administration had specified twenty areas where it was seeking changes. NAFTA supporters in the U.S. business community and agricultural groups justifiably breathed a sigh of relief; so did the governments of Mexico and Canada, which issued positive statements. The strong messages from the Senate, the business community, Washington trade think tanks, and America's NAFTA partners had clearly influenced Trump's advisers, and ultimately, the president.[97] However, Rich Trumka, the fiery leader of the AFL-CIO, reminded Trump of his campaign promises to his blue-collar base. "Working people have lived with the failure of NAFTA, and Donald Trump made big promises to fix it.[98] NAFTA needs to be completely rewritten. . . . Small changes around the edges—or the insertion of the disastrous TPP provisions—are not acceptable and would be the ultimate in hypocrisy," Trumka said in a July 14 statement. Trump had acknowledged that health care and North Korea were more complicated than he expected. He would probably add trade to that list before too long.

The Trump administration's second trade priority was number one for virtually everyone else: China. China played a constructive role during the Great Recession, when its powerful, continuous economic growth and voracious demand for commodities sustained much of the world. But for U.S. companies, the optimism that accompanied China's entry into the WTO in 2001 vanished long ago.[99] After WTO accession, China quickly became the manufacturing arm of the world, with sudden devastating impact on U.S. industries. Despite its commitments to liberalize, China continued to favor its state-owned enterprises, unwilling to accept the loss of jobs that would result from closing them down.[100] China's overcapacity in many industries,[101] starting with steel and aluminum, had caused damage to competitors all over the world. China continued its extensive use of state subsidies to prop up various sectors.

China also seemed relentlessly focused on developing, and dominating, the industries of the future. As Fred Hiatt wrote in the *Washington Post*: "China is not operating by the same rules[102] as everyone else. . . . China has found ways to suck technologies from western companies with giving them equal access to its market." The hope that China's economic liberalization would produce political liberalization had proven naïve, and there was no longer that much economic liberalization either. According to a survey done by the American Chamber of Commerce in China, four out of five U.S. companies felt less welcome[103] than they had a few years earlier, citing unclear laws with inconsistent enforcement, as well as increasing protectionism and restrictions on foreign investment.

President Trump and his team had correctly concluded that the U.S.-China trade relationship was working against the United States. Unfortunately, reaching that conclusion did not provide much guidance as to what steps to take to improve the situation. If President Trump and his advisers started a trade war with China, China had plenty of its own weapons with which to retaliate: switching airplane purchases from Boeing to Airbus, cracking down on U.S. food imports, and possibly making it more difficult for Apple to sell iPhones in China. Moreover, the Trump administration discovered quickly that the United States needed to maintain a constructive relationship with China, particularly in trying to map out a cooperative strategy for dealing with the increasingly ominous threat posed by North Korea's nuclear weapons.

It certainly made no sense to threaten the U.S. relationship with Mexico and Canada when the strength of the North American economy and North American manufacturing provided an essential counterweight to China. Trump's decision to abandon the TPP was probably the most counterproductive move possible for a new administration seeking leverage against China and influence in the Asia-Pacific region. While the move undoubtedly pleased many of Trump's working-class supporters, it was a historic step, signaling a withdrawal of the United States from the Asia-Pacific and potentially ceding the region to China. Victor Shih, an expert on China's political economy at the University of California San Diego, said, "The U.S. will be seen as an unreliable partner both economically and perhaps even in the security area."[104]

Given limited options, Trump soon moderated his rhetoric toward China. In his first meeting with China's president Xi Jinping, in early April, Trump concluded that China was no longer a currency manipulator. The leaders put in place a "100 Day" plan to begin considering adjustments in the trade relationship[105]; at the same time, Trump told Xi that the terms of a trade agreement[106] would be much better for China if Xi helped the United States deal with the

North Korean nuclear threat. In May, the Trump administration announced its first trade success with China[107]: the lifting of the ban that had prevented U.S. beef from entering China for fourteen years. China also increased access for U.S. financial firms. But in exchange for the concession of beef, the United States opened our market to processed chicken from China, which alarmed consumer advocates and food safety experts.

In contrast to dealing with NAFTA, the Senate offered Trump little advice on China. The hard truth was that no one had found a magic bullet, or bullets, for dealing with China. Six months into the Trump administration, the U.S.-China trade relationship looked very much like a continuation of the same tough choices and intractable dilemmas that had faced the Obama administration, except that Trump had abandoned the TPP and weakened alliances with countries that had previously cooperated in efforts to pressure China to reduce overcapacity in steel and other industries and meet its WTO obligations.

As the G-20 nations met in Hamburg, Germany, in July, the threat posed by the Trump's Section 232 investigation on the impact of steel imports on U.S. national security hung over the world economy.[108] Steel represented one of the most persistent trade problems for the United States, going back to the 1970s. The U.S. market depended on a substantial amount of foreign steel, but massive overcapacity globally had caused the level of imports to soar in 2014 and 2015, causing great harm to domestic steel companies. While the U.S. industry had successfully reduced imports through antidumping and counter-vailing duty actions, those actions could not effectively address the problem of China's overcapacity that was flooding the world. The Trump administration wanted a new, global solution and turned to the rarely used Section 232. At the G-20, President Trump declined to join a strong statement by the other nineteen nations about the dangers of protectionism. America's trade partners knew that Trump owed his narrow victory to his Rust Belt support and that the president, himself, hated to disappoint his supporters.

At the same time, however, the G-20 provided a stark reminder of how strongly other countries were resisting America's economic nationalism. Meeting in Brussels on route to the G-20, Prime Minister Shinzo Abe of Japan and President Donald Tusk of the European Union announced that Japan and the EU had reached a major trade agreement.[109] The EU and Japan had been negotiating for several years, but the announcement, made with great fanfare, was a sharp stick in the eye of the protectionist American president. Two of the world's largest economies were deepening their trade and investment ties in a preferential trade agreement that would disadvantage U.S. exporters in both Japan and the EU. European tariffs on Japanese autos would be reduced; so would Japanese tariffs on European cheese.

The announcement sent the clearest possible message: major countries were not being bullied by, or emulating, Trump's America First policy. The United States ran the serious risk of being left out and left behind as other nations made trade deals with their preferred partners. That precise concern had prompted Obama, McConnell, and Ryan to come together behind TPP in 2015. In 1993, Bill Clinton had said that "America must compete, not retreat" from world commerce.[110] Now, twenty-four years later, America faced the same choice. Most of the senators believed that the combination of protectionism and isolationism was still a loser's game. If Lighthizer and Ross were such tough negotiators, they should start negotiating because other nations were moving ahead.

CLIMATE CHANGE DENIAL

Hostility to immigration and international trade formed the hard core of Donald Trump's populist appeal that drove his presidential campaign. By comparison, Trump's opposition to aggressive action to combat climate change received less attention, but his position was clear enough. In 2012, Trump had called climate change "a hoax" concocted by China to advantage its manufacturers.[111] During the campaign, he promised, if elected, to withdraw the United States from the Paris Agreement on climate change.[112] His forceful commitment roused the crowds in his campaign rallies in West Virginia and other coal states.

Still, Trump's supporters in the business community harbored the hope that this was simply campaign rhetoric. They noted that Trump and family members had joined an ad in 2009 urging Obama to push the global climate change pact being negotiated in Copenhagen.[113] The president's daughter, Ivanka, and son–in–law, Jared Kushner, were reported to be particularly interested in the issue. During the transition, Ms. Trump invited Al Gore, probably the world's most famous advocate of strong action to combat climate change, to Trump Tower to meet with the president-elect and her.[114]

Harsh reality set in quickly enough. During the transition, Trump cast his lot squarely with the climate change deniers by picking Scott Pruitt to head the EPA. Once in office, the Trump administration went on what John Podesta, senior adviser to President Obama on climate change, described as "a rampage to endanger the planet."[115] Trump took steps to eliminate the limits on carbon pollution and increase domestic oil and coal production. He moved to weaken vehicle-efficiency standards, undoing a far-reaching agreement that the auto companies had reached with the Obama administration.[116] He increased importation of oil from the Canadian tar sands. Trump's budget proposed a stunning 31 percent reduction[117] for EPA—deeper cuts than even what Pruitt had requested—and abolished the office of climate adaptation.

Still, although Trump had moved rapidly to issue his travel ban and withdraw the United States from the TPP, he put off a decision on whether to withdraw from the Paris accord. On May 31, as the president traveled to Europe on his first foreign trip, a decision seemed imminent. The *New York Times* reported that "a divided White House staff, anxious executives, lawmakers and foreign leaders were fiercely competing for President Trump's ear."[118]

The Senate had a long record of accomplishment on domestic environmental protection, going back to its leadership on the original Clean Air Act of 1963.[119] On climate change, the Senate held some of the earliest hearings to bring public attention to the issue, and Al Gore had dramatized the threat with his book *Earth in the Balance* while serving in the Senate in 1991.[120] In 1997, President Bill Clinton, with the strong urging of Vice President Gore, signed the Kyoto Protocol, the first concrete effort to implement the UN commitment made in 1992 to combat climate change.[121] However, a few months before, the Senate had resoundingly voted 95–0 on a nonbinding resolution sponsored by Democrat Robert Byrd and Republican Chuck Hagel opposing any agreement that did not include the rising economies of China and India.[122] The force of the Senate's concerns about Kyoto shaped the Obama administration efforts as it approached global negotiations on climate change.

Obama came to office favoring strong action to reduce carbon emissions. Polls showed broad concern among Americans about the threat of climate change. George W. Bush had demonstrated increasing urgency on the issue in his last eighteen months in office, and John McCain, in his presidential campaign, endorsed a cap–and–trade system to reduce carbon emissions.[123] But any emerging consensus favoring action did not include the Senate, where the division on climate change reflected the chasm between the Republicans and Democrats on the Environment and Public Works Committee, and the increasingly committed opposition of McConnell from the coal state of Kentucky.

For many years, the Environment Committee's ranking Republican was James Inhofe (R–OK), a leading climate change denier, friend of the fossil fuels industry, and most prominent supporter of Pruitt, the Oklahoma attorney general.[124] At the same time, the ranking Democrat was Barbara Boxer (D–CA), one of the country's most fervent environmentalists. Boxer and Inhofe became friends,[125] and their "odd couple" alliance produced major legislation to improve the nation's transportation infrastructure, and even to enhance the regulation of toxic chemicals. But they worked together successfully in part by recognizing that they would never agree on climate change. Boxer's retirement did not change the dynamic on the committee. The new ranking Democrat,

Tom Carper (D-DE), was similarly liberal in his views; John Barrasso (R-WY), the new chairman of the committee, shared Inhofe's passion for fossil fuels, particularly Wyoming coal, and climate change denial.

Obama's leadership on climate change faltered early in the face of Republican resistance and the 2009 failed expectations for the international climate change talks in Copenhagen.[126] Certainly too, the depth of the Great Recession made concern about climate change less compelling than immediate measures to rescue the economy. When the House passed a cap-and-trade bill to limit carbon emissions in 2009, senators from both parties blocked its passage, with Rust Belt Democrats joining the overwhelming majority of Republicans.[127] In the off-year elections of 2010, the Tea Party, with funding from a network of organizations created by Charles and David Koch, used cap-and-trade as a political weapon that helped the Republicans take control of the House.[128] Along with health care, climate change had become the hottest political issue dividing Democrats and Republicans.

Obama, seemingly chastened by the defeat, retreated on the issue until after his reelection in 2012. But continued study of the issue convinced Obama that the threat to the planet was increasingly urgent. "My top science adviser, John Holdren,[129] periodically will issue some chart or report or graph in the morning meetings, and they're terrifying," Obama said. Soon after the 2012 election, Obama surprised a group of prominent historians by saying, "If we don't do anything on the climate issue, all bets are off."[130]

Recognizing that legislation could not succeed, the president instructed his aides to put together a program for reducing emissions through regulations.[131] They concluded, based on the 2007 Supreme Court decision in *Massachusetts v. EPA*, that the Clean Air Act gave the EPA the authority to issue regulations of dangerous pollutants. In 2014, President Obama unveiled the first draft of what would become the Clean Power Plan (CPP). The CPP would require the states to reduce overall greenhouse gases (GHGs) from electricity by 33 percent below 2005 emission levels by 2030.[132] The states were required to submit a plan describing how they would achieve such reductions; if a state failed to produce such a plan or requested an extension, the federal government would draft a plan for it, and EPA would directly impose it.

To both its supporters and its opponents, CPP represented a strikingly ambitious plan. Secretary of State John Kerry noted that it would contribute to the closure of several hundred coal-fired power plants, showing the seriousness of the U.S. commitment to strong measures.[133] The regulatory push outraged Obama's Republican opponents, led by McConnell. Kentucky, traditionally a leading coal producer, was already suffering from a severe loss of coal industry jobs.[134] The concerted pushback by the coal industry and its advocates would make the 2010 battle look like a walk on the beach.

The Copenhagen talks had fallen far short[135] because China and India had refused to take on binding obligations. Obama learned from that experience that no consequential international agreement would be possible—or, harkening back to the Byrd-Hagel resolution on the Kyoto Protocol, acceptable to the Senate—unless and until the major developing economies made commitments along the same lines as those of major developed countries. Obama believed that any agreement had to be led by the two largest emitters, the United States and China.[136] He initiated talks with China's president Xi Jinping at a get-acquainted summit meeting in June 2013. Encouragingly, they reached agreement to seek progress toward a pact to reduce emissions of hydrofluorocarbons (HFCs), a powerful planet-warming chemical used in air conditioners and refrigerators. That progress paved the way for months of negotiations between China and the United States, led by Podesta and Todd Stern, the Obama administration's climate change envoy, on the terms of a new climate accord that would become the Paris Agreement.[137]

China had always resisted such agreements, but the toxic levels of pollution in China had convinced Mr. Xi that the time for positive action had come. Obama's Clean Power initiative persuaded China that the United States was seriously committed, giving Podesta and Stern leverage they needed to negotiate.[138] In November 2014, the presidents announced a historic agreement committing both countries to significant reduction in emissions and providing the springboard to a global agreement.[139] A year later, in Paris, the United States led the negotiations of 195 nations to reach the most significant climate change agreement in history.

Predictably, the Republican offensive against Obama's climate change policies found McConnell in the quarterback position. For a Kentucky senator, McConnell had shown little interest in coal for most of his career. "As a lawyer in Louisville, was I paying attention to coal?[140] Not much," he noted. Even after leaving Louisville for the Senate in 1985, his interest remained limited. His 2016 memoir does not contain a single mention of "coal" or "coal miners." But after Obama took office and pledged action on climate change, "McConnell positioned himself as coal's bulwark—a central element of his across-the-board campaign to thwart the president politically," wrote James Rowley and Paul M. Barrett in *Bloomberg Business Week*.[141]

It was an uphill and, in many ways, a quixotic struggle. Kentucky's coal production had topped out in 1990.[142] Market forces, rather than Obama's policies, particularly the availability of cheap natural gas, caused 250 coal–fired power plants across the country to shut down, or convert to natural gas. "It's a last stand; the forces arrayed against coal are too powerful to resist," said David Doniger, director of the climate program at the National Resources Defense

Council (NRDC).[143] "The trouble with last stands though is they can go on for a long time, and McConnell is a very determined fighter."

McConnell began a concerted effort to block Obama's climate change agenda long before the Paris talks concluded. Legislation was futile; he recognized that even with a Republican majority in both houses of Congress, he could never get the two-thirds needed to override the president's veto. He embarked instead on a novel and bold approach, writing to all fifty governors to enlist the support of as many as possible in lawsuits challenging the Clean Power regulations.[144] Ultimately, an unprecedented twenty-eight states would join the lawsuits. McConnell also formed an unlikely alliance with Harvard Law professor Laurence Tribe, perhaps the best-known liberal legal scholar in the country and Obama's mentor when he was a law student at Harvard University.[145]

On March 17, 2015, Tribe, representing Peabody Energy, the nation's largest coal company, testified before the subcommittee on Energy and Power of the House Energy and Commerce Committee.[146] Submitting a fifty-three-page legal analysis, Tribe contended that "the absence of EPA legal authority in this case makes the Clean Power Plan, quite literally, a 'power grab.' EPA is attempting an unconstitutional trifecta: usurping the prerogatives of the States, Congress and the Federal Courts—all at once." While other respected legal scholars strongly argued that EPA was acting within its authority, Tribe's unmatched stature, his liberal credentials, and his long relationship with Obama gave his argument powerful legal and political impact. "As the iconic left-leaning law professor Laurence Tribe put it," McConnell wrote, "the administration's effort goes 'far beyond its lawful authority.'"

On November 27, 2015, just before the UN Climate conference in Paris convened, McConnell offered a stern warning to the 195 countries coming to negotiate. "It would obviously be irresponsible for an outgoing president to purport to sign the American people to international commitments based on a domestic energy plan that is likely illegal, that half the states have sued to halt, that Congress has voted to reject and that his successor could do away with in a few months' time," he wrote in an op-ed that appeared in the *Washington Post*.[147] "The president's international negotiating partners at [the] conference should proceed with caution before entering into an unattainable deal with this administration, because commitments the president makes there would rest on a house of cards of his own making."

Despite McConnell's grim admonition, 195 nations forged ahead to reach a successful and historic conclusion in Paris. Senator Sheldon Whitehouse (D-RI), one of ten senators attending the negotiations, stated: "The last political bastion of the fossil fuel industry worldwide is now the American Republican Party.[148] No Republican was able to come with us. The fossil fuel industry would never let them. Pretty soon there will be no one left on the shrinking denial island but the fossil fuel industry, the Koch Brothers and their front groups—and the Republican members of Congress."

But that last bastion was a formidable one. On February 8, 2016, Mc-Connell's legal/political strategy paid off as the Supreme Court stayed the implementation of the Clean Power Plan, pending resolution of the legal challenges to the CPP that had been brought by twenty-eight states.[149] Ordinarily, when health, safety, and environmental regulations are challenged, the courts allow the regulations to go into effect while litigation over their validity goes forward. The courts have traditionally tilted toward protecting health, safety, and the environment during the pendency of litigation. The Supreme Court decision came as a surprise, particularly since the D.C. Court of Appeals had denied a stay. It is hard to disagree with the assessment of Jonathan H. Adler, a law professor at Case Western University:[150]

> EPA's arguments against the stay were undermined by the Agency's own statements about the potentially revolutionary nature of the CPP. . . . EPA repeatedly emphasized that the CPP represented the most ambitious climate-related undertaking in the agency's history and crowed that the plan would lead to the complete restructuring of the energy sector. . . . An unprecedented assertion of regulatory authority may itself have justified an unprecedented exercise of the Court's jurisdiction to stay the agency's action.

The drumbeat of opposition continued. The Senate Environment Committee held a series of seven hearings, highlighting what the Republican majority saw as every objectionable aspect of CPP.[151] In April 2016, the committee Republicans issued a paper titled "Lessons from Kyoto," pushing back against what Inhofe called "Paris' empty promises."[152] The paper noted that the Senate had "called up and defeated every new energy tax and regulation" for twenty years, beginning with its 95–0 rejection of Kyoto. As always, the Republicans failed to note that the Paris Agreement had responded to the central concern expressed by senators over the Kyoto Protocol: it contained commitments by China, India, and the other developing economies. But the opponents' arguments now focused completely on the alleged effect of the Paris agreement on U.S. jobs and the economy, and the claim that the commitments, even if honored, would produce a miniscule reduction in carbon.

With Trump nearing his decision on Paris, other senators beyond the vehement opponents began weighing in. Through a series of letters and resolutions led by Tom Carper, Chris Murphy (D-CT), and Ben Cardin (D-MD), the Senate Democrats pressed Trump to stay in the Paris agreement. Whitehouse, emerging as the toughest Democratic attack dog on this issue, ripped "the fossil-fuel funded denial machine that controls the Republican Party.[153] It will do its best to change the subject. To muddy the waters. To cast doubt. To use its anonymous, dark, political money to thwart progress."

On May 3, Susan Collins, who often stood alone in carrying the once-proud mantle of moderate Republicanism, joined Cardin in a powerful letter to Secretary of State Rex Tillerson.[154] They noted that the United States had suffered from fifteen extreme weather events in 2016, causing damage of more than $1 billion. The senators argued that "combatting climate change presents exciting possibilities for U.S. competitiveness. Private sector partnerships with U.S. research institutions make the U.S. the world's leader in climate innovation." Cardin and Collins noted that many of the global energy giants are voluntarily applying a 2 degree Celsius "stress test" to their business models to better plan for a less carbon-intensive future—which should be compelling to the former CEO of ExxonMobil. Concluding with the observation that virtually every country in the world had signed the Paris accord, and 65 percent had fully joined by specifying what their voluntary "nationally determined contributions" would be, the senators urged the administration to keep America's "seat at the table."

Other Republican senators jumped into the discussion of whether the United States should remain in the agreement. Bill Cassidy expressed concern that U.S. energy exports might face a border tax levied by the European Union if we withdrew. "There would be a great irony, as we continue to lower our carbon footprint if we were penalized," Cassidy noted.[155] Foreign Relations Committee chairman Bob Corker expressed the view that without Obama's climate regulations in place, there was no urgent reason to withdraw: "All it does is hack off our allies when we have got other fish to fry . . . with that same group of people."[156] Shelley Moore Capito, from another leading coal state, wondered whether "we would be better off staying in the agreement to make it more realistic, make it make better sense, bring other people to the table, rather than totally walk away from it."[157] But Barrasso argued that the agreement was a "great deal"[158] for countries like China and India, who would gain a "leg up" on the United States in terms of energy security.

Even as McConnell, Barrasso, and Inhofe dug in, many senators had a broad enough perspective to consider the economic consequences for the United States if we retreat from the path toward clean energy. Trump had already boosted China's leadership in world trade by taking the United States out of the Trans-Pacific Partnership (TPP). Now, the risk was that Trump "will also cede American leadership on clean energy to other major powers, most notably China," wrote Podesta.[159]

Grover Norquist, the longtime leader of the anti-tax movement, who continued to wield enormous influence in Republican circles, commented: "Everyone who hates Trump wants him to stay in Paris.[160] Everyone who respects him, trusts him, voted for him, wishes for him to succeed wants him to pull out." If Mr. Trump pulls out, Norquist added, the message is: "I kept my word."

Many of America's leading corporations and executives urged the president to stay in the agreement. In January, 630 businesses and investors signed an open letter to then president-elect Trump and Congress, calling on them to continue supporting low-carbon policies, investment in a low-carbon economy, and American participation in the Paris accord.[161] Companies including GE, DuPont, Hewlett-Packard, Apple, Amazon, Unilever, Morgan Stanley, Microsoft, Mars, and Ingersoll Rand strongly countered the economic arguments offered by Bannon, Pruitt, and the coal companies. "By expanding markets for innovative clean technologies, the agreement generates jobs and economic growth.[162] U.S. companies are well-positioned to lead in these markets," the companies stated in full-page advertisements that ran in the *New York Times*, the *Washington Post*, and the *Wall Street Journal*.

The overwhelming majority of the Senate Democrats favored staying in the Paris Agreement. On May 25, twenty-two Senate Republicans signed a letter urging the president to make a "clean break" and abandon the agreement.[163] Commending the president for signing fourteen executive orders to roll back Obama's climate initiatives, the senators argued that staying in the Paris agreement "would subject the United States to significant litigation risk that could upend your administration's ability to fulfill its goal of rescinding the Clean Power Act," they contended. Lindsey Graham chided his colleagues, saying on CNN that pulling out of the Paris accord was "a statement that climate change is not a problem, is not real."[164]

At the G-7 meeting in Italy ending on May 27, after three days of contentious discussions that included lobbying by Pope Francis, Trump declined to endorse the Paris accord. The final communique by the G-7 acknowledged that the United States needed more time to reach its decision, but the tenor of the discussions was unmistakably grim. Chancellor Angela Merkel, Europe's strongest leader, expressed bitter disappointment:[165] "The whole discussion about climate was very difficult, not to say unsatisfactory. There's a situation where it's six—if you count the European Union, seven—against one." Newly elected French president Emmanuel Macron said that he told Trump it "was indispensable for the reputation of the United States and for the Americans themselves that the Americans remain committed" to the climate agreement.[166] If Trump remained torn over the decision, as appears possible, being lectured to in Europe by Merkel, Macron, and other leaders undoubtedly tilted the balance. After those unpleasant meetings, he would honor his campaign pledge to his supporters, demonstrate his "America First" populism, and show his contempt for international agreements and institutions, as well as European leaders.

On June 1, President Trump announced that the United States would withdraw from the Paris climate accord. Trump described the decision as "a reassertion of America's sovereignty."[167] He contended that the Paris agreement "handicaps the United States economy in order to win praise from the very foreign capitals and global activists that have long sought to gain wealth at our country's expense. They don't put America first. I do, and I always will. I was elected to represent the citizens of Pittsburgh, not Paris." It was as concise a statement of his philosophy as could possibly be offered. One senior White House official characterized disappointing European allies as "a secondary benefit" of Trump's decision to withdraw.[168]

The full impact of Trump's decision on the U.S. economy will play out over the next five to ten years. Some business leaders, most notably Michael Bloomberg, believe that companies were already making their decisions based on a low-carbon future, and that the progress was irreversible.[169] "The net impact to our emissions performance is likely zero to negligible," said Andy Karsner, a senior energy official and negotiator in the Bush administration.[170] "I don't actually believe for a moment that a withdrawal from Paris is tantamount to abating our efforts, direction or momentum toward increased penetration of clean-energy technologies. Washington does not have the power to put the genie back in the bottle." About thirty states, led by California, New York, and Washington, have adopted mandates for utilities to increase their use of renewable energy, and Trump's decision on Paris or the Clean Power Act will not change those state standards.[171] Nor is the debate about climate change and renewable energy simply a divide between "blue states" and "red states." The five leading states, in terms of electricity generated from wind—Kansas, Iowa, North Dakota, South Dakota, and Oklahoma—are all "red states" that strongly supported Donald Trump in the presidential election.[172]

In making the decision, Trump and his populist advisers led by Stephen Bannon were not thinking about *those* red states. They were pursuing their "Rust Belt" strategy, playing to their base in the closely contested states of Ohio, Pennsylvania, Michigan, and Wisconsin, as well as Kentucky and West Virginia, which by now have become Republican strongholds in presidential elections. "When forced to choose between keeping promises to his base or broadening his appeal, President Trump always seems to choose his base," said Michael Steele, who was a senior aide to former House Speaker John A. Boehner.[173]

Whatever the political calculation that prompted the decision, or the future economic impact, leaving the Paris accord represented a major retreat from American leadership in the world. Some 195 countries supported the Paris agreement; Trump's withdrawal placed the United States in a group of three opponents, joining Syria and Nicaragua. Mary Robinson, the former president of Ireland and United Nations special envoy, said, "The U.S. reneging on its commitment to the Paris agreement renders it a rogue state."[174]

Virtually overnight, diplomatic relationships established over many decades began to change. The shift of global leadership from the United States to China, already jump-started by Trump's abandonment of the TPP, dramatically accelerated. Chinese premier Li Keqiang, meeting in Berlin with Chancellor Merkel, said that his country remained committed to the fight against climate change and to participating in the international efforts to bring about a greener world.[178] After his meeting in Berlin, Mr. Li headed to Brussels to underscore China's climate change commitment to the European Union. Zhang Haibin, a professor at Peking University who specializes in international environmental policy, noted that China could not fill the leadership void alone: "Instead, we'll need to work closely with the European Union and the Basic Countries," referring to a negotiating bloc that included Brazil, South Africa, and India as well as China.[179] "Collective leadership will be more important." That is to say, China-led collective leadership. And certainly China, already the world's leader in the solar industry, welcomed the economic opportunities presented by renewable energy that Washington—although not Sacramento or Albany—seemed ready to walk away from.

Could the Senate have done anything that would have persuaded Trump not to withdraw the United States from the Paris Agreement? The Senate had the historic credentials to play an influential role. Working with Democratic and Republican presidents, the Senate had spearheaded every significant piece of environmental legislation since the original Clean Air Act of 1963. However, through the Byrd-Hagel resolution, the Senate had stated emphatically that America would not support an international agreement to combat climate change unless and until China, India, and other advanced developing nations were willing to assume equivalent obligations. In 2009, the Senate had stopped Obama's cap-and-trade legislation in its tracks, showing its unwillingness to impose additional costs on the economy while the United States was struggling to escape the deepest downturn since the Great Depression. Now China, India, and the other advanced developing nations had agreed to take on equivalent obligations, and the U.S. economy was showing sustained strength. It would have been natural, and potentially influential, for the Senate to make its views known on whether the United States should stay in the Paris Agreement given the changed circumstances and just how much was at stake.

Given Trump's desire to respond to his political base and stick a finger in the eye of the Europeans, it is possible that nothing could have swayed him. Still, a stronger Senate, with Republican leaders who had broader vision, probably could have tried. Twenty-two Republican senators had signed the letter calling for the president to withdraw from Paris, but thirty Republican senators did not sign on, despite the urging of McConnell, Cornyn, and Barrasso. Corker, the chairman of the Foreign Relations Committee, had already expressed his skepticism that leaving the Paris agreement was in the interest of the United States. He could have convened high-profile hearings to consider the ramifications of staying in, or leaving, the accord. Past Republican chairmen of the Foreign Relations Committee Charles Percy (R-IL) and Richard Lugar (R-IN) were men who combined an understanding of the economy, the environment, and America's place in the world. It is hard to envision Percy or Lugar allowing President Trump to decide an issue of this magnitude about America's place in the world without real Senate involvement.

By taking no action beyond kibitzing, the Senate allowed the president to make a decision of enormous implications that went against the strong majority of the country, and what would have been a strong majority of the Senate if members voted on their true beliefs. "Most Republicans still do not regard climate change as a hoax," said Whit Ayres, a Republican strategist who advised Marco Rubio's presidential campaign. "But the entire climate change debate has now been caught up in the broader polarization of American politics." Of course, that is exactly why we need a Senate: to rise above the polarization when the issue is important enough. Our system recognizes the need for strong presidential leadership, but not one-man rule, particularly where the futures of our children and grandchildren—not to mention our standing as leader of the free world—are affected.

· 13 ·

Reconsidering the Senate

TWO WEEKS IN OCTOBER

*A*gainst the grim backdrop of recent natural disasters in Texas, Florida, Puerto Rico and the Virgin Islands, and the mass killing in Las Vegas, events of the first two weeks of October provided a clear reminder of the radical nature of Donald Trump's presidency as well as the toll taken by the long period of Congressional dysfunction. But they also vividly illustrated the central role that the Senate, and, indeed, individual senators can play, as the balance wheel in our political system—the nation's mediator—when they rise above partisanship.

President Trump, frustrated by the inability of Senate Republicans to repeal and replace the Affordable Care Act, made good on his periodic threats to sabotage the ACA. On October 12, the administration announced an executive order designed to push people into insurance plans with skimpier benefits, generally referred to as "junk insurance plans," and slashing funds used to help people enroll in the ACA.[1] Later that day, the administration announced that it would no longer make payments to insurers that enabled them to reduce the deductibles and co-payments for lower-income Americans, rattling already shaky insurance markets.[2] A federal district court judge had ruled in 2016 that the Obama administration had overstepped by authorizing payments that had not been appropriated by Congress, and the Trump administration based its action on that ruling.

Earlier in the same week, the Trump administration laid out its demands that Democrats would have to meet before the president would agree to legislation protecting the "Dreamers" by maintaining the Deferred Action for Childhood Arrivals (DACA) program.[3] The administration's requirements included construction of a border wall, elimination of key federal grants for sanctuary cities and a fundamental overhaul of the legal immigration. The

231

September 5 announcement by Senate Minority Chuck Schumer and House Minority Leader Nancy Pelosi that they had reached agreement in principle with the president on legislation to protect the Dreamers constituted a rare moment of bipartisanship and progress. For those committed to protecting the Dreamers, it seemed like a moment too good to be true. The president's new list of demands made it clear that it had been.

On October 11, U.S, Mexican and Canadian negotiators met in Washington in the fourth round of talks to renegotiate NAFTA. Trump's extraordinary attacks on NAFTA and Mexico had quieted, and professional negotiators from all three countries were dealing with the demands and concerns of their numerous constituencies, and preparing to explore the tradeoffs necessary to for a successful negotiation. But during a visit by Canadian Prime Minister Justin Trudeau, President Trump casually restated his willingness to withdraw from NAFTA if United States demands were not met.[4] No one believed that Mexico or Canada would bow to any extreme U.S. demands to change NAFTA provisions to favor the U.S., and it appeared unlikely that Trump, or his U.S. Trade Representative Robert Lighthizer, would settle for modernization of NAFTA that would be welcomed by Mexico, Canada and the business communities in all three countries. With countless industries having built a North American supply chain based on NAFTA, the economic impact of a breakdown in the negotiation was incalculable, but would be enormous. The political repercussions of a breakdown, particularly in a Mexican presidential election year, could be seismic. NAFTA helped reverse a long history of Mexican hostility and distrust toward the United States, but Trump's fiery rhetoric had undermined three decades of progress in weeks, destroyed decades of progress in weeks, reawakening an anti-American sentiment in Mexico tha had been dormant.[5]

Also in the week of October 9, EPA administrator Scott Pruitt announced that the Trump administration was formally terminating the Clean Power Plan, the regulatory initiative of the Obama administration to reduce emissions from power plants to meet U.S. commitments made in the Paris agreement on climate change.[6] The decision came as no surprise, given Trump's repudiation of the Paris agreement, and Pruitt's leadership in opposing the Clean Power Plan as Oklahoma Attorney General. Eliminating the Clean Power Plan made it less likely that the United States will meet the commitments made in Paris, since coal and natural gas-fired power plants presently contribute about one-third of America's CO2 emissions.[7] It also continued, and underscored, America's retreat from leadership in the global effort to combat climate change.

On October 13, President Trump disavowed the nuclear pact with Iran by refusing to certify that Iran was complying with the terms of the pact.[8] The decision to decertify did not end the United States' involvement in the agreement; rather, it passed the buck to Congress to decide if sanctions should be re-imposed. But the president's decision cast doubt on the U.S. commitment to the treaty, potentially isolating the U.S. as the other signatories indicated that they had no plans to leave the treaty. The Obama administration had reached three landmark international agreements in 2015: the Paris agreement, the Trans-Pacific Partnership, and the Iran nuclear agreement. Each agreement represented years of painstaking negotiation with many other countries, with adversaries as well as allies. His successor had jettisoned two, and created serious doubt about the U.S. commitment to the third.

This flurry of actions by the Trump administration clearly demonstrated the regressive right-wing nature of Trump's domestic policy, and the Trump-Bannon commitment to disrupt the world by remaking America's place in it. "There's a new and scary spring in his step," said Clifford Kupchan, chairman of the Eurasia Group, a global consulting firm. "He could be entering a new phase of fuller takedowns of agreements and institutions."[9] The Senate faced the choice of whether to check the president in a series of areas, and if so, how to do it.

Health care quickly took center stage, as it had all year. For months, Lamar Alexander and Patty Murray had been quietly sharing ideas about a legislative fix to shore up the Affordable Care Act (ACA). When McConnell's legislative efforts with the Graham-Cassidy bill failed in September, Alexander and Murray immediately accelerated their work, meeting with a broad range of affected constituencies, and holding the first Senate hearing of the year on the ACA, to fashion legislation that could stabilize the insurance markets. On October 17, Alexander and Murray announced that they had reached agreement on a plan to fund the subsidies, known as cost-sharing reduction payments, for two years, reimbursing insurance companies for lowering deductibles, co-payments and other out-of-pocket expenses for lower-income customers. The agreement would also restore millions of dollars for advertising and outreach activities to publicize insurance options available in the health law's open enrollment period, starting on November 1.[10] To attract support of Republican governors and some conservatives, the Alexander-Murray deal would give the states increased flexibility in some of the choices they offered to consumers. State governments would find it easier to obtain waivers from some the requirements of the ACA, but there would be explicit protections for low-income people and people with serious diseases. The senators' bill quickly attracted 24 co-sponsors, twelve from each party.[11]

Senator Schumer praised the agreement as a model for how the two parties could work together. "I don't expect the Republicans to give up their goal of repealing the ACA," Schumer said. "But in the meantime, stabilizing the system, preventing chaos and stopping the sabotage is in everybody's interest."[12] While House Freedom Caucus members immediately objected to the deal, and President Trump changed his view from day to day, the bipartisan support in the Senate, and the angry public response to the Republican efforts to repeal or gut the ACA, made enactment of the legislation likely. "In my view, this agreement avoids chaos," Senator Alexander said, "and I don't know a Democrat or Republican who benefits from chaos."[13]

The challenge of protecting the Dreamers, an issue on which Congress had repeatedly failed, confronted the Senate again. Trump had been all over the map: running a vicious anti-immigrant campaign, promising a border wall, and appointing Jeff Sessions to be Attorney General; refusing to continue DACA but giving Congress six months to fix it; expressing his love for the Dreamers and seemingly agreeing with Schumer and Pelosi to work together to protect them. The Senate found a successful formula for immigration legislation in 2013, thanks to the bipartisan "Gang of Eight; strong support from a group of Republicans is essential. Helping the Dreamers should be much easier than obtaining comprehensive immigration reform. Lindsey Graham remains strongly committed, continuing to push the Dream Act with Dick Durbin, his Democratic co-sponsor. Thom Tillis (R-NC), a first-term senator, has emerged as a strong new player on the immigration issue. He approached Durbin earlier in the year to express his commitment to do something to help protect the Dreamers. In September, along with Republicans Orrin Hatch and James Lankford (R-OK), Tillis introduced the Succeed Act, a bill that would create a pathway to citizenship for the Dreamers, although with more stringent requirements and tougher restrictions than the Durbin-Graham Dream Act. Tillis' bill quickly drew criticism from both sides; liberals criticized it as openly harsh, while conservatives described it as amnesty, with a slightly conservative wrinkle. John Cornyn, the Senate Republican whip who also chairs the Senate subcommittee on immigration expressed his admiration: "He's a pretty courageous guy." Ali Noorani, executive director of the pro-reform National Immigration Forum, said: "He's been a new player . . . on an issue where we've frankly been starved for new talent."[14]

For Democrats, shielding the approximately 800,000 Dreamers from deportation is probably their highest legislative priority in the closing months of Trump's first year. Schumer and Pelosi's three- month deal with Trump to increase the debt limit and fund the government until mid-December gives them considerable leverage with White House, since Democratic votes will be needed to keep the government open. In the battles over health care, Susan Collins, Lisa Murkowski and John McCain showed that legislation can be stopped by as few as three senators who were willing to stand against the Republican leader and the White House. But enacting legislation requires genuine bipartisan cooperation, which means support from a substantial contingent of the Senate Republicans. With Tillis, Hatch, Lankford and Cornyn embracing the cause of the Dreamers, the critical mass of Republicans necessary for Senate passage could be building. The Republican senators who are supportive of the Dreamers will undoubtedly prove to be key players in the December showdown. Because of unrelenting opposition from most House Republicans, the president's position is likely to be decisive.

Health care and immigration present complex, emotionally-charged issues, but they represent familiar terrain. Legislating successfully will require wisdom and courage, but the senators have devoted years of work to these issues and understand them quite well. In contrast, President Trump's handling of the Iran nuclear pact puts the Senate in uncharted waters. There is no precedent for Trump's decision to throw this hot potato to Congress, while retaining the authority to reject their advice or action, and terminate America's involvement in the agreement. As Josh Rogin observed in the *Washington Post*: "the president combined tough-sounding rhetoric about reversing part of President Obama's legacy with a too-clever-by-half plan to avoid doing the heavy lifting himself. Now Congress is left with the mess while the international community scratches its head."[15]

In fact, the administration has a strategy that can be discerned. According to Rogin's reporting, Secretary of State Rex Tillerson has been working quietly for weeks with Senator Bob Corker, chairman of the Foreign Relations Committee, and Senator Tom Cotton (R-ARK) on legislation to amend the Iran Nuclear Agreement Review Act. The proposal would effectively change the terms of the deal by imposing new sanctions "triggers" if Iran gets close to nuclear weapons capability and negating the "sunset" provisions easing restrictions on Iran in the deal's out years. As Secretary Tillerson explained, the United States must "either put more teeth into this obligation that Iran has undertaken...or let's just forget the whole thing. We'll walk away and start over."[16]

The administration obviously sees this as a way of putting pressure on Congress and our international partners to toughen the agreement. However, as Wendy R. Sherman, former Under Secretary of State and lead negotiator for the Iran agreement, wrote: "[The president] hopes Congress will pass new legislation to address concerns that were never part of the nuclear agreement's original mandate. If Congress complies, such unilateral action to change a multilateral agreement will effectively kill it. . . . Whether the Trump administration's decertification unravels the deal quickly or slowly, unjustified unilateral American action will give the Iranians the moral high ground, allowing them to rightly say it was the United States, not them, who killed the deal...This decision will breach the trust of America's partners and isolate our country."[17]

Corker and Ben Cardin, the ranking Democrat on the Foreign Relations Committee, bear the principal burden of responding to the president's ill-conceived action. That seems fair since they strongly believe that the Senate should be partners in formulating America's foreign policy. Corker and Cardin crafted the 2015 legislation which gave Congress a limited role in reviewing the Iran agreement before it went into effect. They also took the lead in strengthening sanctions against Iran, North Korea and Russia earlier this year, and restricting Trump's ability to waive the Russia sanctions. The Senate, with Corker and Cardin in the lead, faces a fundamental choice. They can collaborate with President Trump in a course of action that will inevitably lead to the United States leaving the agreement. Alternatively, the senators can tell the president that they oppose any action that leads to the United States withdrawing from an agreement with which Iran is complying. They can express their views privately, but they should also express them publicly, in statements and a Senate resolution. They may not persuade President Trump to stay in the Iran agreement, but our allies and our adversaries, as well as the American people, need to know that the Senate was not complicit in his decision.

At the same time, the Senate Republican leaders on trade, particularly Orrin Hatch and Chuck Grassley, began to assess how to block a potential move by President Trump to pull the United States out of NAFTA. The *Financial Times* reported a rising concern in the Senate and in the U.S. business community that the administration's chief trade negotiator, USTR Robert Lighthizer, were making "'poison pill' proposals intended to force a collapse of increasingly bitter negotiations."[18] A decision by Trump to withdraw the United States from NAFTA would be a major test of the Constitutional division of powers. "Many presidents have torn up security treaties on their own march. But there are not any examples where a president has terminated a trade agreement [unilaterally], which gets at the central power of Congress," said Gary Hufbauer of the Peterson Institute of International Economics, one of the world's leading trade experts.[19] Although NAFTA has always been unpopular in the House, particularly among Democrats, the Senate has traditionally been more supportive. "Congress has a ton of power," said Phil Levy, a former trade adviser to president George W. Bush. "The question is whether they are willing to use it."[20] The politics of trade pose more fascinating cross-currents than the politics surrounding the Paris agreement on climate change, but the possibility of a withdrawal from NAFTA raises the same basic question: whether the Senate will stand by and allow the country to submit to one-man rule.

Also, during the turbulent first two weeks of October, two of the most independent Republicans, Bob Corker and Susan Collins, who had been publicly agonizing about whether to stay in the Senate, reached their decisions. Corker, the former mayor of Chattanooga and successful builder, announced that he would not seek a third term in 2018.[21] Collins, the former Senate staffer and state Cabinet officer, who had been contemplating a race for governor in Maine, decided that she could serve Maine and the country better by staying in the Senate.[22]

In mid-October, the political fate of a third independent-minded Republican senator hung by a thread. Jeff Flake, a fifth generation Arizonan from a ranching family, entered politics after serving as a Mormon missionary, and being inspired by Barry Goldwater's principled conservatism. Flake even headed the Goldwater Institute before getting elected to the House of Representatives in 2000 and the Senate in 2012. In 2016, Flake steadfastly refused to support Donald Trump even after Trump seized the Republican presidential nomination. By the summer of 2017, Flake had seen enough. He borrowed the title of Goldwater's book—"the conscience of a conservative"—and wrote an astonishing indictment of Trump's dangerous presidency and the Republican Party that abandoned its principles to support him.

Viewing the threat that Trump's reckless policies and divisive behavior posed to the nation, Senator Flake wrote: "Under our Constitution, there simply are not that many people who are in a position to do something about an executive branch in chaos. As the first branch of government (Article I), the Congress was designed expressly to assert itself in just such moments. It is what we talk about when we talk about 'checks and balances.' Too often we observe the unfolding drama along with the rest of the country, passively all but saying 'someone should do something' without seeming to realize that someone is us."[23] Flake's outspoken book evoked admiration in the country, and loathing within the Republican Party. Facing certain defeat in the Republican primary, Flake announced his decision on October 24 not to seek re-election, acknowledging that there was no longer a place for someone with his views in the Republican Party. Explaining his decision on the Senate floor, Flake said: "We must stop pretending that the degradation of our politics and the conduct of some in the executive branch are normal."[24]

The decisions of Corker, Collins, and Flake would impact the Senate powerfully, and the contrasting outcomes were revealing. Bob Corker always saw himself as a "citizen-legislator," and followed the Tennessee tradition of Howard Baker and Bill Frist, both of whom announced early that they planned to limit their time in the Senate. He made no secret of his frustration with the Senate's gridlock, and his inability to bridge the partisan divide on taxes and the budget, and financial regulation. Corker had, in fact, given serious thought to leaving the Senate after one term. At the time Corker was making his decision, he was involved in an extraordinary, bitter, continuing battle with President Trump. Corker had questioned Trump's competence, called the White House "an adult day care center," and said that only the senior administration officials containing Trump protected the country against chaos and the possibility of World War III.[25] His decision not to seek re-election gave Corker complete independence, and he undoubtedly believed, quite rightly, that he was serving the country by speaking hard truths about the dangerous president.

Susan Collins, in her fourth term, had not missed a vote in her entire 20-year Senate career.[26] She had carved out a special place in the Senate and the country as the most moderate Republican, a bridge to the Democrats, and a perennial thorn in the side of Mitch McConnell. Experienced, principled, and willing to stand alone, Collins provided the decisive vote and the leadership to ensure that President Obama's economic stimulus would become law in early 2009. She was the only Republican senator who maintained the position that Judge Merrick Garland should receive a hearing after Obama nominated him. And more recently, Collins played a key role in thwarting every one of McConnell's efforts to repeal the ACA. It was inconceivable to those who knew her that Collins would choose to leave the Senate at a time when the Trump presidency posed such a threat to the country, and characteristically, she chose to stay, and fight. Senators on both sides of the aisle expressed delight at Collins's decision.

The decisions of Corker and Collins came against the backdrop of an extraordinary, intensifying rift within the Republican Party. Stephen Bannon, the architect and driving force behind Trump's fierce populist campaign, had left the White House and returned to Breitbart News. Now, in the name of "Trumpism," Bannon turned his rhetorical blowtorch and formidable fund-raising skills to recruiting extreme, anti-government candidates to challenge incumbent Republican senators.[27] Bannon won a striking victory on September 26 when former Alabama State Supreme Court Justice Roy Moore, best known for his fervent religious views, which included designing and commissioning a 2½ ton monument of the Ten Commandments for the courthouse, defeated Luther Strange who had been appointed to the Senate when Jeff Sessions left to become Attorney General.[28] Propelled by an outpouring of evangelical supporters, Moore won decisively, despite a $10 million advertising blitz funded by allies of Senator McConnell, and the tepid endorsement of President Trump. Exultant, Bannon moved ahead, lining up similarly extreme candidates to take on other Republican senators.

McConnell became majority leader after the 2014 elections because he had successfully obstructed Obama's presidency and prevented the emergence of extreme Republican nominees who would have lost Senate seats. Now three years later, McConnell found himself criticized by Trump as a weak, effectual leader, and the principal target of the populist insurgency, which saw him as epitomizing Washington's failed establishment—the "swamp" that Trump had promised to "drain." Yet President Trump, turning to his highest legislative priority—tax reform—could not afford to alienate McConnell, or any of the Republican senators.

John McCain, fighting incurable brain cancer, emerged as the most eloquent critic of both the Trump presidency and McConnell's dysfunctional Senate. In fact, Trump and McConnell faced the same fundamental problem. The American political system is designed to prevent one- man rule, and over time has evolved to prevent one-party rule as well. The moments in our history when one party could govern without some help from the other are almost non-existent. If the president and the majority leader wanted legislative accomplishments, they needed each other, but they also needed some degree of Democratic support. Indeed, Trump and McConnell needed "the system" to work, and yet both of them—each in his own way—had done great damage to its ability to do so.

ASSESSING THE SENATE'S LONG DECLINE

Donald Trump and his extraordinary presidency tend to blot out everything else on the political landscape, or distort it. While the Senate faces the unique and unprecedented challenge of responding to, and containing, Trump, no one should lose sight of how long the Senate was failing before Trump was elected. The Senate's long downward spiral raises serious questions about its ability to respond to Trump, questions that I believe are being answered in a mixed, but mostly encouraging, way. At the same time, the Senate needs to come to grips with its problems and restore its strength going forward. Hopefully, the Trump presidency will be mercifully brief, but America will always need a respectably functioning Senate that is not paralyzed by partisanship and gridlock.

The Senate's long decline is, of course, closely tied to the overall deterioration of our politics, our political culture, and our national government. In the early 1990s, a quarter century ago, important books by E. J. Dionne Jr. (*Why Americans Hate Politics*), Thomas Byrne Edsall and Mary D. Edsall (*Chain Reaction*), and Kevin Phillips (*Boiling Point*) painted a troubling picture of America's increasingly poisonous politics and a government failing to address fundamental issues. But the Senate's decline has also proceeded on its own separate and distinctive path, increasingly unable to overcome partisanship. Since the Senate's ability to serve as the "nation's mediator" relies on the senators' ability to find common ground, its failure to transcend partisanship strikes at the heart of its special mission.

This is first and foremost a profound failure of Senate leaders. Looking back at the leadership of the great Senate of Mike Mansfield and Republican leaders Everett Dirksen and Hugh Scott, we see a leadership characterized by mutual trust and respect, recognition of the importance of bipartisanship, and an abiding commitment to making the Senate work to take collective action in the national interest. Of course, when there were substantial contingents of moderate Republicans and conservative Democrats, it was much easier to form cross-party alliances. But even as the composition of the Senate changed in the 1970s and 1980s, Senate leaders communicated and collaborated to keep the Senate working. Robert Byrd and Howard Baker formed a special relationship of trust, particularly because of their remarkable collaboration in the fight to win Senate approval of the Panama Canal treaties. Byrd and Bob Dole continued the pattern of collaboration and the record of accomplishment. It may have helped that they both served as majority and minority leaders, but what mattered most was their commitment to the Senate.

The last effective leadership team was Tom Daschle, the liberal Midwestern Democrat, and Trent Lott, the conservative southern Republican. They disagreed on virtually every issue, but they established a relationship that helped steer the Senate through the stormy impeachment trial of Bill Clinton, the fair allocation of committee slots and funding when the Senate divided 50–50, and the testing and emotional period after 9/11. Ironically, Lott, who served in the House as a young man and hated the Senate when he first arrived, grew to appreciate its special role and, over time, became a leading advocate of bipartisanship (which, admittedly, is often easier once out of office).

The Senate's long decline certainly did not go unnoticed. Scholars, journalists, political analysts, and senators themselves all lamented the loss of the Senate that they remembered. What is striking is how little effort the recent Senate leaders made to combat it. This is particularly true for Mitch McConnell and Harry Reid, who presided over the long, bleak decade where the trajectory of the Senate's decline was steepest. Nobody questions that they were working hard in two of the most challenging jobs possible, but they devoted all their energy to leading their respective caucuses into the next round of partisan warfare rather than worrying about the health of the institution.

Previous Senate leaders approached their responsibilities very differently. In 1977, Robert Byrd and Howard Baker, the new Senate leaders, faced an internal challenge because James Allen (D-AL) had found a new way to tie the institution in knots. Traditionally, when the Senate invoked cloture on a bill or a nomination, that signaled the end of the debate was near. Senator Allen, a keen student of the Senate rules, spotted the opportunity to prolong debate by filing many amendments before cloture was invoked, and then, after cloture, calling up the amendments one by one and utilizing quorum calls to waste Senate time. Allen road tested his new tactic in 1976, with great effect, against the antitrust legislation known as Hart-Scott-Rodino. Allen's filibuster ended only because all senators wanted to complete the legislation to honor Phil Hart (D-MI), a beloved colleague who was dying of cancer.

The next year, when the Senate took up complex legislation to deregulate the price of natural gas, James Abourezk (D-SD) and Howard Metzenbaum (D-OH) launched their own post-cloture filibuster. Majority Leader Byrd, working with Vice President Walter Mondale presiding over the Senate, and with Minority Leader Baker's acquiescence, crushed the filibuster, outraging many senators on both sides of the aisle. Byrd and Baker came away understanding that they needed to convince the Senate to change its rules to address the threat of post-cloture filibusters. At the beginning of the next Congress, the Senate, by a vote of 78–16, approved a package of significant changes, negotiated by an ad hoc committee appointed by the leaders that restricted the use of the post-cloture filibuster.

Byrd and Baker did not stand by, letting filibusters proliferate, comity erode, and the Senate be crippled when they saw a serious problem. They did not avert their eyes to the threat to the Senate, wait for some better time to deal with the problem, or pretend the problem would solve itself. They stepped up quickly because they recognized their responsibility to be leaders of the Senate rather than just a leader of the Senate Democrats and a leader of the Senate Republicans.

By now, everyone recognizes the many factors that have contributed to the decline of our politics, including: the cost of campaigns; the impact of the shrill and contentious twenty-four-hour media; a political conversation increasingly conducted on Facebook and Twitter; a fivefold increase in the number of lobbyists in the last thirty years; gerrymandered districts; and members fearful of being "primaried." These and other factors have contributed to increased polarization that has ultimately produced gridlock.

But it was not inevitable that the Senate would succumb to those factors so completely. The Senate leaders failed, and, frankly, the senators, in both parties, failed to insist that the problems of the Senate be seriously addressed. The Senate is a group of one hundred men and women, all of whom are extremely intelligent and exceptionally determined; otherwise, they would not have reached the Senate. It is safe to assume that although they have major policy differences, most, if not all, of the senators want to be part of a Senate that is respected and serving the American people. It is shocking that they stood by and allowed the Senate, one of the rocks of the Republic, to continue to decline.

It does not require much imagination to come up with a process that would have enabled meaningful changes to be considered. By 2011, the Senate had gone through the grueling battles of the first two years of the Obama administration. The next year would witness a presidential election and Senate elections, with control of the White House and the Senate completely uncertain. That would have been an ideal time to consider changes in the

Senate rules and practices that would work for the majority, the minority, and the individual senators. The stars aligned similarly in 2015. Under those circumstances, would it have been so difficult to fashion rules to deal with executive and judicial nominations that would have been fair to both parties? We will never know, since McConnell and Reid made no effort to initiate a meaningful process. Instead, they allowed the Senate to lurch from crisis to crisis, congratulating themselves on last-minute deals to avert disasters—until they could no longer reach those agreements.

There is a clear record of nearly three decades of serious decline, and a historical backdrop that shows the Senate, by its nature, to be "procedurally fragile,"[29] a wonderful description offered by John C. Roberts, a law professor and former Senate committee staffer. The concept of "unlimited debate" causes the Senate to tilt toward paralysis. The ad hoc fixes that began with the adoption of cloture in 1917 have not been sufficiently strong or supple to overcome the obstruction by individual senators, or the obstruction of a determined minority party. We need to look anew at the Senate so that it can serve its vital function in the twenty-first century.

The process should start from an agreement about what our country needs and expects from the Senate. Although the country has changed dramatically since its founding, the framers' original concept retains great value. The Senate should be an institution whose members bring wisdom, experience, and independent judgment to bear on the full range of domestic and foreign policy issues. The Senate should act as a thoughtful, moderating force to the passions of the time that may find expression in the president and rip through the House of Representatives.

That much is easy, and today's senators, like their predecessors, have the requisite wisdom and experience to contribute to the national interest, if they exercise a degree of independent judgment rather than lining up as partisan warriors. The question becomes how the Senate avoids the obstruction and polarization that have so damaged its performance.

The Senate has not done a comprehensive review of its rules and procedures since 1979. As far back as 2005, Trent Lott wrote: "The Senate, in my view, had become increasingly dysfunctional.[30] . . . It was time we gave all the rules a thorough and fair review. How many of them were simply archaic? And were there new rules we could adopt in the interest of efficiency and consensus?" No such review occurred, and the Senate's paralysis intensified.

In my view, the Senate should commit to empower a panel to conduct a comprehensive review in 2019, with the intent of putting in place necessary changes in rules and procedures when the Senate convenes in 2021 after the next presidential election. The panel could be cochaired by two distinguished former senators, but it should also include knowledgeable outside experts as well as respected representatives of the public. Without prejudging what such a review panel would ultimately recommend, several areas of concern warrant special attention.

ADDRESSING AND REMEDYING "PROCEDURAL FRAGILITY"

The Senate should do its work through substantial, considered debate. Robert Byrd, the longest-serving senator and its greatest institutionalist, distinguished between "extended debate" and "unlimited debate," for obvious reasons.[31] "Extended debate" is what is needed for understanding the issues, allowing for amendments that improve the legislation and for compromises to emerge that bring members with diverse views toward common ground. "Unlimited debate" sounds like an invitation to obstruction and paralysis, and that has proven to be exactly the case.

The late Barbara Sinclair, perhaps the most respected political scientist studying the Senate, described in 1989 "the hyper-exploitation of prerogatives under the rules.[32] . . . The majority uses procedural devices to prevent debate and action on the minority's agenda, and the minority reciprocates by blocking the majority's agenda." Other experts have referred to "the Senate syndrome," whereby the minority threatens to filibuster[33] and the majority responds by moving to quickly cut off debate and deny the minority the ability to offer amendments. Over time, obstruction has become a routine and expected part of Senate life, and the senators come to accept it in the same way that Washingtonians live with traffic jams or Metrorail breakdowns. It is important to remember that it was once different. In the entire decade of the 1970s, the Senate invoked cloture to end filibusters forty-three times. In the 113th Congress (2013–2014) alone, the Senate invoked cloture 187 times.

The obstruction has caused the Senate's productivity to be dramatically reduced.[34] In the four years of Jimmy Carter's presidency, Congress passed 2,046 bills. Comparing four-year periods of subsequent presidents: during the Reagan presidency, 1,722 bills passed; during the presidency of George H. W. Bush, 1,927. In Bill Clinton's first four years, 1,200 bills passed; in George W. Bush's first term, it was 1,313. During the first four years of the Obama presidency, Congress passed 540 bills. That is a striking decline, even acknowledging that the Affordable Care Act and the Dodd-Frank financial reform were huge legislative undertakings.

Recorded votes have also declined sharply. In the five Congresses of the 1970s, the Senate took an average of 1,135 votes. By contrast, in the five Congresses of the 2000s, the Senate took an average of 665 votes—a reduction of 41 percent. The nation's challenges had not decreased, but the Senate's productivity certainly has.

The United States is not the only country that faces the challenge of balancing majority power and minority protection in its legislature. All the leading democracies seem to grapple with the challenge of the filibuster; the United Kingdom, Australia, Canada, and South Korea are all debating legislation that seeks to protect minority rights while in some way limiting the filibuster. In South Korea, for example, the National Assembly Advancement Act, passed in 2012 and implemented in 2014, requires three-fifths of the lawmakers to agree to put a bill up for a vote during a plenary session.[35] This bill was intended to protect minority rights in the Assembly but quickly faced criticism for slowing down business. In February 2016, the main opposition party in South Korea set what might be a global record for filibustering—192 hours of speeches from approximately thirty-eight lawmakers. But in all these countries, the use, or threat, of the filibuster is an exception, not the rule, for conducting parliamentary business. The filibuster is employed for controversial legislation, and while it is a delaying tactic, filibusters are not generally effective in killing legislation.

Of course, the Senate once worked that way; resort to the filibuster was reserved for exceptional cases, particularly the historic clashes over civil rights. But that changed dramatically over time. John C. Roberts has written: "Restraint in the use of obstructive practices arose from recognition of the Senate's procedural fragility[36]—every senator realized that under its loose rules, chaos would result if each senator fully exploited his rights, and that each senator's own pet bills were vulnerable to reciprocal obstruction." Roberts went on to contend that "the Standing Rules must be changed to recognize that the old consensus controls of restraint and cooperation[37] that kept the filibuster weapon from destroying the Senate's work are no longer functioning." He urges a return to the Senate's traditional view: "to re-establish the filibuster as an instrument of extended debate,[38] not knee-jerk obstruction, [and] to confine the filibuster, to issues of real importance."

Senators Jeff Merkley (D-OR) and Tom Udall (D-NM) have suggested the most direct and effective way to both "reestablish" the filibuster and "confine" it: requiring the return to the talking filibuster. No longer should "the mere threat of a filibuster suffice to kill a bill[39] as the Senate shrugs and goes on to other business," as Congressman Tom McClintock (R-CA) has observed. Conservative columnist George Will has also endorsed the return to the talking filibuster.[40]

Closely related to the abuse of the filibuster is the use of the "hold," a formal tactic by which any senator could stall a bill or the nomination process. In his 2005 memoir, Trent Lott expressed puzzlement about how the "hold," originally respected as a temporary courtesy to ensure that a senator with a special interest in a matter would have the opportunity to participate in debate, had morphed into a tool for blocking consideration of legislation or a nomination for an indefinite time. But as far back as 1989, Barbara Sinclair quoted a frustrated senator:

> It used to mean that putting a hold on something meant simply that you would be given twenty-four hours' notice that this thing would come up, so you could prepare for that. And of course, when you put a hold on something, it puts the people, the sponsors, on notice that you had some problems and it would be in their interest to come and negotiate with you. But four or five or six years ago, it started to mean that if you put a hold on something, it would never come up. It became, in fact, a veto.[41]

Even in the 1980s, the party leaders made several attempts to return to the former interpretation of holds. For example, on December 6, 1982—thirty-five years ago—Majority Leader Howard Baker announced on the Senate floor: "In these final two weeks . . . holds will be honored only sparingly and under the most urgent circumstances. . . . Senators are aware, of course, that holds . . . are matters of courtesy by the leadership on both sides of the aisle and are not part of the standing rules of the Senate."[42] Baker's admonition had no real impact. "As long as members are willing to back their holds with actual extended debate,"[43] Sinclair observed, "the leaders are faced with an impossible situation when floor time is short."[44]

Since that time, the use of "holds" has further proliferated. Now it is common for a senator to place a hold on a nomination or a piece of legislation because the senator is angry about some unrelated issue. Frequently, a senator will place a hold on numerous nominations at once. Several senators, led by Ron Wyden, have objected to anonymous holds, and have had some success in getting daylight put on them. But no one seems to ask the more basic question: Why should there be any holds, beyond a short courtesy period?

The Senate also seems to be unique in the world in permitting "non-germane," that is, "irrelevant," amendments. The Senate is the only legislative body that can be debating transportation or energy or foreign aid and suddenly find itself considering amendments on abortion, gun control, or school prayer. The Senate recognizes that non-germane amendments should at some point be limited, so Senate rules require that after cloture is invoked, all amendments must be germane. But that requirement produces a situation in which the majority leader increasingly feels the pressure to invoke cloture as soon as possible—sometimes even before the debate has begun—angering the minority. The Senate could join with the other parliaments in the world and require that all amendments be "germane," that is, relevant to the underlying subject matter. Senators have many opportunities to express their views on any and every issue. They should not have license to speak on the Senate floor during a legislative debate on some irrelevant issue, disrupting debate on the issue that the Senate is considering.

Senate floor time is a precious commodity, particularly as the legislative year goes on. Thus, these three significant changes—returning to "real filibusters," recognizing that holds are only a temporary courtesy, and eliminating non-germane amendments—could reduce obstruction and restore the Senate to a body where serious debate occurs on important issues. A full review of the Senate rules and practices would undoubtedly identify other valuable changes that could be made. It should be possible to guarantee to any president that his executive and judicial nominations will be taken up within ninety days, or some other specified amount of time. It should also be possible to establish that if a unanimous consent agreement cannot be reached, the minority party's right to offer some number of amendments would be ensured. The Senate's operations could be improved significantly, increasing floor time for real debate and reducing the frustration that senators feel today.

REBALANCING THE "LEADER-DRIVEN" SENATE

With its commitment to "unlimited debate" and proceeding by "unanimous consent," its consideration of "non-germane" amendments, its submission to "holds," and its vulnerability to filibusters and the threat thereof, the Senate has always been extremely difficult to manage. Gary Hart (D-CO) once described the Senate of his time as a "controlled madhouse," and it often walked the narrow ledge between paralysis and chaos. Consequently, the Senate will always need strong and effective leaders. But at its best, the Senate maintained a healthy balance between the leaders, the committees, and the individual senators. The leaders played an essential role but did not dominate the institution. The committees, and the individual senators, would not allow it. Regrettably, the Senate has lost that balance, and will recover on a lasting basis only when it finds a way to restore it.

Ross K. Baker, the Rutgers political scientist and one of the greatest students of the Senate, got a unique perspective on the modern Senate being "embedded" in Harry Reid's staff in 2008 and 2012. "In the intimate confines of a Senate committee, personal ties and common interests promote bipartisanship," Baker noted.[45] "It would be safe to say that the world of the committees is a less contentious place than the Senate floor.[46] The committee is the realm of 'regular order,' the systematic and methodical processing of legislation by policy specialists backed up by professional committee staffs."

The legislative process always provides plenty of room for politics and partisanship. "The Senate floor is a more free-wheeling place of political combat, of partisan cut and thrust, and a place where, in a time of political polarization, points can be scored against the opposition," Baker wrote. But the senators need to stand up for the importance of the work that their committees are doing. They need to insist that serious legislative work be done in the committees rather than in ad hoc, partisan task forces. The committees will produce legislation that is substantively stronger and more likely to command broad, bipartisan support and public confidence.

Of course, the Republican effort to "repeal and replace" the Affordable Care Act illustrates the fundamental differences between two possible approaches. If there was ever an issue that required real substantive expertise and a bipartisan approach, it was the challenge of repairing the health care system. When the process starts with the committees, it immediately starts with the substance, including such novel ideas as holding comprehensive hearings. When the process starts with the leadership, it becomes partisan from day one. The American people would have expected the Senate to produce a much more generous bill through a much less partisan process than the House. Ideally, the leaders of the two committees of jurisdiction would have told McConnell and Schumer: "We've got this. The committee staff will keep your staff very current on what we're doing."

McConnell's approach was not only a shocking departure from the Senate's best practices; it was radically different than anything that an experienced Senate watcher could remember. Hopefully, this vivid example of the leader's overreach will be the catalyst for the committees, and the individual senators, to push back and provide a needed rebalance to the institution.

Given the fact that the Senate has failed over a long period, some individual soul searching by senators is in order. The Senate cannot counteract all the forces that have polarized our politics, but it should make efforts to minimize polarization rather than worsen it. It should build trust rather than destroy it. In 2012, looking at the Reid-McConnell dynamic, I suggested that the Senate needed new leaders. In 2014, I wrote the Senate would work much better with a different Republican leader. That was before McConnell's unprecedented refusal to take up the Garland nomination and his unprecedented effort to ram the health care bill through the Senate. McConnell's memoir is aptly titled *The Long Game*; I certainly see a possibility that as the Russia investigation moves inexorably forward, McConnell will decide it is in his interest to play a role in forcing Trump to resign. But I do not believe the Senate can restore itself until the Republicans have a new leader. The Senate would benefit greatly if a Democrat and Republican, or a team of Democrats and Republicans, put themselves forward to provide new leadership. It would be a dramatic departure from tradition, but a dramatic departure, in the interest of bipartisanship and a new start, is sorely needed.

The voters of their states have given the hundred senators one of the greatest privileges that the Republic can bestow. It is natural that the senators will seek to maximize their individual impact; their speeches, press appearances, and proposed bills and amendments all matter. But it is also crucial that they contribute to making the Senate work—as the nation's mediator; as the check on presidential overreach and House extremism; and as an institution that finds common ground to take collective action in the national interest.

It is far more difficult today to be a senator than it was in an earlier era. Senators are constantly bombarded by the demands of constituents, interest groups, the media and the sheer challenge of representing one million people of Montana or thirty-nine million people of California. The ease of air travel and the demands of fundraising have drastically reduced the amount of time that senators spend together building personal friendships based on trust and mutual respect. But the senators are not powerless victims; they can do things to improve the situation. If they understand that their weekly caucus lunches are partisan pep rallies, they should have fewer caucus lunches, or more bipartisan committee lunches. They should emulate the example of Mark Warner, who is well known for bringing groups of senators together for dinner.[47] They should learn from the experience of Barbara Mikulski, who retired at the end of 2016. She worked for years to mentor the expanding contingent of women senators in both parties, creating a bipartisan "zone of civility" through monthly dinners.[48] It is no accident that in recent years, women senators, Democrats and Republicans, have been among the most effective legislators and builders of consensus in the Senate.

The senators work in an acrimonious political culture that seems to offer little reward for substance and sees moderation and compromise as weaknesses. The senators are simultaneously practitioners and victims of the "permanent campaign." But there remain great rewards for being "in the arena," as Theodore Roosevelt memorably described it.[49] Despite all the challenges, a substantial number of senators constantly demonstrate the wisdom, judgment, and independence that always characterized the outstanding senators. They attract and value the high-quality staff needed to help them, and they build and maintain the personal relationships needed to legislate successfully. The best senators understand and reflect Mansfield's wisdom: their individual agendas do not ultimately matter; it is the Senate, and the nation, that matter. What is most urgently needed is for senators to act like senators, not partisan operatives. They should not mirror, and even exacerbate, the nation's divisions. They were sent to Washington to overcome them.

A Note on Sources

$\mathcal{I}$ was at one time a Senate insider, but that ended thirty years ago. I know very few of the current or recent senators or staff members, and I did not feel it would be appropriate to talk to such a small sample, so I didn't. I am not a journalist, so I did not attempt to write a book based on interviews. Consequently, this book relies on what I learned about the Senate while working there in the 1970s and 1980s; the research that allowed me to write *The Last Great Senate*; and following the Senate closely through press coverage, particularly from the *New York Times* and *Washington Post*. Part II of the book—the Senate during the first six months of the Trump presidency—is exclusively based on my observations about the Senate's performance based on the superb journalism of many terrific reporters and columnists who provided a first look at an extraordinary period of American political history. I have also benefited from the rapid-fire series of books in the past five years depicting the increasingly broken Senate.

I particularly appreciate the regular reporting and coverage of the Senate by Paul Kane, Carl Hulse, Jennifer Steinhauer, Sheryl Gay Stolberg, and Jonathan Weisman, and the more general political analysis by Dan Balz, E. J. Dionne Jr., Norman Ornstein, Gerald Seib, George Will, Peggy Noonan, Paul Krugman, David Leonhardt, Ezra Klein, and William Galston. Special thanks go to Joshua Green for his superb 2011 article "Strict Obstructionist," about Senator Mitch McConnell when he was minority leader, and to Marc Fisher for his more recent profile of McConnell while majority leader.

With respect to recent books about the Senate, I benefited from the wisdom and insight of David A. Corbin, *The Last Great Senator: Robert C. Byrd's Encounters with Eleven U.S. Presidents* (2012); Neil MacNeil and Richard A. Baker, *The American Senate: An Insider's History* (2013); Robert G. Kaiser, *Act of Congress: How America's Essential Institution Works and How It Doesn't* (2013);

Senator Olympia Snowe, *Fighting for Common Ground: How We Can Fix the Stalemate in Congress* (2013); Alec MacGillis, *The Cynic: The Political Education of Mitch McConnell* (2014); Steven S. Smith, *The Senate Syndrome: The Evolution of Procedural Warfare in the Modern U.S. Senate* (2014); Richard A. Arenberg and Robert B. Dove, *Defending the Filibuster: The Soul of the Senate* (2015); Ross K. Baker, *Is Bipartisanship Dead?: A Report from the Senate* (2015); Senator Trent Lott and Senator Tom Daschle, *Crisis Point: Why We Must—and How We Can—Overcome Our Broken Politics in Washington and across America* (2015); Nick Littlefield and David Nexon, *Lion of the Senate: When Ted Kennedy Rallied the Democrats in a GOP Congress* (2015); and Senator Mitch McConnell, *The Long Game* (2016). I believe that Bob Kaiser's *Act of Congress* will become a classic, although that probably became inevitable when that great political reporter got Senator Chris Dodd and Congressman Barney Frank, two brilliant legislators and raconteurs, to be his principal sources.

While writing, I spent some time trying to make the case that our political system was in crisis—polarized, paralyzed, and dysfunctional—when I realized that it was the only thing that everyone agreed on: virtually a "given." Some of the books that analyze the situation thoughtfully include Amy Gutman and Dennis Thompson, *The Spirit of Compromise: Why Governing Demands It and Campaigning Undermines It* (2012); Frances E. Lee, *Insecure Majorities: Congress and the Perpetual Campaign* (2016); and James E. Campbell, *Polarized: Making Sense of a Divided America* (2016). Several important books from the early 1990s remind us just how long our political system—once the pride of our country—has been failing: E. J. Dionne Jr., *Why Americans Hate Politics* (1991); Thomas Byrne Edsall and Mary D. Edsall, *Chain Reaction: The Impact of Race, Rights, and Taxes on American Politics* (1991); and Kevin Phillips, *The Politics of Rich and Poor* (1990) and *Boiling Point: Democrats, Republicans and the Decline of Middle-Class Prosperity* (1993).

I borrowed my own thinking and writing from *The Last Great Senate* for limited parts of this book, particularly the discussions of Senate leaders Mike Mansfield, Howard Baker, Bob Dole, and Trent Lott. My section on the impeachment trial of President Clinton comes almost completely from Peter Baker's superb book, *The Breach: Inside the Impeachment and Trial of William Jefferson Clinton*. I also relied heavily on Baker's equally superb *Days of Fire: Bush and Cheney in the White House* (2013) for background on the run-up to the Senate's authorization for the Iraq war; on Timothy Geithner's *Stress Test: Reflections on Financial Crises* (2014) for background on the Senate's handling of the Troubled Assets Relief Program (TARP) and economic stimulus legislation; and on Rich Arenberg and Bob Dove, two premier Senate experts, for their knowledge of the filibuster and their account of the series of battles between Senate leaders that resulted in the triggering of the "nuclear option."

Barbara Sinclair, the eminent political scientist, passed away in March 2016. Her books and articles about the Senate, and the Congress generally, constitute a matchless body of insightful work. No one wrote more knowledgably about the changing political and legislative environment on Capitol Hill over the past forty years. It was a special privilege for me to meet Barbara in 2012; we had breakfast near the UCLA campus, and I gave her a copy of *The Last Great Senate*. I was delighted later when she told me that she liked it very much, although I learned much more from her than she did from me.

My thinking owes a special debt to Norm Ornstein, whom I met in 1977 while he was trying to reorganize the Senate committees and I was trying to write an ethics code for the Senate, and his collaborator Tom Mann. *It's Even Worse Than It Looks: How the American Constitutional System Collided with the New Politics of Extremism* (2012), Norm and Tom's superb book, and its subsequent editions—"worse than it was"; "worse than you think"—will be enduring classics because they capture a central truth about this depressing period of political dysfunction. My thinking and writing certainly confirm Ornstein and Mann's view that years before Donald Trump started his campaign for the presidency, the blame for our current political plight fell asymmetrically, attributable to the seemingly endless movement of the Republican Party to the right, producing extremism, obstruction, and ultimately gridlock on Capitol Hill and in Washington.

While some readers will dismiss this as simply the view of a partisan Democrat, I ask them to remember that many Senate Democrats worked with George W. Bush on his highest legislative priorities—tax cut and education reform—which helped them become law. This contrasted starkly with the complete lack of Senate Republican cooperation that Barack Obama encountered from day one of his presidency, even as America was on the edge of a second Great Depression. The legacy of Tom Mann and Norm Ornstein also includes their seminal work in 2006, *The Broken Branch: How Congress Is Failing America and How to Get It Back on Track*. It was worse than you think earlier than you think; we are long overdue for a comeback.

Notes

CHAPTER 1. McCONNELL'S POWER PLAY

1. Russell Berman, "Congress's Surprisingly Productive Year," *The Atlantic*, December 23, 2015.

2. Carl Hulse, "McConnell Vows a Senate in Working Order, If He Is Given Control," *New York Times*, March 3, 2014.

3. Mitch McConnell, *The Long Game: A Memoir* (New York: Sentinel 2016), 239.

4. "McConnell Reviews Senate Accomplishments in 2015," CBS News, December 19, 2015.

5. Berman, "Congress's Surprisingly Productive Year," quoting Sarah Binder.

6. Michael Bowman, "U.S. Congress Ends 2016 with Rare Show of Bipartisanship," *VOA News*, December 20, 2015.

7. Sam Levine, "Mitch McConnell Apparently Is Having 'An Almost Out-of-Body Experience' with Obama," *Huffington Post*, May 13, 2015.

8. Tom Daschle and Trent Lott, *Crisis Point: Why We Must—and How We Can—Overcome Our Broken Politics in Washington and across America* (New York: Bloomsbury Press, 2016). See, for example, Olympia Snowe, *Fighting for Common Ground: How We Can Fix the Stalemate in Congress* (New York: Weinstein Books, 2013); George Packer, "The Empty Chamber: Just How Broken Is the Senate?" *New Yorker*, August 9, 2010, 38–50; Thomas E. Mann and Norman J. Ornstein, *It's Even Worse Than It Was: How the American Constitutional System Collided with the New Politics of Extremism* (New York: Basic Books, 2016, revised edition).

9. Daschle and Lott, *Crisis Point*, 1.

10. Daschle and Lott, *Crisis Point*, 4.

11. Joshua Green, "Strict Obstructionist," *The Atlantic*, January–February 2011.

12. Green, "Strict Obstructionist."

13. David M. Herszenhorn, "It's a Stretch, but Mitch McConnell Is Reaching across the Aisle," *New York Times*, April 24, 2016.

14. McConnell, *The Long Game: A Memoir*, 212.

15. McConnell, *The Long Game*, 212.

16. Rebekah Metzler, "Tea Party Candidates Hard to Come by in 2014 Races," *U.S. News and World Report*, February 21, 2013; McConnell, *The Long Game*, 240.

17. Burgess Everett and Glenn Thrush, "McConnell Throws Down the Gauntlet: No Scalia Replacement under Obama," *Politico*, February 13, 2016.

18. Everett and Thrush, "McConnell Throws Down the Gauntlet."

19. Jonathan Adler, "Again on the Erroneous Argument That the Senate Has a 'Constitutional Duty' to Consider a Supreme Court Nominee," *Washington Post*, March 15, 2016.

20. Mike DeBonis and Julian Eilperin, "Republican Governor of Nevada Brian Sandoval Being Considered for Supreme Court," *Washington Post*, February 24, 2016.

21. Manu Raju, "In Reversal, Jerry Moran Says He Does Not Favor Hearings for Merrick Garland," CNN *Politics*, April 1, 2016.

22. Pema Levy, "Blocking Scalia's Replacement Could Put GOP Senators in a Bind, Poll Shows," *Mother Jones*, February 22, 2016.

23. Elaine Godfrey, "The Judge Chuck Grassley Can't Ignore," *The Atlantic*, June 8, 2016.

24. David M. Drucker, "McConnell: Vacant Supreme Court Seat Won the Election for Trump," *Washington Examiner*, April 7, 2017.

CHAPTER 2. IN THE SHADOW
OF MANSFIELD'S GREAT SENATE

1. Jonathan Martin, "Book Depicts the 'Last Great Senate,'" *Politico*, March 27, 2012.

2. Jack Doyle, "The Kefauver Hearings, 1950–1951," PopHistoryDig.com, April 17, 2008. Quotes in this section from *Life* and *Time* also come from Doyle's article.

3. H. W. Brands, *The General vs. the President: MacArthur and Truman at the Brink of Nuclear War* (New York: Doubleday, 2016).

4. John F. Kennedy, *Profiles in Courage* (New York: Harper and Brothers, 1957).

5. William S. White, *Citadel: The Story of the U.S. Senate* (New York: Harper and Brothers, 1957).

6. J.Y. Smith, "Sen. McClellan Dies in His Sleep at 81," *Washington Post*, November 29, 1977.

7. Thomas Mallon, "'Advise and Consent' at 50," *New York Times Sunday Book Review*, June 25, 2009.

8. Scott Simon, "At 50, A D.C. Novel with Legs," *Wall Street Journal*, September 2, 2009.

9. White's famous observation in *Citadel*, 68, recently quoted by Michael Tomasky, "The South Shall Not Rise Again," *The Daily Beast*, June 29, 2015.

10. George Packer, "The Empty Chamber: Just How Broken Is the Senate?" *New Yorker*, August 9, 2010.

11. This summary of Mansfield's leadership first appeared in my book, *The Last Great Senate: Courage and Statesmanship in Times of Crisis* (New York: PublicAffairs Books, 2012), 14–17. It draws principally on two superb books about Mansfield: Don Oberdorfer, *Senator Mansfield: The Extraordinary Life of a Great American Statesman and Diplomat* (Washington: Smithsonian Books, 2003), and Francis R. Valeo, *Mike Mansfield, Majority Leader: A Different Kind of Senate 1961–76* (New York: M. E. Sharpe, Inc., 1999).

12. *Congressional Record*, November 11, 1963.

13. Shapiro, *The Last Great Senate*, 327.

14. Shapiro, *The Last Great Senate*, xvii–xviii; 212–13.

15. David A. Corbin, *The Last Great Senator: Robert Byrd's Encounters with Eleven U.S. Presidents* (Washington: Potomac Books, 2012).

16. The discussion of the qualities of the senators and Mansfield's Senate largely draws on what I wrote in *The Last Great Senate*, xiv–xv.

17. President Carter's distaste for politics and the legislative process is discussed in *The Last Great Senate*, 43–44. My analysis drew on several biographies of President Carter, most notably Charles O. Jones, *The Trusteeship Presidency: Jimmy Carter and the United States Congress* (Baton Rouge: Louisiana State University Press, 1988), 1–9.

18. The political pressures on Howard Baker and Frank Church are discussed in *The Last Great Senate*, at 141, 145–46. Baker's quote—"Why now? Why me?"—came from a memorable interview that I had with him on October 22, 2008.

19. The financial rescue of New York City, summarized here, is described in great detail in *The Last Great Senate*, 185–200.

20. David Broder, "McConnell's Unlikely Role Models," *Washington Post*, December 3, 2006; John Dickerson, "Mitch McConnell's Refreshing Candor," *Slate*, December 10, 2014; statement of Senator Mitch McConnell, January 8, 2014.

CHAPTER 3. FROM BAKER AND DOLE TO GINGRICH AND LOTT

1. The discussion of Ronald Reagan's victory and the Senate election of 1980 is taken from Shapiro, *The Last Great Senate* (New York: Public Affairs, 2013), 351–54; 362–63.

2. The introduction to Howard Baker comes from Shapiro, *The Last Great Senate*, 26, 35.

3. Tom Daschle and Trent Lott, *Crisis Point* (New York: Bloomsbury Press, 2016), 108–9.

4. J. Lee Annis Jr., *Howard Baker: Conciliator in an Age of Crisis*, 2nd ed. (Knoxville: Howard Baker Center for Public Policy, University of Tennessee, 2007), xix.

5. The description of Bob Dole's evolution as a legislator and leader comes from Shapiro, *The Last Great Senate*, 364–65.

6. Sean Wilentz, *The Age of Reagan: A History 1974–2008* (New York: Harper Perennial, 2009), 147–48.

7. Matthew Dallek, "Bipartisan Reagan-O'Neill Social Security Deal in 1983 Showed It Can Be Done," *U.S. News and World Report,* April 2, 2009.

8. The discussion of Dole's leadership comes from *The Last Great Senate,* 364–65.

9. Neil MacNeil and Richard A. Baker, *The American Senate: An Insider's History* (Oxford: Oxford University Press, 2013), 348–49.

10. The discussion of Iran-Contra is based primarily on senators William S. Cohen and George J. Mitchell, *Men of Zeal: A Candid Inside Story of the Iran-Contra Hearings* (New York: Viking, 1988).

11. Cohen and Mitchell, *Men of Zeal,* 308–9.

12. The discussion of the Bork fight is based primarily on Lou Cannon, *President Reagan: The Role of a Lifetime* (New York: PublicAffairs, 1991), 724–26; Jules Witcover, *Joe Biden: A Life of Trial and Redemption* (New York: HarperCollins Publishers, 2010), 171–84; 197–214; 219–25; Adam Clymer, *Edward M. Kennedy: A Biography* (New York: William Morrow and Company, 1999), 416–28.

13. Clymer, *Edward M. Kennedy,* 417–19.

14. Clymer, *Edward M. Kennedy,* 424.

15. Cannon, *President Reagan,* 726.

16. Clymer, *Edward M. Kennedy,* 427.

17. Clymer, *Edward M. Kennedy,* 424, quoting Linda Greenhouse, *New York Times,* October 8, 1987.

18. Clymer, *Edward M. Kennedy,* 420–21, 426.

19. Adrienne LaFrance, "Down with Lifetime Appointments," *Slate,* November 12, 2013.

20. Lou Cannon, *President Reagan: The Role of a Lifetime* (New York: PublicAffairs, 1991), p. 724.

21. Leonard Fein, "Furor over Bork Amounts to a Celebration of Republican Democracy," *Los Angeles Times,* October 23, 1987.

22. Joe Biden, *Promises to Keep: On Life and Politics* (New York: Random House, 2007), 210.

23. Susan Rasky, "Congress Regains Its Voice on Policy in 1987–88 Sessions," *New York Times,* October 24, 1988.

24. Ezra Vogel, *Japan as Number One: Lessons for America* (New York: Harper, 1979); Clyde V. Prestowitz Jr., *Trading Places: How We Are Giving Our Future to Japan and How to Reclaim It* (New York: Basic Books, 1988); *Frustrated auto workers took a sledge hammer:*

25. Jonathan Weisman, "Gephardt Keeps Talking Trade," *New York Times,* December 27, 2003.

26. Howard Kurtz, "Between the Lines of a Millionaire's Ad," *Washington Post,* September 2, 1987.

27. Susan Schwab, *Trade-Offs: Negotiating the Omnibus Trade and Competitiveness Act* (Boston: Harvard Business School Press 1994), 117–54.

28. Schwab, *Trade-Offs.*

29. Michael Oreskes, "Senate Rejects Tower 53–47; First Cabinet Secretary Veto since '59; Bush Confers on New Choice," *New York Times,* March 10, 1989.

30. Oreskes, "Senate Rejects Tower 53–47."

31. E. J. Dionne Jr., "Washington Talk: Working Profile: Paul M. Weyrich; "It's Straight and Narrow for Architect of the Right," *New York Times*, March 16, 1989.

32. John G. Tower, *Consequences: A Personal and Political Memoir* (Boston: Little Brown, 1991), 350–52.

33. Tower, *Consequences*, 352–57.

34. Trent Lott, *Herding Cats: A Life in Politics* (New York: Regan Books, 2005), 112–18.

35. Lott, *Herding Cats*, 118.

36. Adam Clymer, "Confrontation in the Gulf; Congress Acts to Authorize War in Gulf; Margins Are 5 Votes in Senate, 67 in House," *New York Times*, January 13, 1991.

37. Clymer, "Confrontation in the Gulf."

38. Maureen Dowd, "The Supreme Court; Conservative Black Judge, Clarence Thomas, Is Named to Marshall Court Seat," *New York Times*, July 2, 1991.

39. Dowd, "The Supreme Court."

40. Jane Mayer and Jill Abramson, *Strange Justice: The Selling of Clarence Thomas* (Boston: Houghton Mifflin Company, 1994), 227–44.

41. Mayer and Abramson, *Strange Justice*, 291–323.

42. Richard Berke, "The Thomas Nomination: Senators Who Switched Tell of Political Torment," *New York Times*, October 16, 1991.

43. Roxanne Roberts, "'It Was Just Awful': The Clarence Thomas Hearings, in the Words of Those Who Were There," *Washington Post*, April 9, 2016.

44. Emma Gray, "Why Anita Hill's 1991 Testimony Is So Haunting Today," *Huff Post*, April 15, 2016.

45. Emma Green, "A Lot Has Changed in Congress since 1992, the 'Year of the Woman,'" *The Atlantic*, September 26, 2013.

46. Elizabeth Kolbert, "Dole Campaign Will Be Bringing Out Its Secret Weapon: The Candidate's Sense of Humor," *New York Times*, October 4, 1996.

47. Neil MacNeil and Richard A. Baker, *The American Senate: An Insider's History* (Oxford, UK: Oxford University Press, 2013), p. 351.

48. Sidney Blumenthal, *The Clinton Wars* (New York: Farrar, Straus and Giroux, 2003), 159.

49. David Rosenbaum, "The Budget Struggle: Clinton Wins Approval of His Budget Plan as Gore Votes to Break Senate Deadlock," *New York Times*, August 7, 1993.

50. Glenn Kessler, "History Lesson: More Republicans Than Democrats Supported NAFTA," *Washington Post*, May 9, 2016.

51. Warren Rudman, *Combat: Twelve Years in the U.S. Senate* (New York: Random House, 1996), 242–43.

52. John C. Danforth, *Faith and Politics: How the "Moral Values" Debate Divides America and How to Move Forward Together* (New York: Viking Penguin, 2006),143.

53. Interview with Keith Kennedy, Senator Hatfield's senior staffer, November 11, 2010, while writing *The Last Great Senate*.

54. William Eaton, "Senate Majority Leader Mitchell to Step Down," *LA Times*, March 5, 1994.

55. Peter Baker, *The Breach: Inside the Impeachment Trial of William Jefferson Clinton* (New York: Scribner, 2000), p. 262.

56. Interview with Senator Bob Packwood, July 19, 2010.

57. Cohen and Mitchell, *Men of Zeal*.

58. Lott, *Herding Cats*, 125.

59. Lott, *Herding Cats*.

60. Sean Theriault, *The Gingrich Senators: The Roots of Partisan Warfare in Congress* (New York: Oxford University Press, 2013).

61. Interview with Senator Alan Simpson, February 2, 2010.

62. Norman J. Ornstein and D. David Eisenhower, *Lessons and Legacies: Farewell Addresses from the Senate* (Reading, MA: Addison-Wesley, 1997).

63. All quotes from the speeches of the retiring senators come from Ornstein and Eisenhower's *Lessons and Legacies*.

64. Eric Pianin and John F. Harris, "President, GOP Agree on Balanced Budget Plan," *Washington Post*, May 3, 1997.

CHAPTER 4. BIPARTISANSHIP TRIED, LOST, AND FOUND

1. Linda Greenhouse, "*Bush v. Gore*, A Special Report; Election Case a Test and a Trauma for Justices," *New York Times*, February 20, 2001; Adam Cohen, "Has Bush v. Gore Become the Case That Must Not Be Named?" *New York Times*, August 15, 2006.

2. Gore's speech was universally regarded as "graceful" and "statesmanlike." See, for example, "The End at Last," *The Economist*, December 14, 2001; Brent Baker, "Bob Woodward Still Marvels at Gore's 'Statesmanlike' Speech," *Media Center Cybercart*, November 7, 2001.

3. Edward M. Kennedy, *True Compass: A Memoir* (New York: Twelve, 2009), 488.

4. Kennedy, *True Compass*, 489.

5. Kennedy, *True Compass*, 493.

6. Kennedy, *True Compass*, 494.

7. Alan Greenspan, *The Age of Turbulence: Adventures in a New World* (New York: The Penguin Press, 2007), 218.

8. Greenspan, *The Age of Turbulence*, 219.

9. Greenspan, *The Age of Turbulence*, 221.

10. Greenspan, *The Age of Turbulence*, 223.

11. John F. Harris and Dan Balz, "Delicate Moves Led to Tax Cut," *Washington Post*, May 27, 2001.

12. Harris and Balz, "Delicate Moves Led to Tax Cut."

13. Harris and Balz, "Delicate Moves Led to Tax Cut."

14. Harris and Balz, "Delicate Moves Led to Tax Cut."

15. Harris and Balz, "Delicate Moves Led to Tax Cut."

16. Harris and Balz, "Delicate Moves Led to Tax Cut."

17. Harris and Balz, "Delicate Moves Led to Tax Cut."

18. Senator Robert C. Byrd, *Losing America: Confronting a Reckless and Arrogant Presidency* (New York: Norton, 2004), 19.

19. Byrd, *Losing America*, 27–31.

20. Byrd, *Losing America*, 28.

21. Byrd, *Losing America*, 32.

22. Byrd, *Losing America*.

23. Byrd, *Losing America*, 29.

24. Greenspan, *The Age of Turbulence*, 224.

25. Byrd, *Losing America*, 47–51.

26. Byrd, *Losing America*, 105–7.

27. David Firestone, "For Homeland Security Bill, A Brakeman," *New York Times*, July 31, 2002.

28. Peter Baker, *Days of Fire: Bush and Cheney in the White House* (New York: Anchor, 2014), 135.

29. Baker, *Days of Fire*, 144.

30. Baker, *Days of Fire*.

31. Baker, *Days of Fire*, 181.

32. Baker, *Days of Fire*, 207.

33. Baker, *Days of Fire*, 207–8.

34. Baker, *Days of Fire*, 208–9.

35. Baker, *Days of Fire*, 210.

36. Olympia Snowe, *Fighting for Common Ground: How We Can Fix the Stalemate in Congress* (New York: Weinstein Books, 2013), pp. 198–99.

37. Baker, *Days of Fire*, 210–11.

38. Baker, *Days of Fire*, 211.

39. Baker, *Days of Fire*, 223.

40. Kennedy, *True Compass*, 495.

41. Kennedy, *True Compass*, 495.

42. Byrd, *Losing America*, 164–65.

43. Byrd, *Losing America*, 173–74.

44. Byrd, *Losing America*, 173.

45. Byrd, *Losing America*.

46. Byrd, *Losing America*, 176.

47. George Herring, *From Colony to Superpower* (New York: Oxford, 2008), 949.

48. Peter Baker, *Days of Fire*, 228.

49. Senator John Danforth, *Faith and Politics: How The "Moral Values" Debate Divides America and How to Move Forward Together* (New York: Viking Penguin, 2006), 7.

50. Danforth, *Faith and Politics*, 76.

51. Mitch McConnell, *The Long Game: A Memoir* (New York: Sentinel, 2016), 33–35, 72; Alec MacGillis, *The Cynic: The Political Education of Mitch McConnell* (New York: Simon & Schuster Paperbacks, 2014), 9–11.

52. MacGillis, *The Cynic*, 1.

53. Stephen Collinson, "Harry Reid's Complicated Legacy," CNN, March 27, 2015.

54. McConnell, *The Long Game*, 159.

55. Baker, *Days of Fire*, 478–81; 511–12.

56. Baker, *Days of Fire*, 507.

57. Baker, *Days of Fire*, 515.

58. Baker, *Days of Fire*, 518.

59. Baker, *Days of Fire*, 525.

60. Baker, *Days of Fire*, 526.

61. McConnell, *The Long Game*, 161–66.

62. McConnell, *The Long Game*, 162.

63. McConnell, *The Long Game*, 163.

64. McConnell, *The Long Game*, 164–65.

65. Baker, *Days of Fire*, 570; McConnell, *The Long Game*, 165–66.

66. Baker, *Days of Fire*, 582.

67. Baker, *Days of Fire*.

68. Baker, *Days of Fire*, 607–8.

69. McConnell, *The Long Game*, 170.

70. McConnell, *The Long Game*, 172.

71. McConnell, *The Long Game*, 173.

72. Baker, *Days of Fire*, 615.

73. McConnell, *The Long Game*, 174.

CHAPTER 5. OBAMA'S FIRST TERM:
STRICT OBSTRUCTIONISM

1. This chapter title comes from Joshua Green's insightful article. Joshua Green, "Strict Obstructionist," *The Atlantic*, January–February 2011 issue.

2. Mitch McConnell, *The Long Game: A Memoir* (New York: Sentinel, 2016), 173.

3. McConnell, *The Long Game*, 185.

4. McConnell, *The Long Game*, 184.

5. Green, "Strict Obstructionist."

6. Green, "Strict Obstructionist"; Carl Hulse and Adam Nagourney, "Senate G.O.P. Leader Finds Weapon in Unity," *New York Times/International Herald Tribune*, March 18, 2010.

7. McConnell, *The Long Game*, 185.

8. Timothy Geithner, *Stress Test* (New York: Broadway Books, 2015), 256.

9. Geithner, *Stress Test*, 277.

10. Geithner, *Stress Test*, 258.

11. Green, "Strict Obstructionist."

12. Carl Hulse, "Maine Senators Break with Republican Party on Stimulus," *New York Times*, February 10, 2009.

13. Hulse, "Maine Senators Break with Republican Party on Stimulus."

14. Hulse, "Maine Senators Break with Republican Party on Stimulus."

15. Manuel Rogi-Franzia and Paul Kane, "Two Moderate GOP Senators Give Big Voice to Little Maine," *Washington Post*, February 16, 2009.

16. Hulse, "Maine Senators Break with Republican Party on Stimulus."

17. McConnell, *The Long Game*, 190.

18. McConnell, *The Long Game*, 191.

19. McConnell, *The Long Game*, 193.

20. McConnell, *The Long Game*, 191.

21. Norm Ornstein, "The Real Story of Obamacare's Birth," *The Atlantic*, July 6, 2015.

22. Ornstein, "The Real Story of Obamacare's Birth."

23. Ornstein, "The Real Story of Obamacare's Birth."

24. Ornstein, "The Real Story of Obamacare's Birth."

25. David Herszenhorn and Robert Pear, "Health Policy Is Carved Out at Table for 6," *New York Times*, July 27, 2009.

26. See, for example, Robert Reich, "Why the Gang of Six Is Deciding Health Care for Three Hundred Million of Us," *Huff Post The Blog*, September 21, 2009.

27. McConnell, *The Long Game*, 191.

28. David Drucker, "Baucus Optimistic over Bipartisan Health Care Progress," *Roll Call*, July 9, 2009.

29. Julie Rovner, "What the 'Gang of Six' Wants from the Health Care Bill," *NPR WAMU*, September 9, 2009.

30. Alex Isenstadt, "Town Halls Gone Wild," *Politico*, August 3, 2009; Don Gonyea, "From the Start, Obama Struggled with Fallout from a Kind of Fake News," *NPR WAMU*, January 10, 2017.

31. Julie Rovner, "In Health Care Debate, Fear Trumps Logic," *NPR*, August 28, 2009.

32. Alexander Bolton, "Gang of Six Health Care Reform Negotiations on the Verge of Collapse," *The Hill*, September 4, 2009.

33. Bolton, "Gang of Six Health Care Reform."

34. Bolton, "Gang of Six Health Care Reform."

35. Olympia Snowe, *Fighting for Common Ground* (New York: Weinstein Books, 2013), 191–205.

36. Alec MacGillis, *The Cynic* (New York: Simon and Schuster, 2014), 106.

37. Ornstein, "The Real Story of Obamacare's Birth."

38. Ornstein, "The Real Story of Obamacare's Birth."

39. Ornstein, "The Real Story of Obamacare's Birth."

40. Molly Ball, "Harry Reid Goes Down Fighting," *The Atlantic*, March 27, 2015.

41. Ball, "Harry Reid Goes Down Fighting."

42. Jason Zengerle, "Who Will Do What Harry Reid Did Now That Harry Reid Is Gone?" *New York Magazine*, December 27, 2016.

43. Ornstein, "The Real Story of Obamacare's Birth."

44. McConnell, *The Long Game*, 196–97.

45. McConnell, *The Long Game*, 197.

46. Ornstein, "The Real Story of Obamacare's Birth."

47. Ornstein, "The Real Story of Obamacare's Birth."

48. Ornstein, "The Real Story of Obamacare's Birth."

49. MacGillis, *The Cynic*, 106; Geithner, *Stress Test*, 386.

50. Robert G. Kaiser, *Act of Congress: How America's Essential Institution Works, and How It Doesn't* (New York: Alfred A. Knopf, 2013), 75–76, 199–202.

51. Kaiser, *Act of Congress*, 144.

52. Kaiser, *Act of Congress*, 80–81.

53. Geithner, *Stress Test*, 317–18, 327–29.

54. John Cassidy, "The Volcker Rule: Obama's Economic Adviser and His Battles over the Financial-Reform Bill," *The New Yorker*, July 26, 2010.

55. Cassidy, "The Volcker Rule."

56. Cassidy, "The Volcker Rule."

57. Cassidy, "The Volcker Rule."

58. Cassidy, "The Volcker Rule."

59. Kaiser, *Act of Congress*, 76–83.

60. Kaiser, *Act of Congress*, 201.

61. U.S. Senate Committee on Banking, Housing and Urban Affairs, "Dodd and Shelby Issue Joint Statement on the Progress of Financial Reform," December 23, 2009.

62. U.S. Senate Committee on Banking, Housing and Urban Affairs, "Dodd and Shelby Issue Joint Statement."

63. Geithner, *Stress Test*, 417.

64. Geithner, *Stress Test*.

65. Nina Easton, "Bob Corker: Washington's Dealmaker," *Fortune*, December 9, 2010; Kaiser, *Act of Congress*, 245–54.

66. Kaiser, *Act of Congress*, 267–68.

67. Cassidy, "The Volcker Rule."

68. Cassidy, "The Volcker Rule."

69. Cassidy, "The Volcker Rule."

70. Cassidy, "The Volcker Rule."

71. Brady Dennis, "Congress Passes Financial Reform Bill," *Washington Post*, July 16, 2010.

72. Dennis, "Congress Passes Financial Reform Bill."

73. Interview with Senator Levin, August 6, 2010.

74. George Packer, "The Empty Chamber," *New Yorker*, August 9, 2010.

75. Jonathan Alter, *The Center Holds: Obama and His Enemies* (New York: Simon and Schuster Paperbacks, 2013), 5.

76. Fox News, "Obama Wins Senate Approval of START Nuclear Pact with Russia," December 22, 2010.

77. Liz Montgomery and Shailagh Murray, "Congress Votes to Extend Bush-Era Tax Cuts until 2012," *Washington Post*, December 17, 2010.

78. Thomas E. Mann and Norman J. Ornstein, *It's Even Worse Than It Was* (New York: Basic Books, 2016), 8.

79. Mann and Ornstein, *It's Even Worse Than It Was*, 9–11.

80. Mann and Ornstein, *It's Even Worse Than It Was*, 7.

81. Mann and Ornstein, *It's Even Worse Than It Was*, 15.

82. Mann and Ornstein, *It's Even Worse Than It Was*.

83. Mann and Ornstein, *It's Even Worse Than It Was*, 15–16.

84. Mann and Ornstein, *It's Even Worse Than It Was*, 21.

85. Mann and Ornstein, *It's Even Worse Than It Was*.

86. Mann and Ornstein, *It's Even Worse Than It Was*, 22.

87. Mann and Ornstein, *It's Even Worse Than It Was*, 18–19.

88. Mann and Ornstein, *It's Even Worse Than It Was*, 18.

89. Mann and Ornstein, *It's Even Worse Than It Was*, 17.

90. Mann and Ornstein, *It's Even Worse Than It Was*, 25.

91. Mann and Ornstein, *It's Even Worse Than It Was*.

CHAPTER 6. OBAMA'S SECOND TERM:
THE FISCAL CLIFF AND THE NUCLEAR OPTION

1. Fareed Zakaria, "Can America Be Fixed?" *Foreign Affairs*, January–February 2013 issue.

2. Ezra Klein, "Goodbye and Good Riddance, 112th Congress," *Washington Post*, January 4, 2013.

3. Ira Shapiro, "Senate Holds Key to Fixing Washington," CNN.com, January 15, 2013; Ira Shapiro, "Say Goodbye to Gridlock in Washington," CNN.com, April 1, 2013.

4. Manu Raju and Ginger Gibson, "Reid, McConnell Reach Filibuster Deal," *Politico*, January 24, 2013.

5. Lori Montgomery, "Senate Passes First Budget in Four Years," *Washington Post*, March 23, 2013.

6. Seung Min Kim and Carrie Budoff Brown, "Judiciary Panel OKs Immigration Bill," *Politico*, May 22, 2013.

7. Jackie Kucinich, "Senate Panel Passes Two Gun-Control Measures," *USA Today*, March 12, 2013.

8. Ben Protess and Jessica Silver-Greenberg, "Senate Report Said to Fault JPMorgan," *New York Times*, March 4, 2013.

9. Eric Garcia, "'Too Big to Fail' Is Still a Problem. Here's How D.C. Wants to End It," *The Atlantic*, July 29, 2013.

10. Philip Rucker and Rosalind S. Helderman, "Turning on Charm, Obama Tries to End Gridlock," *Washington Post*, March 7, 2013.

11. Paul Kane, "Amid Obama's 'Charm Offensive,' A Quest for Common Ground," *Washington Post*, March 15, 2013.

12. Jonathan Alter, *The Center Holds: Obama and His Enemies* (New York: Simon and Schuster), 371.

13. Dana Bash, "Mikulski Makes History While Creating 'Zone of Civility' for Senate," CNN.com, March 17, 2012.

14. Daniel Halper, "Sessions on Secret 'Fiscal Cliff' Negotiations: 'The Senate Now Operates Like the Russian Duma,'" *Weekly Standard*, December 12, 2012.

15. Ashley Parker and Jonathan Martin, "Senate, 68 to 32, Passes Overhaul for Immigration," *New York Times*, June 27, 2013.

16. Seung Min Kim, "Senate Passes Immigration Bill," *Politico*, June 27, 2013.

17. Parker and Martin, "Senate, 68 to 32, Passes Overhaul."

18. Richard A. Arenberg and Robert B. Dove, *Defending the Filibuster: The Soul of the Senate* (Bloomington: Indiana University Press, 2015 [first edition, 2012]).

19. Alexander Bolton, "Udall, Merkley and Harkin Unveil Filibuster-Reform Resolution," *The Hill*, January 4, 2013.

20. Ira Shapiro, *The Last Great Senate* (New York: PublicAffairs, 2012), 228–32.

21. Arenberg and Dove, *Defending the Filibuster*, 138–39.

22. Arenberg and Dove, *Defending the Filibuster*, 173–74.

23. Arenberg and Dove, *Defending the Filibuster*, 174.

24. Arenberg and Dove, *Defending the Filibuster*, 174–75.

25. Arenberg and Dove, *Defending the Filibuster*, 176–77.

26. Arenberg and Dove, *Defending the Filibuster*, 174–77.

27. Arenberg and Dove, *Defending the Filibuster*, 179.

28. Arenberg and Dove, *Defending the Filibuster*, 181–82.

29. Arenberg and Dove, *Defending the Filibuster*, 182.

30. Arenberg and Dove, *Defending the Filibuster*, 182.

31. Arenberg and Dove, *Defending the Filibuster*, 183–84.

32. Arenberg and Dove, *Defending the Filibuster*, 185.

33. Arenberg and Dove, *Defending the Filibuster*, 186.

34. Arenberg and Dove, *Defending the Filibuster*.

35. Arenberg and Dove, *Defending the Filibuster*, 189–90.

36. Arenberg and Dove, *Defending the Filibuster*, 190.

37. Arenberg and Dove, *Defending the Filibuster*, 191.

38. Arenberg and Dove, *Defending the Filibuster*, 191.

39. Arenberg and Dove, *Defending the Filibuster*, 192.

40. Arenberg and Dove, *Defending the Filibuster*, 193.

41. Arenberg and Dove, *Defending the Filibuster*.

42. Arenberg and Dove, *Defending the Filibuster*, 195.

43. https://www.brainyquote.com/quotes/quotes/s/samrayburn390211.html.

44. Arenberg and Dove, *Defending the Filibuster*, 107.

45. Jonathan Weisman, "Reid's Uncompromising Power Play in Senate Rankles Republicans," *New York Times*, January 9, 2014.

CHAPTER 7. POLITICS UPENDED

1. Burgess Everett and Seung Min Kim, "McConnell Goes Underground on Trump," *Politico*, October 10, 2016.

2. Everett and Kim, "McConnell Goes Underground on Trump."

3. Carrie Levine, "Super PACs, 'Dark Money' Groups Eschew Presidential Race for Senate," Center for American Integrity, November 8, 2016.

4. Jim Geraghty, "Chuck Schumer: Democrats Will Lose Blue-Collar Whites but Gain in the Suburbs," *National Review*, July 28, 2016.

5. Frank Bruni, "Show Us the Money," *New York Times Magazine*, December 16, 2001.

6. Burgess Everett, "Joe Sestak's Last Stand against the Democratic Party," *Politico*, April 7, 2016.

7. Gabrielle Levy, "Why Pick Chuck Schumer to Lead the Democrats in the Senate?" *U.S. News and World Report*, April 19, 2015.

8. Alexander Bolton, "Schumer May Shatter Fundraising Records," *The Hill*, April 16, 2015.

9. Connor Simpson, "Chuck Schumer Is Washington's Best Matchmaker," *The Atlantic*, August 18, 2012.

10. Alexander Bolton, "Sen. Schumer's Stock on the Rise," *The Hill*, June 25, 2013.

11. Burgess Everett and Elana Schor, "Senate Democrats Settle on Leadership Team, Sanders Elevated," *Politico*, November 16, 2016.

12. Alexander Bolton, "Vulnerable Dems Ready to Work with Trump," *The Hill*, November 28, 2016.

13. Alexander Bolton, "Schumer Reaches to Left," *The Hill*, March 31, 2015.

14. Sarah Mimms, "Chuck Schumer: Passing Obamacare in 2010 Was a Mistake," *The Atlantic*, November 25, 2014.

15. Jennifer Bendery and Arthur Delaney, "Senate Democrats Already Willing to Work with Trump Administration," *Huffington Post*, November 16, 2016.

16. Jonathan Martin, "Angry Democrats Study the Tea Party's Playbook," *New York Times*, January 23, 2017.

17. Michael Sainato, "Bernie Sanders Puts the Democratic Party in Check," *Observer*, February 5, 2017.

18. Jordain Carney, "Liberals Rip Schumer as 'Unfit' to Lead Democrats," *The Hill*, August 7, 2015.

19. Letter of James Madison to Thomas Jefferson, October 24, 1787, *The Founders' Constitution*, vol. 1, ch. 17, doc. 2, University of Chicago Press.

20. Federalist Paper #263.

CHAPTER 8. CONFIRMATION BATTLES
OVER THE PRESIDENT'S TEAM

1. Michael Oreskes, "Senate Rejects Tower, 53–47; First Cabinet Veto since '59; Bush Confers on New Choice," *New York Times*, March 10, 1989.

2. Tim Weiner, "Theodore C. Sorensen, 82, Kennedy Counselor, Dies," *New York Times*, October 31, 2010.

3. Gwen Ifill, "Settling In: Anatomy of a Doomed Nomination; The Baird Appointment: In Trouble from the Start, Then a Firestorm," *New York Times*, January 23, 1993; Richard L. Berke, "Judge Withdraws from Clinton List for Justice Post," *New York Times*, February 6, 1993.

4. Eric Schmitt, "Pentagon Nominee Withdraws Name," *New York Times*, January 10, 1994.

5. Tim Weiner, "Lake Pulls Out as Nominee for C.I.A., Assailing Process as Endless Political Circus," *New York Times*, March 18, 1997.

6. Jeff Zeleny, "Gregg Ends Bid for Commerce Job," *New York Times*, February 12, 2009.

7. Jeff Zeleny, "Daschle Ends Bid for Post; Obama Concedes Mistake," *New York Times*, February 3, 2009.

8. Steve Holland, "Susan Rice Withdraws as Secretary of State Candidate," *Reuters*, December 14, 2012.

9. Krishnadev Calamur, "Donald Trump's Choice for National Security Adviser Has One Priority: Combatting 'Radical Islamic Terrorism,'" *The Atlantic*, November 18, 2016.

10. Bryan Bender and Andrew Hanna, "Flynn under Fire for Fake News," *Politico*, December 5, 2016.

11. Lena Williams, "Senate Panel Hands Reagan First Defeat on Nominee for Judgeship," *New York Times*, June 6, 1986.

12. Hans A. Von Spakovsky, "Here's Why Jeff Sessions Is the Perfect Pick for Attorney General," Fox News, November 18, 2016; Robert Knight, "Restoring Justice," *Washington Times*, January 15, 2017.

13. Nahal Toosi and Alex Isenstadt, "Trump Taps Nikki Haley to Be UN Ambassador," *Politico*, November 23, 2016.

14. Caitlin Emma and Michael Stratford, "Trump Selects DeVos as Education Secretary," *Politico*, November 23, 2016.

15. Robert Pear, "Tom Price, Obamacare Critic, Is Trump's Choice for Health Secretary," *New York Times*, November 28, 2016.

16. Julie Hirschfeld Davis, Binyamin Applebaum, and Maggie Haberman, "Trump Taps Hollywood's Mnuchin for Treasury and Dines with Romney," *New York Times*, November 29, 2016; Julie Hirschfeld Davis, "Wilbur Ross, Billionaire Investor, Is Said to Be Trump's Commerce Pick," *New York Times*, November 24, 2016.

17. Jeremy W. Peters and Maggie Haberman, "Trump Picks Elaine Chao for Transportation Secretary," *New York Times*, November 29, 2016.

18. Michael D. Shear, "Trump Picks Mick Mulvaney, South Carolina Congressman, as Budget Director," *New York Times*, December 16, 2016.

19. Katy Tur and Benjy Sarlin, "Gingrich, Giuliani, Priebus Eyed for Top Jobs in Trump White House: Sources," NBC News, November 7, 2016; "Rudy Giuliani Is in the Lead to Be Trump's Secretary of State," *Fortune (Reuters)*, November 15, 2016.

20. Jessie Hellmann, "Trump Leaning toward Romney for Secretary of State," *The Hill*, November 22, 2016.

21. Duncan Hunter, "Choosing Two of America's Finest Leaders," *Washington Times*, November 12, 2017; Tom Bowman, "100 Days In, Trump's Generals Seen as a Moderating Force," NPR, April 28, 2017.

22. Nicholas Fandos, "Trump Expands Search for His Secretary of State," *New York Times*, December 4, 2016.

23. Michael D. Shear, "Trump Lines up Establishment Republicans to Vouch for Rex Tillerson," *New York Times*, December 13, 2016.

24. Peter Nicholas, Michael C. Bender, and Carol E. Lee, "How Rex Tillerson, a Late Entry to Be Secretary of State, Got Donald Trump's Nod," *Wall Street Journal*, December 14, 2016.

25. Samantha Michaels, "Tillerson's Tenure at Exxon Mobil Includes Suits Alleging Torture," *Newsweek*, January 14, 2017; Paul Barrett and Matthew Philips, "Can ExxonMobil Be Found Liable for Misleading the Public on Climate Change?" *Bloomberg Week*, September 7, 2016.

26. Suzanne Goldenberg, "ExxonMobil Gave Millions to Climate-Denying Lawmakers Despite Pledge," *The Guardian*, July 15, 2015.

27. Josh Rogin, "Inside Rex Tillerson's Long Romance with Russia," *Washington Post*, December 13, 2016.

28. Ed Crooks and Jack Farchy, "Exxon Considers Its Course after Sanctions Hit Russian Ambitions," *Financial Times*, September 30, 2014.

29. David Filipov, "What Is the Russian Order of Friendship, and Why Does Rex Tillerson Have One?" *Washington Post*, December 13, 2016.

30. Nick Wadhams and Margaret Talev, "Tillerson Visited White House Often over Russia Sanctions," *Bloomberg Politics*, December 12, 2016.

31. Mark Mazzetti, "Mike Pompeo, Sharp Critic of Hillary Clinton, Is Trump's Pick to Lead C.I.A.," *New York Times*, November 18, 2016.

32. Greg Miller, "Senate Confirms Mike Pompeo as CIA Director," *Washington Post*, January 27, 2017.

33. Coral Davenport and Eric Lipton, "Trump Picks Scott Pruitt, Climate Change Denialist, to Lead E.P.A.," *New York Times*, December 7, 2016.

34. Davenport and Lipton, "Trump Picks Scott Pruitt."

35. Davenport and Lipton, "Trump Picks Scott Pruitt."

36. Coral Davenport, "Senate Confirms Scott Pruitt as E.P.A. Head," *New York Times*, February 17, 2017.

37. Davenport, "Senate Confirms Scott Pruitt."

38. Davenport, "Senate Confirms Scott Pruitt."

39. Oliver Milman, "Donald Trump Presidency a 'Disaster for the Planet,' Warn Climate Scientists," *The Guardian*, November 11, 2016.

40. Erica Chenoweth and Jeremy Pressman, "This Is What We Learned by Counting the Women's Marches," *Washington Post*, February 7, 2017.

41. Nicole Gaudiano, "Schumer Set to Oppose 8 Trump Nominees," *USA Today*, January 30, 2017.

42. Russell Berman, "The Senate Delays a Key Nomination Hearing," *The Atlantic*, January 9, 2017.

43. Robert Iafolla, "U.S. Senate Hearings Delayed for Three Wealthy Trump Nominees," *Reuters*, January 10, 2017.

44. Bridget Bowman, "Top Senate Democrats List Requirements for Trump Nominees," *Roll Call*, December 22, 2016.

45. Russell Berman, "How Democrats Paved the Way for the Confirmation of Trump's Cabinet," *The Atlantic*, January 20, 2017.

46. Mallory Shelbourne, "Schumer Regrets Dems Triggering 'Nuclear Option,'" *The Hill*, January 3, 2017.

47. Paul Kane, "Senator Susan Collins Pushes Approval of Jeff Sessions for Attorney General," *Washington Post*, January 7, 2017.

48. Abby Phillip and Mike DeBonis, "Without Evidence, Trump Tells Lawmakers 3 Million to 5 Million Illegal Ballots Cost Him the Popular Vote," *Washington Post*, January 23, 2017.

49. David Weigel, "Booker Opposes Sessions, Saying 'Law and Order without Justice Is Unobtainable,'" *Washington Post*, January 11, 2017.

50. Eric Lichtblau, "Jeff Sessions, as Attorney General, Could Overhaul Department He's Skewered," *New York Times*, November 18, 2016.

51. Eric Lichtblau and Matt Flegenheimer, "Jeff Sessions Confirmed as Attorney General, Capping Bitter Battle," *New York Times*, February 8, 2017.

52. Dana Goldstein, "Betsy DeVos, Pick for Secretary of Education, Is the Most Jeered," *New York Times*, February 3, 2017.

53. Goldstein, "Betsy DeVos, Pick for Secretary of Education."

54. *Los Angeles Times* Editorial Board, "Betsy DeVos Embarrassed Herself and Should Be Rejected by the Senate," *LA Times*, January 19, 2017.

55. Robert Pear, "Tom Price, H.H.S. Nominee, Drafted Remake of Health Law," *New York Times*, November 29, 2016.

56. Dan Diamond, "5 Trump Health Care Promises That Won't Become Reality," *Politico*, May 1, 2017.

57. M.J. Lee, "Trump Gives a Boost to Obamacare Repeal, but Doesn't Solve GOP's Problems," CNN Politics, March 1, 2017.

58. Vann R. Newkirk II, "Why Do Tom Price's Potential Conflicts of Interest Matter?" *The Atlantic*, January 19, 2017.

59. Newkirk, "Why Do Tom Price's Potential Conflicts of Interest Matter?"

60. Newkirk, "Why Do Tom Price's Potential Conflicts of Interest Matter?"

61. Newkirk, "Why Do Tom Price's Potential Conflicts of Interest Matter?"

62. Judy Stone, "Draining the Swamp? Not with Tom Price as Head of Health," *Forbes*, January 17, 2017.

63. M. J. Lee, "Democrats Call for Ethics Probe of Trump HHS Nominee Tom Price," CNN Politics, January 5, 2017.

64. Matt Flegenheimer, "Republican Senators Vote to Formally Silence Elizabeth Warren," *New York Times*, February 7, 2017.

65. Eric Lichtblau and Matt Flegenheimer, "Jeff Sessions Confirmed as Attorney General, Capping Bitter Battle," *New York Times*, February 8, 2017.

66. James Hohmann, "The Daily 202: Lamar Alexander Is Dragging Betsy DeVos across the Finish Line to Become Secretary of Education," *Washington Post*, January 18, 2017.

67. Brady Dennis and Juliet Eilperin, "Hundreds of Current, Former EPA Employees Urge Senate to Reject Trump's Nominee for the Agency," *Washington Post*, February 6, 2017.

68. Leigh Ann Caldwell, "Betsy DeVos Vote: Pence's History-Making Tie Breaker Confirms Controversial Education Secretary," NBC News, February 7, 2017.

69. Michelle Chang, "Trump Still Hasn't Filled Top Jobs, and He Has (Mostly) Himself to Blame," *FiveThirtyEight*, July 3, 2017.

70. Chang, "Trump Still Hasn't Filled Top Jobs."

71. Chang, "Trump Still Hasn't Filled Top Jobs."

72. Josh Barro, "Trump Is Taking His Time to Fill More Than 500 Key Jobs, and That Could Stymie His Agenda," *Business Insider*, February 28, 2017.

73. Chang, "Trump Still Hasn't Filled Top Jobs."

CHAPTER 9. THE GORSUCH NOMINATION:
WHEN NO COMPROMISE IS POSSIBLE

1. James D. Zirin, *Supremely Partisan: How Raw Politics Tips the Scales in the United States Supreme Court* (Maryland: Rowman & Littlefield, 2016), 7, 55; John Dean, *The Rehnquist Choice: The Untold Story of the Nixon Appointment That Redefined the Supreme Court* (New York: Free Press, 2001).

2. Robert Dallek, *Flawed Giant: Lyndon Johnson and His Times, 1961–1973* (Oxford: Oxford University Press, 1998), 556–64.

3. Dallek, *Flawed Giant.*

4. Dallek, *Flawed Giant.*

5. Dallek, *Flawed Giant.*

6. Richard J. Ellis, *The Development of the American Presidency* (London: Routledge, 2012), 511–18.

7. Tom Howell Jr., "Justices Roberts, Kennedy Fall from GOP Favor after Recent Supreme Court Decisions," *Washington Times,* July 19, 2015.

8. Alan Rappeport and Charlie Savage, "Donald Trump Releases List of Possible Supreme Court Picks," *New York Times,* May 18, 2016; Ben Kamisar and Lydia Wheeler, "Trump Soothes the Right with List of Supreme Court Picks," *The Hill,* May 18, 2016.

9. Rappeport and Savage, "Donald Trump Releases List of Possible Supreme Court Picks."

10. Lawrence Baum and Neal Devins, "How the Federalist Society Became the de facto Selector of Republican Supreme Court Justices," *Slate,* January 31, 2017.

11. Rappeport and Savage, "Donald Trump Releases List of Possible Supreme Court Picks."

12. Julie Hirschfeld Davis and Mark Landler, "Trump Nominates Neil Gorsuch to the Supreme Court," *New York Times,* January 31, 2017.

13. Davis and Landler, "Trump Nominates Neil Gorsuch."

14. Alicia Parlapiano and Karen Yourish, "Where Neil Gorsuch Would Fit on the Supreme Court," *New York Times,* February 1, 2017.

15. Michael D. Shear, Mark Landler, Matt Apuzzo, and Eric Lichtblau, "Trump Fires Acting Attorney General Who Defied Him," *New York Times,* January 30, 2017.

16. Peter W. Stevenson, "The Real Reason Senate Democrats Are Going to Oppose Judge Gorsuch for the Supreme Court," *Washington Post,* March 30, 2017.

17. Davis and Landler, "Trump Nominates Neil Gorsuch."

18. Thomas Fuller, "'So-Called' Judge Criticized by Trump Is Known as a Mainstream Republican," *New York Times,* February 4, 2017.

19. Sean Sullivan, "Gorsuch Calls Attacks on Federal Judges 'Disheartening' and 'Demoralizing,'" *Washington Post,* March 21, 2017.

20. Matt Flegenheimer, "Democrats' Line of Attack on Gorsuch: No Friend of the Little Guy," *New York Times,* March 13, 2017.

21. Adam Liptak, Peter Baker, Nicholas Fandos, and Julie Turkewitz, "In Fall of Gorsuch's Mother, A Painful Lesson in Politicking," *New York Times,* February 4, 2017.

22. Neal K. Kaytal, "Why Liberals Should Back Neil Gorsuch," *New York Times*, January 31, 2017.

23. Jordain Carney, "Progressives Set to Declare Victory on Gorsuch, One Way or the Other," *The Hill*, April 6, 2017.

24. Paul Kane, "Senate Democrats Vastly Outspent by Right in Gorsuch Fight," *Washington Post*, March 18, 2017.

25. Kane, "Senate Democrats Vastly Outspent by Right in Gorsuch Fight."

26. Kane, "Senate Democrats Vastly Outspent by Right in Gorsuch Fight."

27. Adam Liptak, "An 'Ideological Food Fight' (His Words in 2002) Awaits Neil Gorsuch," *New York Times*, March 18, 2017.

28. Liptak, "An 'Ideological Food Fight.'"

29. Burgess Everett and Seung Min Kim, "Gorsuch Battle Brings Senate to the Brink of a New Low," *Politico*, March 30, 2017.

30. Matt Flegenheimer, "Gorsuch Tries to Put Himself above Politics in Confirmation Hearing," *New York Times*, March 20, 2017.

31. Tessa Berenson, "How Neil Gorsuch Could Dramatically Reshape Government," *Time*, March 19, 2017.

32. Emily Bazelon and Eric Posner, "The Government Gorsuch Wants to Undo," *New York Times*, April 1, 2017.

33. Charlie Savage, "Neil Gorsuch Helped Defend Disputed Bush-Era Terror Policies," *New York Times*, March 15, 2017.

34. Lydia Wheeler, "American Bar Association Gives Gorsuch Its Best Rating," *The Hill*, March 10, 2017.

35. Michael McConnell, "I Served with Judge Gorsuch. This Is My Reflection on His Character," *The Hill*, February 10, 2017.

36. Alexander Bolton, "Schumer a No on Gorsuch, Will Urge Dems to Oppose," *The Hill*, March 23, 2017.

37. Rebecca Savransky, "McConnell: Gorsuch Will Be Confirmed This Week," *The Hill*, April 2, 2017.

38. Everett and Kim, "Gorsuch Battle Brings Senate to the Brink of a New Low."

39. Everett and Kim, "Gorsuch Battle Brings Senate to the Brink of a New Low."

40. Matt Flegenheimer, "Senate Republicans Deploy 'Nuclear Option' to Clear Path for Gorsuch," *New York Times*, April 6, 2017.

41. Flegenheimer, "Senate Republicans Deploy 'Nuclear Option.'"

42. Ali Rogin, "Senate Approves 'Nuclear Option,' Clears Path for Neil Gorsuch Supreme Court Nomination Vote," ABC News, April 6, 2017.

43. Flegenheimer, "Senate Republicans Deploy 'Nuclear Option.'"

44. Flegenheimer, "Senate Republicans Deploy 'Nuclear Option.'"

45. Flegenheimer, "Senate Republicans Deploy 'Nuclear Option.'"

46. Julie Hirschfeld Davis, "Joe Biden Argued for Delaying Supreme Court Picks in 1992," *New York Times*, February 22, 2016.

47. Davis, "Joe Biden Argued for Delaying Supreme Court Picks in 1992."

48. Davis, "Joe Biden Argued for Delaying Supreme Court Picks in 1992."

49. Elana Schor, Seung Min Kim, and Burgess Everett, "Collins Pushes to Preserve Legislative Filibuster," *Politico*, April 6, 2017.

50. Jordain Carney, "McConnell Shoots Down Trump's Call to End the Filibuster," *The Hill*, May 2, 2017.

51. Paul Kane, "Gorsuch Vote Makes McConnell-Schumer Relationship Look Bad. It Might Get Better," *Washington Post*, April 6, 2017.

52. Kane, "Gorsuch Vote Makes McConnell-Schumer Relationship Look Bad."

53. Kane, "Gorsuch Vote Makes McConnell-Schumer Relationship Look Bad."

54. Kane, "Gorsuch Vote Makes McConnell-Schumer Relationship Look Bad."

55. Kane, "Gorsuch Vote Makes McConnell-Schumer Relationship Look Bad."

56. Kane, "Gorsuch Vote Makes McConnell-Schumer Relationship Look Bad."

57. Kane, "Gorsuch Vote Makes McConnell-Schumer Relationship Look Bad."

58. Adam Liptak, "Confident and Assertive, Gorsuch Hurries to Make His Mark," *New York Times*, July 4, 2017.

59. Liptak, "Confident and Assertive."

60. Thomas L. Friedman, *Thank You for Being Late: An Optimist's Guide to Thriving in the Age of Accelerations* (New York: Farrar, Straus, and Giroux, 2016).

CHAPTER 10. INVESTIGATING THE RUSSIAN CONNECTION

1. Colin Campbell, "Deborah Ross' ACLU Leadership Looms Large in US Senate Race," *The Charlotte Observer*, September 30, 2016.

2. Gideon Resnick, "North Carolina GOP Senator Jokes about Shooting Hillary Clinton," *The Daily Beast*, October 31, 2016.

3. Simone Pathe, "Can This North Carolina Democrat Become the Next Kay Hagan?" *Roll Call*, March 20, 2016.

4. David Graham, "The North Carolina Governor's Race Is Finally Over," *The Atlantic*, December 5, 2016.

5. Resnick, "North Carolina GOP Senator."

6. Colin Campbell, "US Sen. Richard Burr Says 2016 Will Be His Last Run for Elected Office," *The Charlotte Observer*, July 20, 2016.

7. Catherine Ho, "Nervous Republicans Ramp up Spending in North Carolina as Senate Race Tightens," *Washington Post*, September 1, 2016.

8. Matt Bai, "Obama vs. Boehner: Who Killed the Debt Deal?" *New York Times*, March 28, 2012.

9. Ho, "Nervous Republicans."

10. Elana Schor, "Leahy to Be Top Democrat on Appropriations Committee," *Politico*, November 16, 2016.

11. Donald Trump, "@realDonaldTrump," Twitter, June 18, 2013.

12. Donald Trump, "@realDonaldTrump," Twitter, June 18, 2013.

13. Matthew Nussbaum, "The Definitive Trump-Russia Timeline of Events," *Politico*, March 3, 2017.

14. Donald Trump, "@realDonaldTrump," Twitter, November 10, 2013.

15. Tal Kopan and Jim Sciutto, "Donald Trump Says Russia Isn't to Blame for MH17, Despite Evidence," CNN, October 15, 2015.

16. Gail Collins, "Trump and Putin, in the Barn," *New York Times*, December 16, 2016.

17. Linda Qiu, "Did Vladimir Putin Call Trump 'Brilliant'?" *Politifact*, September 8, 2016.

18. Donald Trump, "Donald J. Trump Foreign Policy Speech," Trump/Pence, April 27, 2016.

19. Meghan Keneally, "Trump Says Putin Better Leader Than Obama in Military Town Hall," ABC News, September 7, 2016.

20. Brianna Gurciullo, "Graham Rips Trump's 'Nonsensical' Foreign Policy Speech," *Politico*, April 27, 2016.

21. "Trump's Been Talking about His Business Interests in Russia for 30 Years," *The Atlantic*, May 10, 2017.

22. Michael Crowley, "All of Trump's Russia Ties, in 7 Charts," *Politico*, March/April 2017.

23. Nicole Gaouette, "Intel Chief: Presidential Campaigns under Cyber attack," CNN, May 18, 2016.

24. David Sanger and Nick Corasaniti, "D.N.C. Says Russian Hackers Penetrated Its Files, Including Dossier on Donald Trump," *New York Times*, June 14, 2016.

25. Eric Bradner, "Trump: DNC Hacked Itself," CNN, June 15, 2016.

26. James Rogers, "After DNC Attack, Hacker Guccifer 2.0 Claims Hillary Clinton 'Dossier' Leak," Fox News, June 21, 2016.

27. Michael Shear and Matthew Rosenberg, "Released Emails Suggest the D.N.C. Derided the Sanders Campaign," *New York Times*, July 22, 2016.

28. Jonathan Martin and Alan Rappeport, "Debbie Wasserman Schultz to Resign D.N.C. Post," *New York Times*, July 24, 2016.

29. Nancy Youssef and Shane Harris, "FBI Suspects Russia Hacked DNC; U.S. Officials Say It Was to Elect Donald Trump," *The Daily Beast*, July 25, 2016.

30. David Sanger and Eric Schmitt, "Spy Agency Consensus Grows That Russia Hacked D.N.C.," *New York Times*, July 26, 2016.

31. Damian Paletta and Devlin Barrett, "Obama Says Experts Tie Russia to DNC Hacking," *Wall Street Journal*, July 27, 2016.

32. Cory Bennett, "Russia-Linked Hacker Leaks House Democrats' Cell Phones, Emails," *Politico*, August 12, 2016.

33. Cory Bennett, "Suspected Russian DNC Hackers also Hit GOP, Researchers Say," *Politico*, August 13, 2016.

34. Robert Windrem and William M. Arkin, "Trump Told Russia to Blame for Hacks Long before 2016 Debate," NBC News, October 10, 2016.

35. Dana Priest, Ellen Nakashima, and Tom Hamburger, "U.S. Investigating Potential Covert Russian Plan to Disrupt November Elections," *Washington Post*, September 5, 2016.

36. Barney Henderson, "Barack Obama and Vladimir Putin Hold 'Blunt' Meeting at G20," *The Telegraph*, September 5, 2016.

37. Damian Paletta, "U.S. Intelligence Chief Suggests Russia Hacks of Democratic Party Groups," *Wall Street Journal*, September 7, 2016.

38. John Wagner, Jose A. DelReal, and Anne Gearan, "Trump Praises Putin at National Security Forum," *Washington Post*, September 8, 2016.

39. Cristiano Lima, "Trump on RT: Johnson Shouldn't Debate; Russian Election Interference 'Probably Unlikely,'" *Politico*, September 8, 2016.

40. Kyle Cheney and Sarah Wheaton, "The Most Revealing Clinton Campaign Emails in WikiLeaks Release," *Politico*, October 7, 2016.

41. "Transcript of the Second Debate," *New York Times*, October 10, 2016.

42. "Transcript of the Second Debate," *New York Times*, October 10, 2016.

43. "Transcript of the Second Debate," *New York Times*, October 10, 2016.

44. Mark Hensch, "Trump: 'I Love WikiLeaks,'" *The Hill*, October 10, 2016.

45. "Transcript of the Third Debate," *New York Times*, October 20, 2016.

46. "Transcript of the Third Debate," *New York Times*, October 20, 2016.

47. Zoya Sheftalovich, "Russia Cheers Trump Victory," *Politico*, November 9, 2016.

48. Bryan Bender, "Trump Names Mike Flynn National Security Advisor," *Politico*, November 17, 2016.

49. Tom Hamburger, Rosalind Helderman, and Michael Birnbaum, "Inside Trump's Financial Ties to Russia and His Unusual Flattery of Vladimir Putin," *Washington Post*, June 17, 2016.

50. Maggie Haberman, Matthew Rosenberg, Matt Apuzzo, and Glenn Thrush, "Michael Flynn Resigns as National Security Advisor," *New York Times*, February 13, 2017.

51. "A Transcript of Donald Trump's Meeting with *The Washington Post* Editorial Board," *Washington Post*, March 21, 2016.

52. Steve Mufson and Tom Hamburger, "Trump Adviser's Public Comments, Ties to Moscow Stir Unease in Both Parties," *Washington Post*, August 5, 2016.

53. Alexander Burns and Maggie Haberman, "Donald Trump Hires Paul Manafort to Lead Delegate Effort," *New York Times*, March 28, 2016.

54. Nicholas Confessore, Mike McIntire, and Barry Meier, "Trump Campaign Chief's Firm Got $17 Million from Pro-Russia Party," *New York Times*, June 27, 2017.

55. Henry Meyer, "Trump Advisor in Moscow Scolds U.S. as Hypocritical on Democracy," *Bloomberg Politics*, July 7, 2017.

56. Josh Meyer and Kenneth Vogel, "Trump Campaign Approved Adviser's Trip to Moscow," *Politico*, March 7, 2017.

57. Sara Murray, Jim Acosta, and Theodore Schleifer, "More Trump Advisers Disclose Meetings with Russia's Ambassador," CNN, March 4, 2017.

58. "Trump Campaign Guts GOP's Anti-Russia Stance on Ukraine," *Washington Post*, July 18, 2016.

59. Jeremy Smith, "Roger Stone Claims to Be in Contact with WikiLeaks Founder," *Roll Call*, August 9, 2016.

60. Nolan McCaskill, Alex Isenstadt, and Shane Goldmacher, "Paul Manafort Resigns from Trump Campaign," *Politico*, August 19, 2016.

61. Roger Stone, "@RogerStoneJr," Twitter, August 21, 2016.

62. Roger Stone, "@RogerStoneJr," Twitter, October 3, 2016.

63. "WikiLeaks' 'October Surprise' Fails; Assange Promises More to Come," Fox News, October 4, 2016.

64. Kyle Cheney and Sarah Wheaton, "The Most Revealing Clinton Campaign Emails in WikiLeaks Release," *Politico*, October 7, 2016.

65. Philip Bump, "Is There Actually Evidence That Trump Allies Had a Heads-Up on What WikiLeaks Was Doing?" *Washington Post*, October 12, 2016.

66. Jim DeFede, "Trump Ally Roger Stone Admits 'Back-Channel' Tie to WikiLeaks," CBS Miami, October 12, 2016.

67. Michael Schmidt, Matthew Rosenberg, and Marr Apuzzo, "Kushner and Flynn Met with Russian Envoy in December, White House Says," *New York Times*, March 2, 2017.

68. Ivan Nechepurenko, "Carter Page, Ex-Trump Advisor with Russian Ties, Visits Moscow," *New York Times*, December 8, 2016.

69. "Donald Trump on Russia, Advice from Barack Obama and How He Will Lead," *Time*, December 7, 2016.

70. David Sanger, "Obama Strikes Back at Russia for Election Hacking," *New York Times*, December 29, 2016.

71. Schmidt, Rosenberg, and Apuzzo, "Kushner and Flynn Met with Russian Envoy in December."

72. Schmidt, Rosenberg, and Apuzzo, "Kushner and Flynn Met with Russian Envoy in December."

73. Krishnadev Calamur, "Flynn's Calls with Russia's Ambassador: Who Knew What, and When?" *The Atlantic*, February 14, 2017.

74. Donald Trump, "@realDonaldTrump," December 30, 2016.

75. Ellen Nakashima and Greg Miller, "FBI Reviewed Flynn's Calls with Russian Ambassador but Found Nothing Illicit," *Washington Post*, January 23, 2017.

76. Rebecca Morin, "Trump: No Computer Safe from Hacking," *Politico*, December 31, 2016.

77. Donald Trump, "@realDonaldTrump," January 3, 2017.

78. Donald Trump, "@realDonaldTrump," January 4, 2017.

79. David Sanger, "Putin Ordered 'Influence Campaign' Aimed at U.S. Election, Report Says," *New York Times*, January 6, 2017.

80. "Background to 'Assessing Russian Activities and Intentions in Recent US Elections': The Analytic Process and Cyber Incident Attribution," *Office of the Director of National Intelligence*, January 6, 2017.

81. Michael Shear and David Sanger, "Putin Led a Complex Cyberattack Scheme to Aid Trump, Report Finds," *New York Times*, January 6, 2017.

82. Shear and Sanger, "Putin Led a Complex Cyberattack Scheme."

83. Louis Nelson, "Trump Says Hacking Had 'No Effect on the Outcome of the Election," *Politico*, January 6, 2017.

84. Liz Kreutz, "Hillary Clinton Condemns Donald Trump's 'Insults' of 'Genuine War Hero' John McCain," ABC News, July 18, 2015.

85. Victoria McGrane, "John McCain Has Emerged as a Leading Republican Dissenter," *Boston Globe*, February 6, 2017.

86. Richard Gooding, "The Trashing of John McCain," *Vanity Fair*, November 2004.

87. Todd Purdum, "The Man Who Never Was," *Vanity Fair*, November 2010.

88. Ben Schreckinger, "Trump Attacks McCain: 'I Like People Who Weren't Captured,'" *Politico*, July 18, 2017.

89. Burgess Everett, "Why McCain Refuses to Go Maverick on Trump," *Politico*, August 29, 2016.

90. "McCain Turns Bush on Iraq War Surge," *Washington Times*, August 21, 2008.

91. Brandon Carter, "McCain: Putin a Greater Threat Than ISIS," *The Hill*, May 29, 2017.

92. John McCain, "Statement by Senators McCain and Graham on Sanctions against Russia and the Situation in Ukraine," Press Release, April 28, 2014.

93. Jacob Pramuk, "McCain, Graham Say They Will Seek 'Stronger Sanctions' on Russia," CNBC, December 29, 2016.

94. John McCain, "Statement by SASC Chairman John McCain on President Trump's Phone Call with Vladimir Putin," Press Release, January 27, 2017.

95. McCain, "Statement by SASC Chairman John McCain."

96. McCain, "Statement by SASC Chairman John McCain."

97. Lindsey Graham, "Biography," from his Senate website.

98. "Graham Very Hawkish on ISIS and Assad, More Troops, More Trump Action," Fox News, April 9, 2017.

99. Max Greenwood, "Graham: Calling Climate Change a 'Hoax' Bad for GOP," *The Hill*, May 28, 2017.

100. Josh Rogin, "Graham: Trump Slashing of State Dept. and Foreign Aid Funding Would Be 'Dead on Arrival' in Congress," *Washington Post*, February 28, 2017.

101. Rachel Weiner, "Immigration's Gang of 8: Who Are they?" *Washington Post*, January 28, 2013.

102. Shawn Zeller, "As a Senator, Hillary Clinton Got Along with the GOP. Could She Do So as President?" *Roll Call*, September 26, 2016.

103. Jennifer Steinhauer, "Foreign Policy's Bipartisan Trio Becomes Republican Duo," *New York Times*, November 26, 2012.

104. Alan Rappeport, "Lindsey Graham Enters White House Race with Emphasis on National Security," *New York Times*, June 1, 2015.

105. Jess Byrnes, "Graham: I Won't Vote for Trump," *The Hill*, May 6, 2016.

106. Austin Wright and Seung Min Kim, "Trump in Graham's Cross Hairs as Russia Probe Kicks Off," *Politico*, March 15, 2017.

107. Eugene Scott, "Graham: I Will Never Be Satisfied Until We Punish Russia," CNN, February 2, 2017.

108. Scott, "Graham: I Will Never Be Satisfied Until We Punish Russia."

109. Adam Entous, Ellen Nakashima, and Greg Miller, "Sessions Met with Russian Envoy Twice Last Year, Encounters He Later Did Not Disclose," *Washington Post*, March 1, 2017.

110. "*Face the Nation* Transcript, January 15, 2017: Pence, Manchin, Gingrich," *Face the Nation*, January 15, 2017.

111. Greg Miller, Adam Entous, and Ellen Nakashima, "National Security Adviser Flynn Discussed Sanctions with Russian Ambassador, Despite Denials, Officials Say," *Washington Post*, February 9, 2017.

112. Josh Dawsey, Alex Isenstadt, Tara Palmeri, and Eli Stokols, "Flynn Resigns as National Security Adviser," *Politico*, February 13, 2017.

113. Entous, Nakashima, and Miller, "Sessions Met with Russian Envoy Twice Last Year."

114. Alexander Bolton, "Schumer Calls for Sessions to Resign," March 2, 2017.

115. Karoun Demirjian, Ed O'Keefe, Sari Horwitz, and Matt Zapotosky, "Attorney General Jeff Sessions Will Recuse Himself from Any Probe Related to 2016 Presidential Campaign," *Washington Post*, March 2, 2017.

116. "Transcript: Everything President Trump Had to Say at His First Solo News Conference," *Los Angeles Times*, February 16, 2017.

117. Bridget Bowman, "Bipartisan Senators Call for New Committee on Russian Hacking," *The Hill*, December 18, 2016.

118. Charles Schumer, "Schumer Remarks Calling for Senate Select Committee to Investigate Russian Interference in 2016 Election," Press Release, December 18, 2016.

119. Jordain Carney, "Schumer Asks for Review of 'Political Interference' in Russia Investigations," *The Hill*, March 6, 2017.

120. Rebecca Savransky, "McConnell Stands Firm: No Select Committee Needed to Investigate Russian Meddling," *The Hill*, December 20, 2016.

121. Austin Wright and Martin Matishak, "How the Senate's Russian Meddling Probe Almost Blew Up," *Politico*, January 1, 2017.

122. Max Greenwood, "Top Senate Dem: 'Grave Concerns' about Independence of Russia Probe," *The Hill*, February 25, 2017.

123. Emmarie Huetteman and Michael Schmidt, "Devin Nunes Puts Credibility of House Panel He Leads in Doubt," *New York Times*, March 23, 2017.

124. Martin Matishak and Cory Bennett, "Key Moments from the House Intelligence Committee's Russia Hearing," *Politico*, March 20, 2017.

125. Mark Hensch, "Nunes Regrets Briefing Trump before Intelligence Panel," *The Hill*, March 23, 2017.

126. Karoun Demirjian, Greg Miller, and Philip Rucker, "Nunes Admits Meeting with Source of Trump Surveillance Documents on White House Grounds," *Washington Post*, March 27, 2017.

127. Louis Nelson, "Graham: Nunes Is Running 'an Inspector Clouseau Investigation," *Politico*, March 28, 2017.

128. Emmarie Huetteman, "Mike Conaway Emerges from Relative Obscurity to Lead House Russia Inquiry," *New York Times*, April 16, 2017.

129. Austin Wright and Martin Matishak, "Senate Steps Up As House Russia Probe Fails," *Politico*, March 29, 2017.

130. Paul Kane, "Burr and Warner: In the Spotlight, and Arm in Arm, on Russia Probe," *Washington Post*, March 30, 2017.

131. Devlin Barrett, Adam Entous, and Philip Rucker, "President Trump Fires FBI Director Comey," *Washington Post*, May 10, 2017.

132. Devlin Barrett and Philip Rucker, "Trump Said He Was Thinking of Russia Controversy When He Decided to Fire Comey," *Washington Post*, May 11, 2017.

133. Matthew Rosenberg and Matt Apuzzo, "Days before Firing, Comey Asked for More Resources for Russia Inquiry," *New York Times*, May 10, 2017.

134. Julie Vitkovskaya and Amanda Erickson, "The Strange Oval Office Meeting between Trump, Lavrov and Kislyak," *Washington Post*, May 10, 2017.

135. Peter Baker and Julie Hirschfeld Davis, "Trump Defends Sharing Information on ISIS Threat with Russia," *New York Times*, May 16, 2017.

136. Matt Apuzzo, Maggie Haberman, and Matthew Rosenberg, "Trump Told Russians That Firing 'Nut Job' Comey Eased Pressure from Investigation," *New York Times*, May 19, 2017.

137. Jordan Fabian, "Trump Asked Comey to End Flynn Investigation: Report," *The Hill*, May 16, 2017.

138. Callum Borchers, "Three Prongs of the Russia Investigation, Explained," *Washington Post*, June 15, 2017.

139. Rebecca Ruiz and Mark Landler, "Robert Mueller, Former F.B.I. Director, Is Named Special Counsel for Russia Investigation," *New York Times*, May 17, 2017.

140. Adam Entous and Ellen Nakashima, "Trump Asked Intelligence Chiefs to Push Back against FBI Collusion Probe after Comey Revealed Its Existence," *Washington Post*, May 22, 2017.

141. Entous and Nakashima, "Trump Asked Intelligence Chiefs to Push Back."

142. Philip Rucker and Ashley Parker, "President Trump Faces His Hardest Truth: He Was Wrong," *Washington Post*, March 20, 2017.

143. Karoun Demirjian, "Senate Intelligence Committee Subpoenas Documents from Flynn in Russia Probe," *Washington Post*, May 10, 2017.

144. "Treasury Unit to Share Records with Senate for Trump-Russia Probe: WSJ," *Reuters*, May 12, 2017.

145. Dana Milbank, "These Republicans Could Set the Comey Disaster Right," *Washington Post*, May 10, 2017.

146. Terri Rupar, "McConnell Also Says He Wants to Hear from Comey," *Washington Post*, May 17, 2017.

147. Seung Min Kim, "Senate Judiciary Committee to Investigate Comey Firing, Clinton Email Probe," *Politico*, June 14, 2017.

148. Paul Kane, "On Capitol Hill, the Race Is On to Get the First Crack at Comey," *Washington Post*, May 18, 2017.

149. Brian Naylor, "McCain Promises 'Change Is Coming,'" NPR, September 4, 2008.

150. Elaine Godfrey, "What Does Chuck Grassley Fear?" *The Atlantic*, April 13, 2016.

151. Russell Berman, "The Senate Republican Calling 'Nonsense' on President Trump," *The Atlantic*, June 9, 2017.

152. Todd Ruger, "Feinstein Breaks Glass Ceiling for Women on Senate Judiciary," *Roll Call*, November 17, 2016.

153. Bruck, "The Inside War."

154. Wright and Kim: "Trump in Graham's Cross Hairs."

155. Burgess Everett, "Comey Will Testify before Senate Committee Next Thursday," *Politico*, June 1, 2017.

156. Matthew Flegenheimer and Emmarie Huetteman, "Senate Intelligence Committee Leaders Vow Thorough Russian Investigation," *New York Times*, March 29, 2017.

157. Seung Min Kim, "Senate Judiciary Committee to Investigate Comey Firing, Clinton Email Probe."

158. Ellen Nakashima and Karoun Demirjian, "Intelligence Officials Rogers and Coats Said They Won't Discuss Specifics of Private Conversations with Trump," *Washington Post*, June 7, 2017.

159. Kyle Cheney and Josh Gerstein, "Coats and Rogers Refuse to Say If Trump Asked Them to Sway Russia Probe," *Politico*, June 7, 2017.

160. Cheney and Gerstein, "Coats and Rogers Refuse to Say If Trump Asked Them to Sway Russia Probe."

161. Cheney and Gerstein, "Coats and Rogers Refuse to Say If Trump Asked Them to Sway Russia Probe."

162. Cheney and Gerstein, "Coats and Rogers Refuse to Say If Trump Asked Them to Sway Russia Probe."

163. Cheney and Gerstein, "Coats and Rogers Refuse to Say If Trump Asked Them to Sway Russia Probe."

164. "Comey Testimony: Highlights of the Hearing," *The New York Times*, June 8, 2017.

165. James Comey, "Statement for the Record," Senate Select Committee on Intelligence, June 8, 2017.

166. Josh Gerstein and Kyle Cheney, "Comey Blasts White House for 'Lies, Plain and Simple,'" *Politico*, June 8, 2017.

167. "Comey Testimony: Highlights of the Hearing."

168. "Full Transcript and Video: James Comey's Testimony on Capitol Hill," *New York Times*, June 8, 2017.

169. "Full Transcript and Video: James Comey's Testimony on Capitol Hill."

170. Emmarie Huetteman, "Senate Democrats Call for Sessions's Russia Testimony to Be Public," *New York Times*, June 11, 2017.

171. Mallory Shelbourne, "Wyden Calls for Sessions to Testify in Open Hearing," *The Hill*, June 11, 2017.

172. Huetteman, "Senate Democrats Call for Sessions's Russia Testimony to Be Public."

173. Charlie Savage, Emmarie Huetteman, and Rebecca Ruiz, "Highlights from Attorney General Jeff Sessions's Senate Testimony," *New York Times*, June 13, 2017.

174. Max Greenwood, "Franken Fires Back at Sessions after Testimony," *The Hill*, June 13, 2017.

175. *Politico* Staff, "Transcript: Jeff Sessions' Testimony on Trump and Russia," June 13, 2017.

176. *Politico*, "Transcript: Jeff Sessions' Testimony on Trump and Russia."

177. Savage, Huetteman, and Ruiz, "Highlights from Attorney General Jeff Sessions's Senate Testimony."

178. *Politico*, "Transcript: Jeff Sessions' Testimony on Trump and Russia."

179. Philip Rucker and Karoun Demirjian, "Trump Says He Has No 'Tapes' of Comey Conversations," *Washington Post*, June 22, 2017.

180. Michael D. Shear and Maggie Haberman, "Friend Says Trump Is Considering Firing Mueller as Special Counsel," *New York Times*, June 12, 2017.

181. George J. Mitchell and William Cohen, *Men of Zeal* (New York: Penguin Books, 1989).

182. Jo Becker, Matt Apuzzo, and Adam Goldman, "Trump's Son Met with Russian Lawyer after Being Promised Damaging Information on Clinton," *New York Times*, July 9, 2017.

183. Karoun Demirjian, "Senators Strike Comprehensive Deal to Increase Russia Sanctions," *Washington Post*, June 12, 2017.

184. Demirjian, "Senators Strike Comprehensive Deal."

185. Peter Baker and Sophia Kiskovsky, "Trump Signs Russian Sanctions into Law, with Caveats," *New York Times*, August 2, 2017.

186. David Ignatius, "On Russia Sanctions, Trump Has a Point," *Washington Post*, August 3, 2017.

187. Max Greenwood, "Trump Thanks Putin for Cutting US Diplomats: 'We Want to Reduce our Payroll,'" *The Hill*, August 10, 2017.

CHAPTER 11. CATASTROPHIC HEALTH CARE

1. Sheryl Gay Stolberg and Robert Pear, "Obama Signs Health Care Overhaul Bill, with a Flourish," *The New York Times*, March 23, 2010.

2. Alexander Bolton and Silla Brush, "Republicans Block Wall Street Reform Bill," *The Hill*, April 27, 2010.

3. Robin Bravender and Gabriel Nelson, "Republicans Blitz Obama over EPA's 'Anti-Industrial' Regulations," *The New York Times*, September 28, 2010.

4. David Fahrenthold, Paul Kane, and Lori Montgomery, "How McConnell and Biden Pulled Congress Away from the Fiscal Cliff," *Washington Post*, January 2, 2013.

5. Jennifer Steinhauer, "Republican Freedom Caucus's Revolt in House Is Stoked Back Home," *New York Times*, October 19, 2015.

6. Frank Rich, "The Billionaires Bankrolling the Tea Party," *New York Times*, August 28, 2010.

7. Michael Leahy, "Is the Biggest Threat to Speaker of the House John Boehner the 'Young Guns' in His Own Party?" *Washington Post*, May 19, 2011.

8. Lisa Mascaro and Noam Levey, "With a Push from Trump, House Republicans Pass Obamacare Overhaul," *Los Angeles Times*, May 4, 2017.

9. Jeff Zeleny, "G.O.P. Captures House, but Not Senate," *New York Times*, November 2, 2010.

10. Cristina Marcos, "GOP Expands House Majority," *The Hill*, November 4, 2014.

11. Paul Krugman, "The Obamacare Replacement Mirage," *New York Times*, April 11, 2016.

12. "Patient Protection and Affordable Care Act," Public Law 111-148, March 23, 2010.

13. Glenn Kessler, "How Many Pages of Regulations for 'Obamacare'?" *Washington Post*, May 15, 2013.

14. Margot Sanger-Katz, "Grading Obamacare: Successes, Failures and 'Incompletes,'" *New York Times*, February 5, 2017; Glenn Kessler, "Confused by Obamacare? Here Are Answers to Key Questions," *Washington Post*, October 27, 2016.

15. Cody Cain, "Obamacare Architect Ezekiel Emanuel: Donald Trump Has an Opportunity 'to Do Enormous Good'—or to Create 'Chaos,'" *Salon*, December 3, 2016.

16. Jonathan Alter, *The Center Holds: Obama and His Enemies* (New York: Simon & Schuster, 2014).

17. Jeryl Bier, "Obamacare Website No Longer Addresses 'You Can Keep Your Doctor,'" *The Weekly Standard*, August 24, 2016.

18. Tom Cohen, "Rough Obamacare Rollout: 4 Reasons Why," CNN, October 23, 2013.

19. Stephen Collinson, "Obamacare Rollout Disaster Is a Political Embarrassment and an Opening for the Republicans," *Business Insider*, October 22, 2013.

20. Adam Liptak, "Supreme Court Upholds Health Care Law, 5–4, in Victory for Obama," *New York Times*, June 28, 2012.

21. Liptak, "Supreme Court Upholds Health Care Law."

22. "A Guide to the Supreme Court's Decision on the ACA's Medicaid Expansion," *Kaiser Family Foundation*, August 2012.

23. Alter, *The Center Holds*.

24. "Coverage for Pre-Existing Conditions," HealthCare.gov.

25. Sarah Kliff (ed.), "Obamacare's Individual Mandate, Explained," *Vox*, July 2, 2015.

26. Reed Abelson and Margot Sanger-Katz, "Explaining the Health Payments That Trump Has Called 'Ransom Money,'" *New York Times*, April 14, 2017.

27. Katherine Greifeld, "What Obamacare Repeal Could Mean for Medicaid: Quick Take Q&A," *Bloomberg*, January 26, 2017.

28. "Medicaid Financing," Medicaid.gov.

29. David Leonhardt, "The Fight for Obamacare Has Turned," *New York Times*, February 28, 2017.

30. Leonhardt, "The Fight for Obamacare Has Turned."

31. Heayoun Park and Margot Sanger-Katz, "The Parts of Obamacare Republicans Will Keep, Change or Discard," *New York Times*, March 6, 2017.

32. Julie Appleby, "What If You Could Take It with You? Health Insurance, That Is," NPR, February 28, 2017.

33. Sarah Mimms, "Chuck Schumer: Passing Obamacare in 2010 Was a Mistake," *The Atlantic*, November 25, 2014.

34. Eduardo Porter, "America's Inequality Problem: Real Income Gains Are Brief and Hard to Find," *New York Times*, September 13, 2016.

35. Eric Pianin, "It Could Take 3 Years for Republicans to Replace Obamacare," *Business Insider*, December 1, 2016.

36. Margot Sanger-Katz and Heayoun Park, "Obamacare More Popular Than Ever, Now That It May Be Repealed," *New York Times*, February 1, 2017.

37. Rachana Pradhan, "Liberals Mount Campaign to Save Obamacare," *Politico*, December 7, 2016.

38. Pradhan, "Liberals Mount Campaign to Save Obamacare."

39. Pradhan, "Liberals Mount Campaign to Save Obamacare."

40. Pradhan, "Liberals Mount Campaign to Save Obamacare."

41. Pradhan, "Liberals Mount Campaign to Save Obamacare."

42. Pradhan, "Liberals Mount Campaign to Save Obamacare."

43. Alexander Bolton, "McConnell: We'll Start Obamacare Repeal on Day One," *The Hill*, December 6, 2016.

44. Thomas Kaplan and Robert Pear, "Senate Takes Major Step toward Repealing Health Care Law," *New York Times*, January 12, 2017.

45. Erin Kelly, "Obamacare Takes First Real Step Closer to Repeal after Senate Vote," *USA Today*, January 11, 2017.

46. Kelly, "Obamacare Takes First Real Step."

47. Kelsey Snell, "18 Million Would Lose Insurance in First Year of Obamacare Repeal without Replacement, CBO Report Says," *Washington Post*, January 17, 2017.

48. Snell, "18 Million Would Lose Insurance."

49. Nathaniel Weixel, "Rival Senate Healthcare Group Seeks to Make Waves," *The Hill*, May 14, 2017.

50. Susan Collins, "Senators Collins, Cassidy to Introduce ACA Replacement Plan to Expand Choices, Lower Health Care Costs," Press Release, January 17, 2017.

51. Bruce Westerman, "Medicaid Block Grants Give States More Freedom," *The Hill*, March 21, 2017.

52. Burgess Everett, Rachael Bade, and Rachana Pradhan, "GOP Split over Medicaid Imperils Obamacare Plans," *Politico*, January 23, 2017.

53. Kimberly Leonard, "Governors Disagree on Future of Medicaid Expansion, Obamacare," *U.S. News & World Report*, February 27, 2017.

54. Rachana Pradhan, "GOP Governors Fight Their Own Party on Obamacare," *Politico*, January 13, 2017.

55. Alison Kodjak, "From Birth to Death, Medicaid Affects the Lives of Millions," NPR, June 27, 2017.

56. Kyle Cheney, "Freedom Caucus Thwarts Boehner, Ryan—and Now Trump," *Politico*, March 26, 2017.

57. Darius Tahir, "Boehner: Republican Won't Repeal and Replace Obamacare," *Politico*, February 23, 2017.

58. Tahir, "Boehner: Republican Won't Repeal and Replace Obamacare."

59. Rich Lowry, "Heed the Protests," *National Review*, February 14, 2017.

60. David Weigel, "Freedom Caucus Backs ACA 'Repeal and Replace' That Counts on Private Health Care," *Washington Post*, February 15, 2017.

61. Hannah Fingerhut, "Support for 2010 Health Care Law Reaches New High," *Pew Research Center*, February 23, 2017.

62. Jeremy Peters, "Patience Gone, Koch-Backed Groups Will Pressure G.O.P. on Health Repeal," *New York Times*, March 5, 2017.

63. Peters, "Patience Gone."

64. Peters, "Patience Gone."

65. Peters, "Patience Gone."

66. Peters, "Patience Gone."

67. Peters, "Patience Gone."

68. Peters, "Patience Gone."

69. Robert Pear and Thomas Kaplan, "House Republicans Unveil Plan to Replace Health Law," *New York Times*, March 6, 2017.

70. Pear and Kaplan, "House Republicans Unveil Plan to Replace Health Law."

71. Pear and Kaplan, "House Republicans Unveil Plan to Replace Health Law."

72. Sean Sullivan, Mike DeBonis, and Kelsey Snell, "Trump Stands with House GOP on Proposal to Revise Obamacare, Spokesman Says," *Washington Post*, March 10, 2017.

73. Dan Mangan, "House GOP Releases Plan to Repeal, Replace Obamacare," CNBC, March 6, 2017.

74. Yasmeen Abutaleb, "Factbox: Republican Obamacare Plan Would Repeal Medicaid Expansion, Taxes," *Reuters*, March 7, 2017.

75. Abutaleb, "Factbox."

76. Mike DeBonis, Kelsey Snell, and Sean Sullivan, "Obamacare Revision Clears Two House Committees as Trump, Others Tried to Tamp Down Backlash," *Washington Post*, March 9, 2017.

77. DeBonis, Snell, and Sullivan, "Obamacare Revision Clears Two House Committees."

78. DeBonis, Snell, and Sullivan, "Obamacare Revision Clears Two House Committees."

79. DeBonis, Snell, and Sullivan, "Obamacare Revision Clears Two House Committees."

80. DeBonis, Snell, and Sullivan, "Obamacare Revision Clears Two House Committees."

81. Jonathan Chait, "Mitch McConnell's Trumpcare Plan Is to Lose Fast," *New York Magazine*, March 22, 2017.

82. Dan Diamond, "5 Trump Health Care Promises That Won't Become Reality," *Politico*, May 1, 2017.

83. Madeline Conway, "Trump: 'Nobody Knew That Healthcare Could Be So Complicated,'" *Politico*, February 27, 2017.

84. DeBonis, Snell, and Sullivan, "Obamacare Revision Clears Two House Committees."

85. Dan Mangan, "Trump Endorses GOP Replacement Plan for Obamacare, Says 'Let's Get It Done,'" CNBC, March 7, 2017.

86. Byron York, "Why Can't House Repeal Obamacare? Because a Lot of Republicans Don't Want To," *Washington Examiner*, April 27, 2017.

87. Eliza Collins and Herb Jackson, "Republican Moderates Reject Group Talks with House Freedom Caucus," *USA Today*, March 30, 2017.

88. Mike DeBonis, Ed O'Keefe, and Robert Costa, "GOP Health-Care Bill: House Republican Leaders Abruptly Pull Their Rewrite of the Nation's Health-Care Law," *Washington Post*, March 24, 2017.

89. DeBonis, O'Keefe, and Costa, "GOP Health-Care Bill."

90. DeBonis, O'Keefe, and Costa, "GOP Health-Care Bill."

91. Alan Rappeport, "Dealt a Defeat, Republicans Set Their Sights on Major Tax Cuts," *New York Times*, March 26, 2017.

92. Peter Sullivan and Jessie Hellmann, "Freedom Caucus Gets to Yes on Healthcare," *The Hill*, April 26, 2017.

93. Thomas Kaplan and Robert Pear, "House Passes Measure to Repeal and Replace the Affordable Care Act," *New York Times*, May 4, 2017.

94. M. J. Lee, "House Republicans Pass Bill to Replace and Repeal Obamacare," CNN, May 4, 2017.

95. Margot Sanger-Katz, "Who Wins and Who Loses in the Latest G.O.P. Health Care Bill," *New York Times*, May 4, 2017.

96. Reed Abelson and Katie Thomas, "In Rare Unity, Hospitals, Doctors and Insurers Criticize Health Bill," *New York Times*, May 4, 2017.

97. Abelson and Thomas, "In Rare Unity."

98. Abelson and Thomas, "In Rare Unity."

99. Dan Mangan, "Obamacare Deductibles Are on the Rise for 2017, along with Monthly Premiums," CNBC, October 26, 2016.

100. Carolyn Johnson, "Iowa Obamacare Program on Verge of Collapse as Congressional Uncertainty Takes Its Toll," *Washington* Post, May 3, 2017.

101. Danielle Kurtzleben, "Even without Congress, the Trump Administration Can Still Redo Obamacare," National Public Radio, March 29, 2017.

102. "Fact Check; Obamacare Is Not in a 'Death Spiral,'" CBS News, January 10, 2017.

103. Matthew Yglesias, "Tom Cotton Slams House GOP Health Bill: 'Pause, Start Over. Get It Right, Don't Get It Fast,'" *Vox*, March 9, 2017.

104. Leigh Ann Caldwell and Andrew Rafferty, "After CBO Report, Senate Republicans Aim for Better Health Care Bill," NBC News, May 24, 2017.

105. Jennifer Haberkorn and Elana Schor, "Bipartisan Health Care Talks Pick Up Steam in Senate," *Politico*, May 16, 2017.

106. Haberkorn and Schor, "Bipartisan Health Care Talks."

107. Haberkorn and Schor, "Bipartisan Health Care Talks."

108. Haberkorn and Schor, "Bipartisan Health Care Talks."

109. Haberkorn and Schor, "Bipartisan Health Care Talks."

110. Haberkorn and Schor, "Bipartisan Health Care Talks."

111. Haberkorn and Schor, "Bipartisan Health Care Talks."

112. Seung Min Kim and Elana Schor, "How Schumer Kept Dems United on Obamacare," *Politico*, June 28, 2017.

113. Julie Hirschfeld Davis, "Trump's Budget Cuts Deeply into Medicaid and Anti-Poverty Efforts," *New York Times*, May 22, 2017.

114. Jessie Hellmann and Nathaniel Weixel, "GOP Senators Bristle at Trump's Medicaid Cuts," *The Hill*, May 23, 2017.

115. Kelsey Snell, Damian Paletta, and Mike Debonis, "Even Some Republicans Balk at Trump's Plan for Steep Budget Cuts," *Washington Post*, May 23, 2017.

116. Michael Hiltzik, "The Costs of Trump's Sabotage of Obamacare Already Are Showing up in Rate Hikes," *Los Angeles Times*, May 16, 2017.

117. M. J. Lee and Lauren Fox, "One Week. 52 Senators. Can Mitch McConnell Get It Done?" CNN, June 23, 2017.

118. Robert Pear, "13 Men, and No Women, Are Writing New G.O.P. Health Bill in Senate," *New York Times*, May 8, 2017.

119. Pear, "13 Men, and No Women."

120. Olivia Beavers, "Ex-Medicare Head: GOP Using 'Sabotage, Speed and Secrecy' to Pass ObamaCare Repeal," *The Hill*, June 11, 2017.

121. Adam Cancryn, "Secrecy Boosts GOP's Obamacare Repeal Push," *Politico*, June 20, 2017.

122. Steven T. Dennis and Laura Litvan, "Health Bill Setback for McConnell Sets Stage for Final Push," *Bloomberg Politics*, June 27, 2017.

123. Sean Sullivan, Juliet Eilperin, and Kelsey Snell, "Senate GOP Leaders Will Present Health Bill This Week, Even as Divisions Flare," *Washington Post*, June 20, 2017.

124. Sullivan, Eilperin, and Snell, "Senate GOP Leaders Will Present Health Bill This Week."

125. Lauren Fox, "Conservatives on Capitol Hill Anxiously Await Health Care Bill," CNN, June 20, 2017.

126. Paige Winfield Cunningham, "The Health 202: Here's What's in the Senate Health-Care Bill," *Washington Post*, June 22, 2017.

127. Thomas Kaplan and Robert Pear, "Senate Health Bill in Peril as C.B.O. Predicts 22 Million More Uninsured," *New York Times*, June 26, 2017.

128. Marc Fisher and Sean Sullivan, "Mitch McConnell, America's No. 1 Obstructionist Is Trying to Make Big Things Happen," *Washington Post*, June 30, 2017.

129. Clare Foran, "GOP Senator Dean Heller Won't Support Senate Healthcare Bill," *The Atlantic*, June 23, 2017.

130. Robert Pear and Jennifer Steinhauer, "G.O.P. Rift over Medicaid and Opioids Imperils Senate Health Bill," *New York Times*, June 20, 2017.

131. Brooke Singman, "Senate Health Care Bill: 4 Key Republicans Come Out against GOP Plan," Fox News, June 22, 2017.

132. Paul Kane, "If These Two Republicans Can't Agree, the Senate Can't Pass Its Health-Care Bill," *Washington Post*, June 29, 2017.

133. Juliet Eilperin, Sean Sullivan, and Ed O'Keefe, "Senate Democrats Seek New Allies in Effort to Scuttle Obamacare Overhaul: Republican Governors," *Washington Post*, July 10, 2017.

134. Daniella Diaz, Lauren Fox, and Phil Mattingly, "Senate Bill: New Version Unveiled, Cornyn Closes 'the Door' on Extending Date to Vote," CNN, June 26, 2017.

135. Manu Raju, Phil Mattingly, and Ashley Killough, "McConnell Delays Vote on Health Care Bill until after July 4 Recess," CNN, June 27, 2017.

136. Campbell Robertson, Dave Philipps, Jess Bidgood, and Emily Cochrane, "Senate Republicans Lie Low on the Fourth, or Face Single-Minded Pressure," *New York Times*, July 4, 2017.

137. David Weigel, "A Town Hall in Kansas Shows Republican Struggles with Health-Care Bill," *Washington Post*, July 6, 2017.

138. Weigel, "A Town Hall in Kansas."

139. David Wright, "GOP Sen. John Hoeven Comes Out against Health Care Bill," CNN, July 6, 2017.

140. Burgess Everett, "GOP Senators Call for McConnell to Shorten August Recess," *Politico*, July 30, 2017.

141. Fisher and Sullivan, "Mitch McConnell, America's No. 1 Obstructionist."

142. Caroline Kenny, "Trump Confirms He Called Health Care 'Mean,'" CNN, June 26, 2017.

143. Audrey Carlsen and Haeyoun Park, "Which Party Was More Secretive in Working on Its Health Care Plan?" *New York Times*, July 10, 2017.

144. Juliet Eilperin and Amy Goldstein, "McConnell Says GOP Must Shore Up ACA Insurance Markets If Senate Bill Dies," *Washington Post*, July 6, 2017.

145. Eilperin and Goldstein, "McConnell says GOP Must Shore up ACA Insurance Markets."

146. Eilperin and Goldstein, "McConnell says GOP Must Shore up ACA Insurance Markets."

147. Jordain Carney, "McConnell Signals Doubts about ObamaCare Vote," *The Hill*, July 6, 2017.

148. "McConnell Nixes Part of Senate Vacation to Deal with Backlog," *New York Times*, July 11, 2017.

149. Molly Ball, "Why D.C. Hates Ted Cruz," *The Atlantic*, January 26, 2016.

150. Manu Raju, "Cruz Accuses Mitch McConnell of Telling a 'Flat-Out Lie,'" *Politico*, July 24, 2015.

151. Jon Greenberg, "PolitiFact Sheet: Understanding Ted Cruz's Health Care Amendment and Preexisting Conditions," *Politifact*, July 17, 2017.

152. Bob Bryan, "Ted Cruz's Plan to Save the Senate Healthcare Bill Is Gaining Steam—But It Might Not Fix Republicans' Biggest Problem," *Business Insider*, July 8, 2017.

153. Kelsey Snell, Sean Sullivan, and Juliet Eilperin, "McConnell Delays August Recess to Complete Work on Healthcare Bill, Other Issues," *Washington Post*, July 11, 2017.

154. Alan Fram, "New GOP Health Bill Likely Keeping Obama Tax Boosts on Rich," *Washington Post*, July 11, 2017.

155. Juliet Eilperin, Sean Sullivan, and Ed O'Keefe, "Senate Republicans' Effort to 'Repeal and Replace' Obamacare All but Collapses," *Washington Post*, July 18, 2017.

156. Lucia Mutikani, "Eight to 10 Republicans Have Concerns on Healthcare Bill: Collins," Reuters, July 16, 2017.

157. Jennifer Steinhauer, "Old Truth Trips up G.O.P. on Health Law: A Benefit Is Hard to Retract," *New York Times*, July 18, 2017.

158. Elise Viebeck, Paul Kane, and Ed O'Keefe, "McCain Returns to Senate for Health-Care Vote to Emotional Applause from Colleagues," *Washington Post*, July 25, 2017.

159. John Bresnahan, "McConnell Gets a Win in Obamacare Repeal Opening Round," *Politico*, July 25, 2017.

160. Thomas Kaplan and Eileen Sullivan, "Health Care Vote: Senate Rejects Repeal without Replace," *New York Times*, July 26, 2017.

161. Kaplan and Sullivan, "Health Care Vote."

162. Paul Krugman, "The Sanctimony and Sin of G.O.P. 'Moderates,'" *New York Times*, July 27, 2017.

163. Juliegrace Brufke, "Johnson, McCain, Graham Seek Assurance 'Skinny Repeal' Isn't the Final Bill," *The Daily Caller*, July 27, 2017.

164. Ed O'Keefe and Paul Kane, "The Week John McCain Shook the Senate," *Washington Post*, July 28, 2017. The description of events on the Senate floor is taken from this vivid article.

165. Matt Flegenheimer and Thomas Kaplan, "'Time to Move On': Senate G.O.P. Flouts Trump after Health Care Defeat," *New York Times*, August 1, 2017.

166. Adam Cancryn, "Alexander, Murray plan bipartisan hearings to shore up Obamacare," *Politico*, August 1, 2017.

167. Matt Flegenheimer and Maggie Haberman, "Mitch McConnell's 'Excessive Expectations' Comment Draws Trump's Ire," *New York Times*, August 9, 2017.

168. Matt Flegenheimer, "Deepening Rift, Trump Won't Say if Mitch McConnell Should Step Down," *New York Times*, August 10, 2017.

169. Leigh Ann Caldwell and Andrew Rafferty, "Republican Senators Defend McConnell after Trump Attacks," *NBC News*, August 11, 2017.

170. Olivia Beavers, "Hatch Defends McConnell against Trump's Attacks," *The Hill*, August 10, 2017.

CHAPTER 12. AMERICA VERSUS THE WORLD

1. Mujib Mashal, "U.S. Senators, in Kabul, Urge Filling of Vacancies," *New York Times*, July 5, 2017.

2. Stephen R. Weissman, "Congress and War: How the House and the Senate Can Reclaim Their Role," *Foreign Affairs*, January–February 2017; Ira Shapiro, *The Last Great Senate: Courage and Statesmanship in Times of Crisis* (New York: Public Affairs, 2012), chapters 4, 8, 9, 13, and 16.

3. Janell Ross, "From Mexican Rapists to Bad Hombres, the Trump Campaign in Two Moments," *Washington Post*, October 20, 2016.

4. Fred Imbert, "Donald Trump: Mexico Is Going to Pay for the Wall," CNBC, October 28, 2015.

5. Jeremy Diamond, "Donald Trump: Ban All Muslim Travel to the U.S.," CNN Politics, December 28, 2015.

6. Brian Bennett (interviewed by Robert Siegel), "Jeff Sessions Takes Strong Anti-Immigration Views to Justice Department," National Public Radio, February 9, 2017.

7. Ana Gonzalez-Barrera, "More Mexicans Leaving Than Coming to the U.S.," *Pew Research Center Hispanic Trends*, November 19, 2015.

8. Ana Gonzalez-Barrera and Jens Manuel Krogsted, "U.S. Immigrant Deportations Declined in 2014, but Remain Near Record High," *Pew Research Center*, August 31, 2016.

9. Maya Rhodan, "Are the Syrian Refugees All 'Young, Strong Men'?" *Time*, November 20, 2015.

10. Dan Merica, "Trump Signs Executive Order to Keep Out 'Radical Islamic Terrorists,'" CNN Politics, January 30, 2017.

11. Aaron Blake, "Trump's Travel Ban Is Causing Chaos—and Putting His Unflinching Nationalism to the Test," *Washington Post*, January 29, 2017.

12. "Statement of Senator Tom Carper on Executive Order Blocking Refugee Resettlement, Suspending Entry of Immigration from Muslim-Majority Countries," *U.S. Fed News Service*, January 31, 2017.

13. Mallory Shelbourne, "McCain, Graham: Trump Order May Become 'Self-Inflicted Wound' in Terrorism Fight," *The Hill*, January 29, 2017.

14. Aaron Blake, "Whip Count: Here's Where Republicans Stand on Trump's Controversial Travel Ban," *Washington Post*, January 31, 2017.

15. Blake, "Whip Count."

16. Blake, "Whip Count."

17. Rebecca Savransky, "Portman: Trump's Order 'Not Sufficiently Vetted,'" *The Hill*, January 29, 2017.

18. Jason Williams and Dan Horn, "Cincinnati Now a 'Sanctuary City.' What's That Mean?" *Cincinnati Enquirer*, January 30, 2017.

19. Sean Sullivan, "Leading Republican Senators Criticize Trump's Refugee and Travel Ban—48 Hours Later," *Washington Post*, January 29, 2017.

20. Alexander Bolton, "McConnell: Trump's Proposal on Muslims Inconsistent with American Values," *The Hill*, December 8, 2016.

21. Kelsey Snell and Abby Phillip, "McConnell: We Don't Have Religious Tests in This Country," *Washington Post*, January 29, 2017.

22. Thomas Fuller, "'So-Called' Judge Criticized by Trump Is Known as a Mainstream Republican," *New York Times*, February 4, 2017.

23. Mark Landler, "Appeals Court Rejects Request to Immediately Restore Travel Ban," *New York Times*, February 4, 2017.

24. Matt Zapotosky, David Nakamura, and Abigail Hauslohner, "Revised Executive Order Bans Travelers from Six Muslim-Majority Countries from Getting New Visas," *Washington Post*, March 6, 2017.

25. Matt Zapotosky, "Second Federal Judge Blocks Revised Trump Travel Ban," *Washington Post*, March 16, 2017.

26. Jaweed Kaleem and Kurtis Lee, "Trump Faces Major Hurdles—and His Own Words—in Challenging Rulings against His New Travel Ban," *LA Times*, March 16, 2017.

27. Matt Ford, "A Make-or-Break Moment for Trump's Travel Ban," *The Atlantic*, May 8, 2017.

28. Melanie Zanona, "More Than a Dozen Attorneys General Support Lawsuit against Trump Ban," *The Hill*, February 6, 2017.

29. Statement of the American Civil Liberties Union: "ACLU and Other Groups Challenge Trump Immigration Ban after Refugees Detained in Airports Following Executive Order," January 28, 2017.

30. *Wall Street Journal* Roundup, "Corporate Criticism of Trump's Travel Ban Moves beyond Tech," *Wall Street Journal*, January 30, 2017.

31. Mark Hensch, "598 Colleges Have 'Concerns' on Trump Travel Ban," *The Hill*, February 3, 2017.

32. Elaine Glusac, "Trump's Travel Ban Draws Growing Opposition from Tourism Executives," *New York Times*, February 1, 2017.

33. Peter Baker and Michael D. Shear, "Trump Softens Tone on Islam but Calls for Purge of 'Foot Soldiers of Evil,'" *New York Times*, May 21, 2017.

34. Rafael Bernal and Mike Lillis, "Trump Signs Orders on Border Wall, Immigration Enforcement," *The Hill*, January 25, 2017.

35. Bernal and Lillis, "Trump Signs Orders on Border Wall."

36. Statement of Senator Tom Carper on Executive Action to Build a Wall along the U.S. Southern Border, January 26, 2017.

37. Jordain Carney, "Senate Dems Introduce Bill to Rescind Trump Border Wall, Immigration Order," *The Hill*, March 16, 2017.

38. Andrew Taylor (Associated Press), "Congress Reaches $1 Trillion Deal to Fund Government but Provide Little for Trump's Priorities," *Chicago Tribune*, May 1, 2017.

39. Statement of Senator Dianne Feinstein on Immigration Executive Order Implementation, February 21, 2017.

40. Julia Preston and John H. Cushman Jr., "Obama to Permit Young Migrants to Remain in U.S.," *New York Times*, June 15, 2012.

41. Dara Lind, "It's Official. Trump Is Keeping 750,000 Unauthorized Immigrants Safe from Deportation," *Vox*, June 16, 2017.

42. Lind, "It's Official."

43. Alexander Bolton, "McConnell: I'm Very Sympathetic to 'Dreamers,'" *The Hill*, February 17, 2017.

44. Annie Lowrey, "Trump's Anti-Immigration Policies Are Scaring Eligible Families away from the Safety Net," *The Atlantic*, March 24, 2017.

45. Vivian Yee, "Immigrants Hide, Fearing Capture on 'Any Corner,'" *New York Times*, February 22, 2017.

46. David Muir and Devin Dwyer, "Trump: 'Time Is Right for Immigration Bill,' Open to Giving Some Legal Status," ABC News, February 28, 2017.

47. Rafael Carranza (*Arizona Republic*), "Sessions Directs Felony Charges against Repeat Illegal Immigrants," *USA Today*, April 11, 2017.

48. Matt Zapotosky and Sari Horwitz, "Sessions Tells Prosecutors to Bring More Cases against Those Entering U.S. Illegally," *Washington Post*, April 11, 2017.

49. Zapotosky and Horwitz, "Sessions Tells Prosecutors to Bring More Cases."

50. Adam Liptak, "Appeals Court Will Not Reinstate Trump's Revised Travel Ban," *New York Times*, May 25, 2017.

51. Michael D. Shear and Adam Liptak, "Supreme Court Takes Up Travel Ban Case, and Allows Parts to Go Ahead," *New York Times*, June 26, 2017.

52. Patrick Gillespie, "Trump Hammers America's 'Worst Trade Deal,'" CNN Money, September 27, 2016.

53. Ana Swanson, "Trump Will Have the Power to Move Swiftly on Trade," *Washington Post*, November 9, 2016.

54. Charlie Campbell, "Donald Trump's Pledge to Withdraw U.S. from TPP Opens the Door to China," *Time*, November 21, 2016.

55. Darren Samuelsohn, "The 'Political Hacks' Trump Says Are Doing Trade Deals Are Actually Career Government Employees," *Politico*, September 26, 2016.

56. Maggie Haberman, "Donald Trump Says He Favors Big Tariffs on Chinese Exports," *New York Times*, January 7, 2016.

57. Michael Kranish and Marc Fisher, *Trump Revealed* (New York: Charles Scribner's Sons, 2016), 275.

58. Jonathan Weisman, "Trade Authority Bill Wins Final Approval by Senate," *New York Times*, June 24, 2015.

59. James Gerstenzang, "Senate Approves NAFTA on 61–38 Vote; Trade: Passage in Upper House Had Been Expected," *LA Times*, November 21, 1993.

60. Alexander Bolton, "McConnell Praises Obama for a Change," *The Hill*, May 5, 2015.

61. Ian Bremmer, "The Era of American Global Leadership Is Over. Here's What Comes Next," *Time*, December 19, 2016.

62. Hal Shapiro and Lael Brainard, "Fast Track Trade Promotion Authority," *Brookings Institution*, December 1, 2001.

63. Clyde H. Farnesworth, "Congress Is Expected to Keep Pressing for Trade Legislation," *New York Times*, April 18, 1987.

64. "Clinton Loses Fast Track Trade Bill," *Congressional Quarterly Almanac*, 1997.

65. Paul Blake, "In Pushing TPP, President Obama Says He Has 'Better Argument' Than Trump or Clinton," ABC News, August 2, 2016.

66. Mireya Solis (interviewee), "Japan Boosts the Trans-Pacific Partnership," *Council on Foreign Relations*, August 7, 2013.

67. Nelson Schwartz and Bill Vlasic, "By Announcing New Jobs, Corporations Help Themselves Too," *New York Times*, January 17, 2017.

68. Tim Worstall, "Memo to Trump—20% Mexican Import Tariff Means Americans Pay for the Wall," *Forbes*, January 27, 2017.

69. Ben Jacobs, Dominic Rushe, and David Agren, "Trump-Mexico Relations Hit New Low after 20% Border Wall Tax Mooted," *The Guardian*, January 27, 2017.

70. Tracy Wilkinson and Brian Bennett, "Trump Has First Meeting with Mexico's Pena Nieto amid Tense Relations," *LA Times*, July 7, 2017.

71. Azam Amed, "Preparing to Meet Trump, Mexican Leader Seeks Common Ground," *New York Times*, January 23, 2017.

72. Eduardo Porter, "Mexico's Potential Weapons If Trump Declares War on NAFTA," *New York Times*, January 24, 2017.

73. Ana Swanson and Damian Paletta, "Trump Says He Will Not Label China Currency Manipulator, Reversing Campaign Promise," *Washington Post*, April 22, 2017.

74. Mark Landler, "Blind Spots in Trump's Trade Tirade against Germany," *New York Times*, May 30, 2017.

75. Vicki Needham, "Why Trump Is Fighting Canada on Softwood Lumber and Dairy," *The Hill*, May 2, 2017.

76. Peter Baker, "Trump Abandons Trans-Pacific Partnership, Obama's Signature Trade Deal," *New York Times*, January 23, 2017.

77. Don Lee, "Trump Wants to Cut Bilateral Trade Deals, But What If Nobody Comes to the Table?" *LA Times*, July 12, 2017.

78. Kate Linthicum, "Mexico's Bargaining Chips with Trump? How about a Corn Boycott," *LA Times*, March 29, 2017.

79. Linthicum, "Mexico's Bargaining Chips with Trump?"

80. Joseph Parilla, "How US States Rely on the NAFTA Supply Chain," *Brookings*, March 30, 2017.

81. Vicki Needham, Megan R. Wilson, and Rafael Bernal, "Trump Sparks Rush of NAFTA Lobbying," *The Hill*, June 21, 2017.

82. Eric Martin and Justin Sink, "U.S. Chamber Said to Tell Mexico It Will Defend NAFTA Deal," *Bloomberg Politics*, December 8, 2016.

83. Mitra Tag, "Trump Administration Taking 'Constructive' Stance on NAFTA," *Reuters*, April 24, 2017.

84. Damian Paletta, "Trump Considers Order That Would Start the Process of Withdrawing from NAFTA," *Washington Post*, April 26, 2017.

85. Paletta, "Trump Considers Order."

86. Paletta, "Trump Considers Order."

87. Tara Palmeri, Adam Behsudi, and Seung Min Kim, "Republicans Tell Trump to Hold Up on NAFTA Withdrawal," *Politico*, April 26, 2017.

88. Palmeri, Behsudi, and Kim, "Republicans Tell Trump to Hold Up."

89. Sean Higgins, "Trump Vows 'Big Changes or We're Going to Get Rid of NAFTA,'" *Washington Post Examiner*, April 18, 2017.

90. Matthew Korade, Adam Behsudi, and Louis Nelson, "Trump Picks Lighthizer to Serve as U.S. Trade Representative," *Politico*, January 3, 2017.

91. Vicki Needham, "Senate Confirms Trump's Chief Trade Negotiator," *The Hill*, May 11, 2017.

92. Needham, "Senate Confirms Trump's Chief Trade Negotiator."

93. Statement of Senator Maria Cantwell, Hearing on the Nomination of Robert Lighthizer to Be U.S. Trade Representative, March 14, 2017.

94. Alexander Panetta, "U.S. Lawmakers Balk at NAFTA 'Tweaks,' Urge Tough Stance against Canada," *Canadian Manufacturing*, March 15, 2017.

95. Statement of Senator Debbie Stabenow, Hearing on the Nomination of Robert Lighthizer to be U.S. Trade Representative, March 14, 2017; Melissa Nann Burke, "Stabenow—Close Loopholes in Buy America Law," *Detroit News*, March 31, 2017.

96. Julie Hirschfeld Davis, "Trump Sends NAFTA Renegotiation Notice to Congress," *New York Times*, May 18, 2017.

97. Rosie Gray, "Trump Backs Away from Terminating NAFTA," *The Atlantic*, April 26, 2017.

98. Statement of AFL-CIO president Rich Trumka, "Make-or-Break Moment in NAFTA Renegotiation Plans," July 19, 2017.

99. Evelyn Chang, "More and More American Companies Have Decided Their Big China Opportunity Is Over," CNBC, December 8, 2016.

100. Paul Carsten (*Reuters*), "US Tech Companies Are Partnering with Chinese Firms to Survive in China," *Business Insider*, January 29, 2015.

101. Frank Tang, "China's Bid to Cut Production Overcapacity in Heavy Industries 'Losing Steam', Study Suggests," *South China Morning Post*, December 1, 2016.

102. Fred Hiatt, "Trump Could Transform America's Relationship with China. Here's How." *Washington Post*, January 15, 2017.

103. Fred Hiatt, "China Is Bent on World Domination—But Not in the Way You Think," *Washington Post*, May 7, 2017.

104. Peter Baker, "Trump Abandons Trans-Pacific Partnership, Obama's Signature Trade Deal," *New York Times*, January 23, 2017.

105. David Nakamura and Emily Rauhala, "U.S. and China End Summit with 100-Day Plan to Boost Trade and Cooperation," *Washington Post*, April 7, 2017.

106. Mark Landler, "Trump Says China Will Get Better Trade Deal If It Solves 'North Korean Problem,'" *New York Times*, April 11, 2017.

107. Shawn Donnan, "Critics Pan Trump's 'Early Harvest' Trade Deal with China," *Financial Times*, May 14, 2017.

108. Michael Birnbaum and Damian Paletta, "At G-20, World Aligns against Trump Policies Ranging from Free Trade to Climate Change," *Washington Post*, July 7, 2017.

109. James Kanter, "The EU-Japan Deal: What's in It, and Why It Matters," *New York Times*, July 6, 2017.

110. Lawrence Malkin, "Clinton Lays Out Open-Trade Policy with Equal Terms for Market Access," *New York Times*, February 27, 1993.

111. Kate Sheppard, "Trump Says He Didn't Call Climate Change a Hoax. But He Did," *Huffington Post*, September 26, 2016.

112. Michael D. Shear and Coral Davenport, "World Awaits President's Decision on U.S. Future in Paris Accord," *New York Times*, June 1, 2017.

113. Philip Bump, "In 2009, Donald Trump Endorsed Action on Climate Change. Three Months Later, He Disparaged It," *Washington Post*, June 9, 2016.

114. Robinson Meyer, "Why Did Ivanka Summon Al Gore to Trump Tower?" *The Atlantic*, December 6, 2016.

115. John Podesta, "Trump Is on a Rampage to Endanger the Planet. Now It's Up to Us to Save It," *Washington Post*, March 28, 2017.

116. Dave Boyer, "Donald Trump to Ease Obama-Era Rule on Auto Fuel Economy Standards," *Washington Times*, March 15, 2017.

117. Valerie Volcovici and Timothy Gardner, "EPA Hit Hardest as Trump Budget Targets Regulators," *Reuters*, March 16, 2017.

118. Michael D. Shear and Diane Caldwell, "Trump Advisers Wage Tug of War before Decision on Climate Deal," *New York Times*, May 30, 2017.

119. Ira Shapiro, *The Last Great Senate: Courage and Statesmanship in Times of Crisis* (New York: PublicAffairs, 2012), 84–87.

120. Glenn Kessler, "Kerry's Claim That He Organized the 'Very First' Hearings on Climate Change," *Washington Post*, March 18, 2015.

121. Peter Baker, *Days of Fire: Bush and Cheney in the White House* (New York: Doubleday, 2013), 95.

122. Baker, *Days of Fire.*

123. Baker, *Days of Fire*, 588.

124. Coral Davenport, "E.P.A. Head Stacks Agency with Climate Change Skeptics," *New York Times*, March 7, 2017.

125. Matthew Daley (AP), "Senate's Odd Couple: Boxer, Inhofe Forge Unlikely Alliance," *The Oklahoman*, September 18, 2016; Ashley Halsey III, "Bipartisan Senate Bill Would Fund Transportation for Six Years," *Washington Post*, June 23, 2015.

126. Julie Hirschfeld Davis, Mark Landler, and Coral Davenport, "'Terrifying' Path of Climate Crisis Weighs on Obama," *New York Times*, September 8, 2016.

127. Davis, Landler, and Davenport, "'Terrifying' Path of Climate Crisis."

128. Davis, Landler, and Davenport, "'Terrifying' Path of Climate Crisis."

129. Davis, Landler, and Davenport, "'Terrifying' Path of Climate Crisis."

130. Davis, Landler, and Davenport, "'Terrifying' Path of Climate Crisis."

131. Davis, Landler, and Davenport, "'Terrifying' Path of Climate Crisis."

132. Davis, Landler, and Davenport, "'Terrifying' Path of Climate Crisis."

133. Davis, Landler, and Davenport, "'Terrifying' Path of Climate Crisis."

134. Davis, Landler, and Davenport, "'Terrifying' Path of Climate Crisis."

135. Davis, Landler, and Davenport, "'Terrifying' Path of Climate Crisis."

136. Davis, Landler, and Davenport, "'Terrifying' Path of Climate Crisis."

137. Davis, Landler, and Davenport, "'Terrifying' Path of Climate Crisis."

138. Davis, Landler, and Davenport, "'Terrifying' Path of Climate Crisis."

139. Davis, Landler, and Davenport, "'Terrifying' Path of Climate Crisis."

140. Paul M. Barrett and James Rowley, "And Now, I'll Show You Climate Change!" *Bloomberg Business Week*, December 28, 2015.

141. Barrett and Rowley, "And Now, I'll Show You Climate Change!"

142. Barrett and Rowley, "And Now, I'll Show You Climate Change!"

143. Barrett and Rowley, "And Now, I'll Show You Climate Change!"

144. Barrett and Rowley, "And Now, I'll Show You Climate Change!"

145. Barrett and Rowley, "And Now, I'll Show You Climate Change!"

146. Testimony of Laurence H. Tribe, House Committee on Energy and Commerce, Subcommittee on Energy and Power, March 17, 2015.

147. Mitch McConnell, "Obama Takes His Reckless Energy Plan to the United Nations," *Washington Post*, November 27, 2015.

148. Sheldon Whitehouse, "It's Time for Corporate Leaders to Push Congress on Strong Climate Action," *Medium*, January 5, 2016.

149. Tracy Hester, "The Supreme Court Suspends Obama's Clean Power Plan: Changing the Law on Staying Put," *Forbes*, February 18, 2016.

150. Jonathan Adler, "Supreme Court Puts the Brakes on the EPA's Clean Power Plan," *Washington Post*, February 9, 2016.

151. Hannah Hess, "Paris Agreement: Republicans Ramp Up Their Offensive," *E&E Daily*, April 26, 2017.

152. Senate EPW Committee Releases White Paper: Lessons from Kyoto: Paris Agreement Will Fail National Economies and the Climate, April 21, 2016.

153. Zoe Carpenter, "Senator Sheldon Whitehouse on the Fossil-Fuel Industry's 'Web of Denial,'" *Nation*, July 13, 2016.

154. Letter of senators Susan Collins and Benjamin Cardin to Secretary of State Rex Tillerson, May 3, 2017.

155. Hannah Hess, "Paris Agreement: Senators Fret as Trump Decision Looms," *E&E News Reporter*, May 4, 2017.

156. Hess, "Paris Agreement."

157. Hess, "Paris Agreement."

158. Hess, "Paris Agreement."

159. Podesta, "Trump Is on a Rampage."

160. Podesta, "Trump Is on a Rampage."

161. Lydia O'Connor, "More Than 600 Companies Urge Trump Not to Renege on Climate," *Huffington Post*, January 10, 2017.

162. Alanna Petroff, "CEOs Make a Final Urgent Plea: Don't Pull Out of Paris Accord," CNN *Money*, June 1, 2017.

163. Michael Biesecker (AP), "22 GOP Senators Want US to Pull Out of Paris Climate Accord," *US News and World Report*, May 25, 2017.

164. Shear and Caldwell, "Trump Advisers Wage Tug of War"; Harriet Sinclair, "Graham Says Calling Climate Change 'Hoax' Bad for GOP, Thinks Trump Should Sign Paris Deal," *Newsweek*, May 18, 2017.

165. Alison Smale and Steven Erlanger, "Wary of Trump, Merkel Doubts U.S. Is Solid Ally," *New York Times*, May 29, 2017.

166. J. Weston Phippen, "Trump's Paris Climate Accord Indecision," *The Atlantic*, May 27, 2017.

167. Philip Rucker and Jenna Johnson, "Trump Announces U.S. Will Exit Paris Climate Deal, Sparking Criticism at Home and Abroad," *Washington Post*, June 1, 2017.

168. Ashley Parker, Philip Rucker, and Michael Birnbaum, "Trump's Deliberative Verdict? The Same as His First Instinct," *Washington Post*, June 2, 2017.

169. Hiroko Tabuchi and Henry Fountain, "Bucking Trump, These Cities, States and Companies Commit to Paris Accord," *New York Times*, June 1, 2017.

170. Steven Mufson, "States, Firms Vow to Press Ahead with Climate Policies," *Washington Post*, June 2, 2017.

171. Mufson, "States, Firms Vow to Press Ahead"; Javier C. Hernandez and Adam Nagourney, "California's Governor Steps in to Lead Charge on the Climate," *New York Times*, June 8, 2017.

172. Justin Gillis and Nadja Popovich, "The View from Trump Country, Where Renewable Energy Is Thriving," *New York Times*, June 8, 2017.

173. John Wagner, "By Upending Paris Accord, Trump Buoys His Political Base," *Washington Post*, June 3, 2017; Peter Baker, "Rejecting Popular Deal, the President Bets Big on His Core Supporters," *New York Times*, June 2, 2017.

174. Somini Sengupta, Melissa Eddy, and Chris Buckley, "Defiant Other Countries Reaffirm Fight against Climate Change," *New York Times*, June 2, 2017.

175. Brad Plumer, "The Climate Deal, and What a U.S. Departure Would Mean," *New York Times*, June 1, 2017; Keith Bradsher, "China Turns Economic Engine toward Clean Energy Leadership," *New York Times*, June 6, 2017.

176. Sengupta, Eddy, and Buckley, "Defiant Other Countries."

CHAPTER 13. RECONSIDERING THE SENATE

1. Margot Sanger-Katz, "What We Know About Trump's Twin Blows to Obamacare," *New York Times*, October 12, 2017.

2. Sanger-Katz, "What We Know About Trump's Twin Blows to Obamacare."

3. Michael D. Shear, "White House Makes Hard-Line Demands for any 'Dreamers' Deal, *New York Times*, October 12, 2017.

4. Ana Swanson, "Trump's Tough Talk on NAFTA Raises Prospect of Pact's Demise," *New York Times,* October 11, 2017.

5. Kate Linthicum, "A new report shows just how much Trump has hurt Mexico's view of the U.S., *LA Times,* September 14, 2017.

6. Lisa Friedman and Brad Plumer, "E.P.A. Announces Repeal of Major Obama-Era Carbon Emissions Rule," *New York Times,* October 9, 2017.

7. Friedman and Plumer, "E.P.A. Announces Repeal of Major Obama-Era Carbon Emissions Rule."

8. Mark Landler and David E. Sanger, "Trump Disavows Nuclear Deal, but Doesn't Scrap It," *New York Times,* October 13, 2017.

9. Peter Baker, "Promise the Moon? Easy for Trump. But Now Comes the Reckoning," *New York Times,* October 14, 2017.

10. Thomas Kaplan and Robert Pear, "2 Senators Strike Deal on Health Subsidies that Trump Cut Off," *New York Times,* October 17, 2017.

11. Dylan Scott, "The Perilous Path for Alexander-Murray to become a law," *Vox,* October 19, 2017.

12. Kaplan and Pear,"2 Senators Strike Deal"

13. Kaplan and Pear,"2 Senators Strike Deal"

14. Seung Min Kim, "The GOP senator who might cut a Dreamers deal," *Politico,* October 11, 2017.

15. Josh Rogin, "Trump's Iran Trap for Congress," *Washington Post,* October 16, 2017.

16. Rogin, "Trump's Iran Trap for Congress."

17. Wendy R. Sherman, "Trump is Going to Make a Huge Mistake on the Iran Deal," *New York Times,* October 9, 2017.

18. Shawn Donnan, "Bitter differences over Nafta break into the open," *Financial Times,* October 17, 2017.

19. Donnan, "Bitter Differences over Nafta"

20. Donnan, "Bitter Differences over Nafta"

21. Michael Collins, "Sen. Bob Corker will not run for re-election," *USA Today,* September 26, 2017.

22. Katharine Q Seelye, "Senator Susan Collins Will Not Run for Governor of Maine," *New York Times,* October 13. 2017.

23. Jeff Flake, "My Party is In Denial About Donald Trump," *Politico,* July 31, 2017, an excerpt from his book *Conscience of a Conservative: A Rejection of Destructive Politics and a Return to Principle* (2017).

24. Sheryl Gay Stolberg, "Jeff Flake, A Fierce Trump Critic, Will Not See Re-election to the Senate," New York Times, October 24, 2017.

25. Philip Rucker and Karoun Demirjian, "Corker calls White House 'an adult day care center' in response to Trump's latest Twitter tirade," Washington Post, October 8, 2017.

26. Paul Kane, "Susan Collins's near retirement speaks directly to the frustrations of Washington," *Washington Post,* October 13, 2017.

27. Jonathan Easley, "Bannon-tied group kicks off brutal GOP primary season," *The Hill,* October 11, 2017.

28. Jonathan Martin and Alexander Burns, "Roy Moore Wins Senate G.O.P. Runoff in Alabama," *New York Times*, September 26, 2017.

29. John C. Roberts, "Gridlock and Senate Rules," *Notre Dame Law Review* 88, no. 5 (June 2013): 2191.

30. Trent Lott, *Herding Cats: A Life in Politics* (New York: Harper Paperbacks, 2006), 284.

31. Robert C. Byrd, *The Senate 1789–1989: Addresses on the History of the United States Senate*, volume II (Washington: GPO, 1991): 162.

32. Barbara Sinclair, *Unorthodox Lawmaking: New Legislative Processes in the U.S. Senate*, 4th edition (Washington, DC: CQ Press, 2011).

33. Steven Smith, *The Senate Syndrome: The Evolution of Procedural Warfare in the Modern U.S. Senate* (Norman: University of Oklahoma Press, 2014).

34. Report of the Brookings Institute, *Vital Statistics on Congress, Chapter 6*, January 9, 2017.

35. "South Korean MPs 'Set World Filibuster Record,'" bbc.com/news/world-asia-35704123, March 2, 2016.

36. John C. Roberts, "Gridlock and Senate Rules," *Notre Dame Law Review* 88, no. 5 (2013): 2189.

37. Roberts, "Gridlock and Senate Rules," 2208.

38. Roberts, "Gridlock and Senate Rules," 2189.

39. Tom McClintock, "How and Why the Senate Must Reform the Filibuster," *Imprimis* 46, no. 1 (January 2017).

40. Senator Jeff Merkley and Senator Tom Udall, "Filibuster Rules Changes Epitomize the Senate," *The Government Affairs Institute at Georgetown University*, http://gai.georgetown.edu/filibuster-rules-changes-epitomize-the-senate/; Poopdogcomedy, "NM-Sen: Organized Labor & Sierra Club Back Udall-Merkley-Harkin Filibuster Reform," *Daily KOS*, January 12, 2013.

41. Barbara Sinclair, *The Transformation of the U.S. Senate* (Baltimore: Johns Hopkins University Press, 1989), 130.

42. Sinclair, *The Transformation of the U.S. Senate*, 131.

43. Sinclair, *The Transformation of the U.S. Senate*.

44. Sinclair, *The Transformation of the U.S. Senate*.

45. Ross K. Baker, *Is Bipartisanship Dead? A Report from the Senate* (Boulder: Paradigm Publishers, 2015), 35.

46. Baker, *Is Bipartisanship Dead?* 37.

47. Ross K. Baker, *Is Bipartisanship Dead?* 49.

48. Erica Lovley, "Senate Women's 'Civility Pact,'" *Politico*, February 4, 2011.

49. Speech of then-former President Theodore Roosevelt, *The Man in the Arena*, at the Sorbonne, Paris, France, April 23, 1910.

Index

About the Author

Ira Shapiro began his long Washington career with a summer internship with Senator Jacob Javits (R-NY) the day after he graduated from Brandeis University in 1969. Since then, Shapiro served as a senior Senate staffer for twelve years, negotiated trade agreements during the Clinton administration—earning the rank of ambassador—practiced law, and became chairman of the National Association of Japan-America Societies. He is the author of *The Last Great Senate: Courage and Statesmanship in Times of Crisis*, a critically acclaimed narrative history of the Senate in the 1970s. A local newspaper described his 2002 congressional campaign as "the antidote to cynicism that he promised to deliver." He is currently president of Ira Shapiro Global Strategies, LLC, and a senior adviser to the Albright Stonebridge Group.